THE POWE
IN THE LAI

It does not matter where you look or what examples you select, you will see that every form of enterprise, every step in material progress, is only undertaken after the land monopolist has skimmed the cream off for himself, and everywhere today the man or the public body who wishes to put land to its highest use is forced to pay a preliminary fine in land values to the man who is putting it to an inferior use, and in some cases to no use at all. All comes back to the land value, and its owner for the time being is able to levy his toll upon all other forms of wealth and upon every form of industry. A portion, in some cases the whole, of every benefit which is laboriously acquired by the community is represented in the land value, and finds its way automatically into the landlord's pocket. If there is a rise in wages, rents are able to move forward, because the workers can afford to pay a little more. If the opening of a new railway or a new tramway or the institution of an improved service of workmen's trains or a lowering of fares or a new invention of any other public convenience affords a benefit to the workers in any particular district, it becomes easier for them to live, and therefore the landlord and the ground landlord, one on top of the other, are able to charge them more for the privilege of living there.

WINSTON S. CHURCHILL, *in a speech in Edinburgh,*
July 17, 1909

THE POWER IN THE LAND

An Inquiry into Unemployment, the Profits Crisis and Land Speculation

Fred Harrison

Shepheard-Walwyn (Publishers) Ltd

© Fred Harrison, 1983

First published 1983 by
Shepheard-Walwyn (Publishers) Limited,
26 Charing Cross Road (Suite 34),
London WC2H 0HY

British Library Cataloguing in Publication Data

Harrison, Fred
  The power in the land.
  1. Macroeconomics
  I. Title
  339   HB171

ISBN 0-85683-067-4

Typeset by Alacrity Phototypesetters, Banwell Castle, Avon
Printed and bound in Great Britain by Biddles Ltd, Guildford

Acknowledgements

This book would have been written by Vic Blundell, but for his lifelong dedication to the instruction of mature students who have sought solutions to social problems through an understanding of the science of political economy. The duty to write the book, then, fell to one of his pupils, and it is with pleasure that I express my deep gratitude to him for the generous help that he gave me in the development of some of the key ideas contained in this work.

Some of the research was undertaken while globe-trotting on assignments for my newspaper, *The Sunday People*. A succession of Editors have flown me to locations that made it possible to witness at first hand the workings of the land market in places as diverse as Hong Kong and Sydney, Athens and Kingston (Jamaica). When the Sunday deadlines were met, I was able to switch to on-the-spot investigations that extended my appreciation that the world is one single economy, and that we must work together to find solutions that will serve the common interest. I thank my Editors, whose unwitting role in the production of this book absolves them from any responsibility for the views expressed herein.

Many people helped me during my travels, and I would particularly like to acknowledge the assistance received from Walter Rybeck in Washington, Allan Hutchinson in Melbourne and the late Professor Philip Finkelstein in New York.

Writing is the most civilising of man's arts, but for its dedicated practitioners it is also the most anti-social. And so I record with humility my greatest debt, which is to my wife Rita and daughter Nina, who bore my absence from family routines with fortitude.

Contents

THE UNFREE MARKET

1

The Fatal Mistake

When Mae West told reporters 'I never say "No!" to a good offer', she was not adding yet another one of those sexually suggestive throwaway phrases to the list that made the Hollywood actress famous. She was referring to the land deals that enabled her to build a fortune estimated at around $45m. Her wheeling-dealing gave the late Miss West a mysterious influence which was immeasurably more powerful than her ability to attract men with her celluloid sex. For deals such as those she shrewdly executed in California's San Fernando Valley are at the source of the problem that periodically afflicts the global economy.

The honey-tongued actress commanded the power to disrupt the productive process because industrial society, quite simply, was built on a mistake. The free market, which Adam Smith called 'the invisible hand', was supposed to be the guiding mechanism which equalised the multiplicity of interests and decisions in the economy; it was supposed to aggregate these in such a way that the potential conflicts between private goals would be removed within a harmonious social framework. The mistake made by the founding fathers of the Industrial Revolution in the 1780s — the inventors of new-fangled machines and the entrepreneurs who capitalised on the new factory-based processes of mass production — was to accept and institutionalise land monopoly. The British people, from the Clyde in Scotland to the Thames in the south-eastern corner of England, brought together human skills and material resources in a unique combination, and built a new economic edifice on a corrupt foundation. The good life for *all* was technically capable of achievement, but was not allowed to be fully realised.

The 1980s are the bicentenary of that quantum jump which was the Industrial Revolution. However, that event, unparalleled in the history of mankind, is recalled not for the pleasing possibilities that it offered, but for the exploitation which ruptured economic relationships and generated social tensions. Over thirty million people are jobless in the industrialised countries; hundreds of millions more, dependent upon the prosperity of the

11

metropolitan economies for their jobs, are also tramping the streets in the big cities of the Third World. Those who are fortunate enough to be taking home wage packets at the end of the week are nonetheless living with the constant fear that they are the next to be made redundant.

Entrepreneurs — from the captains of multi-national corporations to the self-employed shopkeepers who keep the wheels of commerce ticking over in the corner shops of our High Streets — are equally vulnerable to the pressures of a seemingly pitiless economic system that appears to jeopardise their material welfare no matter how hard they are willing to work.

Everyone is vulnerable, whether he is a capitalist or worker, whether he lives in the 'miracle' economies of West Germany or Japan or the low-productivity countries like Britain. Could it be that the only appropriate response to the malignant forces that undermine the great social institutions and the nuclear family alike is a thoroughgoing revolution — Marxism, perhaps?

The major social and economic friction points derive their existence and logic from the need to compensate for land monopoly, the original structural defect in industrial society. Economists have always skirted around this issue, and have thus been led — by a variety of motives, some honourable (such as humanitarianism), some inspired by the need to protect vested interests — to propose 'solutions' that have merely aggravated the problems. For example, 19th century reformers concluded that poverty could be eliminated through a progressive income tax only; this failed, as the large number of poverty stricken families in the rich nations of Europe and North America would testify (in 1981, 30m. citizens of the richest nation on earth, the USA, were officially classified as living below the poverty line).

The phenomenon of poverty accompanying prosperity will continue as a feature of society so long as we continue to ignore the fundamental problem, which is the failure to deal with the malfunctioning of the land market. Myopically, we will respond to immediate difficulties with short-term solutions designed to ameliorate the effects rather than remove the original causes.

Our investigation celebrates the Industrial Revolution in the belief that reform, rather than another revolution, is all that is required to eliminate repetition of those tragic events that are an indictment of European civilisation.

The thesis examined here is that land speculation disrupts the industrial economy by distorting the distribution of income and contracting the supply of land available for homes and factories, shops and offices and farms. But if we are to accept conventional wisdom, our explanation for the latest recession that began in 1974 and continued into the 1980s is pure nonsense. How can land speculators close down factories, shut High Street shops and throw people onto the dole queues?

We are invited to believe that land, which is fixed in supply, is neutral in the process of production. For example, in his quantitative analysis of the growth of real national income in the western economies, Edward Denison of the Brookings Institution assigns a 0.00% value to land as an input.[1] The only recognition that land might have a negative impact arises in relation to *per capita* income: because the working population is increasing on a fixed amount of land, so land 'subtracted slightly from the growth of national income per person employed'.[2]

From this it follows that the blame for economic recessions cannot be ascribed to those who own the beneficial rights to land. The assumption underlying Denison's view is that land comes onto the market as and when it is required by labour and capital, and that it does so at market-clearing prices determined by competition. This is consistent with the classical theory of perfect competition, but its use for analysing the land market as it is at present constituted reveals a tragic gap in our knowledge.

The causal mechanism is crucial to our analysis, but it is one which even diligent students of the land market have failed to identify. Take, for example, the following account of the West German economy. Investment in real estate via property funds became popular in the late 1960s. This interest intensified into a boom in 1971 and 1972. A slump in the land market followed in 1973, and the 'miracle' economy went into a deep recession in 1974. Are these events no more than a chronological sequence, purely descriptive and with no explanatory content?

The popular explanation for the problems of the 1980s has been the OPEC-inspired rises in the price of oil. As a group, only Marxist economists have consistently denied that the oil price boom in late 1973 initiated the global recession in 1974. Their view is verified by the historical facts; but while *their* alternative explanation is rejected, can we justifiably attribute the burden of responsibility to land speculation? 'Apparently no one has any defensible idea of the relative import played by speculation in contributing to recent land price booms in Canada, New Zealand, Australia, and elsewhere.'[3] We have documented the evidence in four cases — the USA, Britain, Japan and Australia — to defend the view that speculation *was* responsible for the land booms that then provoked the general recession as a result of the unbalanced flow of land onto the market, the distortion in the production costs of firms and the reduction in the spending power of households.

The power to engineer these effects is identified as corrupt. In theory and practice, land monopoly is inconsistent with *laissez faire*: the free market cannot hope to function effectively if it is undermined by a class of people who are not subjected to the rules of competition. Psychologically, land monopoly stimulates the something-for-nothing attitude which serves no justifiable economic or social purpose. Morally, land monopoly is indefensible because it assigns the power to reap the rewards of other people's labours.

Past attempts at resolving the instabilities in the industrial system were doomed to failure because attitudes and knowledge had been distorted by the historians, economists and politicians who neglected the crucial role of land in the productive process.

The classical economists defined the production function in terms of three factors: land, labour and capital. This was subsequently simplified to capital and labour. The analytical concepts, conforming to the perceptions of 'real-world' economists, were adjusted to take account of what was held to be the diminishing importance of land in the dynamic process of urban-based industrial production. 'Land' was conflated into the concept of 'capital', its unique characteristics thereby distilled out of sight. This freed the minority of people who monopolised land to exercise a devastating influence over the course of production, for which capitalists bore the blame. Their activities were secreted behind a veil of ignorance; the connection was lost to the economic doctors who declined to examine all the symptoms. As a result, their prescriptions were muddled and incapable of curing the psycho-social deprivation and material suffering of generations of workers who had the ground cut from beneath their feet.

Thus, the capitalist system appeared to be anarchistic; there was no reliable long-term stability. Is it beyond the wit of man to find a permanent solution to the booms and catastrophic depressions that periodically return to rupture efforts to build a free and prosperous society on the basis of growth sustained over a long period of time?

The task of finding such a solution is urgent, for capitalism is challenged by the socialists whose concepts have been fashioned by Karl Marx. They argue that economic crises are evidence of those 'internal contradictions' which represent the opportunity to revolutionise society. Rational planning would be substituted for the disorder of the market. The Marxist critique has an undeniable plausibility (given present perceptions) which makes it attractive.

> It will always be one of the most appropriate criticisms of free enterprise society that it is quite unable — or rather, unwilling — to use collectivist forms of economic organisation for an attack on slums, poverty, disease and lack of education, while it is able to use all those techniques, repugnant as they are to the business man's mind, when it comes to war...[4]

Thus, subtly, we are presented with the assumption that only collectivist action can solve these problems. Superficially it appears reasonable, for many people lack not the will but the means to act for themselves in their own interests. Because of the persuasiveness of this assumption, we trundle inexorably into corporate and collectivist action while paying lip-service to liberal philosophy based on individualism.

The language in which these issues are debated determines the way in which we construct the answers. Research and policy-making is heavily conditioned by one simple image: the 'class conflict' between capital and labour, a notion lovingly nurtured by Marxists which has been left unchallenged by the ineptness of liberal economists. The Machine exploits Man. Trade Unions exist to Bash the Bosses. And so on. This fraudulent prospectus has dictated the terms of all the reformist debates of the past hundred years. As a consequence, we have been tackling our economic problems in the wrong way because we have perceived them through a prism of language which distorts reality.

A book that rejects the Marxist critique has to accomplish two things if it is to advance the cause of a prosperous liberal society. First it has to exonerate the free enterprise model of the criticisms levelled against it. This does not mean that the individual actions of all capitalists have to be defended, but we do have to show that material deprivation is not a systemic feature of free enterprise (in the way, for example, that the individual's freedom to make decisions is necessarily eliminated from a system that is built on centralised planning). Then, we have to demonstrate that the major economic problems can be remedied while preserving individual freedom; that people who wish to work can earn good incomes with which to finance their needs without placing themselves in a state of dependence on a bureaucracy and public welfare subsidies. How can these ideal goals, which have eluded us for two hundred years despite the strides in science and technology, now be achieved?

Intuitively, people believe that the answer lies buried somewhere in the tax system, which redistributes income, shapes incentives and apportions power. In this they are right, but what changes, in particular, ought to be promulgated? A straightforward programme of tax-cutting is the general answer. President Ronald Reagan and Prime Minister Margaret Thatcher were both elected to office with a remedial programme based on this proposal.

The philosophy under-pinning this approach goes as follows: manifestations such as unemployment are proof of insufficient free enterprise; instability is attributed to a lop-sided economy based on the growth of the public sector; this public sector participation in the economy should therefore be reduced drastically by cutting taxes and reducing direct state involvement in the operation of firms and the lives of families.

This interpretation does not account for the fact that industrial economies have *from their inception* regularly over-stretched themselves into depressions. Each of these boom-slump cycles lasted for two decades, and their main elements have been consistently replicated. The first British cycle (1795 to 1815), which is analysed in Chapter 4, bears striking resemblance to the most recent cycles. Yet during the earliest cycles on both sides of the Atlantic, state interference in the economy was minimal or non-existent. So the uninformed analysis — that we need more of the same capitalism, and less welfare statism — is sterile as an explanation of the underlying problem. There was no golden industrial age to which we can return; we have to look for one in the future. But to find it, we must first identify those injurious causal influences which are common to all the depressions from 1815 to 1975, if they exist. Only then can we define reforms of lasting value.

But even if we are armed with the correct diagnosis of the problem, the definition of a solution would be no easy matter. This is because, for at least two millenia, fiscal policy has been bedevilled by a tendency to avoid coming to terms with the harsh realities of tax policy if — as is inevitably the case — it affects some vital interest.

There are two indivisible sides to the distribution of wealth through social mechanisms: equity and efficiency. Primitive societies fused these two aspects into coherent codes of practice which were consistent with their resources and level of development. This happy state of affairs dissolved with the rise of classical civilization. We have, ever since, been groping for a formula that served the ends of both justice and the optimum needs of the prevailing mode of production, but with little or no success. There is no Sermon on the Mount, or set of rules inscribed on ancient tablets handed down from on high, on which we can draw for guidance.

There have been some ideal opportunities in modern times for redefining the legitimate claims of the public domain on private wealth, but these have been tragically wasted. The American Founding Fathers, for example, had such a unique opportunity. Their perspicacity is exemplified by James Madison, father of the Constitution and fourth President of the US, who put his finger on the problem when he declared in No. 10 of the influential Federalist Papers:

> The most common source of faction, the most durable, has been the unequal distribution of property.[5]

He identified the problem, and noted the risks of dominant groups using tax legislation to 'trample on the rules of justice. Every shilling with which they over-burden the inferior number is a shilling saved to their own pockets'.[6] But he then proceeded to intimidate future generations of law-makers in Congress by attacking as a 'wicked project' any attempt at an 'equal division of property'.[7] By failing to specify how to deal with the most serious problem in civil society — 'the unequal distribution of property' — he immediately preached against a philosophy that might have produced a fiscal policy to neutralise the consequences. And so the New World, populated by refugees on the run from the old tyrannies that were built on the enclosure of common lands, began to recreate those very conditions that had led to the exodus from Europe (see Chapter 10).

What of the canons of taxation provided by Adam Smith? These are generally regarded as profound, and are still cited by free market economists as the guidelines for fiscal policy. But as we shall see in Chapter 2, Adam Smith suffered from the shortcoming that led him to a set of prescriptions which prove, to the present author's satisfaction at least, that he lacked that 'most exact impartiality' which Madison considered to be crucial to the making of tax laws. What, then, do we propose as a third alternative to the limited choice at present on offer from right-wing Conservatives and their opponents, the Marxists?

The major reform that we prescribe is a 100% tax on the annual rental value of all land and a simultaneous reduction in other forms of taxation. In other words, we advocate the 'socialisation' of all ground rents to remove private gain therefrom, but would give free reign to private enterprise within what would now be a free market system. This proposal is not original: in its full-blooded form, it was propounded by Henry George in *Progress and Poverty* (1879).[8] Is it eccentric to suggest that a single tax advocated over a hundred years ago contains the solution to contemporary problems? Readers will judge once they have acquainted themselves with the evidence. Suffice, for the present, to note the seminal importance of this book, which has become economics' leading best-seller.[9] Paradoxically, today few readers will be familiar with the book, yet it continues to wield influence in the councils of power. We can see this, for example, from the strictures on taxation expressed by President Reagan's economic guru, Dr. Arthur Laffer. The Californian professor promoted the 'supply side' economics that were at the heart of the Republican presidential campaign in 1980.

The Laffer Curve, as it became known, is based upon the principle that savings and investment are most likely to accrue to expand productivity when the government is not taxing the people down to the last penny that can be squeezed out of the private sector. Dr. Laffer's authority on fiscal policy is Henry George, whose canons on taxation were 'the essence of what we are talking about', according to this presidential mentor.[10]

Henry George's analysis culminated in a condemnation of land speculation. He advocated a single tax to capture all economic rent for the community's benefit, and the simultaneous elimination of taxes on labour and capital. President Reagan was not ideologically disposed to carry out the full Georgist fiscal programme, however: he had made a million himself out of Californian land deals!

Henry George was called The Prophet of San Francisco. The label was appropriate. He was a fine orator, and his book was written with an unmistakable passion which fired the imaginations of people around the world who sought a practical philosophy which would enable them to both preserve individual liberty and yet restore that primitive cohesion which is vital to a healthy society. The message in *Progress and Poverty* was a simple one. Natural resources have no cost of production, they are God-given, and so they legitimately belong to everyone. The most efficient way of securing a fair distribution of resources is through a tax on land values. Every citizen has a stake in the revenue which then flows into and out of the exchequer coffers. If the government levies that tax and spends the money on socially-necessary projects, there is no need to interfere with the liberties, economic activities or property of anyone; people know what they want and are capable of securing these for themselves *provided that there is no monopoly of land*.

Henry George thus advanced, in addition to his moral theory of property, the hypothesis that a free enterprise economy could operate efficiently only if economic rent was completely taxed out of the arena of private enterprise. The statistical data was not available to enable him to test his theory empirically. He had to rely on impressionist evidence. Even today we are not much better off, for while statisticians spend a great deal of time and money in collating data on capital and labour, they all but ignore the land. This encourages economists to neglect George's macro-economics. For example, Professor Samuelson — in one of the most widely read student textbooks on economics published in the postwar years — reduces Henry George's problematic to an ethical one. The case against private land ownership 'must be attacked or defended in terms of ethical value judgments concerning the proper FOR WHOM resolutions in society'.[11] The *economic* case against the present land tenure system is side-stepped.

Here we shall try to ignore the ethical arguments (not always successfully, as some of the language will reveal). Our purpose is to explore the scientific proposition that land monopoly, and not the free market, must accept the blame for the poverty and human degradation in industrial society.

The enquiry necessarily begins with the 'bible' of the free market, Adam Smith's *The Wealth of Nations*. This was the book that provided the captains of industry and the politicians in Westminster (a body largely composed of landowners) with the theoretical framework and moral justification for the new mode of production. What we discover is that the advocates of capitalism failed to elaborate a scheme that would enable them to attain capitalism's full potential. So for two hundred years the entrepreneurs and their employees have laboured within the framework of an impure model.

This has served the Marxist critics well, for they have been able to attack the *laissez faire* ideal by marshalling evidence derived from a seriously malfunctioning system. That they were pointing to a crippled capitalism has not been an argument used in defence of the free market.

We, in defending the need to establish *laissez faire*, maintain that land monopoly is not one of its intrinsic characteristics. The private appropriation of the *value* of land (as opposed to secure individual possession and use of specific sites) is not a necessary condition for the capitalist mode of production. Capitalism entails the accumulation of wealth based on the provision of goods and services to consumers. It is a two-way exchange: consumers produce wealth in order to exchange it with others — to consume. Land monopoly undermines this creative process because it is a one-way relationship. The monopolist secures legal title to the resources of *nature*, and then claims a portion of the wealth created by others in return for nothing more than the permission to use land. This is the economics of the bandit sanctified by law. The monopolist *per se* does not contribute to production; he is, therefore, an anomalous feature within an otherwise efficient system.

Unfortunately for the free market, even its champions have not served it well. Now, with the eclipse of Keynesianism, we are back in the philosophical vacuum that has regularly afflicted Western society. The political dangers, as we pass through a recession that equals the one of the 1930s, are well known. We do not believe that it was a coincidence that the Japanese government's White Paper in 1981 contained repeated calls for greater 'patriotism', or that in 1982 Japan began to sanitise her military history as the sun rapidly set on the miracle economy.[12]

In the desperate search for explanations and solutions, liberal economists have sought refuge in the theory of a Soviet economist, Nikolai Kondratieff. In 1925, he postulated that capitalist economies rise and decline in 'long waves' of about 50 years duration.[13] The global economy is supposed to be in the trough of the latest such cycle. This view has produced exercises in exhaustive statistical compilation, some of them scholarly,[14] others popular treatments which the authors admit could be interpreted by scientists as smacking of the occult.[15] The problem with Kondratieff is that he did not offer an *explanation* for his cyclical phenomena. Yet without explanations it is impossible to equip the politicians with a package of rational corrective policies.

Unlike the mono-causal theory presented here, analysts who have built on Kondratieff's work have come up with a choice of 'various theoretical explanations'.[16] This choice has not convinced the decision-makers that they are now within reach of a practical solution for the major schisms in the growth trends that occur more regularly than every half-century.[17] The editor of *The Times*, the newspaper of the British Establishment, noted with candour in his valedictory message to his readers:

> The truth is that nobody knows the best way to manage the worst world slump since the 1930s (for economic historians it is a casebook example of a Kondratiev 50-year recession) in a period of endemic inflation. There is no answer in Keynes or Friedman or Marx or anyone else...[18]

Not surprisingly, therefore, politicians are today floundering around indecisively. The debate about how to regenerate the global economy is conducted in over-simplified terms. On the right hand, the conservatives advocate a 'supply side' strategy: revival through higher investment and output of goods and services. Economic liberals, on the left hand, are moved by desperation to cautiously propose a demand-side strategy: a return to government pump-priming, which brings with it the risk of new inflation.

This debate of the deaf is doomed to ultimate failure. This is predictable, because each side is offering a partial truth, recourse to which in the past has produced the state of disarray in which we find ourselves. Reducing interest rates (to stimulate investment), or increasing public expenditure (to increase demand), may have beneficial short-term effects; the passage of time, however, shows that they are of little more value than the placebos handed out by doctors who do not know the cause of the illness that they are invited to cure, but are too vain to admit of their ignorance to their patients.

It is this piecemeal tinkering with parts of the economy, however, which, cumulatively, has built up heavy income taxes, insupportable government deficits, overwhelming disincentives to the wealth-creating processes and has permitted cyclical collapse of the system. They are all hopeless attempts at mitigating the original problem. For too long, now, 'managing the economy' has been a substitute for a radical solution. While it provides power for politicians and jobs for civil servants, it does not create social stability and new wealth. That will be accomplished only when we finally come to terms with the monopoly of land, the one factor which is traditionally omitted from all the equations.

Because we have failed to address ourselves to this major problem, the door has been opened to the extreme left. They triumphantly claim that the capitalist system is about to terminate in one of those epoch-making Big Bangs that constitute the saltatory Marxist theory that history moves in stages, with communism at the pinnacle of human social achievement.

But if, as we claim, land monopoly is not an intrinsic 'contradiction' within capitalism, the corrupting influence can be surgically removed without recourse to social transformation. We do not claim that the fiscal reform recommended here will create an economic system at its best and final stage in human organisation. But capitalism would be equipped to ensure full employment and sustained prosperity, and so able to resist its ideological enemies and last much longer than they would have us believe.

Marx regarded capitalism as the last antagonistic form of class society. Fiscal reform would lay the foundations for the removal of the antagonistic elements and enable us to refine liberal democratic society. This is a sweeping claim, the full justification for which is not elaborated in this book. Other works will have to follow. Meanwhile, establishing how the speculative booms and disastrous slumps can be eliminated from the industrial economy is the first and necessary step in the direction of a happier and more prosperous society.

Notes

1 E. F. Denison, 'Economic Growth', in *Britain's Economic Prospects*, by R. E. Caves and Associates, Washington, DC: Brookings Institution, 1968, p. 236.
2 *Ibid.*, p. 251.
3 D. Hagman and D. Misczynski, *Windfalls For Wipeouts : Land Value Capture and Compensation*, Chicago: American Society of Planning Officials, 1978, p. 123.
4 J. Steindl, 'Capitalism, Science and Technology', in C. H. Feinstein, editor, *Socialism, Capitalism and Economic Growth*, London: Cambridge University Press, 1967, p. 200.
5 *The Federalist Papers* (Introduction by C. Rossiter), New York: The New American Library, 1961, p. 79.
6 *Ibid*, p. 80.
7 *Ibid*, p. 84.
8 H. George, *Progress and Poverty*, centenary edn. 1979, New York: Robert Schalkenbach Foundation.
9 G. Gilder, *Wealth and Poverty*, New York: Basic Books, 1981, p. 42.
10 J. Rees, 'Supply-Side Economist Arthur Laffer', *The Review of the News*, 6.11.80, pp. 47-49.
11 P. Samuelson, *Economics*, Tokyo: McGraw-Hill Koga Kusha, 10th edn., 1976, p. 568.
12 Among other emendations, school textbooks — with the approval of the Ministry of Education — were altered so that the Japanese 'invasion of northern China' was made to read 'advance'. The description of how Korean labourers were forcibly sent to Japan was changed to read 'mobilized'. The diplomatic row that ensued from this reappraisal of history forced the Japanese government to back-track. The new nationalistic mood, however, was firmly established. We cannot predict what this portends for Far Eastern relations. What we do know, however, is that a new 5-year plan for military procurements was adopted, and that there was a proposal to increase the 1983 defence budget by 7.3% (to £6.29 bn.)
13 N. D. Kondratieff, 'The Long Waves in Economic Life', *Lloyds Bank Review*, October 1978.
14 For example, W. W. Rostow, *The World Economy*, London: Macmillan, 1978.
15 J. B. Schuman and D. Rosenau, *The Kondratieff Wave*, New York: Delta, 1972, p. viii.
16 W. W. Rostow, 'The Long Waves in Economic Life', *Lloyds Bank Review*, July 1979, p. 53.
17 Ray admits that 'no more than guesses can be expressed' in the search for the motive power that might drag the British economy out of the Kondratieff trough and into a new phase of sustained growth. G. Ray, 'Innovation in the Long Cycle', *Lloyds Bank Review*, January 1980, p. 26.
18 W. Rees-Mogg, 'My resumption of liberty', *The Times*, 7.3.81.

2

Laissez Faire:
Adam Smith's Version

Adam Smith believed that he was recommending the economics of the free market when he wrote *The Wealth of Nations*. He thought that his theoretical system had, as its dynamic principle, the competitive spirit; that, within the framework of natural justice, economic growth would be enjoyed by the three 'original great orders' which comprised civilized society — the landlords, capitalists and labourers. He was wrong.

Smith was not wrong in thinking that theoretically the economics of capitalist competition could function efficiently to the advantage of all. His error arose from the deduction that his specific system provided such an outcome, that it would secure the dual aim of freeing people to pursue private aims while guaranteeing the natural harmony of the total system. For his was not a description of how to construct a free market: he insulated the landlords from the competitive spirit. Until this is appreciated the science of political economy will be severely limited in its influence on public policy.

For two centuries Smith's book has been the 'bible' for the buccaneering entrepreneurs who built factories and mass-produced cheap goods, and for the rational thinkers — the technologists, scientists and engineers and organisational managers — who trampled theological mysticism under foot in favour of science. But when Smith penned *The Wealth of Nations* he betrayed the spirit of the free market. At the abstract level, his testament promoted a philosophy that relentlessly exposed the special privileges and the monopoly power that politicians and manufacturers tried to invoke to their profitable advantage, but the book also set the seal of approval on an institutional framework that crippled capitalism at its conception. And so Adam Smith's victims were not just the toiling masses who were subjected to the tortuous economic pressures that reduced so many of them to misery. A death blow was also administered to the very idea of the free market.

Laissez faire is now discredited because, by popular agreement, it has failed to work to everyone's satisfaction. It was out of resignation to this 'failure' that the philosophy of the New Deal developed: the belief that a mixed

22

economy would do what the free market was incapable of accomplishing. But the interpretation of the history of industrial society ever since publication of *The Wealth of Nations* has geen grossly defective, which is why the critics have been able to conclude that unrestrained competition is inherently evil. Collective action, collective ownership of capital and centralised bureaucratic planning are now — in degrees varying only according to vested interests — acclaimed as the remedial alternatives.

The analyses have been wrong because the historians and social scientists have taken all the tenets of Adam Smith as necessarily intrinsic to the capitalist market. They have pursued their enquiries into a malfunctioning system without questioning the necessity for those property rights which have underpinned that system; without questioning whether, had a modified configuration of property rights existed, the free market might have achieved its goals without the evil consequences which have beset industrial society. Across the political spectrum, from Marxist left to conservative right, the arguments and counter-arguments have progressed without adequate reflection on whether a reform of the principles of property ownership and the rationale which motivates the owners of these rights might be sufficient to improve the operations of the free market without recourse to those bureaucratic modifications that deny the 'perfect liberty' that Smith wished to attain.

The debate about capitalism as a mode of production, therefore, has been in the terms validated by Adam Smith. But contrary to what he thought he was doing — and his readers interpreted him as doing[1] — Smith developed an economic framework which entailed a fatal element of monopoly power. He wrote about an 'invisible hand' guiding the system to the benefit of everyone, but he recommended the preservation of a structure of property rights which by its very nature struck at the heart of individual liberty and economic prosperity.

Critics, then, are opponents of Adam Smith — not of *laissez faire*. For the freely competitive market system with a capitalistic ethos has yet to be put to trial. Responsibility for the slums of Bolton in the 19th century, and the hunger of the Jarrow marchers in the 20th century, must be laid at the feet of Adam Smith and the politicians and practitioners who happily accepted his values; these tragedies, as we shall see, are *not* a necessary part of *laissez faire* capitalism. The search for a system which combines personal freedom and social stability with economic prosperity for everyone is a realisable dream, and its pursuit must start with an analysis of the defects in the philosophical justification advanced to legitimise the history of western industrial society: *The Wealth of Nations*.

Dr Smith was a careful Scottish scholar. He had taught at the University of Edinburgh, travelled to France where he studied the Physiocratic system of economics, and was an accomplished logician and natural scientist. His great book was not specifically prepared for the Industrial Revolution which was fermenting all around him. He wanted to define the principles of a free and just economic system of relevance to any civilized society. Indeed, surprisingly, he was not well acquainted with the great strides in mechanical inventions which characterised the two decades during which he wrote the book which he published in 1776.[2]

The clues to Smith's fatal errors were contained in his first book, *The Theory of Moral Sentiments* (1759),[3] which was a discourse on ethics. In this, he distorted the way in which income was divided between the landlords and the landless. In doing so, however, he linked 'the invisible hand' with the process, and the free market was generally held to be guilty of what subsequently happened.

Smith knew the facts. The natural fertility of the earth, nurtured by human labour, increased the output that fed a greater multitude. But, he insisted:

> It is to no purpose that the proud and unfeeling landlord views his extensive fields, and without a thought for the wants of his brethren, in imagination consumes himself the whole harvest that grows upon them. The homely and vulgar proverb, that the eye is larger than the belly, never was more fully verified than with regard to him.[4]

Smith insisted that, given the limited capacities of the landlord's belly, he was obliged to 'distribute' his surplus food. The rich 'consume little more than the poor; and in spite of their natural selfishness and rapacity . . . they divide with the poor the produce of all their improvements'. Underpinning the whole structure of Adam Smith's economics was this naive claim that landlords shared the surplus output among every person in society; more than that, however, the distribution was effectively an *equal* one. Of landlords, he said:

> They are led by an invisible hand to make *nearly the same* distribution of the necessaries of life which would have been made had the earth been divided into equal portions among all its inhabitants; and thus, without intending it, without knowing it, advance the interest of the society, and afford means to the multiplication of the species.[5]

So land redistribution was not on the agenda of reforms that might be necessary to improve the new mode of production. For 'the invisible hand' ensured that people enjoyed 'nearly the same distribution' as if the earth had been divided into equal portions among all.

Smith insulated the landlords from criticism by claiming that they were not responsible for the existing distribution of property rights, and that in any event nobody was really excluded from a share of wealth:

> When providence divided the earth among a few lordly masters, it neither forgot nor abandoned those who seemed to have been left out in the

partition. These last, too, enjoy their share of all that it produces. In what constitutes the real happiness of human life, they are in no respect inferior to those who would seem so much above them. In ease of body and peace of mind, all the different ranks of life are nearly upon a level, and the beggar, who suns himself by the side of the highway, possesses that security which kings are fighting for.[6]

All was well, then; the 'fitness' of the system was bestowed with a certain 'propriety and beauty'[7] that was the free market.

Smith appears to confuse the differences between the division of the *products* of the earth, with the *value* of that output as it is exchanged across the stalls in the market towns. Landlords may not hoard all the food that is grown on their land; but nor do they distribute its value on a nearly equal basis, as Smith would have us believe — as any landless beggar sunning himself on the side of the highway could have told the young Professor of Moral Philosophy from Glasgow.

Adam Smith was not a fool, and his attention to detail was meticulous. So we can account for the apparent shallowness of his economic reasoning only in terms of his having to fit reality to his theory. He must, at the outset, have decided that property rights to land should not be distributed in the new industrial system. In doing so, he was hamstringing capitalism.

In *The Wealth of Nations*,[8] Smith attacked the manufacturers who sought to monopolise markets in order to inflate the price of their products; yet while he recognises that rent was a monopoly price for the use of a finite resource, he did not recommend any action to destroy that particular monopoly. He acknowledged that 'perfect liberty' was associated with the need to allocate capital and labout to their most efficient uses, to maximise the output of goods at the lowest possible prices; yet he condoned the under-use or misallocation of land. In sum, then, he expected labour and capital to work their damndest to maximise the welfare of society; yet he sought to protect the landlords, whose income and property rights were not to be invaded for the sake of improving the operations of 'the invisible hand'.

The theoretical formulations in *The Wealth of Nations* could have been used to predict the tragedies which would consequently afflict industrial society. For he offered a perfectly clear hypothesis about the determination of economic rent, containing all the elements of the theory which was later to be popularly associated with the name of David Ricardo. With this theory, Smith predicted that progress was biased in favour of the landlord class.

> ... every improvement in the circumstances of the society tends either directly or indirectly to raise the real rent of land, to increase the real wealth of the landlord, his power of purchasing the labour, or the produce of the labour of other people.[9]

Anticipating Henry George's formulations on the distribution of national income by over a century, Smith even noted that 'The real value of the landlord's share, his real command of the labour of other people, not only arises with the real value of the produce, but the proportion of his share to the whole produce rises with it'.[10] Smith was under no illusions that rent was an unearned income; and here he acknowledges that it was a rising proportion of national wealth, a fund which lent itself peculiarly well to finance those activities that were suitable candidates for public sector expenditure.

But instead of grasping the historic opportunity presented to him of influencing events for the good of all, Smith reinforced the structural defects and human prejudices which were consequently unleashed in all their fury as never before in the history of mankind, given a new dimension by the scale of operations which is a distinguishing characteristic of the industrial mode of production. Whereas in a 'natural' system based on agriculture, suffering arising from exploitation was limited to individual cases or small groups, now it was transformed into the disgusting deprivations of millions, the malevolent disease stretching itself right round the globe in a system which failed to correspond with Smith's vision of natural harmony.

Smith would have abhorred the living portrayal of his system. Unlike his predecessors in the first half of the 18th century,[11] he advocated high wages as a stimulus to hard work. He was anxious about what sociologists today call 'alienation', the dulling effect on the spirits of people who specialised in monotonous conveyor-belt activities in the factory. He was a humane man who recognised that, in addition to self-interest, the virtue of 'sympathy' was a necessary part of the development of individual personality and of civilized society.

The competition of Smith's 'free' market was complemented by the co-operation entailed by the division of labour. Such defects as may arise in the market he sought to attribute to personal motives (as when businessmen conspire to fix prices) rather than to institutional inadequacies. The model that he delineated was not amoral; on the contrary, he saw it as founded on natural justice.

For Smith, natural justice established itself of its own accord for every man, so long as the laws of justice were not violated. Competition was virtuous, and not the naked thing of Marx's nightmares, the operation of some mythical 'law of the jungle' in which the weak are destroyed by the strong. One of Smith's rules was the concept of fair play. He illustrated what he understood by this rule, as it applied to each and every person.

> In the race for wealth, and honours, and preferments, he may run as hard as he can, and strain every nerve and muscle, in order to outstrip all his competitors. But if he should justle, or throw down any of them, the

indulgence of the spectators is entirely at an end. It is a violation of fair play, which they cannot admit of.[13]

The equal opportunity for everyone to strive as hard as he or she could, and be rewarded accordingly, in a growing economy which ensured the employment of all, was an intrinsic part of his vision of the good life. So long as all the participants played the game fairly, according to the rules, all would be well. But what if the rules handicapped some of the players in such a way that there was no fair way in which they could either win the race or even reach the finishing line? What if the rules prevented some of the would-be participants from even joining the game? These were critical questions to which Smith should have addressed himself, for the structure of property rights, and in particular the monopoly of land, biased the system against some of the players.

Smith may, as some have stated, 'laid about the landlords in his rhetoric',[14] but in fact he proposed nothing to deal with them. On the contrary, he sought to excuse the disparity of wealth and income, and was insensitive to the way in which these would interfere with the dynamics of a competitive system.

Adam Smith recognised that rent was exacted by the use of monopoly power,[15] and he did not try to hide his appreciation of that fact. Landlords, he agreed, 'are the only one of the three orders whose revenue costs them neither labour nor care, but comes to them, as it were, of its own accord, and independent of any plan or project of their own'.[16] But he sought to excuse them by invoking a general psychological disposition.

> As soon as the land of any country has all become private property, the landlords *like all other men*, love to reap where they never sowed, and demand a rent even for its natural produce.[17]

Like all other men? To which group in the economy was he referring? He advanced evidence that capitalists and labourers earned their incomes, but was not able to offer any justification for the reapings of the land monopolists; nor could he. So he sought to justify the role of the landlords by claiming that their exactions were the normal psychological failings of all men. He was unwilling to admit that the unwarranted division of income — the result of the exercise of that monopoly power for which he condemned the mercantilists — would disrupt competition.

To maintain his position, he invoked metaphysics; a 'principle of preservation' would correct any malfunctioning in the system, as a result of which even poor, landless people would find jobs as country labourers or urban craftsmen. Unfortunately, that was precisely what the crippled hand could not accomplish for all men, at all times. When landless peasants resorted to the town for work, they joined a labour market which was conveniently placed at

the disposal of the entrepreneurs who were then able to exploit the vulnerability of wage-seekers.[18]

Were the tools available to enable Smith to propose the means by which the
frictions in the market system could be eliminated, so that the system could
operate closer to its theoretical ideal? Before defining an answer, we need to
look at the dynamics of the land market.

Land as a factor of production has certain unique qualities. For practical
purposes, its supply is fixed, at the local level. Ultimately, the world is a
closed economy. To control land, therefore, is to wield total power. But there
is a more fundamental characteristic which differentiates land from capital and
labour: the life span of people and machines is finite; the life of a plot of land is
infinite. This has an important consequence for an economy relying simultaneously on competition and co-operation. Land monopolists can — and
do — refuse to play the game whenever they choose. If they are not satisfied
with the price that they are offered for their land, they can withdraw it from
use without fear. They know that the value of the land is constantly
appreciating, and that the rental revenue they forego today will be recouped
in a few years through an increase in the value of the land (which is the
capitalisation of a given number of years' revenue). People, on the other
hand, cannot play the game for any length of time. If they withdraw their
labour they starve; and there is no way in which their lost wages can be
recovered. Similarly with capital. If the owners withdraw machines, these rot
away; the rate of depreciation can be slowed down, but only at the expense
of maintaining them while they are idle.

When it comes to a confrontation in the market, then, landowners win.
They have time on their side.[19] The system, consequently, malfunctions; and
the usefulness of concepts like supply and demand, equilibrium analysis,
optimum allocation of resources, efficient distribution of income — the analytical tools of the economist — are seriously restricted.

There is only one free market solution to the partial paralysis which is
otherwise present in the industrial system: a fiscal obligation on the possession of land. A tax levied on the market value of *all* land would constitute a
continuous pressure on the possessors, a cost analogous to that on the
capitalist who must maintain his machines while they are idle. If the tax was
levied at a high enough rate, the effect would be immediate. Either people
would use the land to best effect, or, since they could not carry the tax liability
for long while the land was not yielding an income, they would have to
relinquish it to others. The tax on land values, then, would induce those who
possessed land to play the game of competition and co-operation. They could
not withdraw from participation and expect to take the land with them.
Within this fiscal framework the 'invisible hand' would be restored to health
and would be capable of handling, in an orderly way, the multiplicity o

problems with which it is presented by a community of people with scarce resources, limitless wants and a diversity of tastes.

Adam Smith would not accept this solution. It is true that he regarded land values as 'peculiarly' suitable for taxation, since such a tax falls on an economic surplus and could not be passed on to consumers in the price of goods.[20] The levied tax, furthermore, was in no way a disincentive to the enterprise and effort of workers or capitalists. Land, said Smith, was suited to taxation because its value was difficult to conceal, in contrast to the value of capital. A register of land values could easily be compiled, regular valuations carried out and the tax collected at moderate cost. But he, like the landlords who dominated the British Parliament, resisted the application of the tax on the value of *all* land. In fact, he explicitly opposed a tax on the rental income which could be imputed to idle land. His reasons for declaring this position illuminate his ideological orientation.

In his discussion on the 'Taxes upon the Rent of Houses', Smith twice stated that it would be wrong to levy a tax on unused land. 'The ground-rents of uninhabited houses ought to pay no tax,' he declared emphatically.[21] In his review of the position in Holland, he claimed that taxes on uninhabited houses there posed problems for their owners. 'There seems to be a hardship in obliging the proprietor to pay a tax for an untenanted house, for which he can derive no revenue, especially so very heavy a tax,' he wrote.[22] He failed to confront other problems associated with empty houses, such as the hardships of people living in slums and workhouses who would have preferred to live in the buildings which remained empty for durations longer than the normal time lapse between occupants on the move.[23] What stopped the owners from off-loading the tax burden, either by selling the houses or letting them to tenants?

Smith was careful to protect his theory of property with his four famous maxims on taxation, the first of which was that people ought to contribute to the exchequer a proportion of their 'revenue which they respectively enjoy'.[24] The ability to pay was viewed as conditional on income actually being received, rather than potential income that could be imputed to the possession of a revenue-yielding resource. So a person may own a thousand acres which the citizens of London or New York may wish to use for factories, homes or recreation; but because the owner chooses not to let others have access to them (i.e., he decides to forego the potential income), he ought to be free of tax liability. Such was Adam Smith's fair play.

Thus it was that priority was accorded to land monopolists. Smith accurately recorded how people were denied access to marginal coal mines[25] (which could only yield sufficient income to pay for the labour and capital inputs), and to unimproved agricultural land,[26] until they were able to pay rent. This was not just a descriptive account, however. Adam Smith, the champion of mass production, the division of labour and competition as the means to achieving the lowest prices possible for industrial products, prescribed as sound policy the increase in the prices of food and raw materials to generate rent for the land monopolists. These price increases, 'instead of being considered as a public calamity, ought to be regarded as a necessary forerunner and attendant of the greatest of all public advantages'.[27]

When Smith noted that 'rent makes the first deduction from the produce of the labour which is employed upon land',[28] he was prescribing an order of priorities. Yet in a competitive system, economic rent is a surplus *after* the deduction of wages (for labour), and interest (for capital) from the value of output.

Smith could have altered the order in which income was distributed, by encouraging the establishment of a competitive system in which landlords were forced to compete through the introduction of a tax on the value of land. He refused to lend his weight to this fiscal reform, which had at the time been promoted by Newcastle schoolteacher Thomas Spence (who was imprisoned for his impudence).[29] Adam Smith thus established an intellectual tradition of opposition to the special taxation of rent that can be traced through the 19th century classical economists beginning with David Ricardo[30] and on to Herbert Spencer.[31] They all had a crystal-clear appreciation of the theory of economic rent, and they understood the macro-economic impact of land monopoly, but they were ultimately unwilling to advocate a fully-fledged fiscal policy designed to destroy the greatest of the monopolies that undermined the operations of the capitalist system.

This tradition was embodied in the British institutions which were subsequently replicated in the colonies right around the world. While the land monopolists could employ anti-social strikes with impunity, withholding land from those who needed to use it, the story was different for the men and women who worked in the factories. When *they* went on strike, they were severely attacked by the might of the State. A Manchester magistrate condemned 'This species of restraint or coercion', for it might 'be ultimately a great evil as nothing can be more clear than that commerce in every respect should be allowed to be entirely unshakled and free'.[32] Free men in a fair society would have no reason to go on strike, which is an act of desperation; they would have no reason to shackle commerce, for in doing so they cause themselves hardship. But strikes were the name of the game: the rules were originally established by the land monopolists — didn't they withdraw their acres from production when it suited them? These rules had been sanctified by Adam Smith. So working people were forced to use the system of withdrawing their labour as the only counter to the unequal power of the landowner and the capitalist. Thus was born a system grounded on the principles of deprivation and conflict.

Notes

1 Smith offered us 'a theoretical perfect machine — the mechanical operation of an economic stabilizer', according to A. L. MacFie, *The Individual in Society*, London: George Allen & Unwin, 1967, p. 104.

2 C. P. Kindleberger, 'The Historical Background: Adam Smith and the Industrial Revolution', in *The Market and the State*, eds.: T. Wilson and A. S. Skinner, Oxford: Clarendon Press, 1976; and R. Koebner, 'Adam Smith and the Industrial Revolution', *Econ. Hist. Rev.*, 2nd Series, Vol. XI, 1959.

3 A. Smith, *The Theory of Moral Sentiments*, 1759; page references are to the edition published by Liberty Classics, Indianapolis, 1969.

4 *Ibid.*, p. 304.

5 *Ibid.*, italics added.

6 *Ibid.*, pp. 304-305.

7 *Ibid.*, p. 297.

8 Page references are to the Edwin Cannan edition published by The University of Chicago Press, Chicago, 1976.

9 *Ibid.*, p. 275.

10 *Ibid.* Smith appears to contradict himself on this point on p. 335; but this later reference contains no supporting argument, whereas his earlier conclusion — which we accept as the correct one — is fully elaborated. John Stuart Mill arrived at the same conclusion on the distribution of national income in favour of the landlords: see his *Principles of Political Economy*, Bk V, Ch. 2, sec. 5.

11 A. W. Coats, 'Changing attitudes to labour in the mid-eighteenth century', *Econ. Hist. Rev.*, Vol. XI, 1958/9.

12 See *The Theory of Moral Sentiments*, and T. Wilson, 'Sympathy and Self-Interest', in Wilson and Skinner, *op. cit.*

13 *The Theory of Moral Sentiments*, *op. cit.*, p. 162.

14 E. H. Phelps Brown, 'The Labour Market', in Wilson and Skinner, *op. cit.*

15 *The Wealth of Nations*, *op. cit.*, pp. 162, 370.

16 *Ibid.*, pp. 276-277.

17 *Ibid.*, p. 56. Our emphases.

18 *Ibid.*, pp. 74-75.

19 There is one partial exception to this. Where people have borrowed money to speculate in land, the cost of servicing loans during a recession causes some of them to sell at a loss. But the overall effect is the same, for the new owners, buying at attractive prices, then proceed to sit on the land until they reap the speculative profits which were being sought by the previous owners.

20 *Op. cit.*, pp. 370-371.

21 *Ibid.*, p. 370.

22 *Ibid.*, p. 372.

23 A survey in Liverpool in 1773 revealed that 412 of the 6,340 houses were empty, which could not have been the result of a surplus stock: there were 8,000 families resident in the city, which meant that about 2,000 families had to share their homes with others. Rents were calculated to be high — 'very few can be supposed to let under £5', according to J. Aiken, *A Description of the Country from Thirty to Forty Miles round Manchester*, London, 1795, pp. 343, 374.

24 *Op. cit.*, p. 350.

25 'The landlord will allow nobody else to work them without paying some rent, and nobody can afford to pay any.' *Ibid.*, p. 184.

26 *Ibid.*, p. 252.
27 *Ibid.*, p. 253.
28 *Ibid.*, p. 73.
29 Mingay comments on this period: 'Prudence was the counsel that prevailed ... in fiscal matters. The protection of property was the overriding consideration, and no-one knew where economical reform might end — after all, a reassment of the land tax, by now a very modest burden, might prove to be its unforeseen and disastrous consequence'. G. E. Mingay, *English Landed Society in the Eighteenth Century*, London: Routledge & Kegan Paul, 1963, p. 262.
30 D. Ricardo, *Principles of Political Economy and Taxation* (1817), in *The Works of David Ricardo*, London: John Murray, 1888, p. 121.
31 For a critique of his recantation on the land tax issue, which he had delineated in *Social Statics* (1850), see H. George, *A Perplexed Philosopher* (1892), New York: Robert Schalkenbach Foundation, 1946.
32 J. L. and B. Hammond, *The Skilled Labourer 1760-1832*, London: Longmans, Green & Co., 1933, p. 115.

3

Monopoly and the Veil of Secrecy

Conspiracy theories are an unattractive way of attacking the enemy. They generally serve as short-cuts across the gaps of ignorance, substitutes for the painstaking process of accumulating and evaluating evidence for submission to the court of public opinion. And they often conceal a certain timidity, for the loose allegations — splattered over a wide area, not hitting the bull's eye of a sharply-defined target — deny the accused the right to challenge concrete charges and then retaliate against the accusers.

We do, here, identify a grand conspiracy, in the belief that the evidence is forthcoming to substantiate the charges. The specific allegations are that land monopolists, since the Industrial Revolution, have systematically prevented the public from undertaking those inventories that would lift the veil of secrecy that shrouds the land market; that their success arises from the monopolistic structure of the land market; that this has been the greatest anti-social conspiracy in modern history; and that monopolists have been motivated by the knowledge that, paradoxically, government interference — through the fiscal system — is a pre-condition for the creation of freedom and competition in the land market.

A key defining characteristic of capitalism is rationality — the need for long range planning, adaptation of means to ends, and for exact calculation. This specifies the need for information. 'Underlying the planning and its execution are the evaluation and registration of all business facts in precise quantitative terms and the co-ordination of these records as a significant whole.'[1] Thus, through the ledgers laboriously compiled by the book-keepers, the individual entrepreneurs could monitor their performance in relation to their attempts to service their consumers. The records exposed their behaviour to themselves and to their competitors, either directly (through access to the balance sheet) or indirectly (through the prices that they charged based on production costs). No such informative facility was available to chronicle the land market.

Compared to the availability of data and institutions which enable us to talk

33

intelligibly about the 'labour market' or the 'capital market', there is no land market. There are no regularly-published indices of land prices equivalent to the Dow-Jones Industrial Average or the *Financial Times* Ordinary Share Index. The paucity of information on land is a scandal, for it entails a serious limitation on the economic system to operate at an optimum level of efficiency. One scholar, Colin Clark, notes that 'land use and land values now constitute one of the most important questions in the world, but the amount of research effort devoted to them is deplorably small'.[2]

The industrial economy was forced to establish itself without the aid of a centralised institution dealing in land comparable to the London Stock Exchange,[3] where it was possible to find out what was being sold, and at what prices. A notable attempt to create a recognisable land market was made in 1857. A group of London auctioneers established the Estate Exchange in an effort to bring buyers and sellers together, facilitating the efficient use of land within the UK on the basis of the fullest possible dissemination of information.[4] The attempt failed, but the fact that it was made (it had been proposed in 1838) says something about the needs of the economy.[5] More recently, the American Real Estate Exchange was established in San Francisco in 1969. By 1981, it had nearly $7.5bn. in properties on its sales list, double the value of the previous year and an indication that even monopolists will use such outlets when the depressed state of the economy begins to affect them, but on a typical morning, only 75 real estate people and eight traders were found to be dealing on the floor of the exchange.[6]

The absence of an integrated economy-wide land market resulted from the very nature of monopoly power. Labour and capital spontaneously create their factor markets in the course of competing within themselves and with each other for the opportunities to earn income from the creation of new wealth. Land remains largely aloof from this competitive process. As a result, such markets as have developed are localised and depend on the intimate knowledge of real estate agents and advertisements in local newspapers. This places buyers at a severe disadvantage, for their imperfect knowledge about what is happening elsewhere in the economy means that they are ill-equipped to make rational judgments on the 'best buys'.

Despite the monopoly power and the severe imperfections of knowledge entailed in land transactions, economic theorists persist in describing the rent of land as arising from the interplay of supply and demand as these concepts are understood in their classical sense. This account is inconsistent with the facts. According to the theory of perfect competition, landowners play submissive role: they accept the 'left-overs' from economic activity. That is they exact what remains over and above that part of fresh output which is necessary to attract labour and capital into the productive process. In this sense, economic rent is a surplus; it becomes a correct measure of the differential contributions of specific plots of land arising from varying fertility or the advantages accruing to favourable locations.

But this model cannot function once monopoly power is introduced. For material welfare can be optimised by the entrepreneur only if he can calculate the correct inputs of land, labour and capital on the basis of their true relative costs. Land monopolists inhibit these calculations to a frightening degree. The proof is presented in the following chapters. Meanwhile, we anticipate the evidence and elaborate what we consider to be the ideal solution, to provide readers with a touchstone against which to judge the workings of the most imperfectly understood element of the industrial economy, namely, the land market.

The only way of eliminating monopoly power in the land market is to compel owners to compete with each other on a continuous basis. The only efficient method of accomplishing this is to impose an annual tax on the value of all land that is capable of yielding rental income. Owners would thus be obliged to put their land to good use, within the framework of existing social and economic needs, and legal constraints (e.g., zoning). By doing so, they would acquire an income out of which to pay their tax dues.

Thus, they would not be able to hold valuable land vacant. Sites that were needed for recreation, housing, industry, commerce, and so on, would be released, thereby removing the eye-sores of derelict sites in the middle of our great cities. This *ad valorem* tax, which becomes a cost on the right to possess and use land, effectively neutralizes the power of the monopolist to withhold it from use for no better reason than the wish to cash in — at some future date — on the needs of society for a finite resource. It would, furthermore, remove the temptation to force rents above the realistic levels made possible by the best current uses (hope values, as they are known).

Not only would the tax have a dynamic impact on the land market *per se*, but it would also generate a higher level of activity generally. For the tax ought not to be an additional one, but ought to be a substitute for existing taxes. Indirectly, therefore, the land value tax would smooth out the kinks in the labour and capital markets — imperfections which, as we shall see, were in the main originally generated by land monopoly — thereby extending its benefits throughout the economy.

Before this fiscal reform can be introduced, however, legal titles have to be registered and a survey of values undertaken. The Domesday Book is an example of such an exercise. An up-to-date public register of titles facilitates the transfer of land, for it reduces the legal and administrative costs of checking the legitimacy of titles every time a site changes hands. Lawyers have traditionally opposed the registration of titles in Britain. William Petty, in noting the prosperity of Holland in the 17th century (a prosperity which, we venture to suggest, had something to do with the land

tax, the administration of which Adam Smith deprecated), pointed to the
importance of that country's register of titles to land. Proposals to introduce
registers in England, he said, were stridently opposed by the legal profession.[7] Today, there is public access to title documents in Scotland, but not in
England and Wales. In the US, they are scattered throughout the nation, in
records offices that make a systematic collation and examination difficult.

Landowners, of course, have been in the vanguard of the opposition to the
orderly institutionalisation of land (beyond the minimum system required to
guarantee recognition of legal titles). An open register of titles, incorporating
details of acreage and value, would make the owners vulnerable to taxation.
The absence of hard data made it difficult for the post-medieval bureaucracy
to collect land taxes systematically and on a permanent basis. The landed class
which controlled Parliament made sure that the land tax (which did not fall
exclusively on economic rent) was a fluctuating one. In the main, it was raised
during times of war.[8] This was acceptable because it identified landowners
with a patriotic cause and at the same time set limits to the extent and duration
of the tax.

By contrast, data on the employment of labour is carefully monitored.
Statistics are regularly published on the numbers out of work, regional
variations, and the trends in job vacancies. Industrialists are regularly surveyed to establish the utilisation levels of their capital equipment and their
investment intentions. No such concern is expressed about the use of land.

The waste of valuable land has reached crisis proportions in the Western
world, yet governments refuse to establish the extent of the problem. The
cavalier way in which the land market is treated by the politicians can be
illuminated by the British experience. In 1976 the Labour Government's
Secretary of State for the Environment (Peter Shore) declined to establish the
amount of *publicly-owned* vacant land on the grounds of disproportionate
cost.[9] His successor in Margaret Thatcher's Conservative Government
(Michael Heseltine) reversed the cost calculations, and ordered local
governments to create registers of publicly-owned vacant land; but he
declined to take similar action to register *privately-owned* vacant land.

As a result of the nebulous attitudes of the politicians, the exercise in
quantification is left to under-financed scholars[10] and private organisations
which feel an intuitive concern. One of these, the Civic Trust, exists to arouse
pride in the appearance of towns in Britain. Apart from the 137,000 acres in
England and Wales which were officially classified as derelict (1977), the
Trust estimated that 250,000 acres were 'dormant'. Their report[11] is an
indictment of land use; but while a dramatic case was made out in relation to
the visual appearance of neglected sites in the cities, the effect on gross
national product could not be calculated because the extent of the problem is
impossible to judge without a latter-date Domesday Book survey. And it is

now more than 100 years since the last official study into the ownership and value of land has been conducted (*Return of Owners of Land in England and Wales*, 1873).[12]

The economic effects of the veil of secrecy that shrouds the land market have serious political implications. The power wielded by the land monopolist in his various guises is enormous, is growing rapidly and undergoing important transformations. Before the Second World War there were practically no property companies in existence. The land speculator was usually an individual with the cash resources which enabled him to buy shrewdly, await events and then capitalise on this outlay. But by the mid-1970s, about 180 property companies were quoted on the London Stock Exchange. An estimated 10,000 private property companies were active in Britain,[13] about which there is little systematic knowledge. In 1981, Britain's Society of Investment Analysts identified the property sector as the one in which companies were 'secretive' about their dealings. Annual reports were 'long on pictures but short on financial information, or illuminating comment'.[14] This made sense for the land dealers, for by masking their activities behind the veil of secrecy they minimise competition to their financial advantage.

Insurance companies and pension funds have about £30bn. invested in land and buildings, a total that is rapidly increasing each year. In addition, the merchant banks are increasing their stake in the equity of properties developed with their finance in the 1980s. These developments are paralleled throughout the Western world, but their impact cannot be tracked because of the dearth of information on which analytical evaluations have to be based. This was the major finding of research in 1982 by a City of London stockbroker, Christopher Walls, who discovered the alarming extent of our ignorance when he tried to investigate institutional investment in property.

The topic is of crucial importance for our understanding not only of real estate, but also because of the implications for economic regeneration: real estate constitutes to a large extent the credit lending base for UK industry. And in 1982 the institutions invested £2bn. in property, hardly a penny-pinching operation of no concern to people in the rest of the economy.

The study by Walls should have been a routine exercise for an investment advisor, but it rapidly turned into an impossible task. He was confronted with misleading and inaccurate information'; the quality of the official and unofficial statistics was abysmal; the yields from prime property were misrepresented by the simple expedient of shifting the definition of what constituted prime property; and there was no standard practice for declaring the value of assets.

Walls touched on the essence of the problem when he noted that the introduction of a free market in property 'would be very welcome from the point of view of economic efficiency but could be disastrous for some property investors'.[15] The point was well understood by Hammerson, one of the major British property companies whose chairman, Sydney Mason, was quoted in 1977 as stating: 'I would rather have our planning restrictions and no competition'. In 1982, Hammerson raised £70m. through the issue of new shares, while successfully concealing the value of its assets. Walls noted with an evident sense of disbelief:

> I do not know in that particular case which is worse — Hammerson's continued refusal to let its shareholders know what the real value is of what they own, or the Stock Exchange's surprisingly relaxed attitude in letting Hammerson make yet another rights issue without again revaluing its portfolio, or the auditors who can carry on signing an audit certificate (presumably with a straight face) which says that the accounts 'give a true and fair view of the state of affairs of the company and the group' when the property portfolio is stated in the balance sheet at cost and the directors' valuation of the portfolio deliberately excludes the entire reversionary potential of the portfolio.[16]

The indifference towards the influence of land monopoly on the industrial economy is only too apparent; this indifference actually masks a positive discrimination in favour of the interests of the landed class.

Governments direct their policies in favour of supporting rental income.[17] An historical example from the rural sector is the use to which the British Parliament put the Corn Laws. These imposed duties on imported wheat. By restricting international trade, domestic prices rose and ensured high land values and rental income. Adam Smith would presumably have approved of this policy, for it culminated in what he deemed to be 'the greatest of all public advantages' — even though the policy directly contradicted his strictures against trade protectionism. After 1815, and towards the end of the Corn Law period in the 1840s, the effect on consumers was serious; average prices were higher, and the extreme prices were occasionally very much higher, than they would have been if people had been free to eat foreign-grown wheat.[18]

The consequences were serious at the levels of both households and the economy. For example, the Commission on Hand-loom Weavers found evidence that the greatest grievance of the weavers was the price of food. As a result of the high proportion of their wages which they were forced to spend on food, 'their power of purchasing clothes was curtailed, and the home demand for manufactures was checked'.[19] A similar restrictive effect on international trade was felt. Potential customers in foreign lands could not buy goods made in Britain because they could not sell their wheat on the British market.

A contemporary example from the USA is the practice of funnelling federal government money to farmers as an inducement to set aside land and reduce the output of food. This keeps food prices high and retards the living standards of consumers (who would otherwise spend less on food, and more on durable goods). The value of land, moreover, is increased above its competitive market level, which is the ultimate effect of official policy.[20]

An identical effect on social welfare is achieved by the decisions made by individual land monopolists. An example from the urban sector neatly illustrates how speculation restricts economic growth.

Economists traditionally assume that the ceiling on output is set by the rate of growth of population, technical progress and the accumulation of capital; land monopoly is ignored as a brake on the economy. At a London meeting of the Underground Railway Group in February 1927, Lord Ashfield complained bitterly that the Edgware extension of the London Electric Railway had continued to develop its traffic 'at a slower rate than was anticipated'. Why? He offered an explanation: land speculation at the Edgware terminal had forced up prices to a level which restricted purchases. 'This is an evil which besets all railway enterprise,' he declared, and he proposed as a remedy 'some means by which the increment in the value of the land could be appropriated to pay some share of the enormous cost attending the construction of Underground Railways in Greater London'.

The following year, Lord Ashfield's complaint was investigated by the Liberal Party's Industrial Inquiry, the committee of which included Lloyd George and John Maynard Keynes. They reported:

> Lord Ashfield's suggestion applies not only to London and not only to railway undertakings. It applies to all major transport undertakings, and public improvements in every part of the country. The increase in land values might in some cases pay the whole cost of the development and in all cases a large part of it.[21]

This was a familiar story: public expenditure on improved transportation — to cut the costs of travel and extend the range of living and working environments — pushed up land values. This, in itself, is not a weakness of the economic system, provided that the price of land was not forced above the economic surplus — the real rental value of land proportionate to the current output of wealth. Under the present arrangements, however, not only are the socially-created increases in land values privately appropriated, but the monopolistic structure of the land market encourages speculators to force up their asking prices to speculative levels, consequently retarding the process of capital formation and economic growth.

The vital conclusions ought to be obvious, but they have been ignored. Where capitalists cut costs and increase efficiency, land monopolists serve their interests best by increasing costs and decreasing overall efficiency.

Where capitalism raises consumer satisfaction by extending the range of goods and services at lower prices, land monopoly restricts the choice and raises prices. This outcome arises inevitably from the simple truth that the pursuit of speculative rents can reward the monopolists only by curtailing general welfare.

But vacant sites are not the only manifestation of a malfunctioning land market. Monopoly can produce economic inefficiency even when owners *use* their land. For monopoly enables landowners to conceal entrepreneurial inefficiency. If, for instance, the performance of a firm is inadequate to pay wages at the ruling rates, interest on capital investment and rent to land, the proprietors can delude themselves by foregoing the economic rent which they ought, as a bookkeeping exercise, to impute to themselves as landowners. What usually happens is that they pay wages and interest, and disregard rental income. While this situation may be tolerable to the owner-occupying entrepreneurs, resources are not being used to their best advantage so far as the economy is concerned. Output, and therefore welfare, is not being maximised.

Assume that the firm is in a shrinking industry. Competing firms (which rent their land) have to close down or switch to producing goods or services which the consumers want, and for which they are willing to pay a price yielding sufficient returns to justify the employment of all the factors of production. The stark reality of this position can be hidden from the firm which owns its land. Their day of judgment is deferred. But as a result, firms which want to expand in new directions cannot use the land, labour and capital which are tied up in the redundant firm or industry: artificial shortages constrain the aggregate growth of the economy. The inefficient allocation of resources would be quickly terminated by the imposition of a land tax on market-imputed rental income. If a firm was unable to pay that tax *and* meet its wages bill and returns to capital, it would have to change to some other, more desirable and remunerative activity.

Without that tax, there is less inducement on the firm to make the quick adjustments which would raise general welfare. Very often the end for the ailing firms comes when a land speculator moves in and undertakes an 'asset stripping' operation. By shrewdly judging that the land is not being put to its best use, they buy the firm cheaply, terminate the loss-making side of the enterprise and cash-in on the capital value of the land.[22]

Such an operation can contribute usefully to the reallocation of resources. Is this not a justification for profits from land dealing? No. Under the present fiscal regime, asset strippers often keep their new acquisitions idle in the certain expectation of future capital gains. And there is no reason why the desired transformations could not be engineered to everyone's advantage *except* the speculator's. A land tax which completely removed the private gains from land monopoly would induce the changed use of resources. This would result in higher wages and yields on capital (from the pursuit of more profitable lines of production), while simultaneously increasing public revenue from that portion of wealth that was socially created — economic rent.[23]

An examination of the history of Western industrial society will reveal that land monopoly — and not the acquisitive motives of the capitalists — is the constant internal (but not intrinsic) disruptive influence on the system. If the evidence does sustain this conclusion, we will begin to see the significance in the astonishing admission by Marx — which his disciples ignore — that capitalists play a worthwhile role in the creation of wealth:

> The capitalist still performs an active function in the development of this surplus-value and surplus-product. But the landowner need only appropriate the growing share in the surplus-product and the surplus-value, without having contributed anything to this growth.[24]

Had Marx remained consistent, and pursued to its logical conclusion the evidence which he had accumulated, he would have been led to affirm the virtues of the free market unconstrained by land monopoly.[25] His work in Britain would have complemented Henry George's in America, and modern history would have been dramatically transformed.

But this did not happen, and so we now have to reappraise the historical evidence from the beginning in order to acquire a new appreciation of why events unfolded as they did, and how different they might have been if the land monopolist had been removed from the outset. With the new insights, we can then re-evaluate the strategy of the modern economy in the hope of establishing that system of natural harmony and justice to which Adam Smith claimed that he aspired.

Notes

1   W. Sombert, 'Capitalism', in *Encyclopaedia of the Social Sciences*, Vol. III, New York: Macmillan, 1930, p. 198.

2   C. Clark, 'Prospects for Future Collaboration — the Universities' Contribution', in *New Horizons on Land and Property Values*, RICS Technical Information Service, March 1966. For a statement on the paucity of data on real estate in Britain, see comments by Sir Jasper Hollom, Deputy Governor of the Bank of England, *Chartered Surveyor*, March 1977, p. 257. More recently, one of Britain's leading fiscal experts, A. R. Prest, a professor of economics at the London School of Economics, roundly condemned 'the disgraceful inadequacy of information about landownership'. A. R. Prest, *The Taxation of Urban Land*, Manchester: Manchester University Press, 1981, p. 187.

3   From 1804 stockbrokers met in a special building, the Stock Exchange, which
     they erected close to the Bank of England out of funds raised by subscription
     from the profession.

4   F.M.L. Thompson, 'The Land Market in the Nineteenth Century', in
     W.E. Minchinton, *Essays in Agrarian History*, Vol. II, Newton Abbot: David &
     Charles, 1968, pp. 31-32, 40-41.

5   J.H. Clapham, *An Economic History of Modern Britain, 1850-1886*, Vol. II,
     p. 254. The absence of a nation-wide compendium of property information led
     the London-based *Estates Times* to launch its quarterly *Deals Digest* in 1981 to
     provide 'the vital, local information you need for fast, confident decision making
     in valuations, lettings and other deals'.

6   R. Vicker, 'Real Estate', *The Wall Street Journal*, 17.6.81.

7   W. Petty, *Political Arithmetick*, London, 1690, pp. 27-28.

8   C. Hill, *Reformation to Industrial Revolution*, Harmondsworth: Pelican, 1969,
     p. 221.

9   *Hansard*, 25.10.76, col. 235.

10   John Burrows surveyed idle city land for his M.Sc degree at the University of
     London. He reported in *The Times* (26.2.77): 'On average, between three per
     cent and five per cent of city land is vacant, with one half to two-thirds of the total
     outside the inner areas. Within the inner areas, the remaining vacant land forms
     five per cent to 12 per cent of the area. The inner areas of Glasgow and Liver-
     pool and some East End London boroughs have over 10 per cent of their land
     vacant representing some 300 to 400 hectares in each case'.

11   *Urban Wasteland*, London: Civic Trust, 1977.

12   An examination was undertaken into Britain's agricultural land in the 1970s. See
     *Report of the Committee of Inquiry into the Acquisition and Occupancy of Agricultural
     Land* (chairman: Lord Northfield), London: HMSO, Cmnd. 7599, 1979. Its
     value can be judged from the fact that (a) most properties in Britain are urban, and
     (b) as the committee noted — p. 109, para 259 — 'Throughout our work we
     were hampered by the lack of detailed information on many of the topics we
     studied. It is disturbing that so little is known about the pattern of acquisition,
     ownership and occupancy of agricultural land...' In sharp contrast, however,
     selective data was available — where it was needed to facilitate agricultural
     support policy (p. 113, para. 272).

13   'The future of the valuation surveyor', *Chartered Surveyor*, Dec. 1977, p. 135.

14   *Annual Reports Awards Committee*, 1981 Report, Bromley: The Society of
     Investment Analysts, Nov. 1981, pp. 40-42.

15   C. Walls, 'Property and the Operation of the Financial Markets', speech on
     July 1, 1982, to a conference of The Department of Land Economy, Cambridge
     University, and The Cambridge University Land Society, London: Simon &
     Coates, July 1982, p. 5.

16   *Ibid.*, p. 4.

17   There is an exception to this rule, but it has been a transitory phenomenon. Land-
     lords who let out accommodation in the housing market were a target of socialist
     rent control policy. These controls did cause financial hardship. But the majority
     of the original owners have long since vanished, and they have been replaced by
     speculators who paid low prices for rent-controlled properties. They speculate
     on the death of occupants (and in some notorious cases, they have used illegal
     bully-boy tactics to rid themselves of their tenants); their intention is to cash-in
     by selling their properties at de-controlled prices. Rent controls have reduced the

rented sector and thus imposed the hardships on tenants, who have not been able to find the accommodation that they need, and on the economy (the shortage of houses to let has been a critical factor in the immobility of labour).

18 J.S. Nicholson, *History of the English Corn Laws*, London: Swan Sonnenschein, 1904, p. 52.

19 W. Cunningham, *The Growth of English Industry and Commerce in Modern Times*, Cambridge: Cambridge University Press, 1903, Part II, p. 841.

20 H. Hoyt, 'The Urban Real Estate Cycle — Performances and Prospects', Urban Land Institute Technical Bulletin No. 38, p. 15.

21 *Britain's Industrial Future*, the Report of the Liberal Industrial Inquiry (1928), 2nd edn., 1977, London: Ernest Benn, p. 295.

22 For a description of such activity in Britain in the 1950s, see G. Bull and A. Vice, *Bid for Power*, 1958. Jim Slater was one of the most successful asset strippers of the 1960s. For an account of one operation, in which his company, Slater Walker, made a profit of over £7m. by buying Forestal and selling its lands in Africa, South America and Britain, see A. Vice, *The Strategy of Takeovers*, Maidenhead: McGraw Hill, 1971, Ch. 1.

23 An interesting example of inadequate valuation and monitoring procedures is provided by the Crown Estate, the Commissioners of which administer 250,000 rural acres and a vast portfolio of urban property and mineral rights to finance the Queen of England's household. In 1982, just 2% of the Estate's properties were valued. In this case, the Commissioners were not seeking to hide anything. Nonetheless, the result — in terms of an inability to monitor commercial performance properly — was the same. They were criticised by a House of Commons committee because 'we do not consider that the Commissioners can account satisfactorily for their stewardship without presenting a balance sheet which shows the capital assets entrusted to their management'. *Crown Estate Abstract Accounts 1980-81*, House of Commons Committee of Public Accounts, London: HMSO, 1982, p. viii, para. ii.

24 K. Marx, *Capital*, London: Lawrence & Wishart, 1962, Vol. III, p. 623.

25 F. Harrison, 'Gronlund and Other Marxists', in R. V. Andelson, editor, *Critics of Henry George*, Rutherford: Fairleigh Dickinson University Press, 1979.

4

The Power Loom Puzzle

The Industrial Revolution was heralded by a flood of inventions and the accumulation of capital which, in new forms, constituted enormous power with which to produce wealth. Innovation was in the air. People were searching for new ways of producing goods at cheaper cost. The conveyor belt was born. Mass production based on the division of labour and the use of mechanical power could have raised the living standards of everybody. Sadly, for the workers, this was not to be:

> ... without the increase in productive power that is due to industrialization the rise in real wages could not possibly have occurred. The important question is why it was so long delayed. There is no doubt at all that it was delayed; whether there was a small rise, or an actual fall, in the general level of real wages in England between (say) 1780 and 1840 leaves that issue untouched. It is the lag of wages behind industrialization which is the thing that has to be explained.[1]

Explanations for this have been partial and none have taken into account the regressive effect of land monopoly. The Marxist critique has conditioned us to believe that capital and the motives of its owners constitute the problematic area. The acquisitive greed of the capitalists is held to be responsible for large-scale poverty and deprivation.

From the outset the modern factory system has been blamed. Men had been severed from a tranquil, pastoral history and the machine was nominated as Enemy No. 1. Yet this was ironical, for the machine was as much a victim of the early years of industrial society as were the men.

The land monopolists' ability to periodically exact speculative rents — demanding a portion of *tomorrow's* higher level of output *today* — deterred new capital formation. If this hypothesis is correct, it should solve a curious mystery: why the cotton kings of Lancashire were strangely reluctant to expand their businesses by enthusiastically adopting the power loom during the first long-run trade cycle in industrial history. By untangling the webb

44

which shrouds this phenomenon we expect to reveal the inner processes at work in the imperfectly-free market which shackled the machine and postponed the prospect of prosperity for the men who owned or worked with them.

It was over tea with some friends in a hostelry in Matlock, Derbyshire, in 1784, that the Rev. Edmund Cartwright, a country parson and Fellow of Magdalene College, Cambridge, resolved to invent a power loom which would take the backache out of weaving cotton. Hitherto, weaving had been by hand in little cellars and country cottages. But with the invention of the spinning jenny, the manufacturers from Manchester to Glasgow were producing yarn at an unprecedented rate. Output was threatening to race ahead of the capacity to turn it into cloth. This was a problem for new technology to solve, and when he returned to his home in Nottingham, Cartwright set to work on a lathe. He soon produced the first mechanical device for weaving cotton, a major technical breakthrough which promised astonishing results for the leading industry in Britain. Yet it was to be four decades before the manufacturers took up mechanical weaving on a serious scale. Why? Although more efficient than hand-weaving the apparent lack of interest in the invention was attributed by observers at that time to the competition from low-wage hand-weavers. Mr Brougham addressed his fellow Members of the House of Commons in 1817 in these terms:

> It is now found, for the first time in the history of mankind, so low are wages fallen, so great is the pressure of distress, that manual labour is making reprisals on machinery, standing a successful competition with it, beating it out of the market, and precluding the use of an engine, far from costly in itself, which saves three labourers in four. The further introduction of the power loom is actually stopped by the low rate of weavers' wages.[2]

This attempt at an explanation is unconvincing. It is true that this was a period of hunger marches and demands from the cotton weavers for a legally-enforced minimum living wage; a time when brave cavalrymen with swords drawn charged and killed defenceless protestors at Peterloo, in Manchester. But the argument is inconsistent with the timing. In 1808, one estimate put the number of factories using the power loom as only 28 or 30.[3] In 1813 there were about 2,400 power looms in the UK; in 1820 there were a mere 14,150. But then, in the next decade, the number escalated to about 55,000 in 1829.[4] Why, in the third decade of the 19th century — when wages were still low — did entrepreneurs suddenly find the power loom an attractive proposition?[5]

The cotton weavers' wages were low, but this was not due to their having to compete with machines. If anything, the higher output of machine production should have raised wages, and for this there is evidence.[6] One major reason for the level of wages was the competition from migrant Irish peasants, who could learn the weaving technique quickly and were willing to accept lower wages than Englishmen.[7]

Brougham's explanation is also unconvincing because it implies that the entrepreneurs were making sufficient profits — thanks to the low rate of wages and piece rates — to justify continued production under the existing system. This was not the case.[8] Nor does a change in consumer demand offer an explanation. If the foreign markets were restricted during the Napoleonic war, they were not much better when peace came: an impoverished Europe did not act as a significant stimulant to output in the 1820s. A minor boom in 1825 was preceded and followed by business recessions. Yet there was a marked switch to power looms during this decade.

Equally unsatisfactory is the suggestion by Halévy that the rate of take-up of power looms could have been retarded by the threats against the machines from the handweavers.[9] Weavers were no more vigorous in their protests than other groups of workers who, before or since then, believed that their livelihoods were jeopardised by the introduction of machinery; and threats from workers in agricultural or other manufacturing sectors did not deter capitalists from introducing their innovations if there was a profit to be made.

Even less plausible is Halévy's main explanation, that manufacturers would not invest in the power loom because existing capital equipment had not been exhausted. In fact, it is difficult to understand how he could have advanced this argument at all. After describing how the cotton manufacturers had readily adopted machines for spinning the yarn, he continued:

> For the weavers, however, the change involved the complete sacrifice of the old plant, in which much capital had been sunk. It was surely but natural that the forces of resistance should be much stronger in this department and that the critical period of change should be far longer and should entail far greater suffering.[10]

This suggests that Halévy did not understand the structure of the cotton industry at that time, yet on the next page he gave an adequate description of it. The yarn was spun in the factories and then bought by merchants who took it to the weavers to turn into cloth at agreed rates; the cloth was then sold back to the manufacturers for finishing (e.g., dyeing). The merchants had no large fixed capital equipment at risk, and there was no question of the weavers themselves having the power to resist technological innovation in order to preserve the capital value of the looms which they owned. Those looms, while precious to the weavers, were not as vulnerable as Halévy suggests and their owners wielded no influence over the manufacturer, merchant or Parliament such that they could deter new capital formation by fair means or foul. Halévy must have intuitively understood this, for he fell back on the 'low wages' thesis which he believed he had rejected.[11] But he reversed the argument; instead of the machines beating down wages, and thereby making fresh capital formation unattractive, he concluded that the weavers anticipated the mechanical threat to their traditional, independent weaving process by accepting lower wages and thereby removing the incentive to use machinery.[12] This assumes that the slum-dwelling weavers had at some early stage enjoyed reasonably high wages which they could then afford to reduce, an untenable hypothesis according to the historical evidence.

The point at which the power loom would have been introduced was in the factory, alongside the established cotton spinning processes. The factory owners had no weaving machines threatened with redundancy; but they *did* have an incentive to adopt the power loom, to use up some of the surplus yarn which they were now producing. And credit from banks was available for the manufacturers in the biggest growth industry in the leading trade nation in the world.

On top of all this, there was another sound reason for a quick transformation to mechanical weaving. The price of cotton goods slid fast during the first two decades of the 19th century. Profits were squeezed, but could have been raised by the use of the new machines, which would have cut the unit costs of producing the final article. The power loom, as Mr Brougham pointed out, 'saves three labourers in four'. And inventors like Cartwright were not bashful about publicising the efficiency of their mechanical process compared with the traditional way of doing things by hand. Why, then, was investment in the power loom avoided during the formative decades of an industrial society in which innovation and enterprise constituted the motivating ethos?

The answers can be found in the evidence left by William Radcliffe, who chronicled the affairs of the cotton industry for the benefit of future historians. Radcliffe presents us with a paradox. He earned a good living out of trading, yet he was the first industrialist in the history of modern society to systematically campaign for restrictions on trade. From 1800 onwards he fought vigorously to turn public sentiment away from free international trade which, due largely to the popularity of *The Wealth of Nations*, swayed the parliamentarians who formulated national policy. Radcliffe's campaign was tragic not because he failed, but because it was misconceived. He failed to correctly identify his enemy, the landowner; so much so, that he actually ended up by siding with them and supporting their cause. In doing so, he unwittingly multiplied the problems which confronted the industry to which he devoted a lifetimes's work.

Radcliffe believed that Britain should stop exporting her surplus yarn to European and North American countries, where weavers turned it into cloth which then competed with British cloth in the world's markets.[13] Mercilessly

he attacked the Lancashire cotton manufacturers who indulged in what he
called the 'vile traffic' which was — he believed — responsible for impover-
ishing both employers and workers. Convinced that he had isolated the true
cause of the industry's problems, he roundly attacked 'the curse of modern
political economists, and liberal (*meaning retrograde*) march of mind'.

So it came about that, by one of those curious twists of history, the first
major critique of free international trade came from a man who was a leading
capitalist and benefactor of *laissez faire* ! Radcliffe was not pursuing this policy
out of self-interest; he was not attempting to line his pockets with the profits
arising from oligopolistic control over markets. He was responding to an
industry-wide problem. His misdiagnosis of that problem, and the solution
which appeared to commend itself, was to be the first of many more similar
errors perpetrated as the industrial system evolved.

William Radcliffe was a substantial entrepreneur in his own right, but he
did not fit the stereotyped image beloved by socialist critics of capitalism. He
was neither inhumane towards his employees, nor constantly grasping after
profits, nor self-centred to the exclusion of the interests of others. He was
born on a small farm in Lancashire, where he learnt the cotton weaving trade
from his father, who was a small landowner. So industrious was he that he
expanded his business to the point where he was employing 1,000 weavers
scattered over three counties. In the record he left the industry, he referred
to the capital which he had managed to save and he confidently issued a
challenge:

> I can truly say that it had not been got by 'grinding the face of the poor;'
> for my greatest pride was to see them comfortable; and in every trans-
> action with them, my equals and superiors, 'I did by each, as I would they
> should have done to me,' and I challenge enquiry in the circle I moved in,
> that no fact can be found to contradict what I have said; and I give the same
> challenge as to any deviation from this principle to the present day.[14]

From his home in the small town of Mellor he undertook public-spirited
works, such as improving the roads; his reputation grew and he was
appointed to three district commissions and was destined for the magistrate's
bench. But at the age of 40 he uprooted his family and moved to Stockport.
The new factory system proved too strong to resist.

Radcliffe quickly established a sound business just 14 miles from Manchester, the mecca of the cotton industry. But he soon realised that cotton
spinning was going to pose problems. Rather than export the industry's
surplus yarn, why not develop a new process under one roof which would
ensure that the yarn was woven as fast as it was spun? He talked the problem
over with his partner in 1800, but it was not until the following summer that
he worked out his finances and decided to act. Risking his own capital, he

bought premises from Messrs. Olknow and Arkwright and set about constructing a new system with the aid of a handpicked team of workers. Radcliffe had confidence in his eventual success. He had a wager with his partner that he would prove successful within two years: he won the bet.

Radcliffe built on Cartwright's power loom inventions, and in 1803-4 he patented a dressing machine. The business soon yielded him a profit of £100 a week, and money began to roll in from the licences accorded under his patent rights. But there was no question of his trying to steal a march over his competitors in the industry, for in 1811 he set up a club with the aim of diffusing knowledge about the latest mechanical methods of cloth-making. It was one of his proud boasts that he employed more skilled men than he needed, so that some of them could go off to other factories to help manufacturers to master the latest techniques.

Radcliffe was clear about the reason why he originally undertook the risky business of invention, which could have absorbed his capital and left him penniless: the demand for mechanical weaving existed within the industry. At no point in his detailed account of these developments did he complain that entrepreneurs could not obtain bank loans for new investment. Yet despite all his efforts the diffusion of the new technology was painfully slow. Why?

The deterioration in the condition of the weavers began with the termination of what he called the golden years, from 1788 to 1803. The industry went into a decline. Profits and wages were cut back drastically. Within two decades, he recorded, the price of weaving had dropped 'from 17s. (with a profit of 10 to 20 per cent to the master,) to 4s. to the weaver (and no profit to the master!)'. With the decline in price, the employers were forced to reduce wages: '... the masters foresaw the evils this system of lowering the wages would produce, they had no choice left; as they must either go on in this way, or give up their manufacture altogether'.[15] Wages, he declared with emphasis, were *below the bread and water level.*

The power loom was popularly blamed and attacked as a threat to the employment of weavers. These were men who could hardly be expected to understand the macro-economic forces which were responsible for their pitiable condition. Radcliffe was one of the targets of protest: attempts were made to burn down his factory, and stones were thrown through the windows of his home.[16] This was the time of the Luddites, who wished to smash machines on the assumption that they created hardship rather than increased general welfare. Robert Owen, the utopian socialist, believed that he had demonstrated that mechanisation created an increasing gap between consumption and potential production: he was one of the first economic theorists to advance the under-consumption hypothesis as an explanation of economic recession. But if there was under-consumption, this could not be attributed to a lack of demand. For the workers and their families were hungry and over-worked, their homes were small and mean: there was enormous unsatisfied consumer demand. To blame the economic recession in the 1820s on 'over-production' was a perversion of reality.

Radcliffe's experience with technological innovations during his early years in Mellor convinced him that machines could not be held responsible for the plight of the weavers. 'Surely there must be some other cause for their distress, than the interference of the new system, which, in fact, has never yet interfered directly with them at all,' he asked. The new methods of spinning cotton, he pointed out, actually increased the demand for labour and boosted wages.[17] Radcliffe had no doubt about the enemy of his industry: it was that 'Foreign Anglo Junto' which conspired in Manchester to carry off the yarn to foreign lands, there to be spun cheaply and sold in competition with British cloth. By imposing a duty on such exports, he repeatedly informed the Lords and Commoners of Parliament, the British weavers would be able to recover the markets which they had lost to foreign manufacturers. Was this thesis correct?

First, he argued, foreign labour was cheap. In a memorandum to a committee of the House of Commons which he submitted on April 7, 1808, he referred to the foreign manufacturers 'whose labour might be had at half the price such labour was paid for in this country'.[18] If correct, this would have constituted an advantage to Britain's competitors, although the difference in wages would have been partly (if not wholly) offset by the cost of transporting the yarn abroad. But this is an implausible argument; Radcliffe himself had noted how the wages of English weavers were below subsistence level. Many of them lived only with the additional support of money from the poor rates.[19] So there could have been no comparative advantage on this score.

What of profits? Foreign manufacturers were not accepting lower returns than the Lancashire millowners. UK profit margins had been cut right down to the bone, and many manufacturers were eventually rendered bankrupt. Radcliffe had predicted this ruin, and had recorded the drop in yields on capital investment.[20] In a breakdown of the costs of producing a piece of calico of 28 yards length he recorded 'Other expences, including the master's profit', at 1s. in both Blackburn and Elberfeldt.[21]

There were no significant variations in the level of wages and profits, then, to explain the striking development of foreign weaving — or, to put the problem in a different way, the curious incapacity of British manufacturers to exploit their initial innovative advantage by weaving their own yarn at lower costs than their foreign competitors. So we have narrowed down the analysis to one possible explanation: UK rents were so prohibitively high that domestic manufacturers could not expand their premises and productive capacity. How much truth is there in this hypothesis?

Blindly — from the analytical viewpoint — Radcliffe failed to perceive the crucial importance of the differences in one of the costs of production. The rents paid by foreign producers were low,[22] while land values in Britain during this critical period of the industrial revolution were very high. The results of this on the cost of production were, in fact, documented by Radcliffe, who cited them for his readers when he gave a breakdown in the cost of producing 28 yards of calico.[23]

First cost of a piece of calico, 28 yards long

IN BLACKBURN				IN ELBERFELDT		
lb.	oz.	s.	d.		s.	d.
2	4 of Twist, @ 15d.	2	9¾	ditto, @ 1s.	2	3
2	12 of Weft, @13d.	2	11¾	ditto, @ 10d.	2	3½
Paid for weaving, one part in money, and the other, more or less, as the wages ebb and flow, out of the poor's rate — non-payment of rent, and shop bills the weaver is not able to discharge; all of which is the same as money, in a national point of view		6	0	ditto	2	0
Other expenses, including the master's profit, say		1	0		1	0
		12	9½		7	6½

From this we see that the employers were left with a similar profit, and that the difference in the cost of buying twist and weft (the lower cost to foreign buyers being due to their shrewd dealing, according to Radcliffe) was a few pennies. The major difference is in the cost of labour: 4s. Now, if the weaver of Elberfeldt was paying all his living costs, including rent, out of 2s., and given that there was no significant difference in the wages of the Blackburn and Elberfeldt workers, it appears that the English weavers were paying (or having paid for them out of the poor rates) over 4s. in rent! The difference in costs between the two weaving centres is almost wholly attributable to rent. Radcliffe's data is consistent with the general economic facts of the period.

This was a time of great prosperity for the owner of land, who was favoured by the increased locational concentration of industries. The rise in rents began in the 1790s, and reached its zenith in the late years of the second decade, between 1813 and 1820.[24] Speculation was rife. Thorold Rogers condemned the land monopoly which enabled owners to exploit the power

> which the law confers on corporations and private proprietors to withhold land from the market *at a minimum cost*. It will be clear that if the law encourages an artificial scarcity, *it creates an unnatural dearness*. By permitting corporations to hold land in towns, it gives such persons a power of exacting the highest terms possible for the use of their property, by keeping it out of the market till they can enforce their price. To use an American phrase, taken from the slang of speculators, the Russells and the Bentincks, the Cecils, the Portmans, the Grosvenors, and the rest, with the corporations, have had for a long period a ring or corner in the land market, and can force buyers to give famine prices.[25]

There can be no doubt that rent rises were making themselves felt. Radcliffe observed that 'the change from the old system of hand-labour to the new one of machinery operated in raising the price of land . . .'[26] There was, admittedly, a financial burden on the landowners: poor rates were rising. This, however, was something which they could well afford to accept. 'The rise of the poor rate was certainly vexatious,' wrote Halévy, 'but was compensated by the rise of land values. A farm of 100 acres counted for very little, but when this insignificant piece of land became the site of an entire suburb of some large town, the owner found his property better worth having.'[27]

The mill owners had to buy or rent more land before they could undertake investment in new technology and reorganise their plants to combine the process of spinning, weaving and finishing the cloth. If rents were at a realistic market level (i.e., the surplus above the returns to labour and capital), this would have been a paying proposition. But rents were penal. A capitalist who undertook the expansion of his factory, and installed the power looms, would have had to have accepted an uncompetitive rate of return on his capital. So it was necessary to retain the use of an obsolete process of production by letting the hand weavers in their damp cellars carry the burden of the rents! Not until 1818 to 1820 did the pressure of speculative rents ease off: and that was when the entrepreneurs undertook their capital investment and modernisation programmes.

The macro-economic influences of the land monopolist were hidden from the public consciousness. This does not mean that the victims could not see the visible effects of land speculation. 'It is well known that vile and loathsome buildings, probably the property of some opulent landowner, yield from the misery of their inmates a far larger rent than the plots on which the most luxurious and convenient mansions are built.'[28] But the way that the exploiters distorted the allocation of resources and the pattern of consumption, and the whole range of matters — social and environmental — which constitute the human condition, were well concealed from the political and economic decision-makers of the time.

This is not to admit that the processes could not have been correctly analysed. Radcliffe provided a remarkably detailed account of the causal connection between the development of land values, technological advances and the growth of output.[29] When the machine was introduced into the process of spinning yarn there was an immediate demand for new space. Old loom-shops were inadequate, so that 'every lumber-room, even old barns, cart-houses, and outbuildings of any description were repaired, windows broke through the old blank walls, and all fitted up for loom-shops. This source of making room being at length exhausted, new weavers' cottages with loom-shops rose up in every direction; all immediately filled'. And along with the increase in wages, rents doubled and trebled. As Radcliffe put it, 'the plough was wholly indebted to the shuttle', although — he claimed — many landlords did not seem to appreciate this fact. Radcliffe was anxious about the fact that the landlords were insufficiently concerned about the commercial welfare of the cotton industry.[30] He warned the landlords that 'the landed and agricultural purses were filled even to the brim by every article produced from the soil, or the farm yard being raised in price in proportion to the advanced labour and profit above-mentioned. *This source held out even when the income from manufacturers and commerce had gone to the continent with the raw material, cotton yarns; but unless this new system checks its decline, it cannot hold out much longer!*'[31]

The weavers were obliged to spend long hours in a damp atmosphere in confined workrooms, often cellars near streams; the dampness was necessary to keep the thread supple. The power loom afforded the prospect of dry, healthy working conditions in new factories, as Radcliffe persisted in pointing out. But the machine could not come to their aid: it, too, was a victim of land monopoly.

The cotton weavers were trapped in a captive labour market. Ideally, they should have been free to decline to work in the industrial sector, which they would have done had their land not been confiscated from them and their forefathers. The entrepreneurs should have had to have *attracted* them off the land. Wages and working conditions would have had to have been at least as good as what the self-employed farmer/artisan could provide for himself.

But the freedom to decide one's future was effectively denied to the workers and those who saved or borrowed to go into business on their own account. Labour and capital were united as victims of the land monopolists, and there was greater sympathy between them than is generally admitted. During the agitations of the time, the weavers who combined to press for higher wages did not propose that these should come out of existing profits: they recommended that prices should be raised. And there were sympathetic employers (Radcliffe was not alone) who did want to raise wages. The landlords in Parliament looked upon these proposals with horror. A general rise in wages would have come out of the 'surplus' of the nation's product, which would have entailed a reduction in rental income.

Fortunately for the land monopolists, they had a reliable spokesman in the Home Secretary, Lord Sidmouth, the owner of considerable estates. Sidmouth used spies to watch over, and prosecute, the hungry workers. When it was discovered that magistrates could use existing laws to enforce a minimum living wage he acted promptly in the House of Lords: the laws were repealed.[32] Consequently, with both man and machine shackled to a particularly severe phase of exploitation by the land monopolists, the owners of labour and capital found themselves competing with each other instead of cooperating to their mutual advantage.

The landed class did not relent on its demands. The squeeze on profit margins threatened to put many manufacturers out of business, the fate which did in fact await many of them. Radcliffe was aware of the criticisms levelled against landlords, who 'have been censured for raising their rents at this period, and subsequently still higher'. But he did not begrudge them their exactions. He was, after all, receiving rents from his farms in Mellor.

> If every manufacturer or merchant (for it is to this class I am alluding) will now only fancy himself to have been one of these land-owners at that time, and lay his hand upon his heart and say what *he* would have done under the circumstances I have been stating, I think there is not *one* of these theoretical censors that would be found to cast a second stone.[33]

Under the ruling system of property rights and taxation laws, of course, Radcliffe was right in predicting how the urban capitalists would have responded had they anticipated the trend in land values. But this does not justify what happened, nor did it relieve Radcliffe of the responsibility for correctly apportioning guilt for the problems which ensued.

The problems of the cotton industry can be illuminated in theoretical terms. Rent is an economic surplus, the amount left over from production once labour and capital have received their share — a share determined through competition for the opportunity to use the available resources to create new wealth. The amount which is received by capitalists and labourers has to be sufficient to attract them into the most rewarding activities, and enable them to reproduce over time. If landowners are under the pressure of competition, they will be forced to accept the surplus, and no more. In the absence of any inducement to compete, monopoly power enables them to demand a disproportionately large share of output. They are in the happy position of the highwayman who can demand 'Your money or your life', but with no risk of retribution. For they control the hangman through the legislature!

By imposing increasing demands on the wealth-creating agencies, or by refusing to reduce their exactions as the value of output declines, land monopolists eat into the share which ought to go to labour and capital as wages and interest. This is an irrational situation which cannot last for long. The system must break down. Capital is withdrawn when yields become unacceptably low, and investors are deterred from undertaking fresh capital formation. Labour goes hungry and either dies or suffers from malnutrition. Aggregate output contracts, and sooner or later the landlords are forced by realities to accept a cut-back in their rents — or to hold their land idle, in the certain expectation that, sooner or later, the demand for their land will yield the rents they originally demanded.

For the cotton industry in Radcliffe's time, unfortunately, there was no fiscal mechanism to force down rents to market levels. The increasing speculation in land forced up rents, squeezed interest and wages, and deterred manufacturers from investing money in power looms. By forcing rents beyond the point of merely appropriating the economic surplus, they were effectively demanding a slice of future output in the current period. This inherently unstable situation must, as it did, lead to a general recession.

The insights which we can extract from a review of William Radcliffe's record of the cotton industry have not been exhausted. We will allude to one more, for it has significant general relevance. In 1815, with the end of the Napoleonic war, the landlords were anxious about the prospect of a decline in their revenue. Cheap imports would force down the price of food, and thereby compel a reduction in rents. Once again the landlords demanded a Corn Law which would protect their privileged status. So while industry was required to compete, the landlords in Parliament were able to make an exception of their 'special' case. Radcliffe intervened on their side.[34] He argued that farmers were entitled to a secure domestic market, free from the threat of foreign competition, so that they might expand output to meet demand and thereby reduce their prices. This, in fact, is not the economic effect of protection. In reality, the landlords benefit from an artificial price rise, by capitalising the inflated prices into higher rents and selling prices of land. So, unwittingly, Radcliffe supported Parliamentary action which was expressly designed to aggravate the problem which confronted his industry! He realised that the Corn Bill would increase the food prices paid by workers, and that he would have to pay more for the three sacks of flour which he used every week with which to make paste for his factory. Had he used this as a clue, he could have seen that reduced wheat prices meant higher living standards for the workers, higher profits for the industry and a greater ability to withstand any advantage which foreign competitors might enjoy.

Nevertheless, we have to be tolerant towards Radcliffe. He was an entrepreneur and innovator who wanted nothing more than the freedom to increase the material wealth and spiritual well-being of himself, his employees and his country. Adam Smith, on the other hand, had enjoyed far more leisure time in which to reflect on matters of economic theory, and yet he had failed to warn the public of the horrible results arising from his defence of the landlords' right not to be taxed if they chose not to release their land for use by others. It was not until 1840 that P. J. Proudhon, the French anarchist philosopher, published a book that alerted the world (if it wished to listen) to the way in which land monopoly encouraged labour and the owners of capital to adopt restrictive practices as a defensive response to the original monopoly in land.[35]

Contemporary historians, who as a group have concentrated on the affairs of the aristocracy and the issues of state, have compounded our problems by their neglecting to study the impact of land monopoly on the first infant industrial system. Prof. Hoskins declared of this period:

> ... the land inside the older towns was acquiring a scarcity value, above all in the towns that were surrounded by open fields, so that they could now grow outwards, and a steady rise in the price of land for building was added to the rise in the price of borrowed money. Possibly, too, the building trade was invaded by a new class of speculator who made conditions even worse than they need have been by extracting high profits out of the unprecedented demand for cheap houses. No one has studied this particular class of parasite, how he worked, in what opulence his descendents live today forgetful, or perhaps ignorant, of the origin of their wealth. Their forebears would make a fruitful study.[36]

As the towns grew, noted the Hammonds, 'the spaces of common within their borders became more valuable, and they were appropriated by the powerful classes'.[37] These two students of working class history were almost right to conclude that the advance in the value of ground rents during the Industrial Revolution was such that 'any pupil of Adam Smith would have put a tax on the immense wealth created in the new industrial towns and taken off the heavy burdens on food, clothing and the materials of industry'.[38] This is exactly what *ought* to have happened, but was precisely what did not happen, thanks in no small part to the compromise in the teaching of Adam Smith. Had he indeed been an enlightened fiscal counsellor, the evolution of modern Western society would have been transformed for the good of all, beyond all recognition.

Notes

1 J.R. Hicks, *A Theory of Economic History*, Oxford University Press, 1969, p. 148. See also E.J. Hobsbawm, 'The British Standard of Living, 1790-1850', *Economic History Review*, X (1957).

2 Quoted in J.L. and B. Hammond, *The Skilled Labourer 1760-1832*, London: Longmans, Green & Co., 1933, p. 71. Credence to this view has been lent by a modern Marxist historian, E.P. Thompson, *The Making of the English Working Class*, Harmondsworth: Penguin, 1968, p. 309.

3 E. Halévy, *England in 1815*, London: Ernest Benn, 1960, p. 290.

4 Hammonds, *op. cit.*, p. 72.

5 Although they were aware of this astonishingly slow rate of growth, the Hammonds subscribed to the thesis that wages were forced down by competition from the machines. *Ibid.*, p. 71. In fact, the share of industry using power looms was too small before the 1820s to influence the level of wages.

6 F. Collier, *The Family Economy of the Working Class in the Cotton Industry 1784-1833*, Manchester University Press, p. 43.

7 'The evidence suggests, therefore, that as the English and Scots handloom weavers left the trade, or died, their places were taken by low-grade Irish labour at starvation rates of wages.' A. Redford, *Labour Migration in England*, Manchester University Press, 1964, p. 42.

8 Halévy, *op. cit.*, p. 292. For evidence of a drop in the price of cotton, see testimony of James Kay, a Bury cotton manufacturer, in a House of Commons committee report, cited in *English Economic History*, eds.: A.E. Bland, P.A. Brown and R.H. Tawney, London: G. Bell, 1933, p. 501.

9 Halévy, *op. cit.*, p. 289.

10 *Ibid.*, p. 290

11 *Ibid.*, p. 289, n. 2.

12 *Ibid.*, p. 293

13 W. Radcliffe, *Letters on the Evils of the Exportation of Cotton Yarns*, Stockport, 1811.

14 W. Radcliffe, *Origins of the New System of manufacture commonly called power-loom weaving*, Stockport, 1828, p. 17.

15 *Ibid.*, pp. 16, 106-7.

16 Hammonds, *The Skilled Labourer*, *op. cit.*, pp. 278-9.

17 *Op. cit.*, pp. 54, 62, 66.

18 *Ibid.*, p. 49.

19 The Speenhamland system of wage subsidies was introduced in 1795 to try and deal with this problem. 'These allowances out of local rates were meant to keep labour above the starvation level at least. The system of outdoor relief, designed as a local expedient, spread rapidly throughout the country. Although they probably prevented much actual starvation, the wage subsidies did not keep real wages from falling.' A.D. Gayer, W.W. Rostow, and A.J. Schwarts, *The Growth and Fluctuation of the British Economy 1790-1850*, Oxford: Clarendon Press, 1953, p. 56.

20 *Op. cit.*, pp. 48, 15-16.

21 *Ibid.*, p. 92.

22 *Ibid.*, p. 63.

23 *Ibid.*, p. 92.

24 F.M.L. Thompson, 'The Land Market', *op. cit.*, and R.J. Thompson, 'An

Enquiry into the Rent of Agricultural Land in England and Wales during the Nineteenth Century', in *Essays in Agrarian History, op. cit.*

25   J.E.T. Rogers, *Six Centuries of Work and Wages*, London: Swan Sonnenschein & Co, 1903, p.486. Our emphases.

26   *Op. cit.*, p.59.

27   *Op. cit.*, p.283.

28   Rogers, *op. cit.*, p.426. Aston, in his *Picture of Manchester* (1810), observed that attention in the city had been 'too minutely directed to the value of land to sacrifice much to public convenience or the conservation of health'. Cited by Hammonds, *The Town Labourer 1760-1832*, London: Longmans, Green & Co., 1919, p.45.

29   *Op. cit.*, pp.58 and 65 ff.

30   *Ibid.*, pp.48, 69, 70n.

31   *Ibid.*, p.56: our emphasis.

32   See, e.g., the account of the weavers' strike of 1818, and the masters' plan for a minimum wage, in Hammonds, *The Skilled Labourer*, pp.109-126; on Sidmouth, *ibid.*, pp.86-7, 90-1 and 315.

33   *Op. cit.*, pp.66-7.

34   *ibid.*, p.176ff.

35   P.J. Proudhon, *What is Property?* New York: Dover Publications, Inc., 1970, translated by B.J. Tucker, pp.183-184. Proudhon recognised the cathartic role of recessions when, having described how the idle land monopolist exploited labour and capital, he added: 'Here, then, we have a society which is continually decimating itself, and which would destroy itself, did not the periodical occurrence of failures, bankruptcies, and political and economical catastrophes re-establish equilibrium, and distract attention from the real causes of the universal distress' (*ibid.*, p.185).

36   W.G. Hoskins, *The Making of the English Landscape*, Harmondsworth: Pelican, 1970, p.226.

37   *The Town Labourer, 1760-1832, op. cit.*, p.44.

38   *Ibid.*, p.214.

A THEORY OF RECESSIONS

5

Speculation: a US Hypothesis

Pre-industrial modes of production were coherent. They functioned as stable systems over very long periods of time without generating problems. The crises which disturbed them from some normal level of activity can be ascribed, in the main, to external influences over which there was no control. Hunter-gatherers may have gone hungry at times because the herds failed to return to the traditional grazing grounds. In agrarian systems, famines occurred because of inclement weather. This is not to deny that problems did not originate from within the system. Over-zealous hunting can deplete the available stock of animals in a tribe's territory; over-intensive cultivation can turn soil into a dust bowl. But these were aberrations, cases of unwise, irregular, self-destructive, management of affairs by individuals, and were not entailed by the mode of production itself.

Because these systems were stable, over very long periods of time, scholars classified them as 'stagnant' societies. But the peoples themselves were content. They were culturally equipped to deal with deviant cases within their ranks, and they developed elaborate rituals to explain, if not to control, the 'acts of god'.

Industrial society, by contrast, has in its short life been riddled with regular economic crises which appear to be caused directly by malfunctioning elements of the system itself. If the record is to be believed, capitalism suffers from internal contradictions which preclude stable production of goods and services over a long period of time.

The view that the industrial mode of production based on the private ownership of capital was inherently defective was promoted at a very early stage by left-wing critics. One was Robert Owen, who attributed unemployment to 'under-consumption'. His solution was to create small, self-contained communities. Members would share a communal ethic and earn their living by agriculture and industry in which machinery would be carefully controlled. Owen's scheme was promoted in the House of Commons during the first major industrial recession, in the late 1810s. It was advocated in 1817 by De Crespigny, who placed great store by the claim that people were rendered unemployed by the advance of technology.[1] The theoretical critique from the left was advanced by Frederick Engels in *The Condition of the Working Class*, who argued that capitalism operated through cyclical fluctuations and that therefore the system had to create and maintain a permanent reserve of workers. Karl Marx elaborated on the inevitability of these characteristics. Anarchy reigned because of the multiplicity of individual decisions: entrepreneurs could not have perfect knowledge of the state of the developed market. Furthermore, the maldistribution of income as a result of private ownership of capital meant that labour could not buy back all that it produced. From this, it followed that at certain times there would be 'over-production'. The excess of goods in relation to demand would set in motion a recession, because entrepreneurs were forced to cut back on output and new investment. Only planning from the centre — where the decision-makers had an overview of the total system — would eliminate the risk of wrong decisions. This would create a rational programme of economic activity. Only social ownership of the means of production would ensure that the rate of consumption was tailored to output. In a word — socialism.[2]

The over-production thesis did not mean that recessions were always caused by the inability of labour to buy up the goods which it produced. Marx said that rising wages also caused crises, for among capitalists 'the stimulus of gain is blunted'.[3] Attempts to make up for a decline in the rate of profit, by increasing aggregate profit, merely reinforces the over-production of commodities on sale in the market. Marxists, therefore, have got it both ways. Either there are recessions because the wages of labour are too low, or because wages are too high! And in both cases capital is said to be unable to adjust itself smoothly, and this results in dis-equilibrium.

There have been many theoretical attempts from the time of Marx to Keynes to explain why the modern industrial economy staggers from one recession to another with the predictability of the seasons. All the variables — trends in national income, consumption of durable goods, fresh formation of fixed capital, phases in the innovation of consumer goods and processes of production — have been scrutinized in the search for the cause of trade cycles. Most of these attempts are of a descriptive rather than explanatory character.

With the fall from popularity of the Keynesian doctrine — the tools of which failed to assist the politicians to prevent or even to ameliorate the recession which struck the capitalist West in the 1970s — there has been a hiatus in public policy formation. In desperation, there has been a fall-back to simplistic 'solutions' like the monetarism which found popularity in Britain in the early 1980s. These, however, have been attempts at sitting tight in the hope of happier days to come, relying on the principles of sound budgeting for individual households rather than for nations.

With one major exception, no-one has offered land speculation as the possible explanation for cyclical recessions. This hypothesis was advanced by Henry George. Land speculation, he said, was not the only cause of depressions; but it was 'the great initiatory cause'.[4]

George was not satisfied with conventional 'explanations'. How could it be, he wondered, that there was 'under-consumption' when people were hungry, poorly clothed, badly housed? They were willing to consume more — what stopped them? And how could it be that there was 'over-production' by capitalists who were supposed to be in search of profits? Supply might be larger than demand for a particular product at a given moment in time; but what stopped the entrepreneur from cutting his price, selling off his goods and smoothly moving into a more profitable field of activity?

George concluded that land monopoly was to blame. It operated at two different levels of intensity. Speculation caused depressions by enabling people to demand prices which were extraordinarily high: effectively, the monopolists demanded a part of *tomorrow's* output *today*. The effect of this is to milk the returns to capital and/or labour. But this can only be tolerated up to a point, beyond which it becomes uneconomic to employ either capital or labour; unemployment ensues. Secondly, land monopoly enables speculators to hold land idle in the expectation of future capital gains. This is the wait-and-see strategy. As a result, scarce land is withheld from production — in itself preventing new employment — and as a consequence of the contraction in supply, this pushes up the level of rents of land in use. This has the effect of bankrupting some firms which would otherwise be profitable and competitive.

> Production [wrote Henry George] therefore, begins to stop. Not that there is necessarily or even probably, an absolute diminution in production; but that there is what in a progressive community would be equivalent to an absolute diminution of production in a stationary community — a failure in production to increase proportionately, owing to the failure of new increments of labour and capital to find employment at the accustomed rates.[5]

This produces 'a partial disjointing of production and exchange', which manifests itself in apparent over-production and under-consumption. A decline in output continues until one or a combination of three things happens:

(1) the speculative advance in rents terminates;

(2) an increase in the efficiency of capital and/or labour results in an increase of income and a readjustment of the distribution in relative shares going to the factors of production; or

(3) labour and capital reconcile themselves to lower returns in wages and interest.

Henry George provided an account of how recessions cause the collapse of banks, the bankruptcy of firms and the panic of speculators who find that they have to finance loans at high interest rates for land which is suddenly seen to be over-valued. He used largely impressionistic evidence to support his theory. For this he cannot be criticised, for it is only in recent years that statisticians have produced data in anything like sufficient quantity and quality to enable us to elaborate the theory in a scientific manner.

Our first problem concerns periodicity. The waves in the trade cycle move in regular sequences. The shortest, terminating every four or five years, is the one which concerns democratic politicians most. They feel obliged to keep wary eyes on the economic indices in case these predict unfavourable events coinciding with election time. The most important cycle is of 20-year duration. The cyclical trends in the movement of phenomena like population, migration, immigration and house building were first fully elaborated by Simon Kuznets for the USA.[6] The importance of these long cycles is that they terminate in slumps, the amplitudes of which are greater than those experienced during the course of the upswing of the cycle. This is because inventory investment and other volatile forms of investment coincide with a downturn in the building programme, thereby creating a severe recession.[7] But Kuznets has admitted that, while there is no difficulty in identifying the long swings, there is a problem in explaining them.[8] He had to content himself largely with describing the phenomena.

Does the land speculation hypothesis fit into the 20-year cycle? In the 1930s Homer Hoyt, then a post-graduate student at the University of Chicago, investigated the trends in land values in Chicago over the remarkably long period of 100 years. He discovered a regular cycle of 18-year duration.[9] His data is considered to represent the general trend in real estate values in the USA over the period up to the 1930s.[10] Hoyt has since up-dated his material, and his results are listed in Table 5:I. They fit neatly into the sequence of business cycles. A peak in land values is missing. Its absence may be explained by the threat and advent of the world war, which disturbed the benign psychological outlook which is necessary for speculation. Consequently, the peak of this cycle was eliminated.[11]

But what if the trends in land values were simply a response to other variables in the economy? We expect to see a rise in land values, for as national income increases, so does the surplus, or economic rents. Rising land values, then, are a derived phenomenon. So how can we justifiably ascribe the primary power to cause recessions to the land market, the income for which is itself dependent upon the functioning of the labour and capital markets? Is it not possible that a downturn in national income then results in a drop in land

TABLE 5:I
USA 1818–1929

Peaks in land values[1]	Building cycle peaks[2]	Economic recessions
1818	—	1819
1836	1836	1837
1854	1856	1857
1872	1871	1873
1890	1892	1893
—	1916	1918
1925	1927	1929

urces: 1 Homer Hoyt, 'The Urban Real Estate Cycle — Performances and Prospects', in *Urban Land Institute Technical Bulletin* No. 38, 1950, p. 7.
2 G. Shirk, 'The 18⅓-Year Cycle in Total Construction', *Cycles*, August 1981, p. 149, Figure 1, and C. A. Dauten and L. M. Valentine, *Business Cycles and Forecasting*, Ohio: South-Western Publishing Co., 1974, p. 277. For the booms of the 1830s and 1850s, see also G. F. Warren and F. A. Pearson, *World Prices and the Building Industry*, 1937, p. 99.

alues? This is the popular view: the causal forces are held to be in the pposite direction to the one postulated by Henry George. To prove a usal connection working from land speculation to the wider economy, we eed to trace more than 'a fairly close correspondence'[12] between movements the real estate market and phenomena like the building cycle.

The timings favour Henry George's hypothesis. Table 5:I shows that the eak in land values is reached 12 to 24 months before the economic recession; e., the downturn in land values precedes the decline in general economic rosperity. But this chronological sequence is insufficient to prove cause and fect. Landowners may just be blessed with better predictive foresight than le rest of us (though, in that case, why do so many of them continue to buy nd just as the speculative bubble is about to burst?).

We need to demonstrate a transmission mechanism, one by which ante-edent behaviour in the land market diffuses itself into the factory, office and orner retail store. One such mechanism may be the activity in the con-ruction industry. If land, because of speculation, costs too much, does this urtail construction and thereby dampen activity over a wider sphere of the conomy? The American evidence is tantalising. The peaks in the building ycle *follow* the peaks in land values and *precede* general economic recessions!

This relationship will be investigated in detail in Chapters 8 to 10. First, however, we need a more detailed account of speculative behaviour.

Land speculation is a two-dimensional activity. It is *spatial*. It entails the acquisition of control over a clearly-defined piece of territory, such as land on the fringe of an urban area, or large tracts on the frontiers of a colonising society. It is also *temporal*. Purchases today are calculated to provide a financial gain through resale in the future. Thus, the dealer has to be willing and able to hold onto land for a period of time, and sell when he calculates that prices have reached their most attractive heights.

A useful definition of land speculation has been provided by Prof. Botha. It is, he says, 'an investment over a relatively short period of time in an asset yielding an unrealistically high rate of return accompanied by a relatively low degree of risk'.[13] This contrasts land speculation with speculation in other areas, in which the risk of loss is much greater — for example, in the currency markets. We need to know more about the time scales, however, to see how they relate to the 18-year cycles that have been observed in the US economy.

Botha distinguishes three broad categories of time: secular, long and short-term. In the first case, a second or third-generation land monopolist who sells at a hundred times the original purchase price cannot be said to have speculated; the land was not bought with an intention to capitalise on increasing land values within the lifetime of the buyer. An example of this is the Spanish olive grower who owned five acres near Madrid. He and his family fled from General Franco's army in 1940. The family split itself between London and New York. The parents died, and after the death of Franco the children decided to investigate their ancestral past. They discovered that the five acres that they had inherited were worth £5m. in 1980, just 40 years after the last olive had been picked.[14] During that time, the land had remained idle, but the suburbs of Madrid grew outwards and around the site. So far as the land users of the Spanish capital were concerned, the owner of the five acres was doing a Rip Van Winkle act: he had gone to sleep. Still, the value of the land soared with the prosperity of the community. The children, however, while benefiting from their unearned millions, were not *speculative* owners in the sense which we wish to emphasise for the purposes of this study.[15]

At the other end of the time-scale, people who buy and quickly re-sell land for a profit usually do so for less spectacular gains. This sharp wheeling dealing characterises the tail-end of a cycle in land values, when speculative 'fever' has gripped a wider circle of people who, perceiving the huge gain made by those who bought for rock-bottom prices, decide to gate-crash the market.

The more interesting time-period, for Botha, is the intermediate phase his 'relatively short period' which, in terms of his three categories, is th long period. He cites the example of someone holding land for 10 years, having bought it at agricultural use values and allowing it to lie fallow in the knowledge that urban expansion will force up the price in the fullness of time.

This intermediate time-scale is characterised by a conscious decision to methodically identify and acquire tracts which will eventually be required for development; and the willingness to wait while values rise to obtain a profit well over what can be obtained in the course of normal trading in a competitive market. Botha's example of 10 years was intended to be illustrative. It does not fit well into an 18-year pattern. Intuitively, we would expect speculators who were tutored in the art of dealing in land to buy when prices were at their lowest — at the beginning of a cycle — and sell just before prices reached their peaks: they would sell to the 'mugs' in time to get out of the market before the inevitable crash.

The risky phase of the speculative boom is the last 12 to 18 months. During this period, dealers tend to be the innocents who have entered the market at a very late stage. Most of the profits have been taken by the shrewd dealers, who have held the land for most of the cycle and then withdrawn while the going was good. The latest entrants are those who buy at the speculatively-high prices which bear no relation to the performance of the economy; and they have a rapidly-decreasing margin of time in which to raise their prices, find new buyers and complete the transactions before the alarm bells begin to ring. Thus, we would postulate that a 15 to 16-year period would be the optimum period. This would ensure maximum profits and guarantee a safe withdrawal from the market before the slump. If this time-scale is popularly employed by land speculators, we will have recognised an important element of the dynamics of the 18-year cycle in land values.

The empirical evidence verifies our hypothesis. In the most exhaustive study ever conducted into motives behind the ownership of land on the urban fringe — nearly 700 owners of undeveloped land at the edge of six metropolitan areas in North America were interviewed between 1977 and 1979[16] — it was discovered that the transition in ownership from traditional rural owners to investors and developers 'begins more than 15 years before the land is actually developed for urban use'.[17] Similar time-scales were revealed in a study of 56 vacant sites in South Wales; 64% of the sites were held idle for 15 years or over, and the most popular duration of vacancy was the 15-19 years period (27%).[18] The evidence supports the view that speculators are willing to hold land vacant for a considerable period of time in the expectation of making substantial unearned profits from the needs of society. Providing the purchases are made at the right time, and in the right place, speculation in land conforms to what *Fortune*, the American business magazine, deemed 'a law that seems to make certain you will win'.[19] Thus, there appears to be a

significant synchronisation between the time horizons of speculators, an
the 18-year cycle.

Other features of speculation and land monopoly can be highlighted b
contrasting land with capital as factors of production. In the past, th
differences have been disguised. G. D. H. Cole, a leading left-wing historia
of working-class institutions, exemplifies the perverse insistence on anaes
thetising people from an appreciation of the internal dynamics of the Wester
economic system:

> ... in highly industrialized countries in particular the distinction betwee
> land and capital has lost most of its economic importance, at any rate wher
> a class of great landowners, clearly distinct from other capitalists, ha
> ceased to exist.[20]

Rental income, likewise, is conflated into the catch-all category of propert
income.[21] By blurring the differences, the deleterious influence of the lan
speculator is ascribed to the owner of capital. Yet land and capital are differer
species of phenomena.

For a start, the power acquired by those who buy land depends cruciall
on the unique characteristics of land. The time-horizons are different in th
land and capital markets. Land can be held idle for long periods because it
not perishable. The pressure on landowners in a contest of economic strengt
is far weaker than that which confronts labour and capital. Agricultural lan
will renew itself, and therefore retain its value; owners need not, therefor
capitalise their assets for long periods. Land which derives its value fro
locational advantages presents no problems whatever. But capital in the for
of machines and buildings perishes and must therefore pay for itself within
limited period, during which the capitalist cannot avoid the costs of mainter
ance. There is no escape from this by transforming capital into cash, for unle:
it is employed — by being lent to others — it either depreciates in value as
result of inflation, or does not earn an income (in which case it might as we
be used for consumption).

Furthermore, there is a distinct difference in the ability to finance loar
originally taken out to buy land or accumulate stocks. Except during dee
recessions, banks will continue to lend money when the asset is land, even (c
rather, especially) during uncertain times. This makes it possible to refinanc
loans used to buy land: thus, the speculator can hold out for better pric
which must eventually come his way. Credit to help to finance inventorie
however, is much more difficult to obtain. Credit shortages occur far mo
regularly as a deterrent to stock accumulation. Indeed, the acute cred
shortage associated with the downturn of the shorter, five-year cycles is
direct limitation on accumulation.[22]

The next major class of differences between land and capital relates to th impact on the workings of the economy. Land hoarding results in a contraction in the supply of what is a fixed factor: there is no way of making more land, and reclamation is of no significance. So the price of land is forced up. Firms which are restricted in their choice of locations — because of the need for access to special services, or raw materials, or markets, for example — have two options. They must either increase their product prices, which is not usually possible in a competitive market, or they must absorb the higher cost of rent out of profits. As a result, consumer satisfaction and the output of goods are reduced. Hoarding manufactured goods, however, does not destabilise aggregate demand,[23] and if abnormal profits are made out of a rise in prices, other manufacturers will be attracted into the market. This forces down prices and removes the incentive to hoard goods in warehouses. Manufacturers, then, have every incentive to meet demand at the lowest competitive prices, which raises consumer satisfaction and ensures the full employment of resources.

Finally, consider the money and stock markets. At certain times, principally near the top end of the land value cycle, when people are gripped by speculation mania, the bidding for money to buy land pushes up the rate of interest. This makes it difficult to borrow to finance the formation of new machines on which people rely for new jobs and wealth. Institutions seeking to attract depositors' funds to invest in land force others to raise their interest rates in order to remain competitive. Building societies are an example of this, and as a result low-income earners experience greater difficulty in obtaining mortgages. Speculation in share prices on the stock exchange in the hope of capital gains, on the other hand, reduces the cost of finance to firms, so directly encouraging investment.[24]

Thus, we begin to see that land speculation is a unique economic phenomenon, deriving its power from the ability to play a passive, wait-and-see game, capable of yielding enormous fortunes for shrewd dealers who, as land monopolists, do not contribute anything to the wealth of nations; a power which gives it the ability to inflict severe wounds on the active agents of the wealth-creating process, the workers and their accumulated savings (capital).

Notes

1 The Owen plan was opposed by, among others, Henry Brougham, on the grounds that the real problem was over-population — the poor, it seemed, bred too fast for production to keep up with fertility! See B. Gordon, *Political Economy in Parliament 1819-1823*, London: Macmillan, 1976, p. 65.

2 Socialist planning does not admit of industrial crises. While Menshikov is happy to describe postwar economic recessions in the capitalist West as 'crises', his colleague Khachaturov will only admit of 'minimum efficiency years' in the USSR — and even then the national income is held to be 'less than normal owing to poor harvests'. Who can plan the weather? See S. Menshikov, *The Economic Cycle: Postwar Developments*, Moscow: Progress Publishers, 1975, and T. Khachaturov, *The Economy of the Soviet Union Today*, Moscow: Progress Publishers, 1977, p. 337.

3 *Capital*, Vol. I, *op. cit.*, p. 580.

4 *Progress and Poverty*, *op. cit.*, p. 264.

5 *Ibid.*

6 S. Kuznets, *Capital in the American Economy*, Princeton University Press, 1961.

7 G. F. Warren and F. A. Pearson, *World Prices and the Building Industry*, New York: John Wiley & Sons, 1937, p. 97; R. C. O. Matthews, *The Trade Cycle*, Cambridge University Press, 1959, p. 214, n.1; and A. Shonfield, *Modern Capitalism*, London: Oxford University Press, 1969, pp. 21, n.1 and 28.

8 *Op. cit.*, p. 424.

9 H. Hoyt, *One Hundred Years of Land Values in Chicago*, University of Chicago Press, 1933.

10 H. Hoyt, 'The Urban Real Estate Cycle — Performances and Prospects', in Urban Land Institute *Technical Bulletin* No. 38, June 1950, pp. 7-8, and Warren and Pearson, *op. cit.*, p. 151, Table 4.

11 For a discussion on the distorting influence of the World Wars, see Shonfield, *op. cit.*, p. 27.

12 Thompson, 'The Land Market', *op. cit.*, p. 47.

13 D. J. J. Botha, *Urban Taxation and Land Use*, Report of a one-man Commission appointed by the City Council of Port Elizabeth, South Africa, 1970, p. 23.

14 B. Jordan, '"Abandoned" Madrid plot worth £5m', *Financial Weekly*, 13.6.80.

15 Whatever the motives of the owners, of course, the disruptive effects on the economy are still the same. Madrid, for example, was obliged to urbanise around the vacant site, which meant that rural land was developed needlessly and people were forced to commute to the city that bit further than was necessary.

16 H. J. Brown, R. S. Phillips and N. A. Roberts, 'Land Into Cities', Cambridge, Mass.: Lincoln Institute of Land Policy, 1980, mimeo.

17 Brown *et al.*, 'Land Ownership and Market Dynamics at the Urban Periphery. Implications for Land Policy Design and Implementation', *World Congress on Land Policy 1980*, editors: M. Cullen and S. Woolery, Lexington, Mass.: Lexington Books, 1982, p. 131.

18 M. M. Bruton and A. Gore, 'Vacant Urban Land in South Wales', Cardiff: Dept of Town Planning, University of Wales Institute of Science and Technology Vol. 1, p. 74.

19 'The Strange Leveling Off in Land', *Fortune*, Oct. 1963, p. 124, which note (p. 128): 'True, most US real estate is bought with borrowed money, and the speculative land buyer must pay stiff interest rates, but these will hardly promp

a cut-price sale so long as the land increases in value without a lift of the owner's finger'.

20 G. D. H. Cole, 'Capitalism', *A Dictionary of the Social Sciences*, editors: J. Gould and W. L. Kolb, London: Tavistock Publications, 1964.

21 'We conclude that it is meaningful to distinguish two income shares, which we have termed employment (labour) and property income; that this distinction bears considerable similarity to the Marxian and neo-Keynesian classification of income by class shares, but much less resemblance to neo-classical concepts of "factor shares".' J. King and P. Regan, *Relative Income Shares*, London: Macmillan, 1976, p. 14.

22 Matthews, *op. cit.*, p. 93.

23 *Ibid.*, p. 273.

24 *Ibid.*, p. 61.

6

18-year Cycles: the UK Evidence

The industrial economy regularly falls prey to the vice-tight grip of the jaws of an economic monster. This beast looks innocent enough when represented on graph paper: just two simple lines crossed like the blades of a pair of scissors. Yet the power that is unleashed by the dynamics that are concealed behind these two lines tells us a great deal about why people by the million are subjected to the humiliation of being thrown out of work, and of the scale of the challenge that lies before us if we wish to engineer the appropriate reforms.

Over a period of two decades a remarkable bifurcation opens up in the rate of return derived from the ownership of land and capital. The returns to capital investment diminish, while the returns to land increase. As the gap widens, it becomes increasingly attractive to pump money into land rather than into the creation of new capital. Firms consequently find it increasingly difficult to re-equip themselves with new, higher-productivity machines and buildings. This dampens the capital goods industry, with serious results for employment.

As the process continues, both the internal funds of the average firm (which are used for re-investment) diminish inexorably, and the money on the markets becomes less readily available to entrepreneurs. Speculators who want to borrow for land deals are not confronted with these difficulties, however, and so funds are channelled into an increasingly frenzied land market. It is this scissors movement that periodically cuts the upward trend in economic growth, and which needs to be eliminated if industrial society is to rid itself of traumatic recessions.

The declining rate of return on capital is a well-known phenomenon. It was inferred by the classical economists who argued that the rate of profits on capital shadowed the interest rates on the money markets. 'Accordingly therefore,' wrote Adam Smith, 'as the usual market rate of interest varies in any country, we may be assured that the ordinary profits of stock must vary with it, must sink as it sinks, and rise as it rises. The progress of interest

72

therefore, may lead us to form some notion of the progress of profit.'[1] Smith traced the decline in the rate of interest over a long period of time, and concluded: 'As riches, improvement, and population, have increased, interest has declined'.

Marx popularised the idea of the decline of profits. This could be used to propagate the 'crisis of capitalism' thesis. But the accounts of the long-term trends conceal cyclical movements which are vital for the correct diagnosis of what is happening within an economy.

Statisticians have produced data for the last 100 years which support the scissors hypothesis. But this phenomenon was operating during the first long business cycle in the history of industrial society, between 1795 and 1815. We will now elaborate on that cycle with additional statistical data.

The years 1815-16 have been described as 'one of the most difficult periods in the history of the British economy',[2] followed by an improvement in 1818 and a quick return to depression the following year.[3] The turning point was 1814. Up till that time, there had been no significant increases in money wages except for the textile industry (in the single year 1814), and agricultural money wages showed a consistent decline.[4] But unemployment occurred in every branch of manufacturing industry for which there is evidence. Thus there was no wage pressure on profits (though not for the want of trying: riots and other action broke out throughout the country). Yet profits were low indeed. The first decades of the Industrial Revolution were essentially the story of one industry: textiles, and in particular cotton manufacturing. There was a clear downward trend in the margin of profit. In 1784 the selling price of a lb. of spun yarn was 10s. 11d., and the cost of its raw material 2s. (margin: 8s. 11d.). In 1812 the price was 2s. 6d. and its raw material 1s. 6d. (margin: 1s.). This trend, attests Hobsbawm, was general throughout British industry.[5]

Some contemporary observers decided that capital had become too large, lumpy, and therefore immobile. Ricardo argued against this on the grounds that capital would move to alternative uses if profits were forthcoming. He campaigned vigorously against the corn laws which, he repeatedly told the Commons, were responsible for protecting domestic agriculture (which meant the landowner) and therefore retaining capital in this sector instead of releasing it to other uses.[6]

Various explanations have been advanced to explain the terrible visitations on the British economy during these years. Some of them, besides land monopoly, are valid. Peace with France was declared in June 1814, as a result of which 1.2m men were demobilized over the following three years. The cut-back in military expenditure had a severe effect on the iron industry. *But the seeds of the recession were sown earlier than June 1814.* Urban land values began to soar before the turn of the century. The price of land rendered the construction of canals, houses and factories uneconomic. The production of bricks, for example, declined from 945.1m. in 1811 to 673m. in 1816.[7] Agricultural landowners contributed their share to the distress. Rural land prices had been rising sharply,[8] and when food prices dropped they refused to relieve the pressures on tenants by reducing their rents[9] (which in theory ought to have happened, if landowners passively accepted rent as a 'surplus').

We have to grapple with piece-meal evidence to show the trends and relationships in this first major cycle because statistics were not systematically compiled. Even today the deficiencies in the quantitative evidence present us with a serious difficulty. Economic rent, for example, is not published as a category in its own right; it is incorporated into a catch-all 'rent' category which includes the rents to capital improvements on land. In addition, this category ignores the imputed rent of idle and poorly used land, and freehold land where no rent money changes hands. By lumping rent and interest together, any differences that may exist in the trends are disguised. This problem, however, has been partly dealt with by two economists, Phelps Brown and Weber, who published a study in the *Economic Journal* which revealed a striking fact.[10] The rate of yield on capital in the industrial sector followed the anticipated downward trend. In the 1870s the rate of return was around 17 or 16 per cent; it was about 15 per cent for the last two decades of the century, and dropped to 14 per cent from 1900 to 1913 and fluctuated around the 11 per cent mark during the inter-war years. The authors then disaggregated their figures to show the rate of yield on buildings, which were found to be *upwards*, rising from four to six per cent between 1870 and 1895, and from 3.5 to around five per cent between 1924 and the late 1930s.

The yields were calculated from rents recorded by Schedule A income tax assessments, and these include both economic rent and interest on capital (the buildings). How, then, do we know that the rising yields to 'buildings' in the Phelps Brown and Weber study were to the land component rather than to capital? Adam Smith gives the answer. In his discussion on 'Taxes upon the Rent of Houses',[11] he differentiates between building-rent and ground-rent. 'The building-rent is the interest or profit of the capital expended in building the house,' and interest on this capital behaved the same way as interest on capital in other sectors. 'The building-rent, or the ordinary profit of building, is, therefore everywhere regulated by the ordinary interest of money... Whatever part of the whole rent of a house is over and above what is sufficient for affording this reasonable profit, naturally goes to the ground-rent.' Thus it follows that as general interest rates and yields from capital were declining while 'rent' was increasing, it must have been economic rent (Smith's 'ground-rent') which was rising. So the Phelps Brown and Weber calculations support our hypothesis of opposing trends.[12]

If the percentage increases for the latter decades of the nineteenth century do not seem large, this was due to the annexation of over 11m. square miles of territory by the colonial powers between 1876 and 1914. North American railway lines increased from 30,800 miles in 1860 to 94,200 miles in 1880, making more accessible the prairies of the Middle West and offering cheap transportation of grain to Europe. The newly invented refrigerator ships made possible the large-scale exportation of meat from Australia and New Zealand. From 1880 this directly affected agricultural rents, especially for arable land, until 1895. The decline in demand for home-produced food resulted in distress among tenants; once again, because of the way rent is exacted under monopoly conditions, landlords refused to reduce their demands until many tenants were bankrupt and had to quit farms.[13] The downturn in farming revenue left a reduced surplus (= rent). An appropriately quick response to this, as would occur where tax authorities were taxing *current* values, would have enabled the farmers to continue growing food. For the rate of return on labour and capital would have remained at acceptable levels, but landowners resist downward movements of rents for as long as possible. As a result, thousands of acres fell into disuse and farms deteriorated.

We now have to amplify the thesis that the opposing trends in rents and interest conform to the long swings of business activity.

Collapse comes when the gaps between the two trends have opened up too far. The major recession that follows takes the form of a painful adjustment process. Traditionally, there is a cutback in rents and the selling price of land, which had been raised by speculation to levels which could not be supported by current economic output. For the engine of growth to restart, rents must

TABLE 6:1

*Income Shares as a Percentage of GNP at Factor Cost,
UK 1921-1938*

	Employee compensation	Corporate Profits	Rents
1921-4	58.5	13.0	6.8
1925-9	58.1	12.5	7.5
1930-4	59.3	12.5	9.0
1935-8	58.9	15.0	8.8

Source: C.H. Feinstein, 'Changes in the Distribution of the National Income in the UK since 1860', in J. Marchal and B. Ducros (editors), *The Distribution of National Income*, London: Macmillan, 1968, Table 1, p. 117.

be at some realistic level which leave yields on capital at an acceptable rate
The recession forces people to reappraise their expectations. The interim
unemployment, however, causes much suffering to innocent people who are
not able to protect themselves with income from past savings.

The distribution of national income should provide a test for this hypo
thesis. Table 6:I shows what happened during the interwar cycle in the UK
Rental income is on an upward swing but the trend in corporate profits i
confusing. According to our theory, profits should have slumped at the tail
end of the long swing in business activity; yet here they are shown as rising
Data which supports our theory is provided by Deane and Cole (Table 6:II)
which shows movement in a continuous downward direction.

TABLE 6:II

Distribution of UK national income

	Average Decadel Percentages of total national income	
	Rents	Profits, interest and mixed incomes
1920-29	6.6	33.7
1925-34	8.1	31.2
1930-39	8.7	29.2

Source: P. Deane and W. A. Cole, *British Economic Growth 1688-1959*, Cambridg
University Press, 1962, p. 247, Table 65.

The historical facts, however, suggest that the data in Table 6:I is mor
accurate. Accordingly, we accept these. In doing so, however, we need t
explain the apparent anomalies if we are to preserve the symmetry postulate
by our theory.

If the 18-year cycle in land values began at the end of the war in 1918, i
should have peaked in 1936, followed by the recession 12 to 24 months later
This happened. The interwar years, surprisingly, were a period of almos
continuous growth, in spite of the post 1929 slump.[14] This was induced t
a considerable extent by the problems of the American economy, following
the 1925 land speculation boom. UK unemployment during this recessio
was a regional phenomenon, and the grey image of the hungry '30s wa
more than offset by astonishing economic and social progress.[15] Outpu
rose continuously except for 1926 (the General Strike and the protracted coa
strike) and 1929-1933. The annual average rate of growth of industria

output was 3.1% between 1920 and 1927, rising to 3.7% between 1927 and 1937. The real product per occupied person in the UK in 1932, as a percentage of the level through 1925-29, was 116%. This compared with 83% (USA) and 97% (Germany).[16]

Do the timings of the key events support our theory? Britain experienced a boom in 1919-20. National income rose significantly. If 1900 = 100, national income rose to 124.7 in 1919-20, with *per capita* income at 113.8[17] There was also a staggering boom in land sales — about a quarter of Britain's land changed ownership in just a few years!

> Such an enormous and rapid transfer of land had not been seen since the confiscations and sequestrations of the Civil War, such a permanent transfer not since the dissolution of the monasteries in the sixteenth century. Indeed a transfer on this scale and in such a short space of time had probably not been equalled since the Norman Conquest.[18]

Tenant farmers complained bitterly about the speculation in agricultural land; residential land prices soared as well. 'Land values were high in relation to the income from land,' note Glynn and Oxborrow.[19] So the good start to the postwar growth of output had to be sharply curtailed, according to our theory. It was. Unemployment rose to 9.6% and national income slumped to 110.6 *Per capita* income came down to 102.8 for the years 1921-24. Glynn and Oxborrow calculate the British economy suffered a loss of output of £9,754m. (equivalent to two years income) during the interwar years because of the high rate of under-employment of labour and capital.[20]

The economy settled down to a lower rate of growth, which was sustained, with the two exceptions referred to above, until the late 1930s. Land values reached their peak by 1936.[21] Output peaked in 1937,[22] and began to slide — along with employment — in 1938, just 20 years after the end of the first World War. No-one will blame wage earners or their trade unions, presumably, because as we saw from Table 6:I, the wages and salaries received by employees remained an almost constant fraction of GNP. The average for the cycle was 58.7% and the deviation was plus or minus 0.5%.

At the end of the cycle, however, corporate profits should have been near the bottom. Instead, they were apparently rising. There were a number of reasons for this, of an exceptional nature. First, there were the striking contributions to growth of a once-for-all nature by the motor and electricity industries. The building industry was crucial in reviving activity after 1929. Government policies (tariff protection and import controls) had the general effect of reducing competition and promoting cartels and monopolies 'at the expense, usually, of the consumer'.[23] These were aimed at raising profits. Despite all this, however, the economic alarm bells started ringing in 1938. The recession would have come: the rhythmic pressures of the system would have overridden these counter-cyclical factors. In Britain, unemployment was 40% higher in 1938 than the 1929 level; in the US, unemployment was 14.6% compared with 3.2% in 1929. The slump, however, was cushioned by the intervention of Adolf Hitler. Not all the mistakes of the first World War were to be repeated again. The British Government was better prepared for the next war with Germany, and the economy benefited as a result. Churchill's warnings of Nazi intentions rose to a crescendo in 1934, and on March 4, 1935, the Government issued a White Paper which concluded with these words: 'An additional expenditure on the armaments of the three Defence Services can, therefore, no longer be safely postponed'.[24] Expansion of the aircraft industry had begun the year before. Shipbuilding, which had generally suffered during the early postwar years from foreign competition, received a boost from the requirements of the Royal Navy (mainly cruisers and destroyers) in 1935, and the re-equipment of the Army began in 1936. Expenditure on armaments increased by 250 per cent between 1934 and 1938; expenditure on factory construction amounted to £8.7m. in 1938.[25] So while unemployment generally rose between 1936 and 1938, there was an expansion of work in key industries such as coal, shipbuilding and iron and steel.[26] Profits were boosted, and in 1939 the trend in unemployment came down; men were drafted into the Forces, and Britain swapped an economic tragedy for a human catastrophe. Similar forces were at work in Japan, coming to the rescue of the 'miracle' economy.

The post-World War II trends (Table 6:III) follow such a perfectly satisfactory course that we would be right to exercise caution. We want to know more about timing and the actual yields rather than just relative shares in national income.

The first problem is to decide when the cycle began. Economists using data

TABLE 6:III

*Income Shares as a Percentage of GNP at Factor Cost,
UK 1955-1973*

	Employee compensation	Corporate profits	Rent
1955-59	67.0	18.0	4.5
1960-63	67.4	17.9	5.1
1964-68	67.6	16.8	6.4
1969-73	68.9	13.2	7.6

Source: J. King and P. Regan, *Relative Income Shares*, London: Macmillan, 1976, Table 1, p. 18.

reflecting 20-year cycles in such phenomena as population growth and housebuilding are not able to offer a precise prediction of a forthcoming major slump.[27] We, however, can select 1955 as our starting point. Eighteen years later the land values cycle peaked, and 1974 saw the slide into the deepest recession since the 1930s. So 1955 appears to be arithmetically convenient, but is it historically valid?

The cycle could not have begun earlier. The Labour Party which romped home to power in 1945, despite the wartime credit accumulated by Winston Churchill, introduced drastic measures affecting the land market.[28] Following the Uthwatt Report, the Government introduced a Town and Country Planning Act; among its provisions was the levy of a development charge on additional value accruing to land as a result of the grant of planning permission. This was an absurd piece of legislation, in that it unwittingly encouraged owners to sit tight on their land and wait for the repeal of an unworkable Act when the Conservatives assumed power.

In July 1946, the Government was warned by 167 of its own back-benchers that the proposed legislation was both economically unworkable (for example, it would not eliminate speculation) and did not do sufficient to realise their ethical aspiration — namely, that *all* socially-created land values should be taxed for the benefit of the community. The Government paid no heed, and the Bill became law the following year.

Landowners were correct in their expectations: the development charge was quickly removed from the statute book by the next Conservative administration. But important controls on development of land — and therefore realisation of 'hope' values pinned on it by owners — were retained. It was not until Nov. 2, 1954, that Nigel Birch, the Minister of Works, signalled the beginning of the 18-year cycle with a declaration in the House of Commons that building licences would be dropped. The result of this decision was illustrated by Marriott in his fine study of the land speculators in the early phase of the cycle:

> A week before this blow in favour of the freedom of the market, after fifteen years of varied controls, Gabriel Harrison, a young dealer in property in London, had clinched a deal in Grafton Street, off Piccadilly. Unable to extract a building licence from the Ministry of Works, he had sold a bomb-damaged site next door to the Medici Galleries for £59,000 to a 26-year-old estate agent, Harry Hyams. Immediately he heard that licences were abolished, Harrison cursed his luck and rang up Hyams on the off chance that he might buy the site back. Hyams replied that he would sell it back for £100,000; the end of licensing had changed values somewhat.[29]

So we have our starting point, and it fits perfectly with the timing of the cycles in both land values and business generally. Before the land values cycle began, the yields accruing to labour and capital were on the increase; this trend suddenly reversed as soon as the land values cycle began to bite 12 months later, as can be seen in Table 6:IV, col. 3. The evidence in cols. 1 and 2 reveals a consistent decline in the pre-tax profits of commercial and industrial companies from 1955.[30] Attempts to bolster profits by handing out investment grants did not halt the trend (col. 4).

TABLE 6:IV

	Rate of pre-tax profit, less depreciation, on net assets of industrial and commerical companies: %[1]		All companies gross trading profits *less* stock appreciation *less* capital consumption as % of national income (Col. 4 includes investment grants)[2]	
	(1)	(2)	(3)	(4)
1950	⎫		12.6	
1951	⎪		14.0	
1952	⎬ 16.5		14.1	
1953	⎪		14.0	
1954	⎭		14.2	
1955	⎫		14.6	
1956	⎪		13.1	
1957	⎬ 14.7		12.9	
1958	⎪		12.5	
1959	⎭		13.0	
1960	⎫		13.9	
1961	⎪		11.9	
1962	⎬ 13.0		10.9	
1963	⎪		11.9	
1964	⎭	13.7	12.0	
1965	⎫	12.8	11.5	
1966	⎪	11.3	10.0	
1967	⎬ 11.7	11.7	10.0	10.6
1968	⎪	11.6	10.0	11.2
1969	⎭	11.1	8.3	9.9
1970		9.7	6.7	8.0
1971			6.6	7.8
1972			6.7	7.4

1 A. Glyn and B. Sutcliffe, *British Capitalism, Workers and the Profits Squeeze*, Harmondsworth: Penguin, 1972, p. 66, Table 3.3.

2 G. J. Burgess and A. J. Webb, 'The Profits of British Industry', *Lloyds Bank Rev.*, April 1974, p. 8, Table 2, col. 4.

The story repeats itself for employees, whose post-tax share of the employers' net revenue increased up to the mid-'50s. The trend then reversed itself and began an inexorable slide over the following 25 years (recovering momentarily in the 1970s during the period of Chancellor Anthony Barber's inflationary policies). Labour's increasing share, as we can see from Table 6: V, was an apparent one only. It was due entirely to the exactions of government, which drove a growing wedge into the pay bargaining process and reduced the size of the disposable income of employees.

But the yields from both urban and agricultural land were *increasing* over this period. The Government's Advisory Group on Commercial Property Development, which published its first report in 1975, declared that

> if the value of a development rises faster than construction and associated costs (*the normal position in the last twenty years* though this is not at present so), it will be the site value which will benefit as the residual in the calculation of values.[31]

In the housing sector, during the early phase of the cycle in land values, builders made their money out of the capital improvements upon their land, rather than from the land itself. But as the cycle moved upwards, the position was reversed; profits from the construction of houses were deemed to be modest, while the big returns were made from the land.[32]

Thus the oil price explosion can now be seen to be of secondary importance in the analysis of the recession of the 1970s which reached into the '80s. If the Arab oil exporters were mainly responsible for this recession, the random event — a price rise engineered at the end of 1973 — would remove scientific status from our theory, and the recession becomes an accident which could not have been foreseen in 1955. Yet an economist, if he had used the cycle in land values as his predictive tool, *could* have successfully pinpointed the economic contortions into which the UK economy would have spiralled in 1974 *even if OPEC had never been established.*

Employment is heavily determined by profitability and the rate of investment. A long.run decline in the yields on capital, by inhibiting fresh capital formation out of company funds, should produce a parallel pattern of rising unemployment. This was indeed the case. There was a stable level of employment in the postwar years up to 1955. Then an upward trend in unemployment began. The troughs in the cycles of unemployment rose from 1% in the mid-'50s to 1.5% in the mid-'60s and doubled to 3% in the mid-'70s.

British economists have failed to agree on the causes of the secular decline in profits since 1955.[33] An examination of the testable hypotheses led a policy advisor at the Department of Industry (W. E. Martin) to conclude that 'the reasons for the secular decline in profitability remain something of a

TABLE 6:V

UK Labour Costs and Taxes, 1938-1981

% of employers' net revenue[1]

	Employers' labour cost[2]	Employees' take-home pay	Pay bargain tax wedge[3]
1938	55.6	52.6	3.0
1946	59.1	52.3	6.8
1947	59.2	52.9	6.3
1948	58.1	51.5	8.6
1949	59.0	51.7	7.3
1950	59.2	52.2	7.0
1951	60.2	53.0	7.2
1952	60.5	53.6	6.9
1953	60.1	53.6	6.5
1954	60.4	53.9	6.5
1955	61.8	54.9	6.9
1956	62.7	55.5	7.2
1957	62.8	55.4	7.4
1958	62.7	54.3	8.4
1959	62.3	54.1	8.2
1960	62.5	54.2	8.3
1961	63.4	54.4	9.0
1962	63.7	54.1	9.6
1963	63.0	53.8	9.2
1964	62.9	53.4	9.5
1965	62.9	52.4	10.5
1966	64.1	52.3	11.8
1967	63.9	51.2	12.7
1968	63.2	49.8	13.4
1969	63.1	48.9	14.2
1970	64.7	49.6	15.1
1971	63.7	49.1	14.6
1972	64.1	50.3	13.8
1973	63.3	49.6	13.7
1974	66.2	50.4	15.8
1975	69.4	50.8	18.6
1976	67.2	48.5	18.7
1977	65.7	47.5	18.2
1978	65.8	48.2	17.6
1979	66.4	48.8	17.6
1980	67.8	49.4	18.4
1981	66.7	47.8	18.9

Source: Calculations by R. Burgess of the Economic Study Association from the CSO's annual 'Blue Books' and *National Income and Expenditure of the UK 1946 to 1950*, London: HMSO, Cmnd. 8203, p. 40, Table 27.

1 Excludes capital consumption and stock appreciation.

2 Wages and salaries plus Selective Employment Tax or National Insurance Surcharge.

3 The sum of income tax on wages and salaries and pay of HM Forces, employees' and employers' social security contributions, Selective Employment Tax or National Insurance Surcharge.

mystery'.[34] This assessment is not surprising, given the concepts that were used to investigate the evidence. 'Profits' were defined as 'gross trading profit ... plus rent received', and real rates of return as a percentage of the capital stock of fixed assets 'excluding land because of lack of data'.[35] The trends in rents were concealed, and land was excluded from consideration, effectively wiping out the elements of a solution and leaving the analyst perplexed.

Martin lent credence to the view that political economy was a dismal science, given what he called 'a low rate of return ... of explaining secular movements in income distribution'.[36] However, by reverting to the use of classical concepts, we can begin to shed light on ancient mysteries. In particular, we can now see that trends in both the distribution of national income and yields to the owners of land and capital verify the thesis that land monopoly has a powerful determinative influence on the industrial economy.

There are, however, features of the land tenure theory which at first sight may appear to be equally puzzling, and require explanation. The one which must be raised in the present context concerns the motive to invest in land at the beginning of the 18-year cycle when yields are low. Would it not be more rational to invest in industry where the returns — at least, at this stage of the economic cycle — are high?

Land buying in the early phase assumes — in part — an independent rhythm, determined by long-term expectations based on confidence in future growth of wealth. In the first half of the cycle, rental increases cause a rise in values. As the process gathers momentum, expectations diverge away from the actual performance of the economy; people buy and sell at prices which do not reflect the actual returns which could be expected from rent-paying tenants. During the second half of the cycle 'it is changes in yields which have had most of the effect on increasing values while rents have remained comparatively stable'.[37]

Income is not sacrificed if land is vacant for a long period of time. A high eventual selling price of land results in a recovery of the income stream; income is merely deferred into the future. One of the shrewdest British property developers in the postwar years, Harry Hyams, understood this fact better than most.

Oliver Marriott illuminated the economics of vacant buildings and idle land by analysing a property owned by Hyams.[38] He bought a small shop and office building in Oxford Street and paid a price which assumed a rent of £12,500 per annum. His agents thought that he was joking when he set the rent at £20,000, which was well above the realistic price. The building remained empty for about three years — a prime property in the heart of London's commercial centre. It was finally let for £18,500 per annum, producing a capital value of £270,000. If, however, the rent had been £13,500 (the figure suggested by Hyams' agents), it would have been worth only £200,000 — a difference of £70,000. 'That capital gain would have far outweighed the loss of interest on borrowed money, which could be offset against tax, and the loss of rent, which is worth less than it appears to a high taxpayer. Moreover, no rates had to be paid on empties,' comments Marriott.

But the source of the problem, it must be stressed, is the structure of the property tax which shapes expectations, architecture and the use of land and buildings. The classic example is Centre Point, the 32-storey office tower that stands at the junction of Oxford Street and Tottenham Court Road in London's West End.

Centre Point stood empty for nine years before a Greek shipping company occupied one of the floors in 1975. During that decade, public antipathy for the land speculator intensified, reaching its climax in 1974. Nobody pointed out that the fiscal law — rather than the profit-seeking developer — was responsible for making it possible for a building to remain vacant while its capital value appreciated. Built in 1965 at a cost of £5.5m., Centre Point was worth £56m. in 1980 (excluding the value of 36 maisonettes which are part of the development).

Harry Hyams bore the brunt of criticism, yet he repeatedly proved in the civil courts that he did not deliberately keep Centre Point vacant. Nonetheless, in 1974, a new law was passed — inspired by Edward Heath's Conservative Government, then brought to the statute book by Harold Wilson's Labour Government — that aimed its penalties at Hyams' Oldham Estate, which owned Centre Point. Tories and socialists alike condemned Centre Point as symbolic of what was considered to be the 'unacceptable face of capitalism'. Successive cabinet ministers of both political hues poured execration on the vacant building as a 'scandal' and an 'affront'. But who was *really* to blame?

When the project was conceived in 1958, there was no property tax liability on vacant land or unused buildings. So it was possible to design a building to specifications that made it difficult to let, without the risk of a substantial and recurring tax liability. Centre Point, standing 385 feet high, was intended to accommodate a single tenant. Had tax been payable on the building immediately on completion, the developer would have weighed this in the balance sheet when dictating his requirements to his architect. If the 32 storeys had had to be let quickly, to generate income out of which to pay taxes, different specifications might have been used.

As it was, the owners of vacant property were not liable to a property tax until 1968. A new law made them liable to 50% of the full rate; this was not a burden that was sufficient to change Hyams' expectations, and he began advertising for a single high-quality tenant in 17 countries. The quest was unsuccessful, despite the efforts of several real estate agencies, and it was not until 1974 that Hyams decided to change the company's policy and seek multiple tenancy. It was in 1974 that the penal property tax law was enacted as Section 16 of the Local Government Act. This required a local authority to double, treble, quadruple, and so on, the full property tax for each year that a building stood unused.

Camden Council wanted to invoke the provision against Centre Point, and claimed £1.89m., but abandoned its efforts in February 1976. This was because the law exempted owners who could prove that they had tried their best to let their vacant buildings: Mr Hyams proved that he had made strenuous world-wide efforts to find a tenant, and the council did not want to risk having to test its claim in court. The politicians, responding to public sentiment against speculators who had manifestly enriched themselves in the boom years, had concocted a tax that was long on vindictiveness but short on fiscal sense. It failed to address itself to the need to avoid the deterrent effect of taxing capital improvements, and the encouragement to waste land which was not taxed if left in an unused state.

The fiscal system, then, as Henry George pointed out, encouraged the misallocation of resources by actively rewarding the speculators. The UK evidence vindicates his contention that rent would absorb an increasing proportion of the output produced by an economy, a share which would be exaggerated by the exercise of monopoly power.

George arrived at his conclusions through the use of theory rather than statistical data. In discussing the influence of a rise in population, for example, he concluded:

> The effect of increasing population upon the distribution of wealth is to increase rent, and consequently to diminish the proportion of the produce which goes to capital and labour, in two ways: First, by lowering the margin of cultivation. Second, by bringing out in land special capabilities otherwise latent, and by attaching special capabilities to particular lands.[39]

This distributional effect, with all its implications for social harmony, is disregarded by modern economists, whose treatment of rent can at best be described as complacent. An example is contained in *Economics*, written by Prof. Samuelson of the Massachusetts Institute of Technology. He assured his young readers:

> The Ricardians actually exaggerated the conflict of class interest. While population growth might imply higher rent per acre, they were wrong to think it *had to* imply a larger *percentage share* of GNP going to land... Historically, pure land rent has become a declining fraction of GNP and NNP.[40]

At least three points suggest themselves to disturb this misleading (but all too common) conclusion. First, by considering income trends over a long period like 100 years (which apparently reveal a downward trend for 'rent' in the officially-published figures), the crucial cyclical movements are concealed. Second, the data are incomplete. They do not include rents imputed to land monopolists who fail to put their holdings to rent-yielding uses. Third, class interests and interaction are influenced by individual decisions, whatever the size and trends in the aggregate statistics. For example, the attitudes and interests of thousands are affected by the actions of a few land monopolists who keep land vacant in the middle of an expanding city, thereby compressing socio-economic interaction into smaller spaces and generating unwarranted tensions.

Ricardo, despite the interpretation put on him by Samuelson, fully appreciated that the class conflict arose from the impact of micro-economic decisions. Samuelson[41] quotes a passage from Ricardo which makes the point dramatically:

> A conflict of interests arises between classes. More babies mean lower *per capita* incomes and wage rates; lower wage rates mean higher rent rates per acre of land. Landlords gain as labour loses.

What matters to an entrepreneur who is considering where to open a factory, or a family seeking to build a house, is the cost of a plot of land, not the overall status of rent in the nation's accounts. These national accounts, however, endorse the statements of Adam Smith, Ricardo and Henry George.

Marxist economists are equally inclined to underplay the importance of rent, although we cannot accuse Marx himself of making this mistake. He accepted the classical theory of the tendency for profits to decline in the long run. When it came to rent, however, he was emphatic that both in the industrial and agricultural sectors the share going to landowners was a rising one.

> In so far as commodity-production and thus the production of value develops with capitalist production so does the production of surplus value and surplus-product. But in the same proportion as the latter

develops, landed property acquires the capacity of capturing an *ever-increasing portion* of this surplus-value by means of its land monopoly and thereby, of raising the value of its rent and the price of the land itself ... the landowner need only appropriate *the growing share* in the surplus-product and the surplus-value, without having contributed anything to this growth ... The singularity of ground-rent is rather that together with the conditions which agricultural products develop as values (commodities) ... *there also grows an increasing portion* of these values, which were created without its assistance; and so an increasing portion of surplus-value is transformed into ground-rent.[42]

Marx's theory (which was shared by Adam Smith, David Ricardo, J. S. Mill and Henry George) conformed to the facts.

This observation by Marx (given his ideologically oriented emphasis on capital and the undiscriminating concept of profits, we can call the statement an admission) does not, however, serve the purpose of class conflict and the desire for world revolution. It is an article of faith among Marxists that the decline in the rate of profit is an index of the move towards crises in capitalism which must eventually lead to an overthrow of the existing order and the establishment of socialism. So the fact that beneficial results for yields to capital would follow from a correction of land monopoly holds no attraction. In terms of revolutionary propaganda, it is better to concentrate on the historical decline in the returns to capital.

Associated with this emphasis is the claim that profits decline because the share going to workers in the form of wages and salaries rises.[43] Ergo, we have the makings of pure class struggle. Exploited workers versus the capitalist; who could ask for anything more? The fallacy inherent in this perception is that rising wage demands are said to *cause* a squeeze on profits, which in turn forces a cutback in investment and results in unemployment. To halt this vicious circle, governments are told to control incomes. Incomes policies became a popular feature of postwar European economic management, yet they patently failed to prevent the structural recession which struck in the mid-'70s.

The politicians were unaware of the impact of land monopoly on the operations of the industrial economy. The analyses of their advisors — and, consequently, their policy prescriptions — were distorted by the concepts that were employed. Thus, if the share of national income going to salary and wage earners rose, it followed (using the conventional terms) that the share going to 'profits' declined.[44] But, as Prof. Matthews has noted, 'pointing to a rise in the real product wage is merely another way of restating the phenomenon of the fall in profit share and does not point to one explanation any more than to another explanation. Any fall in profit share would mean a rise in the real product wage, however it arose'.[45] In the evidence adduced for the

UK economy (and shadowed in the other industrialised nations of the West), a fall in 'profit' there certainly was, but this disguised an *increase* in the return to land. Meanwhile, the post-tax share of employers' revenue received by labour over the 18-year cycle was actually declining (Table 6:V).

By retrieving the classical concepts and disaggregating the data, we uncover the crucial conflict in the economy which is concealed by the use of the term 'profit'. Corrective policies differ according to the perception of the economist. Our view is that there has been a serious misdiagnosis of the nature of the problem, and this is consistent with the fact that incomes policies — one of the main corrective measures derived from the orthodox inter- pretation of postwar economic history — have failed. Yet this failure, far from generating a demand for a reappraisal of concepts and evidence, has merely reinforced the demand for more doses of the same treatment. Trade unions, anxious to preserve their share of national income and the structure of differentials, have reacted against constraints on the bargaining processes with ever-growing disruptive measures. This aggravated an already unstable economy, and while the wealth-creating agents locked themselves in mortal combat the economic monster in their midst continued to wreak havoc with impunity.

Notes

1 *Wealth of Nations, op. cit.,* p.99.
2 A.D. Gayer, W.W. Rostow and A.J. Schwartz, *The Growth and Fluctuation of the British Economy 1790-1850,* Oxford: Clarendon Press, 1953, Vol. I, p.136.
3 Clapham designated 1815-20 as 'economically probably the most wretched, difficult, and dangerous in modern English history'. Quoted by Gayer *et. al, ibid.,* p.113.
4 *Ibid.,* p.135.
5 E.J.Hobsbawm, *The Age of Revolution: Europe 1789-1848,* London: Weidenfeld & Nicolson, 1962, p.41.
6 Gordon, *op. cit.,* p.66 and *passim.*
7 Gayer *et al., op. cit.,* Vol. I, p.121. The cycles in brick production between 1702 and 1845 were closely correlated with capital investment aside from the con- struction of residential buildings. *Ibid.,* Vol. II, p.704.
8 For the sharp rise in agricultural rents, see Thompson, 'An Enquiry into Rent', *op. cit.,* pp.59-60.
9 Gayer *et. al., op. cit.,* Vol. I, p.129, n.4, quoting Lord Ernle.
10 E.H.Phelps Brown and B.Weber, 'Accumulation, Productivity and Distribu- tion in the British Economy, 1870-1938', *Econ. J.,* 1953.
11 *Wealth of Nations, op. cit.,* p.366.
12 In the middle of the period studied by Phelps Brown and Weber, from the turn of the century up to the first world war, the trend was on the whole a declining

one. This can be explained by several factors. The Liberål Government was determined to introduce a levy on land values (which produced the constitutional crisis of 1910 and the elections which finally removed from the House of Lords all rights to interfere with budgetary proposals from the Commons). Rent restriction after 1913, and the rise in building costs, also contributed to the uncertainty associated with landownership during this period.

13   C.S. Orwin and E.H. Whetham, *History of British Agriculture 1846-1914*, Newton Abbot: David & Charles, 1971, p.248. Competition for agricultural land near the farming areas of Britain, however, ensured that farming practices were quickly adapted so that higher rents and wages were produced. *Ibid.*, p.286. Agricultural landowners who had urban rents to fall back on — such as the Dukes of Bedford — had less difficulty in weathering the difficulties of this period. *Ibid.*, p.312.

14   C.P. Kindleberger, *The World in Depression 1929-1939*, London: Allen Lane, 1973.

15   J. Stevenson and C. Cook, *The Slump*, London: Jonathan Cape, 1977, expose the myths shrouding this decade while acknowledging the real social and human costs of unemployment.

16   E.H. Phelps Brown and M.H. Browne, *A Century of Pay*, London: Macmillan, 1968, p.234, Table 20.

17   A.R. Prest, 'National Income of the UK 1870-1946', *Econ. J.*, 1948.

18   Thompson, *English Landed Society, op. cit.*, pp.332-3.

19   S. Glynn and J. Oxborrow, *Interwar Britain: a Social and Economic History*, London: George Allen & Unwin, 1976, p.101.

20   *Ibid.*, p.32.

21   E.A. Vallis, 'Urban Land and Building Prices 1892-1969', *Estates Gazette*, May 13, 1972, p.1016.

22   K.S. Lomas, 'Growth and Productivity in the UK', *Productivity Measurement Review*, Vol. 38 (1964).

23   Glynn and Oxborrow, *op. cit.*, pp.111-3. See also L. Hannah, 'Managerial Innovation and the Rise of the Large Scale Company in Interwar Britain', *Econ. Hist. Rev.*, (1974).

24   *Statement Relating to Defence*, Cmnd. 4827, 1935, p.10.

25   C.L. Mowat, *Britain Between the Wars 1918-1940*, London: Methuen, 1955, p.628.

26   D.H. Aldcroft, *The Inter-War Economy: Britain 1919-1939*, London: Batsford, 1973, p.147.

27   For a discussion of these predictions see Shonfield, *op. cit.*, pp.19-22.

28   R. Douglas, *Land, People & Politics*, London: Allison & Busby, 1976, pp.212-215.

29   O. Marriott, *The Property Boom*, London: Hamish Hamilton, 1967, p.1.

30   For the downward trend in company gross trading profits as a proportion of business sales, see K. Coutts, 'Short-run Variations in Company Profits', *Econ. Policy Rev.*, University of Cambridge, March 1978, p.54, Fig. 6.1.

31   *Commercial Property Development*, London: HMSO, 1975, p.32, para. 5.23, our emphasis. Note also that 'Vacant possession farms have consistently out-yielded both equities and general property shares over the past decade in terms of capital appreciation, and land's traditional advantage as a hedge against inflation seems more solid than ever' (*The Farmland Market*, Feb. 1974, p.6). See C.T. Sandford, *Taxing Personal Wealth*, London: George Allen & Unwin, 1971, p.256, for the

mid-'50s as the turning point in the relative attractions of land and capital as investment assets.

32   Economist Intelligence Unit and Halpern and Partners, *Housing Land Availability in the South East*, London: HMSO, 1975, para. 1.32, and *The Role of the Local Authority in Land Programming and the Process of Private Residential Development*, Birmingham: Centre for Urban and Regional Studies, Research Memorandum 80, April 1980, p.15.

33   W.E. Martin, *The Economics of the Profits Crisis*, London: HMSO, 1981, p. 223.

34   W.E. Martin and M. O'Connor, 'Profitability: a background paper', *ibid.*, p. 10.

35   *Ibid.*, p. 12.

36   *Ibid.*, p. 67.

37   *An Analysis of Commercial Property Values 1962-1976*, London: Economist Intelligence Unit, 1977, p. 8.

38   *Op. cit.*, p. 109.

39   *Progress & Poverty, op. cit.*, p. 243.

40   *Op. cit.*, p. 733, n.6, his emphases. See also, for example, A.K. Cairncross, *Home and Foreign Investment 1870-1913*, Cambridge University Press, 1953, p. 8.

41   *Op. cit.*, p. 730.

42   *Capital*, Vol. II, *op. cit.*, pp. 623-4. Our emphases.

43   Glynn and Sutcliffe, *op. cit.*, Ch. 4.

44   For a recent restatement of this position, see G.W. Maynard, 'Factors affecting profitability and employment in UK manufacturing industry, 1960-78', in Martin, *op. cit.*

45   *Ibid.*, p. 219.

7

Under Siege: the Englishman's Castle

House building is the industry most immediately vulnerable to speculation. Through it the land monopolists transmit their cancerous influences into the rest of the system. Land is a vital input, yet the primary importance of the movements in its supply and price remains unchronicled in the learned dissertations.

The crucial role of the house building cycle in relation to general business activity is a well-attested fact. Warren and Pearson have shown that throughout the nineteenth century protracted depressions regularly arrived, in the USA, about three to four years after the downturn in the building cycle.[1]

A British study by the National Economic Development Office drew the conclusion that 'Within the broad heading of investment, investment in private dwellings can be seen to be the most unstable, more unstable even than investment in the manufacturing sector of industry'.[2] This alarming instability has followed a close and predictable relationship with the business cycle in the past and in modern times. The figures for Britain since 1959 reveal that 'private sector house-building is one of the least stable components of GDP and makes a substantial and, recently, a growing contribution to the overall cycle. In general, the private housebuilding cycle is in very close conformity with the overall cycle'.[3] We cannot, however, be satisfied with merely observing a close correlation. We want to know if house building in the UK has had a causal influence on general business prosperity, and if so, what determines the cyclical movements.

There is a firmly-held view in Britain that building cycles conform to movements in interest rates. Furthermore, house building is said to be counter-cyclical — and therefore benign — compensating for trends in the general business cycle. The theory is that interest rates fall during the downswing of business activity, thereby making money cheaper to borrow and so stimulating building: this produces 'the spark that rekindles economic activity', as Grebler put it.[4] During the upswing, however, interest rates rise and make money expensive, thereby detering construction. So decisions as to whether to build or not are allegedly made on the basis of these movements. This hypothesis succeeds in attributing the burden of responsibility for the housing cycle (and, therefore, in part at least, its effects on business generally) to monetary phenomena.

People wishing to make a profit on their investments obviously have to take account of the cost of borrowing money. But to narrow down the rhythm of the housing industry to this explanation is misleading. This becomes serious when dealing with a cycle which has important predictive value: three out of the four recent peaks in investment in private houses in the UK (1959, 1967 and 1971) were followed one year later by a downturn in GDP. (The one exception was 1964, when there was a simultaneous downturn in both trends.)

The interest rate theory is challenged by the facts. In 1957 and 1963 there was an upward movement in both the official Bank Rate (making money dearer) *and* in investment in private houses; in 1961 there was a drop in the Bank Rate *and* a drop in the rate of investment in private houses. For similar contrary evidence we can go back to the late 18th-century.[5] Beginning in the mid-1790s, interest rates were high; house-building, however, proceeded at a vigorous rate.

Prof. Matthews has observed that the interest rate theory has poor explanatory value when related to the major swings in house building,[6] and the most convincing evidence for this conclusion is provided by the US economy. Interest rates were not held to be important in the US,[7] where until 1980 the house-building industry operated on the basis of providing homes within a regime in which mortgages were liable to low and fixed rates of interest. This contrasted with the UK market, where mortgagees have traditionally agreed to variable interest rate payments.[8] Despite the elimination of interest rate uncertainties in the US market, the housing sector has been subjected to cyclical booms and slumps similar to the UK's. If we assume that the British sector is not subjected to unique causal influences, we must search for a factor common to the industries of both countries.

Other explanations have been advanced for the housing cycles. Population growth, for example, which stimulates the demand for homes. As the demand rises, so entrepreneurs offer to construct them at a price. Unfortunately, demographic influences fail to satisfactorily explain the violence of fluctuations in the building cycle.[9] Only the propensity to speculate in land offers a satisfactory general explanation for the booms and busts. Assuming a long-run rise in population and national income, we would expect a stable construction industry servicing the needs of a nation. But if we introduce into such a system the speculator, we guarantee instability. Evidence from the last two cycles in the 19th century illuminates our theory.

The late 1860s and early 1870s are interesting because historians have designated this period as the turning point in the relationship between the economies of North America and Europe: the 'Atlantic economy' was born. One feature of this new interaction was said to be the alternating swings in business activity. As the US economy boomed, so the UK economy slumped, and vice versa in the next phase of the cycle.[10] Cooney used this thesis to explain the downturn in the UK building activity between 1868-73, a period which he views as the peak of the boom.[11] Between 1869 and 1873 there was large-scale emigration to the USA, but Cooney discounts this as a cause of Britain's low house building programme. Most emigrants were young, unmarried and poor. They would therefore have had little effect on domestic construction. More important, in his view, was the export of capital, which was *attracted* to the booming economy of the post-Civil War era. The outflow of funds, then, starved British builders, and caused a reduction in construction.

Our competing hypothesis rests on the movement in land values. Cooney, in searching for an explanation, claimed that details of the movements of rents were lacking. But these were, in fact, available from Norton, Trist and Gilbert,[12] who recorded an alarming increase in rents in the early '70s.[13] In fact, the selling price of land shot up from 1868, fetching 35 to 40 years' purchase. The rise in rental incomes during these few years is attributable to pure economic rent, for building costs were constant until 1872.[14] So attractive were the prices that landowners sold in a market which may have produced the highest volume of transfers in the century.[15] While investment in domestic fixed capital formation declined between 1868 and 1873,[16] a great deal of money was pumped into the purchase of land. The speculators had moved in for the capital gains rather than because they wanted to use land economically. Not only is this the best explanation as to why builders cut back their output, but it also suggests a reason why labour and capital turned their backs on Britain. Migrants vote with their feet. They quit a country to get away from its problems rather than because they are attracted by another homeland, in the same way that people express their dissatisfaction by casting their votes against an existing government rather than for another one. What is more, migrants sailed the Atlantic despite the bad news which was coming back of the stock market panic of 24 September 1869, and the ensuing bank failures, which did little to raise hopes of employment.

Rents and emigration fell in 1874. The selling price of land dropped significantly the following year, and house building surged forward, matched by a rise in industrial output. But land values leapt again in 1877 and 1878; house building was curtailed, and the 20-year life of the current phase of economic growth was over;[17] Britain slumped into a severe recession in the late 1870s. Over 13,000 bankruptcies were declared in 1879, and unemployment among trade union members reached 11 per cent.

TABLE 7:I

Urban land prices 1892-1939 (England)

Price medians, recorded (A) and adjusted to constant 1900 prices (B)

	Residential land £s per acre		Residential building plots: £s per ft frontage	
	A	B	A	B
1892-95	130	130	2.0	2.0
1896-99	890	950	3.1	3.3
1900-04	130	130	4.0	4.0
1905-09	460	400	4.4	4.3
1910-16	250	210	5.0	4.3
1917-21	360	150	—	—
1922-26	270	140	4.4	2.3
1927-30	360	190	4.7	2.5
1931-35	910	580	5.0	3.2
1936-39	870	490	11.0	6.3

Source: E. A. Vallis, 'Urban Land and Building Prices 1892-1969', *Estates Gazette*, May 20, 1972, Table II, p. 1209.

A similar pattern is to be perceived in the events of the 1890s. Land prices leapt in 1896,[18] sales peaked in 1898, and the building programme collapsed in 1899. The economic downturn for the country came in the following year. We can trace this cycle in some detail, thanks to research by Vallis. The story is summarised in Table 7:I. The first column reveals most about the speculative behaviour of people dealing in land by the acre: prices are more unstable than in the second column. Vallis infers the following conclusion: bare land sold on an acreage basis

> may be agricultural land which by reason of its proximity to a town, or the effect of planning proposals, has become potentially suitable for residential development. One would expect to find a wider variation in the per acre price — which could be for quite large areas of land containing a high proportion of 'hope' value — than would be the case with plots sold on a foot-frontage basis, where there is a more direct relationship to the demand for houses at any given time.[19]

Land values in the late 1890s suddenly rose to nearly £900 an acre at recorded prices. This transmitted itself in the form of an immediate and continuing impact on the price of residential plots which the developers were obliged to seek from families wishing to live in their houses. The enormous speculative demands of the owners priced land out of reach of many developers, and pushed final house prices beyond the means of people who wanted to buy homes at that particular time. This, in turn, restricted, and then turned down, economic activity in the building industry. People who ended up paying the higher prices for their homes had to reduce their expenditures on consumer goods, which adversely affected output in the rest of the economy.

The story repeats itself in the early years of the new century. Between 1900-1904, speculation in residential land was low, and housebuilding recovered. Speculation returned with a vengeance in 1905, and house-building slumped — followed by a general downturn in the economy in 1906. Although interest rates collapsed in 1907, housebuilding did not recover (as it should have done, according to the interest rate theory) until 1910. From a peak of 140,000 completed dwellings in 1905, the building cycle crashed to under 40,000 completions in 1909. A slump of this magnitude could not be explained by a shift in interest rates from 3% (1905) to under 5% (1907) and back to 3% in 1908.[20]

Events in London illustrate what happened in these first years of the 20th century. An expanding railway network made transportation cheap and stimulated an increase of migration into the metropolis. This rise in pop-ulation was exploited by landowners, who pushed up the asking prices for their land. Habakkuk has shown what happened.[21] For industrialists, the attractions of a large supply of labour was offset by the rising price of sites;[22] so entrepreneurs did not move into London. For house-builders, a large unsatisfied demand for homes was offset by the cost of land, which made it virtually impossible to build profitably; so they did not build. The capital city of the largest empire ever seen in history was held to ransom by a minority of people who could repress social welfare and economic prosperity by exercising the power of land monopoly.

The foregoing evidence goes beyond a convincing chronological sequence; it provides a causal account. But we need to trace in detail the mechanism by which land speculation transmits its shock waves through the house-building sector into the rest of the economy. Britain in the 1970s has been selected as a case study. But first, a few figures will indicate the size and influence of the economic forces that were at work in the postwar cycle in land values, and the importance of the construction industry to the economy as a whole.

From the beginning of the cycle in 1956, until its end in 1974, the average price of new dwellings on mortgage rose by close on 400%. The basic weekly wage rates of manufacturing industry, however, increased by only 215%, and gross trading profits of companies (at current prices, and before deducting stock appreciation) rose by 236%.[23] In the mid-'70s, the annual value of building and construction work was about £12.5bn., accounting for over 10% of Gross National Product.

From the outset of the cycle, rising prices of houses outpaced building costs, as a result of which building site values rose faster still.[24] Despite the increasing share of the value of housing that was appropriated by land monopolists, however, by 1976 the industry had created a crude surplus of dwellings over households of 800,000. The government, nonetheless, felt obliged to support the Housing (Homeless Persons) Bill introduced by Liberal MP Stephen Ross in 1977. The 2.7m. households which had to accept sub-standard housing[25] were suffering as a direct result of restraints on the housing industry. Builders were unable to satisfy the needs of people who in the last quarter of the 20th century did not freely choose to continue to live in Victorian houses with toilets at the bottom of their gardens.

The reason why so many people are not able to improve their living conditions is told, in part, by the evidence in Table 7:II. Although the interest rate level dropped to a low 5% in 1971, the number of mortgages

TABLE 7:II

UK Housing (Private Sector)

		Price per plot or per hectare (1975 = 100)	Weighted average price per plot: £	Increase over previous year: %	Dwellings completed (000s)
1969		45	828	25	181.7
1970		49	908	10	170.3
1971		56	1,030	13	191.6
1972		94	1,727	68	196.5
1973		146	2,676	55	186.6
1974		145	2,663	nil	140.9
1975		100	1,839	-31	150.8
1976		100	1,848	nil	152.2
1977		106	1,943	5	140.8
1978		129	2,376	22	149.0
1979	1st half	168	3,102	18	
	2nd half	202	3,734.	20	140.4
1980	1st half	243	4,491	20	
	2nd half	238	4,400	-2	126.6
1981	1st half	241	4,467	2	
	2nd half	257	4,766	7	113.0
1982	1st half	268	4,970	4	55.3

Source: Department of the Environment

advanced to house buyers eased off and then dropped continuously from 1972 to 1974. We know that, because of the poor state of a large number of houses (leaving aside the natural desire to further improve on the quality of one's house, even when it is perfectly satisfactory from the point of view of basic amenities), the demand from households for new homes was not fully satisfied. Yet the low interest rates evidently had little impact on the decision to build. Indeed, in 1972 the completion rate of new dwellings peaked, as land prices had reached beyond manageable proportions, and kept on rising into 1973. The cost of a building plot nearly trebled in just three years.

The land monopolist was exonerated, however. Berry, for example, claimed that it was nonsense to accuse landowners of 'holding the nation to ransom.'[26] High land prices, he declared, were the residual sums between building costs and the prices which buyers were willing to pay for roofs over their heads. This is a correct account of what would happen under competitive conditions, but it ignores the reality — the ability of speculators to shrink the supply of the land that they monopolised, and so force up prices to artificially high levels.

By 1974 many builders had used up the land acquired before the boom, and they had to pay astronomical rates if they wished to remain in business. Many of them were unable to do so, and the rate of new house-building declined. Between 1969 and 1974 the price of existing houses was above the selling price of new houses; as a result of the land boom, however, builders were forced to charge prices for new houses which were above the levels for existing dwellings.[27]

The fate of this vital sector of the economy is illustrated by one of the country's most successful post-war house-building companies, Barratt Developments. Its profit margins increased steadily, reaching 24.2% of turnover in 1972, peaking at 25.7% in 1973, and then steadily declined from 20% (1974) to 7.45% in 1977.[28]

The boom in land values squeezed builders and set the economy on a doom course. Land was grossly over-valued, and a collapse in the market had to come. According to William Stern, an American lawyer who helped his father-in-law to build the Freshwater Group into Britain's largest residential property organisation with assets totalling £200m. at one point, 'There has never been such a sudden drop in values as that between January and May 1974'.[29]

So far the supply-side effect of land speculation in reducing the building rate and in raising the price of houses has been emphasised. What of the impact from the demand side, that is, the response of families wishing to buy homes? From Table 7:III we see that the higher cost of buying a house forced a change in the ratio of house prices to earnings; family budgets were squeezed. A larger proportion of the weekly wage had to be paid out in mortgage

TABLE 7:III

	Average new house prices	Average earnings	Retail prices	House prices/earnings ratio
	Per cent increases			
1969	5.2	7.8	5.4	3.50
1970	6.1	12.1	6.4	3.31
1971	15.3	11.3	9.4	3.43
1972	31.5	13.0	7.1	3.99
1973	36.2	13.4	9.2	4.80
1974	6.1	17.8	16.1	4.33
1975	9.4	26.6	24.2	3.74
1976	8.4	15.6	16.5	3.51

Source: The Building Societies Association, *Facts & Figures*, July 1977, p.11, Table A.

repayments or rents. This left less for basic necessities like food, and for durable goods like cars and refrigerators.

Households increased their bank and hire purchase loans (rising from £4.9bn. in 1971 to £9.2bn. in 1973), and divested themselves of stocks and shares (the value of these, including unit trusts and government securities, dropped from £44.5bn. in 1972 to £17.3bn. in 1974). The financial liabilities on households moved up markedly in 1972, largely as a result of the property boom and the increased need to buy consumer goods on credit.[3] There was a squeeze on what the economist calls the liquidity ratio of household budgets (defined as the ratio of personal sector liquid assets such as cash, bank and building society balances — net of borrowing — to personal disposable income),[31] which reduced the demand for articles from the manufacturing sector. Many industrialists, faced with declining demand, reduced stocks and the size of their workforces, and so the process of receding activity was multiplied through the system.

The increase in the value of household physical assets which occurred in 1971-73 — the direct result of the speculative land boom[32] — was poor compensation for the average family, for the rising trend in the net wealth of households as a percentage of personal disposable income peaked in 197 and then slumped.

It was after the land boom had begun that the unions pressed for astonishingly high wages. The higher level of mortgage and rent payments was n the only reason. Workers are not immune from the get-rich-quick syndrome generated by land speculators. But while the heightened activity of trade unions received minute attention and adverse comment, the role of land speculation on house-building and the business cycle was almost totally ignored by the politicans and bureaucrats who formulate national policies.[33]

Land speculation declined in 1975, but the pressure on developers — the men in business to enlarge the housing stock — was maintained. For the Labour Government which came to power in 1974 introduced two new laws, the Community Land Act and the Development Land Tax. These were supposed to help to smooth out the problem of the supply of land to the construction industry, and also ensure that gains from the grant of planning permission were partly appropriated for the benefit of the community. But the private land speculator might just as well have been operating, for the dynamic effect on the economy was just the same. These two laws imposed bureaucratic and fiscal *constraints* on the private land sector, and therefore succeeded in detering people from developing land; while the planning system continued to demonstrate its ineffectiveness in facilitating fresh development at a time when new economic enterprise was urgently needed to drag the economy out of the doldrums.

By 1977 the building industry was still slumbering. The economy was stagnant: unemployment rose past 1.5 m. — 300,000 from the building industry — and the grim picture was only slightly brightened by a drop in price inflation. The terms of trade turned in favour of UK exporters, but manufacturers were not geared up to exploit this advantage and the domestic market was still vulnerable to imported products. The year ended with the rate of interest paid by mortgage holders coming down to a low level. What was happening in the building industry whose prosperity so heavily determined the health of the rest of the economy?

In September 1977 the House-Builders Federation published the results of its Summer State of Trade Inquiry, which recorded the outlook of 259 of its member firms. The builders reported that during the year there had been a marked upturn in the demand for housing. So, linked with the low cost of borrowing money and the ready supply of mortgage funds held by the building societies, the prospects were good: but optimistic forecasts failed to make allowances for land monopoly. We must turn to data in Table 7: IV for the reason.

Clearly the ability to raise money to finance development was a minor difficulty for the industry and there was no shortage of labour and materials; yet there was a low rate of actual construction. Planning permission and infrastructural facilities (i.e. the input of local government) was a more serious obstacle, but the real explanation is to be found in the cost of land. Quite apart from the workings of the Community Land Act, the owners who

TABLE 7:IV

Answers by 259 house builders to the question: 'Given the present outlook for demand, which, if any, of the following considerations affecting the supply of new housing do you think are most likely to impede the ability of your company to meet this demand during the next year or so?' Answers in percentages:

	MAJ	MIN	NO
Lack of building land at viable prices	73.9	19.3	6.8
Inability to obtain infrastructural facilities	21.5	56.6	21.9
Difficulties over obtaining outline permission for proposed developments	39.0	41.5	19.5
Difficulties over obtaining detailed planning permission	44.3	43.9	11.8
Inability to raise development finance	14.1	33.6	52.3
Labour shortages	12.6	37.6	49.8
Materials shortages	5.7	26.7	67.6
Inadequate margins on development projects examined by your company	76.5	17.8	5.7

Source: The House-Builders Federation, *Summer State of Trade Inquiry*, 1977, Table 6.

MAJ = Major impediment; MIN = Minor impediment; NO = No impediment

had acquired land during the earlier boom, when prices were near their peak were in no hurry to sell at a loss. Others, who had chosen to by-pass the opportunities presented by the boom, were in no hurry to sell either. For there is no penalty for the owners who choose to keep land idle; there is furthermore, the reasonable prospect that by waiting long enough the original price expectations *will* be met.

Note, too, that the shortage of building land at viable prices (73.9 per cen of firms declared this to be a major impediment) is only exceeded by th problem of profit margins. Over 76 per cent of the firms expressed pessimisn about profits to be expected on development projects. This re-states th problem of land costs. Given the asking price of land, and the disposabl incomes of prospective house buyers — which set the limit on realistic price — investment in house building would not yield a satisfactory return. Henc the inability of firms to re-employ workers off the dole. By April 1978 hous building had declined further still, and the housing market had returned to the crisis conditions of 1973. The average annual increase in house prices of 11 per cent was higher than the average rise in earnings and retail prices. Family budgets had to provide for a larger proportion of its outgoings on mortgages, which further deflated the economy at a time when Britain's consumer industries desperately needed to start filling their order books.

The influence of land speculation penetrated deep into the social fabric of the urban environment, and generated an irrational psychological response to the tensions created by fewer jobs, poorer homes, and so on. The rise of the electoral strength of the National Front, a racist organisation, occurred *after* the recession of the 1970s had established itself in Britain. The electoral breakthrough came with the council elections and the Westminster by-elections in 1977, each round interspersed with street fighting in London, Birmingham and areas of high concentration of Asians in the north-east. The human convectors for anxieties created by economic distress were black immigrants. Had they not taken our jobs? Were they not occupying our precious houses? Should they not be sent back to their own countries?

This development was a repeat performance of what happened in the 1930s, when Britain experienced the rise in popularity of Oswald Mosley and his anti-semitic Black Shirts. Unemployment rose from 1.2m. in 1929 to over 2.8m. in 1933. Between 1931 and 1935, while people walked on the hunger marches, the speculators were at work : the median price of residential land leaped to over £900 per acre. The highest recorded prices rose from £4,200 in 1927-30 to £18,000 in 1931-35.[34] This upsurge reflected itself in the price of building plots for the families who wanted to live in congenial suburban environments. The price per foot frontage for residential plots more than doubled from £5 (1931-35) to £11 (1936-39).[35] As prices of building materials in the 1930s were declining,[36] the increase in rental income was pure economic rent. The slums of Britain's inner cities, like the East End of London, were economically and psychologically depressing, but thousands of families found that they were trapped — price rises pushed new homes beyond their financial means, thereby destroying expectations of a new environment. These people were the targets for Mosley's recruiting campaign.

Private house building dragged Britain out of the recession. There was a recovery in 1934, due mainly to building.[37] But the developers who were trying to build the estates which are a noted feature of this period found it increasingly difficult to get the land, without which a single brick could not be laid. In 1937 many builders cut back their operations; this was followed by a drop in industrial production in 1938. Public authorities found that they had to provide fewer utilities. The private sector was confronted with a cut-back in demand for consumer durables such as fittings and furnishings, and the rest of the economy suffered from a reduction in income received by people employed in the construction industry. The consequent hardship was fertile ground for Mosley's Black Shirts: they produced the Jew as a scapegoat against whom hatred could be directed.[38]

But the price of renewed prosperity — war — was a heavy one to pay. We would do well to ponder a few sobering questions. What would all the unemployed have done in the mid-1930s if the private developer had not provided work for many of them who lived in the slums of Birmingham and Bolton? Can anyone defend land speculation in this period? If not, why is it defensible at any other time? What would have happened if the war had not intervened? Would the angry masses, so soon after the experience of the early years of the decade, have remained loyal and democratic citizens? Would Mosley have continued to recruit his Black Shirts until some home-grown holocaust materialised?

But it was not just the Englishman's desire for a decent home — his proverbial castle — that was under siege by the land monopolists. A similar situation existed in the US housing market in the early part of the 20th century, as we can see by examining the speculative boom of 1925.[39] Residential construction rose steadily until 1924, when activity levelled off and slumped in 1925. Why? The influence of the interest rate on the incentive to build was 'negligible'.[40] Furthermore, the index of building costs dropped consistently.[41] So what hindered the erection of new homes?

The selling price of land reached speculative peaks, and the rents paid by tenants were on an upward trend which represented an increasing percentage of the total cost of living.[42] Builders were confronted with a shrinking pool of realistically priced land, families were prevented from buying new homes and tenants found it increasingly difficult to meet rental payments to their landlords. Pure economic rent appropriated by the land monopolist was on a rising trend, and it reached a state in the mid-'20s when the downturn in the building industry was inevitable. Construction in the 1930s was inadequate in relation to the needs of households. Yet the vacancy rate for newly built houses rose;[43] this deterred builders from investing resources in the residential sector. In sum, then, the building industry was contributing to the disaster at the end of the 18-year cycle.

We can now see that it is misleading to characterise the house-building cycle as counter-cyclical, which suggests that the cycle is benign — smoothing out the peaks and troughs of general business activity whose rhythmic movements are independent of house-building. At the beginning of an 18-year cycle the price of land is low, whereas the rate of return on capital investments (including the yields on buildings) is high: this encourages an inflow of resources into the housing sector, the growth of which stimulates activity in associated sectors of the economy. Yet no sooner does this constructive process begin, than the seeds of destruction are sown within the interstices of the economy. The returns on land monopoly increase, and the rate of return on capital diminish. House-building, like the other sectors of the economy, eventually fall prey to the speculators; house-building, then, becomes the medium through which the monopolists are able to dictate to a considerable degree the level and intensity of general business prosperity.

In housing, as in other spheres of economic activity, the Marxist analysis, which might have produced enlightened insights into the processes at work, successfully clouded the facts with ideology; this, in turn, distracted effective policy formation. Frederick Engels, for example, wrote a treatise on the housing question. He provided a clinical account of the facts in the late 19th century. There was, he noted, a 'colossal increase in rents', and in the expanding cities the price of land was often inflated to artificial levels.[44] Houses were demolished to make way for speculation.[45] Who benefited? The capitalist who constructed the buildings with his capital? Engels wrote:

> ...although in the meantime the house may have brought in a sum 'which covers five or ten times the original cost price,' we shall see that this is solely due to an increase of the ground rent. This is no secret to anyone in such cities as London where *the landlowner and the house-owner are in most cases two different persons.*[46]

The builder received on average no more than 7% per annum on his investment in the capital improvements on the land, out of which costs such as those for repairs to buildings had to be deducted. As Marx noted: 'The profit from just building is extremely small,' and the 'main profit comes from raising the ground-rent'.[47] Yet having clearly separated out the economic relationships, the distinct motives and the contrasting rates of return derived from land and capital, Engels blamed housing shortages on the capitalist mode of production. The relations between tenant and landowner he derogated to 'a quite ordinary commodity transaction between two citizens'.[48]

A solution to the instability created by speculation was presented to Engels by the Proudhonists of his time. This was the transfer of ground rent to the state,[49] which would have eliminated the benefits of speculation and thus improved the social and physical fabric of the industrial cities. Engels was not willing to entertain this as a solution worthy of socialists.

In the capitalist West, then, alternative ways have had to be devised at least to create the semblance of tackling the building cycles. In the last 50 years, genuine attempts have been made to use house-building as a counter-cyclical tool. Even socialist critics of the capitalist system who have understood the corrupting influence of land monopoly have been misled into believing that this strategy has been successful. According to Harvey, commenting on the US economy:

Cyclical swings in the economy have been broadly contained since the 1930s and the construction industry appears to have functioned effectively as a major counter-cyclical tool.[50]

If true, Washington must have devised a fail-safe mechanism for overriding the causal influences of land monopoly in the postwar years. It is to an examination of the American evidence that we now turn.

Notes

1 *Op. cit.*, p.150. In Britain, a study of turning points in the trade cycle revealed that in 22 of the 26 peaks and troughs recorded between 1842 and 1914, house-building preceded or coincided with the turning points in business activity. See J.P. Lewis, *Building Cycles and British Growth*, London: Macmillan, 1965, pp. 362-363.

2 *Cyclical Fluctuations in the UK Economy*, Discussion Paper 3, London: NEDO, 1976, p.4. This is not peculiar to the British economy. Pribram states of the US: 'The amplitude of the oscillations of building activity far exceeds any similar amplitude in changes of general business activity'. K. Pribram, 'Residual, Differential, and Absolute Urban Ground Rents and their Cyclical Fluctuations', *Econometrica*, Vol. 8, 1940, p.71.

3 *Cyclical Fluctuations in the UK Economy*, *op. cit.*, p.15.

4 L. Grebler, 'House Building, the Business Cycle and State Intervention: I', *International Labour Rev.*, Vol. 33, 1936, pp. 342-3.

5 A.K. Caincross and B. Weber, 'Fluctuations in Building in Great Britain, 1785-1849', *Econ. Hist. Rev.*, 2nd series, Vol. IX, 1956-7, p.285, describe two 18-year building cycles in this period.

6 *Op. cit.*, p.111.

7 C.A. Dauten and L.M. Valentine, *Business Cycles and Forecasting*, Ohio: South-Western Publishing Co., 1974, p.280.

8 In 1981, the Reagan Administration's high interest rates policy forced American mortgage lenders — the savings and loan associations — to adopt a variable interest rate policy.

9 C.E.V. Leser, 'Building Activity and Housing Demand', *Yorkshire Bulletin of Economic and Social Research*, Vols. 3-4, 1951, pp. 138-143.

10 See, e.g. W.A. Lewis and P.J. O'Leary, 'Secular Swings in Production and Trade 1870-1913', *Manchester School of Social and Economic Studies*, 1955, who show that UK building booms in the 1870s and 1890s coincided with protracted slumps in US building.

11 E.W. Cooney, 'Long Waves in Building in the British Economy of the Nine-teenth Century', *Econ. Hist. Rev.*, Vol. 13 (1960-1), reprinted in *British Economic Fluctuations 1790-1939*, eds: D.H. Aldcroft and P. Fearon, London: Macmillan, 1972. Page references are to the latter.

12 'A Century of Land Values', *The Times*, April 20, 1889.

13 Confirmed subsequently by A.K. Cairncross, *Home and Foreign Investment 1870-1913*, Cambridge University Press, 1953, pp. 212-3.

14 K. Maiwald, 'An Index of Building Costs in the UK, 1845-1938', *Econ. Hist Rev.*, 2nd Ser., Vol. VII (1954-5), p.192.

15 Thompson, 'The Land Market', *op. cit.*, p.40.
16 C.H. Feinstein, 'Income and Investment in the UK, 1856-1914', *Econ. Journal* (1961), p.374, Table II.
17 The average per capita rate of growth was 1.1 per cent between 1857 and 1866, and 1.5 per cent up to 1873. Glynn and Oxborrow, *op cit.*, p.18.
18 Vallis, *op. cit.*, p.1209.
19 *Ibid.*, p.1211.
20 Grebler, *op. cit.*, p.348.
21 H.J. Habakkuk, 'Fluctuations in House-Building in Britain and the United States in the Nineteenth Century', *J. of Econ. Hist.*, Vol. 22, 1962, republished in Aldcroft and Fearon, *op. cit.* See pp.265-7 of the latter work.
22 For the sharp rise in industrial land prices between 1900 and 1904, see Vallis, *op. cit.*, pp.1016 and 1209. Median prices more than doubled to £2,600 per acre.
23 *Economic Trends*, Annual Supplement, No. 1, London: HMSO, 1975.
24 R. Turvey, 'The Rationale of Rising Property Values', *Lloyds Bank Review*, Jan. 1962, pp.29-30.
25 *Housing Policy: A Consultative Document*, Cmnd. 6851, London: HMSO, 1977, para. 3.07.
26 F. Berry, *Housing: the Great British Failure*, London: Charles Knight, 1974, pp.142-3.
27 The Building Societies Association's *Facts & Figures*, July 1976, p.8, Table 9.
28 *Estates Gazette*, 13.5.78, p.555.
29 R. Milner, 'Bankrupt Stern gets US family backing', *Sunday Times*, 4.6.78.
30 P. Falush, 'The Changing Pattern of Savings', *National Westminster Bank Quarterly Rev.*, Aug. 1978, p.52.
31 *Ibid.*, p.49, Table II.
32 *Ibid.*, p.50.
33 Academic analysts are equally aloof. In their analysis of cycles in building activity, Dauten and Valentin, *op. cit.*, pp.275-281, succeed in avoiding the word 'land' completely. In her otherwise thorough treatment of *Economic Theory and the Construction Industry* (London: Macmillan, 1974), Patricia Hillebrandt thought that 'cost of land' was worth mentioning three times in 233 pages.
34 Vallis, *op. cit.*, p.1016.
35 *Ibid*, p.1209, Table II.
36 Maiwald, *op. cit.*, p.196, Graph 3.
37 H.W. Richardson, *Economic Recovery in Britain, 1932-9*, London: Weidenfeld & Nicolson, 1967; A.J.P. Taylor, *English History, 1914-1945*, Oxford University Press, 1965, pp.426-9.
38 Grebler, *op. cit.*, p.354, notes that although house-building once again became 'the pillar of British business recovery', there was nonetheless what he called 'its darker side... for there has been only a very inadequate improvement in the provisions of dwellings for the poorest classes'.
39 The role of unrealistically high land prices in depressing building activity received some recognition at the time. See W.H. Newman, 'Building Industry and Building cycles', *J. of Business of the University of Chicago*, Vol. 8, 1935, Part 2, p.18.
40 J.B.D. Derksen, 'Long Cycles in Residential Building: An Explanation', *Econometrica*, Vol. 8, 1940, p.108.
41 *Ibid.*, p.114.
42 *Ibid.*, p.111.

43   US census data is cited by Leser, *op. cit.*, p. 147.
44   F. Engels, 'The Housing Question', in Marx and Engels, *Selected Works*, Vol.
     Moscow: Progress Publishers, pp. 305-6.
45   *Ibid.*, p. 307.
46   *Ibid.*, p. 359. Our emphasis.
47   *Capital*, Vol. II, *op. cit.*, p. 238.
48   *Op. cit.*, p. 308.
49   *Ibid.*, p. 371.
50   D. Harvey, 'Class-Monopoly Rent, Finance Capital and the Urban Revolution
     Regional Studies, Vol. 8, 1974, p. 244.

THE UNITED STATES ECONOMY

8

The Hoyt Heist

Homer Hoyt, the economist who led the field with his study of cycles in land values, believes that the 18-year cyclical trends — in the USA, at any rate — no longer operate. Yet in our analysis of the British economic depression of the mid-'70s a major role was assigned to the causal influence of land speculation, and stress was placed on the predictive value of the 18-year pattern. But if Hoyt is correct, the theoretical value of the 18-year cycle has been extinguished. Its apparent presence in the UK would turn out to be a fluke, a random event of no scientific value in terms of its ability to yield general hypotheses about the effects of land monopoly.

If the speculative influence of the land market has been removed — thereby smoothing out the peaks in the trends in land values — we want to know how this came about. Was it due to institutional innovations, or a change in the psychological motives of investors? Then there is the challenge to Henry George's thesis that speculation is the major cause of recessions. If land speculation had diminished in importance, why is it that the world economy took a deep dive into an economic trough in the 1970s? Was George's analysis at best relevant to a bygone age? On the other hand, could it be that the cycle in land values is alive but disguised, and still operating to undermine the economic system? If it transpires that the latter possibility is correct and relevant to the US economy, we would have discovered a second modern case to verify the 18-year cycle.

Hoyt had no sooner concluded his study of the cycles in Chicago land values than he felt disposed to predict, as early as 1933, that

> the sequence of events just described may in the future be of interest only to historians delving in the habits and customs of 'early machine age culture in the United States,' and the knowledge of the mode of behaviour of forces in the real estate cycle will have no value in forecasting the trend of future events.[1]

Thirty-five years later he concluded that his prescience was warranted. He decided that 'The fluctuations in the real estate cycle which characterised our

109

economy in the 150 years prior to 1933, have ceased'.[2] He reaffirmed this view in correspondence with the present author in 1976, and also when interviewed at his home in Washington — at the age of 83 — in 1978. As one of America's most distinguished land economists, Hoyt's views are authoritative and command respect. A contrary view has to be well-documented. Three sorts of evidence have been collated to show that Hoyt is wrong.

Chicago real estate appraisers were interviewed, to establish whether there was any discernible trend in the values of the land in the city in the post-war years. It will be recalled that, in Chapter 5, the Chicago cycles were reported to be a sound barometer for what was happening in the rest of the economy. To what extent did a pattern emerge in the postwar years, and how did this (a) reflect trends elsewhere in the economy, and (b) sustain the hypothesis that there is a causal relationship between land speculation and industrial depressions?

In addition, it is now possible to evaluate some aggregate data which was not available when Hoyt undertook his Ph.D research in 1930. But our starting point is an examination of the successes and failures of a distinguished land speculator, whose business biography may provide clues and therefore suggest a general pattern. That speculator is none other than Homer Hoyt himself.

Homer Hoyt's grandparents emigrated from Germany in 1853. They settled in South Dakota in the 1880s, and their daughter gave birth to Homer in 1896. Homer recalls that his mother had a burning desire to own land, and this desire was inherited by her son. His earliest impressions of the fortunes to be made from land speculation were acquired while he was living in Chicago in the early 1920s. In 1925 he decided to buy some land in Cicero Avenue But he made a cardinal mistake: he bought at a time when prices were at thei peak, and although he held on to the land for over four years he lost money The price of the land collapsed and he could not find a buyer. That was one o the reasons for his decision to study the history of land values in Chicago fo his Ph.D thesis, upon which he embarked in 1930.

Vacant land, it seemed to Hoyt, was a bad risk: the Chicago venture ha left him 'disgusted' with land which failed to yield an income, and he wa determined not to repeat the mistake. In 1943 he bought some orange grove in Florida. Unfortunately, however, he was to fare no better out of this dea The land was valuable because the US military forces were paying hig prices for the oranges. But when the war ended and the soldiers wei demobilised, the army stopped buying oranges! The bottom fell out of th market, the value of Hoyt's land slumped, and once again he realised that F had bought at the wrong moment: at the peak of the prices. The secret, F told himself, was to buy land early in the cycle in values, and then sell befo. the down-turn. Someone else should be left holding over-valued land who the slump came. These hard-learnt lessons were to stand Hoyt in good stead, and were to help him to become a multi-millionaire.

The postwar years saw the beginnings of a new trend in the United States: the emergence of large shopping centres to suit the needs of the age of the motor car. Hoyt was involved with these enterprises at the outset. He was employed as a consultant to appraise the profitability of the complexes which were planned from coast-to-coast. He earned fat fees in return for his remarkable talent for predicting the income streams which could be expected from these developments. His close study left him in no doubt that the biggest profits accrued to whoever owned the land, which 'skyrocketed'. His interest in vacant land was rekindled.

In 1953 Hoyt bought an interest in 620 acres in Fairfax County, near to Washington DC, for between $200 and $350 an acre. At the time, he recalls, there was a total lack of demand for land. So he was buying in the trough of the cycle, when values were rock bottom. He sold out in 1972 for $7,000 an acre — an average increase per acre of nearly 2,500%, reaping him a profit of $2m. What does this tell about any cycle in values which might have been at work? Hoyt cannot identify when the value of his land started moving up, but he points out that the turning point in the speculative boom was in mid-1973. This is an overall period of 20 years, which is close to the theoretical cycle of 18 years. But the issue is complicated by the fact that the value of the land did not dramatically slump in the recession which followed, for in 1976 Hoyt placed a value of $10,000 an acre on the land which he had formerly owned. Here, then, we have our first feature apparently inconsistent with previous cycles: if the boom in land speculation terminated in 1973, why was it not followed by a collapse in land values?

Hoyt's assessment may have been coloured by his own prospects, which are well illustrated by some of his deals in Florida. This south-eastern corner of the union, sun-soaked and washed by the warm waters of the gulf, has been a traditional hunting- (and burial-) ground for land speculators. Hoyt had successfully completed a number of deals in the postwar years, including one near Fort Lauderdale. He bought a tract with 950 feet fronting onto the Atlantic. Because the land was being eroded by the ocean, no-one was interested in it. So Hoyt bought it for $1,700 a front foot, sank piles into the ocean at a modest cost to protect the coastline, and resold within two years at $3,000 a front foot, netting him $900,000. Other properties were not speedily resold. One of the most speculative of these was a lake of 360 acres used by anglers in Washington County. Hoyt did not own any of the shoreline land, so the property returned an annual loss of nearly $300 — the tax he had to pay on the property. What was the value of the lake? He used a nominal value of $100 an acre, but conceded that valuation was difficult. After all, he had received a number of enquiries from oil prospectors who wanted to explore the lake for black gold, and if any *was* found then the $100 would have to be revised!

But the most illuminating transaction, for our present purposes, was the property called Treasure Beach. Hoyt sent a camera crew to film the Miami coastline from the sky. When the film was developed, he saw how intensive had been the building northwards for 100 miles. The only vacant site of any size which had not been exploited was on Hutchinson Island, in St Lucie County, one mile south of Fort Pierce. This was a golden opportunity, for by the mid-1960s prime sites fronting onto the ocean were scarce. Swiftly, Hoyt bought up four separate tracts — some of it swampland — at $200 a foot front. All told, he paid $1m. Six years later, in September 1972, he sold the land for $3m. to a Fort Lauderdale-based developer, Warren F. McFadden. The developer made a down payment of $400,000, and met his annual payments of $400,000 in 1973 and 1974. In March 1975, however, he defaulted, crippled by the 12% interest he was paying on his mortgages. Hoyt instituted foreclosure proceedings, kept the $1.2m. he had already received from McFadden and recovered his land. McFadden's downfall was a classic example of what happens to the unwary at the peak of a land boom.

The belief that money can be made from nothing — as, for shrewd operators in the land market, it can be[3] — generates a swift flow of short-term funds into speculation. This enables buyers to pay high prices, but unless they re-sell to other speculators before the crisis they are left with over-valued assets which they may not be able to re-mortgage to finance original loans. The demand for funds to speculate in land helps to push up interest rates, and when the bottom falls out of the market the speculators sink into bankruptcy with it. The movement of funds and interest rates are summarised in Table 8:I.

Homer Hoyt was willing to share the crucial lesson of timing in land deals. In 1967 he published the insights which he had acquired in a remarkable document, *Market Value Versus Speculative Value.*[4] This is a guide for successful land speculation. The object of the exercise is to buy land at a price which enabled the speculator to re-sell at a price which included its *future* value. Thus, knowledge of plans to build a new highway or airport, or careful study of the direction of expansion of a growing town, enabled the land dealer to buy at current use value and then hold the land until he could capitalise on future values. 'Often the full value has been added to the price in advance,' in which case it was profitless to buy at such a price. The presence of amenities such as sewerage disposal systems increased the value of land, which is what happened with Hoyt's land in Fairfax County, which in addition had the presence of the nation's capital: 'land values have sky-rocketed'.

TABLE 8:I

	1960	1965	1968	1969	1970	1971	1972	1973	1974	1975 (March)
			FUNDS: Uses and Some Sources, in billions of dollars[1]							
USES										
Investment	27.4	44.4	54.3	60.2	66.4	101.1	114.7	111.3	111.5	
Short-term	13.8	23.4	26.2	35.7	19.0	20.5	42.5	65.5	66.9	
SOME SOURCES										
Savings and Loans Associations	7.3	9.6	10.2	9.5	12.5	28.9	35.8	25.4	20.8	
Mutual Savings Banks	1.5	3.9	4.4	2.8	4.2	9.8	10.2	4.7	3.0	
Real Estate Investment Trusts	(z)	(z)	0.2	0.9	2.1	2.5	4.9	4.5	1.4	
Commercial Banks	9.5	28.6	40.0	17.1	36.5	49.7	74.6	78.2	62.5	
			Selected Money Market Rates[2]							
Prime commerical paper	3.85	4.38		7.83	7.72	5.11	4.69	8.15	9.87	6.06
Euro $ deposits	NA	NA		9.76	8.51	6.59	5.40	9.24	11.01	6.85
Short-term bank loans to business	5.16	5.06		8.21	8.48	6.32	5.82	8.30	11.28	9.94
Federal Reserve discount rate (high and low)	3-4	4-4½		6.00	5½-6	4½-5¼	4½	4½-7½	7½-8	6¾-7¾

(z) = less than $50m.

NA — not available

Sources: 1 Statistical Abstract of the US 1975, Washington DC: US Department of Commerce, Table 765.

After sewer and water lines have been extended to an area, there will of course be a sharp advance in land prices. In order to make a substantial profit on his investment, the buyer must anticipate the possibility or probability of the extension of the utilities before others do.[5]

This ensuing increase in land values results in people paying *twice* for public services. The first payment is made out of taxes for the installation of the basic facilities, such as sewer works; the second when land is bought (either for private homes, factories, shops and offices, or for public amenities such as schools or hospitals) at a price which capitalised the benefits of the publicly-financed facilities.

McFadden had not learnt these basic lessons well enough. He bought land from Hoyt at its full future value, and at a time when interest rates were reaching their peak. One of the institutions which suffered along with McFadden was the Kentucky Mortgage Company, which lost a total of about $2m. on his deals. The company found that when land values levelled off after the 1974 peak it had to re-sell the land of defaulting mortgagees at a time when sellers were willing to accept half of their original asking prices. The Kentucky, however, was not alone. A series of real estate investment trusts (REITs) — operating as the equivalent of secondary banks in Britain in fuelling land speculation — were burnt in the process.

The contribution to our story of the REITs began in 1961 with the Real Estate Investment Trust Act. This law exempted investors from federal taxes on income derived from real estate at the corporate level. This tax break was a powerful incentive for channelling money through the trusts into property. For the investor, a most attractive element of the law was the requirement that trusts had to distribute at least 90% of net income annually to shareholders.

In the early years the REITs concentrated on buying equity in existing properties. This ensured a reliable flow of income and avoided the risks of development, but it missed the chance to earn the substantial profits to be wrung out of speculative enterprises. The speculative phase began in earnest in 1969, and took the form of lending money for buying land and financing buildings. These construction and development REITs proved to be irresistible money-spinning institutions. They secured short-term bank loans a rates sufficiently below their lending rate to provide them with attractiv profit margins. There were additional financial features which encourage the established financial institutions to give their blessings to this new growt industry. The net effect was to turn REITs into 'Everyman's key to th hallowed halls of high finance'.[6]

In 1969 the assets of REITs doubled from $1bn. to $2bn., more tha doubled again by the end of 1970 to $4.7bn. and sustained that rate c growth through 1971, to over $8.1bn.[7] The growth rate accelerated. Banl lent them about $11bn. between 1972 and 1974, and their total assets climbed to over $20bn.

During the 1969-70 period of tight money, which affected the orthodox financial institutions — commercial banks and savings and loans associations — the REITs forged ahead: loans for construction and development rose from $260m. to $2.5bn., a staggering increase of 890%. Operators like Warren F. McFadden agreed to pay hugely inflated prices for land because the trusts were pouring funds into their pockets. Money was no obstacle to any deal which appeared — on paper — to offer bonanza profits. The easy-money period which followed in 1971 aggravated the speculative fever which gripped the economy. Commercial banks increased their construction loans by nearly $3bn. in that one year alone.[8] Prestigious banks, like Chase Manhattan, set up REITs, using their names to sell stocks and debentures to the public.

> The prestigious Chase Manhattan launched a trust with a $50m. line of credit and announced, with fanfare, a public offering of $112m. worth of shares and debentures. Chase's idea was to get into the field of risky short-term, high-interest loans, designed to yield quick profits, by wearing the hat of its REIT affiliate — a game it wouldn't dare to play under its own parent name.[9]

The pressure to find borrowers willing to pay high rates of interest encouraged the less reputable trusts to employ unorthodox business practices. One of these was to agree to defer receipt of interest until the original loan matured, at which time the borrower was obliged to pay back both the capital sum and the interest in one go. This proved tricky, for by law the trusts had to distribute at least 90% of their 'profits' every year. And according to their accounts, these 'profits' included the interest from loans, the actual receipt of which had been deferred. So the trusts could meet their current commitments only by drawing on income from earlier loans or from the sale of shares to the public. They were therefore distributing profits before these had actually been received.[10]

The isolated warnings were ignored. People who are infected with the gambling fever generally refuse to recall the tragic lessons of history, like the collapse of the speculative boom of the mid-1920s (after all, everyone thinks he is holding the winning cards). The speculation continued through 1973, but the yields were starting to come down, and along with them the flow of funds.

At the bottom of the whole operation was the furious trading in land, from which the developers hoped to make their windfall gains. Eventually, however, illusions have to be shattered. The people left holding the land bought at speculatively-high prices have to service their mortgages out of rental income. In the case of vacant land — in the naked condition created by nature — there is no productive economic activity and therefore no income. Where capital improvements, such as shops, offices and warehouses, have been undertaken, rents tend to be at penal rates. They have to be pitched high in order to try and recover the original capital outlay and meet prevailing interest rates. Under these conditions, however, the tenants are not forthcoming. For they can only pay rents out of current income, based on actual output: whereas speculative rents assume a higher, fictitious rate of output based on expectations about the future.

And so the collapse was bound to come. For with buildings standing empty, many people left holding high-priced land find themselves unable to service their mortgages. Speculators and builders alike are forced into bankruptcy, and the weakening foundations brought about the first major collapse in December 1974. Walter J. Kassuba Realty, a Florida building corporation which had invested $550m. into nearly 120 properties, filed for bankruptcy. A dozen REITs found themselves holding $110m. in bad loans. Nearly 200 trusts had mushroomed during the height of the boom; by the end of 1975 the share prices of those which had preferred construction lending had sunk to 78% below book value (book value determined *after* massive writedowns). The bubble had burst. Some REITs disappeared rapidly. Others managed to float on. The Chase Manhattan Mortgage & Realty Trust, the country's largest, clung on until May Day 1978, before it defaulted on more than $38m. in loan notes.[11]

In principle the idea of real estate investment trusts was a sound one, if the objective was to marshall funds in sufficient quantities to enable capital improvements to be undertaken by developers. With a growing population, an aging stock of homes, shops, offices, and industrial buildings requires constant renewal. If the purpose of REITs had been to further this goal, in the pursuit of interest on investment which would ultimately be comparable with yields from other sectors of economic activity, the trusts would have been admirable. The intrinsic defect, however, was the monopolistic basis of the land tenure system, which held out the powerful temptation of enormous, unearned, gains from inflated land prices.

The end of the speculative boom in real estate broke many people. For the resourceful rich, this merely meant having to explore new ways to recover their fortunes. Egyptian film star Omar Sharif lost a great deal of money on his investments in real estate at the time. His solution was a simple one: stop gambling and produce a few more films.[12] But for the hundreds of thousands of wage earners who hoped to fructify their hard-earned savings through REITs, the end of the boom was a disaster.

The diffusion of ownership in the equity of a nation's physical assets was something to which Homer Hoyt had developed an early commitment.

Sitting at a desk in the lobby of a hotel in Washington in 1918, he drafted an article in which he warned that concentrated ownership over land would lead to communism.

> If the concentration of wealth under the legitimate rules of the game should proceed to the point where a few toil little and enjoy disproportionately much and where the many work long and receive disproportionately little, then there will come into existence a reason for revolution.[13]

At the same time, however, he deplored 'the gambling spirit' which served to 'attack the soul of a nation like a dry rot'. Was this not a criticism of the speculative forces which drove up land values to unrealistic peaks? Hoyt did not recognise it as such, for in his analysis of the cyclical upward thrust of land values he emphasised real factors such as the growth of population. The presence of empty offices and shops at the end of the cycle in land values he censured on the grounds of a failure to correctly appraise demand, rather than as being the result of an over-extension of the speculative — i.e. gambling — spirit. As for the downturn in the cycle, this was a historical phenomenon of no relevance to the modern era. Hoyt explained the downturns of the past as a result of monetary deflation. Periodically, the authorities realised that the money supply had got out of hand; the real value of the dollar had declined. So the remedial action was to contract this supply.

> So we had periods of falling prices and wages, unemployment, bankruptcies and foreclosures, which dragged down real estate values to low levels.[14]

This explanation, while it may relieve the consciences of speculators, is a curious one for the economic historian to advance. The rhythmic pattern in the timing of remedial action allegedly taken by governments over a period of one hundred years ought to have alerted Hoyt to its implausibility, thereby opening up other avenues of scholastic enquiry. In any event, he would write off the counter-argument advanced here as of academic interest, for since the second World War, without the discipline of the gold standard, the situation had changed. As a result of the consistent inflation of the money supply, there was little risk of a repeat of past slumps in land values, and thus, in his view, the role of land speculation in de-stabilising the economy is effectively neutralised.

Yet the latest round of land speculation in the US preceded the slump which struck the economy in 1974. The causal connections are uncovered in the next chapter. Meanwhile, however, we have to recognise that land values did not collapse in a way that we might have expected on the basis of historical experience. Treasure Beach, for example, which Hoyt had sold to McFadden in 1972 for $3m., was on the market in May 1978 for $6m. ('I might take \$5m.'). Many people, including foreign buyers — some of them Arabs — showed strong interest. But no deal was concluded, and when re-interviewed in October 1982 Hoyt said that the price had risen to \$9.5m. ('I might take a million less'). The reasons why the land market did not fold like a snowman in a Florida heatwave will be explained in Chapter 19. We can say, however, that a long upward trend in land values terminated in 1974. Nonetheless, while this may be the end of the cycle, we have yet to establish its beginnings in order to verify that a cycle of approximately 18 years duration was operating, a manifestation of both real economic growth in the economy and, grafted onto it, the speculative activities of a relatively few people who were attacking 'the soul of [the] nation like a dry rot'.

Notes

1   *One Hundred Years, op. cit.*, p. 423.
2   Homer Hoyt, *The Changing Principles of Land Economics*, Washington: UL Technical Bulletin No. 60, 1968, p. 11.
3   The profits from land speculation, of course, are recognised as not only legitimate but — for many people — morally defensible. The opportunities presented b the land market, however, have attracted their fair share of fraudulent deals. Fc a documented account of one land swindle perpetrated at this time, by teamste boss Jimmy Hoffa, in Titusville, Florida, see D. E. Moldea, *The Hoffa War* London: Paddington Press, 1978.
4   Originally published by the Urban Land Institute, Washington, DC, reprinte in *According to Hoyt*, 1970, pp. 792-5.
5   *Ibid.*, p. 794.
6   Leland Frederick Cooley and L. M. Cooley, *Land Investment USA*, L Angeles: Nash Publishing, 1973, p. 222.
7   P. A. Schulkin, 'Real Estate Investment Trusts in an Era of Innovation', *R. Estate Review*, Fall 1972, Table I.
8   *Ibid.*, Table 2.
9   D. L. Thomas, *Lords of the Land*, New York: G. P. Putnam's Sons, 1977, p. 2£
10 *Ibid.*, p. 287. For a critique of unorthodox accounting practices used after t REIT crash, see J. B. Levy, 'No Bargain Basement: REIT Accounting Co pounds the Risks for Investors', *Barron's*, 13.6.77.
11 *The New York Times*, 3.5.78.
12 Omar Sharif, *The Eternal Male*, London: W. H. Allen, 1977, pp. 152-3.
13 'Bolshevism and the Laws of Property', originally published in *Open Cc Magazine*, 1918, republished in *According to Hoyt*, pp. 114-15.
14 Homer Hoyt, *The Urban Real Estate Cycle - Performances and Prospects*, Washi ton: ULI Technical Bulletin No. 38, 1950, p. 9.

9

Recycling the Speculators

In 1943 the Chicago Plan Commission published its *Master Plan of Residential Land Use*. Homer Hoyt was Director of the research division. At the time, one-fifth of the city's land was vacant. About 20,000 square miles suitable for urban development sparsely accommodated under 7,000 people, instead of the 274,000 who could have settled there within a neatly developing city.[1]

After the world war, the homes fit for heroes were built in a sprawling fashion outside the city. Fine Illinois agricultural land was eaten up, the community suffered the burden of maintaining unnecessary costs (both public and private), and the city sluggishly struggled to re-adapt itself to peacetime living.

> In recent years the construction boom beyond the corporate limits of Chicago has necessitated the duplication of many public and institutional facilities. Vacant areas closer to the center of the city have been passed by and the development of more distant areas has necessitated the costly extension of power lines, water mains, streets, and other facilities. Premature subdivision has also caused a wasteful dispersion of population through many areas which were only partially built up.[2]

The largest vacant areas suitable for residential use within Chicago were on the southwest side, in a prong of land extending west from Cicero Avenue[3] — where Homer Hoyt, back in the boom of the '20s, had bought land at speculatively-high prices. The commission condemned the effects of vacant land, and analysed the problem in terms of the influence of land speculation. One of its targets was the zoning practices which had supported the speculative motive.

> Improper zoning has been another of the artificial barriers that impeded the development of the city's vacant areas. The original zoning ordinance of 1923 was adopted at the beginning of one of the most active real estate booms in the history of Chicago. It encouraged the holding of much vacant land for apartment and commercial uses and the installation of

119

premature and uneconomic street and utility improvements in anticipation of large speculative profits from rapid absorption of vacant areas into these intensive uses. The total amount of vacant land zoned for apartments was far in excess of the demand for such structures. Single-family dwellings were not constructed on land so zoned *because of high land costs* and the lack of protection from the intrusion of more intensive uses and larger structures.[4]

But while house-building sprawled into the countryside, real estate men were despondent about the prospects of development within the city. They were wryly commenting that the Loop, within the heart of Chicago, 'might as well be returned to the Indians'.[5] Interest in developing land was at a low level. Although land values rose slowly, they levelled off again once the Korean War broke out. The first skyscrapers in the commercial centre did not start to go up until 1955, along with the value of land beneath them.

Chicago is unique in enjoying the information published annually in *Olcott's Blue Book*, which logs the individual values of most of the city's sites.[6] From it we can trace the movement in the value of a quarter-acre on the corner of State and Madison Street which is illuminating. In 1874 it was worth $1,000 a foot front. Waving up and down during the intervening years, it stood at $25,000 a foot front during World War II. As the economy reconverted to peacetime activity, the site's value moved up to $40,000 by 1950. During the three years of the Korean War, however, it slid back to $35,000. It was three years after this further wartime dislocation (in 1956) that the value of the site, right in the middle of Chicago's shopping centre, began the upward climb once again.

Does this date, 1956, suggest our starting point for the sustained post-war growth which would enable us to predict a severe recession 18 years later? The date would appear to fit, for the depression struck 18 years later, in 1974, when over 12m. square feet of new space was added at rents few tenants could afford. By itself, however, this evidence would be classed as impressionistic, and of limited scientific value. However, this does not mean that we are bereft of evidence for the postwar years.

Since 1912 the US Department of Agriculture has systematically collected data on the value of farmland, providing us with the most consistent series of information from which to analyse long-term trends in land values and their implication for the economy. The house building industry, for example, regards trends in farmland values as one of the best indicators of potential changes in residential land prices.[7]

There has been an almost continuous upward trend in farmland values since the Second World War, with the index soaring from 27 in 1944 to 308 in 1978. Can we extract a pattern to support the hypothesis of an 18-year cycle? There was a levelling off in values in the early 1950s, but why take the climb which began in 1954 as our starting point for a post-war cycle? The element of arbitrariness in the selection of dates for turning points is something against which we have to guard. A superficial examination of this data suggests that the 18-year cycle is not evident, for there was no cut-back in the rate of growth right up to 1980.

TABLE 9:1

Residual return to US farm production assets
expressed as % of value of production assets

	Total return to operators and assets	Residual return to production assets
1950	15.7	6.2
1951	15.6	6.2
1952	13.4	4.8
1953	11.9	3.3
1954	11.7	3.4
1955	10.6	2.7
1956	10.3	2.7
1957	9.5	3.0
1958	10.6	4.4
1959	8.1	2.2
1960	8.1	3.0
1961	8.5	3.6
1962	8.3	3.8
1963	8.0	3.7
1964	7.1	3.2
1965	8.3	4.7
1966	8.3	4.9
1967	7.2	3.8
1968	7.1	3.7
1969	7.5	4.2
1970	7.2	4.1
1971	7.3	4.1
1972	8.6	5.6
1973	13.1	10.0
1974	8.9	6.2
1975	7.9	5.4
1976	5.8	3.6
1977	5.5	3.5

Source: E. Melichar, 'The Relationship between Farm Income and Asset Values, 1950-77', Seminar on Food and Agriculture Policy Issues, 1978.

It will be recalled that the theory of the 18-year cycle postulates a bifurcation in the distribution of income to the various factors of production: a decline in the rate of return to capital (thereby squeezing profits and the potential for reinvestment), concomitant with a growth in the returns to land (which therefore attracts speculators). Can we support this hypothesis by penetrating behind the crude figures?

On March 28, 1978, Emanuel Melichar, an economist on the staff of the Board of Governors of the Federal Reserve System, presented the results of his analysis of the income received by the agricultural industry.[8] From the aggregate data, he deducted the returns to labour, management and the imputed income derived from the investment in dwellings, to disclose the residual return to production assets (Table 9:I). This showed a downward movement which terminated in 1955-56, followed by consistent growth to a peak in 1973 — a trend spanning precisely 18 years.

But these residual returns were to capital assets as well as to land. Can we disaggregate the data to determine which productive factor received an increasing proportion of this income? The answer is that we cannot do so satisfactorily, with statistics, for the land has not been valued separately from all capital improvements upon it. Nonetheless, we can safely infer the answer.

As noted in Chapter 6, the long-term rate of return to capital is downward. This is inevitable, given that capital is reproduced in increasing quantities to take advantage of profitable enterprise; competition among capitalists forces down their returns. Land, however, is in fixed supply.[9] It can only go on appreciating in value; but are its *returns* increasing? In the case of US farmland, even if competition failed to reduce the returns to capital, it would not allow the returns to *rise*. For if that happened, capital would be attracted into the industry in response to the abnormal profits, thereby dampening them down. So where there is a rising trend in the residual return to productive assets, we must attribute a rising proportion to land.

The final piece of empirical evidence comes from a young economist in the US Department of Agriculture. At the National Food and Agricultural Outlook Conference held in Washington in November 1978, Larry Walker presented the preliminary results of his comparison of the relative attractions of Iowa farmland compared with other forms of investments.[10] Land, it transpired, was the most profitable. Walker ascertained the relative profitability of investing in farmland by using the rate of return derived from the net cash rent stream, compared with alternative investment opportunities.

The results are presented in Table 9:II, from which Walker drew the conclusion that 'land seems to have been the prudent investment over the long term'. We find that investors in Iowa farmland had to hold their land for decreasing number of years in order to surpass the income from other forms of investment. For example, an investor buying in 1965 had to hold his land

TABLE 9:II

Iowa Farmland Compared with Alternative Investments

Number of years required to hold Iowa farmland until the discounted present value of the net rate of return derived from the net cash rent stream exceeds the discounted present value of the rate of return derived from an alternative investment providing a constant, annual income stream

Rate of Return on alternative investments	1940	1945	1950	1955	1960	1965	1970	1971
3	1	1	1	1	1	1	1	1
4	1	1	8	4	2	1	1	1
5	5	11	17	14	10	3	2	3
6	12	19	24	20	15	7	5	—
7	20	27	27	23	18	11	7	—
8	29	33	—	—	—	13	9	—

Source: L. A. Walker, 'Farm Finance and Real Estate Markers —Situation and Outlook', Washington, DC: US Dept. of Agriculture, (unpublished).

years until the net discounted current value of the rate of return derived from his annual net rent stream surpassed that of an alternative investment providing an annual 6% rate of return, discounted at 6%. Notice, in particular, the cycle. In the period before the early 1950s, the situation was quite different: Iowa farmland was becoming a *less* attractive proposition. We can see from Melichar's data that the residual return to agricultural production assets was declining until 1954. So it would have paid investors to sink their funds into other investments — capital equipment — rather than land. From the mid-1950s, however, once the economy had shaken off the distorting influences of the Second World War and the Korean War, and begun to pick up its growth rhythm, it became increasingly prudent to switch from investment in capital to the hoarding of land.

Although Walker's initial results were from a sample of Iowa farms, his complete analysis of the data from 13 other States indicated similar results. On the basis of the evidence from the agricultural sector, then, we can conclusively state that the 18-year cycle in land values began in 1955, that it attracted the speculators and that this dictated the economy's date with a major slump in 1974. We can now explore the macro-economic effects, along with the evidence available for land values in the urban sector. As the US economy experienced a recession in 1967-68, in which the annual growth rate was halved, it would be useful to break down our study of the land values cycle into two parts.

We begin by looking at the national income data (Table 9:III). These are crude magnitudes; rent, it will be recalled, consists of interest on capital improvements upon the land as well as economic rent paid for the use of land.

TABLE 9:III

*Percentage Distribution of Aggregate Payments,
by Type of Income, in Current Prices*

	Employee compensation	Entrepreneurial income	Dividends and interest	Rent
1959-1968	75.0	10.9	7.1	7.0
1954-1963	74.3	12.4	7.6	5.7
1949-1958	73.1	14.5	7.8	4.6
1944-1953	71.2	17.5	7.3	4.0
1939-1948	69.8	18.9	7.0	4.3

Source: Department of Commerce estimates tabulated in *Historical Statistics of the U Part 1*, Washington: US Department of Commerce, p.238.

itself. But the trends are unmistakeable. From the Second World War until after the end of the Korean War, the Americans were concerned with the manufacture of wealth. Interest in land was at a low ebb, and so the proportion of GNP going to those who were willing to invest their resources in capital goods and employment increased: rental income decreased. The bias in favour of productive wealth is clear. The prospects for creating jobs and improving living standards were increased in response to the need to satisfy the pent-up demands for consumer goods following the world war.

All this changed in the late 1950s. The abnormal, postwar level of demand had been met, and the economy adjusted to 'normality'.[11] And as we saw with the relationships in the UK economy, the trends went into reverse. The percentage of national income going to the receivers of rent started to increase. Wages to labour rose in line with improvements in productivity. Dividends and interest, however, started to slide downwards, along with the income to entrepreneurial talents. The consequences were predictable: the economy was heading for a slump. For with more money and human energy going into the land market the balance in the distribution of funds moved against the owners of capital who needed to reinvest in new technology and higher productivity processes.

The facts support the theory. The ratio of fixed investment of business as a share of GNP was an average 10.8% up to 1957. After this date, however, the US economy acquired a persistent slack in both demand and employment, during which the ratio fell to an average 9%.[12] Attempts were made to remedy this serious situation through a cut in corporate taxes under the provisions of the Revenue Act (1964), which are named after John F. Kennedy, the President who advocated them just before his assassination. This increased post-tax profits and therefore stimulated investment — which was supposed to boost employment and therefore consumption. The fiscal encouragement did improve the ratio of fixed investment as a share of GNP (11% by 1967), and reversed the downward slide in profits in US industry (Table 9:IV).

The Kennedy tax cut has since been cited as a principal piece of empirical evidence in support of the supply-side economics associated with the Administration of President Reagan. Reaganomics, as it has become known, ensured a new level of economic growth as a result of a cut in tax rates, which stimulated output and simultaneously increased exchequer revenue.[13] The maximum tax rate in 1963 was 91%; this was reduced to 77% in 1964 and 70% in 1965. There was a surge in growth: does this piece of fiscal history carry any lessons for the policymakers of the other industrial nations who were not able to engineer such a reversal in the profits trend? And how does this phase in American economic history square with the theory of the 18-year cycle in land values?

TABLE 9:IV

Manufacturing Industry

International comparisons of profitability, 1955-1980: %

	United States	West Germany	United Kingdom
Profit[1] *Shares*			
1955-58	20	38	28
1959-62	20	33	26
1963-67	23	28	24
1968-71	19	27	21
1972-75	18	21	17
1976-80	19[3]	21[3]	15
1976	18	21	12
1977	20	21	19
1978	20	21	20
1979	18	21	14
1980	NA	NA	11
Net rate of return[2]			
1955-58	26	39	17
1959-62	26	30	16
1963-67	34	21	14
1968-71	24	21	11
1972-75	21	15	8
1976-80	21[3]	NA	6
1976	22	16	5
1977	22	17	8
1978	22	18	8
1979	19	NA	5
1980	NA	NA	4

Source: *British Business* (London: Department of Industry), 4 September, 1981, p. 17, and 15 October 1982, p. 272.

1 Defined as net operating surplus as percentage of net value added.
2 Defined as net operating surplus as percentage of net capital stock of fixed assets (excluding land).
3 1976-1979

George Gilder's best-seller, *Wealth and Poverty*, which can be represented as the bible for the exponents of Reaganomics, argued that the Kennedy tax cuts 'brought almost surgically beneficial effects to the economy'.[14] Large post-tax profits meant an increase in investment and a faster rate of economic growth. This proposition has been challenged by Peter Drucker. He claims that the Federal tax cuts prove nothing, for there was a simultaneous sharp increase in state and local taxes.[15] Drucker's assessment is too sweeping; we need to look closely at the economic implications of a reduction in tax before drawing such a conclusion.

The increase in non-federal taxes did neutralize the prospects of a stimulative expansion in demand as registered through an increase in the retail of goods and services. People who receive low or average wages have a relatively high propensity to consume — to spend their money, rather than invest it in stocks and shares or in property. For these people the decrease in federal taxes was offset by state and local taxes to the point where there was no significant rise in net disposable incomes from which to finance higher consumption. The economy in the mid-'60s, therefore, could not grow at a faster rate because there was no 'pull' from families wanting to increase their purchases of washing machines and the like.

Reaganomics, however, emphasises the prospect of increased demand arising as a direct result of an increase in the supply of goods. Supply creates its own demand, the theory known as Say's Law. Gilder places stress on the fact that the cut in tax rates caused a shift in the pattern of investment: *more money went into businesses, and less into real estate*. It was this transformation in the portfolio of asset holders that caused the beneficial effects on the economy, in his view.

In theory, this is correct. People who receive large salaries or income from investments have a high propensity to save, rather than to spend all their post-tax income on current consumption needs. Because of this, then, we would have expected an increase in the flow of money into assets. Unfortunately, however, Gilder forgot his reading of Henry George's *Progress and Poverty*, which he identified as 'one of the great inspirational works of economic literature'.[16] For if the prospects of making speculative gains were still present — that is, if the income tax cuts were not simultaneously offset by an increase in the tax on land values — then it paid to buy land. Furthermore, we can predict on the basis of Ricardo's theory of rent, that the land monopolist will exact the first claim on an increase in net incomes. That is what happened in the US following the Kennedy tax cuts. In each of the five years up to 1964, land values increased by between $24bn. and $32bn. (see graph). In 1965, the increase rose to $35bn. and the decade's peak was in 1966 ($44bn.). The benefits of the cut in taxes were mopped up by the land monopolists through an increase in the capitalisation of land values. The economy slipped into a recession in the last quarter of 1966, while the land monopolists laughed all the way to the bank. And the downward trend in profits was re-established in 1967, heading for the fateful date with history which was ordained to occur in 1974.[17]

US Land Values, 1955-1976

(Annual increases, $bns)

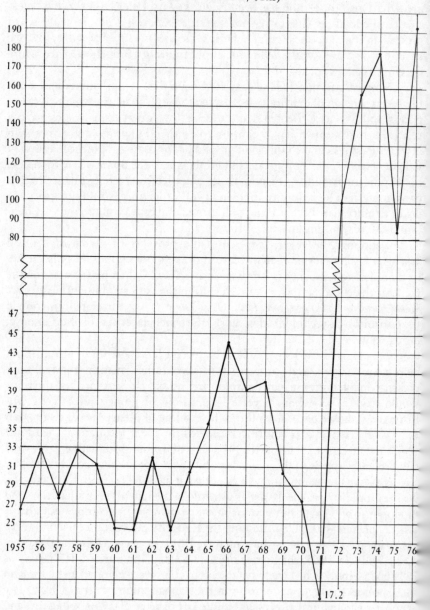

Source: Robert Eisner *et al.*, 'Total Incomes in the US, 1946-1976: A Summar
Report', Gouvieux, France: International Association for Research i
Income and Wealth, 17th General Conference, 1981, Table 14.

In the early phase of an 18-year cycle in land values, the speculative profits to be made out of buying land are necessarily at their lowest. But for anyone who can afford to tie up large sums of money for reasonably long periods (up to 15 years) this is the time to buy, when prices are at their lowest. Not surprisingly, therefore, the market tends to be dominated by institutional buyers along with the newly-rich like Hollywood stars Bob Hope, Lucille Ball and Gene Autry,[18] who amass large sums that need to be safely invested to yield a secure long-term income. Exact data on institutional buyers is not available, but Grace Milgram has been able to show that they increased their land-holdings between 1952 and 1968. Among their tangible assets, the value of their land-holdings increased by 1100% whereas the value of structures rose by 392%.[19] The economic effect of this is that large tracts can be held vacant, or under-used, even though they may be needed by others for more productive uses; for institutions can afford to resist market incentives in the expectation of much higher future gains. Syndicates emerged in the 1950s, pooling funds and helping people to invest the $1 trillion of personal savings which they had accumulated by the end of the decade. 'When a few of the first syndications had vast successes, the demand to "get in" was often fantastic,' reported *Fortune* in September 1961.[20]

Between 1956 and 1966 the market value of real estate rose from $697bn. to $1,261bn., an increase of 81%. Land values rose faster than those for buildings: 95%, or an annual rate of 6.9%, whereas the value of buildings rose by 73% (5.6%).[21] General consumer prices rose by an annual rate of 1.8% over the same period. It clearly paid to invest in vacant land rather than in capital improvements, and this is confirmed by estimates which showed that the value of vacant land increased faster than land under residential, commercial and industrial structures.[22]

The effect of this upward climb on the construction industry was serious. Most builders, by 1963, had acquired their land banks for the following few years, and most of the remaining urban fringe land was owned by speculators, reported *Fortune*. These speculators were sitting pretty, 'planning to sell their land but holding it off the market for an expected future killing'.[23] A survey among members of the National Association of Home Builders in 1964 revealed that they considered lack of market their most important problem. In assessing the data, Michael Sumichrast reported:

> A valid argument can be made that this land price increase is partly responsible for difficulties in selling new homes. It is the price of land which determines the sale price of units to be built. An average $4,567 lot would most likely mean a home selling for $22,500-$25,000. It is obvious that this house is too expensive for the large number of families found in the lower- and middle-income groups. So the increase in the cost of land is a factor in pricing much of the public out of the market.[24]

By 1964, in fact, the price of a site had outstripped other costs. Taking 1957-59 = 100, the index price of a site in that year was 139, building costs were 112 and consumer prices had risen to 108.[25]

As their land was used up, developers had to pay the speculatively high prices. Schmid found that the increase in the price of raw land in 1964 above its agricultural value was between a maximum of 892% and 1,875%, depending on whose data was used,[26] and that this increase was on an accelerating trend.[27]

Thus, the troubles in the building industry foreshadowed the relatively mild recession in the late 1960s. But worse was to follow: the economy, after recovering, was heading for a disaster which was predictable on the basis of an analysis of trends in land values.

Profits were on the downward slide in the non-financial sector.[28] Nordhaus showed that the rate of return on non-financial corporate capital, before tax, had dropped from 15.5% (1953) to 10.5% (1973), and that after tax the figures were 7.9% and 5.4%,[29] even though there was a decline in the burden of taxation on corporations.[30] The economy was being seriously damaged from two angles: industry was a less attractive prospect for investors, and entrepreneurs were finding it increasingly difficult to plough back profits into fixed capital formation — which, to remain competitive and sustain jobs attracting higher wages, ought to be a continuous process for the economy.

The prospect for land speculators was wholly different, as we have seen in our study of farmland. Urban land displayed the same characteristics of rapidly escalating prices and increasing yields. Everybody wanted to get 'a slice of the action', from the small savers who mere magnetised towards REITs to the large institutions anxious to shift their portfolios in favour of property.

By 1971, the consumer price level had risen roughly 60% over the previous 20 years; land in developing areas had shot up by between 400% and 500%.[31] Federal Housing Administration data revealed that, between 1950 and 1970, the estimated value of a new single-family house had increased by about 150%, whereas the market price of the site had risen by about 400%.

But the land boom had not yet reached its peak. In 1974 the Urban Land Institute was commissioned to carry out research by the Department of Housing and Urban Development. The price of land had doubled between 1970-74; developers in six cities surveyed by the ULI reported that the average price of raw single-family dwelling land went from $6,370 per acre to $12,950. This average figure, however, concealed some startling increase — like 300% for raw unzoned land in Dade County, Florida, and 167% for raw townhouse land in Washington, D.C.[32]

The financial effects of these trends was to divert funds from long-term uses to short-term lending (see Table 8:1). Thus, firms found it increasingly difficult to obtain loans to finance the acquisition of capital goods: money-lenders were mainly interested in quick returns arising from deals with speculators. This, in turn, helped to drive up the rate of interest payable by borrowers, making loans accessible only to those who could expect — or hope for — abnormal returns on their deals (which meant from land rather than from machines).

In 1969, land as a proportion of housing costs had risen by 24%, whereas profits from building had declined.[33] By 1973, the stabilising influences of a thriving construction industry on the economy as a whole were ebbing away. Non-residential building slackened off first, followed quickly by home-building. This did not deter the speculators, however, who were anxious to drive their claim stakes into land: 1974 saw the peak turnover in the sale of farmland (42m. acres), thereby boosting the proportion owned by non-farmers.

Before the energy crisis had a chance to contribute its deflationary impact, the consumer market — the object of all productive effort — was weakening. The consumption of durable goods slumped in the first quarter of 1973 along with assets held by households, and general consumption was sluggish by the third quarter. 'The sharp deterioration in household balance sheets appears to have been a major factor in the severity of the economic downturn,' reports Mishkin, who quantified this effect: it was responsible for 40% of the depressive effects during 1973-75.[34] From 1967 to 1974, the cost of shelter — rent paid by tenants, mortgages paid by owner occupiers — rose faster than other costs such as clothing, transport and health.[35] The conditions for collapse rapidly converged on the year 1973, the final 12 months of the cycle in land values. If the record could be completed with a bank collapse, we would have a classic textbook case of the speculation-induced recessions which had repeated themselves throughout the 19th century.

The US National Bank of San Diego provides us with the final piece of the jigsaw. It failed in October, 1973 — a date which absolves OPEC from blame for the recession. The bank went under because of the activities of its major shareholder, C. Arnholt Smith, a close friend of Richard Nixon's and a major real estate speculator in Southern California. The bank had loaned heavily to one of Smith's conglomerates, the Westgate-California Corporation, which between 1967 and 1971 had relied on its property deals for most of its reported pre-tax profits. Smith was sentenced to three years in prison for tax evasion, fraud and theft in June, 1979.

This was the biggest bank failure in 40 years, but it was followed by an even more spectacular disaster. The Franklin National Bank of New York — the 20th largest bank in the US — was declared insolvent in October 1974. Again, property deals were at the source of its troubles. Apart from the loans extended to the San Diego bank, Franklin, which was owned by Italian multi-millionaire Michele Sindona, had money committed to property around the world. Sindona, a one-time financial adviser to the Vatican, owned Società Generale Immobiliare, which built Washington's Watergate complex and owned properties from the Champs Elysées in Paris to Marina Del Ray in Los Angeles. The rapidly-rising values of these properties — on paper — were not enough to enable Sindona to juggle the books and cover up his fraudulent dealings. Franklin was bankrupted in October 1974, despite an unprecedented $1.7bn. loan from the US Federal Reserve and several standby credits (the first, in July 1974, of $100m.) from the state-controlled Bank of Rome.

Sindona had powerful friends, beyond the Mafia links that he was suspected to have cultivated. So when, in 1979, he was charged with 65 counts of fraud arising from the collapse of Franklin, a national Republican Party official in Washington attempted to intervene with the collaboration of P2, the sinister Italian masonic lodge whose activities, when they were exposed in May 1981, led to the fall of the Forlani Government in Rome. Bribery and corruption were among P2's tools. In the Sindona case, the plan was to persuade two cardinals who were senior Vatican financial advisers to speak on his behalf before the US courts.[36] The ploy failed, and Sindona was locked up in prison for 25 years.

The collapse of the San Diego bank did not alert the public to the undercurrents which were fiercely washing away the foundations on which the postwar prosperity of the US economy was built. It was not until the summer of 1974 that J. Bruce Lindeman, an Associate Professor of Real Estate and Urban Affairs at Georgia State University, published the first authoritative warning. He had diagnosed that the land market had over-reached itself and that speculators were thwarting legitimate developers:

> In many suburban areas, speculators are outbidding developers. Outlying land of dubious use potential is trading briskly. The professionals are applauding this activity and proclaiming their faith in its eternal life. Most alarming is the obvious effort being made to bring outsiders into the land market. Vigorous syndication efforts and even the current popularity of dubious land development purchases are hailed as innovative and exciting applications of marketing 'technology' to the 'backward' field of real estate marketing...[37]

But the red flag could be raised only on the basis of disjointed pieces of evidence and the intuition of concerned individuals. The Treasury economists were in no position to objectively analyse the independent effects of the land price variable on the economy, and thereby *anticipate* the looming recession: the data was not available, and so it could not be fed into the

computerised models which are used to predict trends in consumption and
output. The absence of satisfactory data — and principally, a general index of
land prices — is curious, when one considers the trouble to which bureaucracies go to collate statistical evidence ranging from population growth trends
to the price of cabbages in the High ,Streets. Prof. Gunnar Myrdal has
suggested a theory for this critical gap in our knowledge:

> The faults in statistics generally follow an opportunistically biased line.
> Some important facts, for instance those about landownership and tenancy,
> are not only faulty but are often even prevented from being collected, or
> suppressed when collected, by the influence of powerful vested interests.[38]

Although Myrdal was dealing with Third World countries, his hypothesis has
substance for the rest of the 'free' world. In the US, for example, the most open
capitalist country when it comes to public accessibility to information, it is
exceedingly difficult to track down the ownership of land and its area: no
central files exist. In his survey of US land ownership, Gene Wunderlich
noted that landownership was significant 'not only because it is an important
feature of the distribution of a nation's wealth but also because it is thought
to influence the nation's political and social structure'. Despite the importance of the subject, however, 'information is scattered, incomplete, and often
unavailable'.[39] Just how influential the landowning class is, can be illustrated
by the fate of the short-lived Office of Land Use and Water Planning.

The Office was formed in 1973 in anticipation of legislation (which was
subsequently killed on Capitol Hill). In 1975 the Office published a report
which revealed that over 12% — $39bn. — of the federal budget was ear-
marked to be spent on programmes affecting non-federal land. This staggering
expenditure of taxpayers' money was to bolster, in one way or another, the
value of privately-owned land. Senators from the land-rich West were
'incensed' by this revelation, and the intentions behind the Office. Shortly after
the report was published the Senate Appropriations Committee cut off all
funds and closed down the Office.

Its former director, Lance Marston, has since estimated that there was an
increase of at least 20% in land use programmes during the years 1975-78. The
Carter Administration proved no more anxious than its predecessors to study
how public money was being spent on programmes to benefit privately-
owned land.[40]

So the taxpayers bear a double cross: their hard-earned incomes are
channelled by politicians into the pockets of the appropriators of rent, and at
the same time the economic system which creates this wealth is undermined by
those who parasitically exploit it. The extent to which public policies and the
political structure is manipulated by the landowning class is of crucial
importance to any consideration of reform, and it is to this which we now turn.

Notes

1 *Master Plan of Residential Land Use of Chicago*, Chicago: Chicago Plan Commission, 1943, p. 125.
2 *Ibid.*, pp. 115-16.
3 *Ibid.*, p. 113.
4 *Ibid.*, p. 116, our emphasis.
5 C. W. Condit, *Chicago 1930-1970*, Chicago: University Press, 1974, p. 51.
6 The book was started in 1900 by George C. Olcott, and is now (1983) published by the third — and last — generation of the Olcotts.
7 *Economic News Notes*, National Association of Home Builders, Washington, August 1978, p. 2.
8 E. Melichar, 'The Relationship Between Farm Income and Asset Values, 1950-1977', Seminar on Food and Agricultural Policy Issues, Wayzata, Minnesota, 1978.
9 Capital, of course, can be substituted for land in certain cases. But even this works to advantage of the landowner, rather than the owner of capital, once the temporary effects of patents and the advantages of advanced technological knowledge have been removed as barriers to further capital formation. Melichar pointed out, in citing the work of other researchers (*ibid.*, p. 3): '... land prices were rising because the combined effect of two factors: (1) technological advances that lowered unit costs of production, and (2) price support programmes that maintained output prices in the face of the tendency of the technological gains to increase total farm output'.
10 Larry A. Walker, 'Farm Finance and Real Estate Markets — Situation and Outlook', US Dept. of Agriculture, Washington DC (unpublished).
11 E. A. Mennis, 'The Outlook for Corporate Profits', in H. W. Stevenson and J. R. Nelson, *Profits in the Modern Economy*, Minneapolis: University of Minnesota Press, 1967, p. 53.
12 W. H. Heller, 'The Role of Profits in National Economic Policy', in Stevenson and Nelson, *ibid.*, pp. 185-186. Profits of manufacturing corporations averaged 11.4%.
13 B. Bartlett, *Reaganomics: Supply Side Economics in Action*, Westport: Arlington House, 1981, pp. 120-121.
14 *Op. cit.*, p. 186.
15 P. F. Drucker, *Toward the Next Economics*, New York: Harper & Row, 1981, pp. 11-12. The increase in state and local taxes arose because of the need to finance a large number of capital projects, especially schools, that resulted from the creation of a substantial number of new suburban jurisdictions in the mid-'60s.
16 Gilder, *op. cit.*, p. x.
17 A similar explanation can be advanced for the mid-cycle boom and slump in the inter-war years. The Revenue Act (1924) gave taxpayers a 25% reduction retroactive to 1923 income, increased personal and surtax exemptions, and brought the top rate (which had stood at 73% in 1921) down to 46% in 1924. This coincided perfectly with the land boom in 1924/5. Land monopolists converted the dramatic savings in income taxes into higher land values. Andrew Mellon, the Secretary to the Treasury, was impressed with the results of his early experiment in 'supply side' tax-cutting, and the top tax rate was cut to 24%

in 1929. Bartlett, in articulating the need for a fresh round of cuts in the 1980s, failed to see the connection between the reduction in taxes, the way in which the higher net incomes were spent, and the crash of 1929. He merely concludes: 'Unfortunately, the stock market crash and the onset of the Great Depression and later World War II led to severe increases in tax rates' (*op. cit.*, p. 104).

18 H. Kay, 'The Strange Leveling off in Land', *Fortune*, Oct. 1963, p. 129.

19 G. Milgram, 'Estimates of the Value of Land in the US Held by Various Sectors of the Economy, Annually, 1952 to 1968', in R. W. Goldsmith, editor, *Institutional Investors and Corporate Stock – A Background Study*, National Bureau of Economic Research, 1973, pp. 342 and 346.

20 T. A. Wise, 'What to Do with $1,000,000,000,000', republished in *Readings in Economics from Fortune*, editor: R. E. Mulcahy, New York: Holt, Rinehart & Winston, 1967, 3rd edn., p. 115.

21 A. D. Manvel, 'Trends in the Value of Real Estate and Land, 1956 to 1966', in *Three Land Research Studies*, Washington, DC: National Commission on Urban Problems, Research Report No. 12, 1968, p. 1.

22 *Ibid.*, p. 2.

23 Kay, *op. cit.*, p. 128.

24 M. Sumichrast, 'Land Costs are Rising, Survey Confirms', *Economic News Notes*, Special Report, 65-5, Washington DC: NAHB, 1965.

25 A. A. Schmid, *Converting Land From Rural to Urban Uses*, Washington: Resources For The Future, Inc., 1968, p. 9, Table. 3.

26 *Op. cit.*, p. 24. The data was from time series supplied by the Federal Housing Association, which represents medium priced housing, and the National Association of Home Builders, representing somewhat higher-priced housing.

27 *Ibid.*, p. 19. Schmid notes (pp. 24-5): 'Though the quantification of the exact appreciation in the total conversion process awaits better data, it is clear that we are speaking of something which is often measured in hundreds and thousands per cent above farm land opportunity costs. Appreciation of this magnitude seems to deserve public policy attention'.

28 A. M. Okun and G. O. Perry, 'Notes & Numbers on the Profits Squeeze', *Brookings Papers on Economic Activity*, 1970, p. 470.

29 W. D. Nordhaus, 'The Falling Share of Profits', *Brookings Papers on Economic Activity*, 1974, p. 180.

30 *Ibid.*, p. 205. Feldstein and Summers, while challenging the claim that there was a downward trend, agree that pretax net rate of return on corporate capital reached a 30-year low in 1974 of 6.4%. M. Feldstein and L. Summers, 'Is the Rate of Profit Falling?' *Brookings Papers on Economic Activity*, 1977, p. 211.

31 S. Kamm, 'Inflation: Curbing Inflation in Residential Land Prices', *Urban Land*, Washington: ULI, Sept. 1971.

32 'Urban Land Price Inflation: Implications for Public Policy', ULI, Washington DC, 1974, p. II-6. Although unpublished, some of the data is contained in J. T. Black, 'Land Price Inflation', *Urban Land*, Sept. 1974.

33 M. Sumichrast and S. A. Frankel, *Profile of the Builder and his Industry*, Washington, DC: NAHB, 1970.

34 F. S. Mishkin, 'What Depressed the Consumer? The Household Balance Sheet and the 1973-75 Recession', *Brookings Papers on Economic Activity*, 1977, p. 156.

35 *Statistical Abstract of the US*, Washington, DC: US Dept. of Commerce, 1975, Table 688.

36 R. Lustig, 'Secrets of the Vila Wanda', *The Observer*, 31.5.81.

37   J.B. Lindeman, 'Is the Land Boom Coming to an End?' *Real Estate Rev.*, Fall
     1974.
38   G. Myrdal, *The Challenge of World Poverty*, Harmondsworth: Pelican, 1970,
     p.424.
39   G. Wunderlich, *Facts About US Landownership*, Washington, DC: US Dept. of
     Agriculture, Information Bulletin No. 422, 1978, pp. v and 2.
40   P. Meyer, 'Land Rush', *Harper's*, Jan. 1979, p.58.

10

Policies of Pillage

One hundred years after Henry George published *Progress and Poverty*, interest in his proposals for the taxation of land values was revived by President Jimmy Carter's 'troubleshooter' on inflation, Alfred E. Kahn (Chairman of the Council on Wage and Price Stability). He declared:

> I have long held the conviction that it makes absolutely no sense to tax unimproved land in the same way as improved land — that the rental value of the former is, as Henry George observed a long time ago, a genuinely unearned increment, and that taxing it heavily, while reducing correspondingly the taxes on real capital formation, makes excellent sense on grounds both of equity and economics.[1]

A tax which removed the gains of speculation, however, is strongly opposed in the US as an attack on one of the principles of the Founding Fathers.

For the United States of America was founded on a programme of handing over the lands of the continent to private interests. Thomas Le Duc, an historian, has summarised the history to leave us in no doubt that Congress was determined to transfer virgin land not so much to farmers who would develop it, as to speculative intermediaries who would hold it vacant until it could be sold for profit.[2] The relevant Congressional Acts — of 1800, 1820, 1841 and 1862 — fit neatly into the beginning of 18-year cycles in land values, and so gave the stamp of legislative approval to the private pursuit of speculative gains.

The Act of 1800 set a minimum price of $2 an acre. There was no immediate fever of speculation until after 1812, when many buyers decided that they would make a fortune by re-selling to migrants. So much money flowed from the sale of public land that, in 1818, the government repealed all federal taxes. 'Not much of the available capital flowed into farm making... Little of the raw land purchased with these funds, however, went into production; most of it was held idle for speculation.'[3] The financial panic and commercial depression struck in 1819.

The Act of 1820 continued the process of alienating public land; in fact, governmental authorities sought to sell more than the market could absorb. Squatters moved in on virgin land, many of them failing to see why they should pay uneconomically high prices to speculators when they could get in on the act themselves. The boom came in the mid-'30s, the transactions in land peaked in 1836, and the collapse in the economy followed in 1837.

The Pre-Emption Act of 1841 made a token effort at trying to tidy-up the process of disbursing land, by authorising the purchase at the minimum price of up to 160 acres. The speculators, however, worked out a way to overcome this minor difficulty: they formed 'claims clubs' which, by the use of bully-boy tactics and manipulation, ensured that members could obtain holdings of up to 640 acres. This was land obtained at $1.25 an acre, at interest rates ranging from 25% to 50% on borrowed money! Le Duc concludes that 'the only rational explanation of this behaviour is that the borrowers believed that even after paying interest sufficient to double their investment they were making a wise buy'.[4]

After 1847 the federal government increased its donations of land in the states, which Le Duc interprets as 'deficit spending in which the government spent off its capital to support current policies, instead of levying taxes and appropriating the revenue'.[5] This was followed by the Graduation Act (1854) which put almost 40m. acres into private hands. Between 1847 and 1855 the federal government embarked on a programme of land bonuses to veterans: 61m. acres worth of warrants were issued, most of which were sold on the open market to speculators. Le Duc interpreted these land grants as revealing that 'Congress was far less interested in either soldiers or settlers than in speculators'.[6] Land deals peaked in 1854-6, and the economy collapsed in 1857. This was followed predictably by a new act (the Homestead Act[7]), yet 'another stage in the evolution of a set of policies better suited to desocialising capital gains that to harnessing the nation's resources. The interesting thing is that while the real thrust of the land laws was never affirmed as public policy, the declared national objectives were steadily undermined by politicians trading the public property for votes'.[8]

Le Duc summarised the economic effects of this profligacy with public land in an important article.[9] He concluded that the systematic alienation of land, at low prices or in the form of massive grants to states, corporations and settlers, retarded economic development by encouraging the belief that it was more profitable to buy land and hold it vacant than to develop it. In many cases capital improvements were negligible or non-existent.

> By supporting...high rates of interest, the squatter absorbed loan capita that theoretically might otherwise have flowed at lower rates into rea development.[10]

In the 1840s, contemporary testimony agreed that an 8-acre farm was as much as a family could operate without hired help. By over-enlarging their holdings, migrants beggared themselves. Although seriously under-capitalised *qua* farmers, they hoped to capitalise on their good fortune — did they not have a stake in New World real estate?

> The migrants came, they squatted, they tried to control as much choice land as they could and they lived in squalor and penury while they slowly built a farm or waited for a buyer.[11]

Compact settlement was impossible. Consequently the costs of transportation, marketing, education and other social services were raised, and the economy was restrained from growing at its maximum potential.

> ... public policy had not merely stimulated the absorption of capital in land speculation, but had seriously retarded a genuine development built on a rational application of labour and capital to the magnificent but undeveloped resources of the interior.[12]

Land speculation as an explanation for the early slumps is the only hypothesis consistent with American history. In the early period — the first three 18-year cycles — there was nothing present to support the Marxist thesis of miserly capitalists exploiting workers in satanic factories; no 'anarchistic' market so saturated with unplanned surplus goods through over-production as to cause a cut-back in employment. *Yet the country was systematically reduced to recessions in a cyclical pattern which maintained a uniform character and duration from the earliest period of the colony's history to the late stages of the age of so-called mature capitalist 'exploitation'.* Whatever the particular characteristics of the specific time and place over a history spanning 180 years, only the traumatic dislocations of world wars could make this sequence of events falter, and then only temporarily.

Land speculation was the common denominator. If, therefore, the capitalist system was unstable, this was because the market was prevented from developing to its full potential. The monopolistic encumbrance of the land tenure system blocked the free flow of an essential ingredient in the productive process at prices fairly proportionate to its contribution, and distorted the flow of investment funds at fair rates of interest to lubricate the whole system.

Thomas Cochran, in his review of the formative era of the American economy, took a more benign view of the influence of the property market.

> The most money was to be made from townsite planning or from buying the land adjacent to expanding trade centers. Since it was generally thought that there was more money to be made in this way than from the profits of trade or industry, land speculation undoubtedly drew money

from the latter. But in compensation, this activity contributed to the development of banking, credit agencies, mortgage markets, and inland transportation, which in turn increasingly expanded the trader's or manufacturer's national market.[13]

To sustain this view it would have to be shown that the economy could not have developed as extensively (through space) or as intensively (in time) without the lure of speculative profits from land. In New York in 1850, as Cochran notes, 15 out of the 23 citizens worth over $500,000 were involved wholly or mainly in real estate.[14] How much faster could the metropolis have grown without the distractions of land speculation? How much richer the people as a whole if funds were diverted into capital formation rather than circulating within a narrow circle of property dealers battening onto the creative labours of others?

The frontier lands had to be colonised for the land to yield its riches. There was no sound economic reason why the publicly-created share of that wealth should not have been retained to build up the infrastructure of the new commonwealth. All that the legislators needed was a modicum of rationality and a strong sense of justice. However, they were persuaded by the great vested interests that monopoly control of land was a necessary pre-condition of economic development. This view even shapes modern American politics. Some evidence of this must be presented if we are to avoid the mistake of thinking that the problem is not a contemporary political issue. For public policies *are* still designed to promote the financial prospects of monopolists.

The belief that landowners have to be given special encouragement to make profits (always justified on the basis of general social benefits, of course) is well exemplified by a procedure adopted in Chicago in the years after World War II. The cost to the taxpayers of Cook County has to be counted in tens of millions of dollars.

The model adopted in Chicago for leaving this money in the pockets of landowners was simple: for the purpose of the *ad valorem* property tax, the office run by the County assessor grossly under-assessed the value of land and buildings. The assessor was P. J. Cullerton, who was elected to this post in 1958 just as investment in the city's office buildings was accelerating. The beneficiaries — the real estate tycoons who publicly identified themselves as Cullerton's political backers, working actively to re-elect him in November 1970 — were obliged to pay as little as one-third of what they would normally have had to pay in taxes. As a result, the additional tax burden fell on the homeowners.

This practice was exposed by two journalists on the *Chicago Daily News*, William Clements and Charles Nicodemus. By carefully scrutinising the assessor's files on individual skyscrapers, the two reporters discovered that the value of the properties were being written down in a way which was difficult to explain. No explanation was forthcoming, until the newspaper sustained its campaign in the weeks before the 1970 elections and forced Cullerton to give his first Press conference in 12 years.

Cullerton and his aides explained that the tax 'breaks' were justified on the grounds that the rental income received from the tenants, one of the factors taken into account by the assessor, was below anticipated levels. And they argued that without the appropriate downward revision of assessments, new buildings would not have been erected. This, then, was the carrot with which to encourage the developers to erect buildings in the centre of Chicago in areas that might otherwise turn to seedy crime-infested districts.

The difficulty with the explanation, however, was that assessments were often agreed between the assessor's office and the developers *before* the buildings were erected:[15] so there was no way of knowing that the level of rents established by the market would render the buildings uneconomic.

The intricacies of this lucrative model for extracting additional economic surplus out of the public were sardonically summarised by a Chicago architect, Henry Tideman:

> A new building goes onto the tax rolls, normally, at an appraisal distantly related to its cost, higher if the building cost was more, lower if it was less, multiplied by a depreciation factor which is 90% the first year and decreases each year thereafter for fifty years, and then further multiplied by a 'condition factor' which is determined by how well the building is maintained and how well it continues to relate to its neighbourhood. This last is obviously a matter of judgment, and the Assessor's office decided, some time ago, to exercise that judgment in an extensive way. If the taxpayer met certain standards, some of which may be undemonstrable in any single case; if he secured appropriate advance commitments from the Assessor's office; had a project or even an existing building of major size; was appropriately politically connected, which did not preclude his belonging to that other political party; was regarded as appropriately tight-lipped; could demonstrate or claim to have demonstrated — for no files on the matter are kept, as the Assessor says — that his project had not been as profitable at the level informally established by the Assessor, and made an appropriate contribution to the Assessor's campaign fund, then the Assessor's office arbitrarily lowered the 'condition factor' of the building to bring the taxes down to an amount owner and assessor found mutually satisfactory, even if this required a condition factor of only 18% on a major new building.[16]

The Brunswick building on the corner of Dearborn and Washington Streets illustrates the system. Constructed between 1963-5, it is described as 'the largest and most impressive work of concrete framing in the Loop... obviously a distinguished work, superior to anything else of its kind'.[17]

Financially, however, it was allegedly less praiseworthy, claimed the assessor's office and the millionaire real estate dealer who managed the 36-floor skyscraper, Arthur Rubloff.

According to the chief deputy assessor (Russell Johnson) the Brunswick building had its normal assessment reduced by two-thirds. Reason: it had a 'reduced net income' — arising because Rubloff had given 'artificially low rents' to two major tenants.[18] The other tenants in the building paid rents at the market rate.

Not content with this concession, however, Rubloff, with Cullerton's blessings, appealed to the Circuit Court for another reduction under a little-known device called Objection I.[19] The appeal against the *under*-assessment was successful — the tax liability was further cut in half on the grounds that the building was losing money.

The Brunswick building was given a partial assessment 'condition factor' of 30% in 1963, when it was first opened. By 1965 it was fully occupied, and the 'condition factor' ought to have gone up to the top rate. Instead, it remained at the 30% level, until the Objection I appeal reduced it to 18%.[20] The owners saved $2m. during the following five years.[21] In 1969, for example, the tax bill was $479,295, broken down into a $268,539 charge on the building and the remainder on the value of the land. If, however, an 88% 'condition factor' had been used in computing the building portion of the tax bill, as ordinarily would have been the case, the total tax bill would have been $1,020,144. For reasons which at that time were kept confidential, the landlords received a tax break of $540,849 in that one year.[22]

The Brunswick building site of 44,150 sq feet was bought in 1945 at a reported price of $60 a square foot. For the same price it was resold in 1953 and again in 1957. Thus, the site cost the developers $2.6m. Its value in 1978 was estimated to be $225 a square foot, according to one of Chicago's leading real estate appraisers,[23] or a total of $9.9m. If we deduct the cost of knocking down the old buildings in 1957 ($309,050), this leaves a net appreciation in value of $7m., or a rise of over 260% in 20 years.

The economic effects of under-assessment are two-fold. In the short term, it boosts the residual value of the land, and therefore increases the net income stream enjoyed by the landlord. As a consequence, other landowners adjust their expectations upwards. Because of the higher price levels and because it takes longer to secure buyers at the inflated levels, developments which would otherwise have been undertaken are deferred or lost altogether. This achieves, in the medium term, the opposite effect claimed by Cullerton's supporters.

The Chicago model for reinforcing the monopolistic advantages created by the fiscal system had stamped upon it the eccentricities of a particular political machine, the boss of which was Mayor Richard Daley. But the simple fact is that US tax laws and practices institutionalise the disposition to favour land dealers, and this provides encouragement to speculate.

At the local level, property taxes favour the hoarding of vacant land. 'Numerous studies have shown that unimproved suburban land is typically treated with great tenderness by the assessors,' report Clawson and Perloff.[24] This conclusion was endorsed by a Washington task force on housing in 1978, which noted that 'property tax practices, either by design or in-advertance, sometimes work to keep raw land off the market,'[25] a practice for which the government was to blame but for which citizens had to pay in the form of 'land costs . . . being driven up'.[26] Hoyt's tax liability on his Treasure Beach property illustrates the point. In 1979 he was seeking a buyer for the land at a selling price of $7m. But the land was assessed at a value of $2m., and Hoyt paid taxes amounting to 1.2% — $24,000, which is hardly an onerous burden on a property which was up for sale with a multi-million price tag.

Furthermore, however, Federal taxes came to the aid of the speculator to relieve him of even such a minimal financial obligation. Interest payments on mortgages and real estate taxes are deductible when calculating federal income tax. *So it paid to borrow to speculate in land.*

This configuration of tax incentives conspire to encourage urban sprawl and the sub-optimum use of land. It could not have been more wilfully designed if the legislators had deliberately wanted to so arrange affairs as to compel people into removing from the market the scarcest of all factors of production. But we have not yet exhausted the possibilities for land spec-ulation sanctioned by the tax system.

Given the relative rates of taxes on income and capital gains, it pays someone in the super-tax bracket to tie up his assets in vacant land, rather than in resources yielding an annual income from productive enterprise. Hoyt has demonstrated how someone paying a marginal income tax of 80% would make $32,136 more if he invested $100,000 in vacant land which doubled in value in ten years, compared with the same sum invested in a building yielding an annual income.[27] Liability for capital gains can be spread over a number of years, through the use of instalments sales techniques, thereby further minimising the tax burden on shrewd land dealers.

Despite the fact that the tax laws were perpetuating the sordid decay of social relationships and physical structures in the urban ghettos of the union, the politicians on Capitol Hill continued to go out of their way to line the pockets of those who chose to enter the land speculation business.

Tax shelter provisions were tightened up in the 1976 and 1978 laws, because Washington decided that it was wrong for businessmen to be reducing their financial obligations to the community through these devices. The 1976 tax reform act specifically limited the amount of loss from oil and gas tax shelters, cattle feeding, equipment leasing and film-making and from partnerships *other than those in real estate*. The 1978 tax revision went further and limited losses in any trade or business *other than real estate*. Thus, real estate shot to the top of attractive investment opportunities for businessmen wanting to offset 'losses' against other income. But the Revenue Act of 1978, signed by President Carter on Nov. 6, went even further. It reduced the tax rate on long-term capital gains. According to one of the country's leading accountants specialising in tax matters, the effective capital gains rate had been reduced from slightly over 49% to 28%.[28] The effect of this permutation of tax changes was to channel even more money into speculation, tie up land in its vacant state for long periods and therefore drive up prices even further.

The irrationality of these institutional barriers to free market economics in a society ostensibly dedicated to *laissez faire* leads one to the unavoidable conclusion that a powerful group, the landowning class, is able to manipulate the system to safeguard its interests. How else can we account for the paradox whereby politicians and urban planners espouse contradictory policies? They advocate equality of opportunity with respect to employment and housing; renewal of rotting city centres; efficient systems of transportation and social services at minimum costs, and so on — and then proceed to obstruct these goals by giving simultaneous encouragement to those who wish to exploit the land tenure system to their anti-social advantage.

Ignorance may offer a partial explanation, but this does not absolve the scholars who have the responsibility to shed light where there is darkness. The patent failure to understand the implications of policies pursued by the state and federal authorities has led one author, Mary Rawson, to discern a conspiracy.

> American economists who have chosen 'land economics' as their special province in recent decades have almost to a man turned their faces away from a consideration of the property tax as a factor in the problems and policies of urban land use. Furthermore, in their treatments of the property tax they have almost consistently failed to analyse the divergent effects of taxes on land and on buildings, apparently taking the view that to the individual property owner it doesn't matter.[29]

Opposing the lethargy of economists in recent years has been the work of political activists who have penetrated the social and economic implications concealed by the political power of landowners. It became apparent to people representing deprived minority groups that property owners were exercising their control over the political processes to protect and raise the value of their properties by methods such as zoning regulations.[30] As a result, during the 1960s, litigation was instituted to over-ride these.[31] Far from enlightening the public and thereby weakening the vested interest, however, landowners continued to advance their cause by manipulating the electorate. Their strength was their ability to appeal to the average wage earner in his role as land-owning home occupier. The most spectacular recent success is known as Proposition 13.

On June 6, 1978, the voters of California gave their over-whelming support for an amendment to the State's constitution which limited the tax on property to 1%. This cut the state government's revenue from this source from $12bn. to $5bn. Increases in the assessed market value for existing owners were restricted to a maximum of 2% p.a. from the 1975 base. This sharp reduction in public revenue was the outcome of a vigorous campaign instituted and led by two men with interests in property, Howard Jarvis, an executive director of a Los Angeles landlords' association, and Paul Gann, a property dealer.

The state's property tax was moderate by national standards. According to official statistics it stood at around 2%, although one Californian professor of economics, Mason Gaffney, judged the actual rate to be nearer 1% of market values.[32] About 43% of the value of taxable real estate was land value.

The Jarvis-Gann campaign exploited the public's resentment against taxes generally, and it persuaded a majority of the voters that they ought to support the demand for a reduction in taxes falling specifically on land and buildings. The main thrust of their attack was against profligate spending on public services.

Far from reducing overall taxation, Proposition 13 successfully shifted the tax structure from one emphasising property to one which emphasised wages and consumption — a regressive transformation. For if the people of California wanted to maintain the level of social services (police and fire protection, for example) they had to pay out of their other sources of income. Thus, American landowners, like the English barons who saw the virtues of creating an income tax to tap other people's incomes rather than theirs, had succeeded in engineering California's system to their pecuniary advantage.

Proposition 13 came on top of the state's Williamson Land Conservation Act (1965), which theoretically aimed to halt urban sprawl on prime agricultural land. In practice, the Act was turned into a tax shelter by landowners who were marking time until it suited them to capitalise on the value of their assets. Owners were given tax relief that could amount to more than 90% in exchange for their agreement to freeze their land from development for 10 years. They were, however, free to seek the cancellation of the freeze at any time they chose. By the time Proposition 13 had passed into law, California had lost an estimated $120m. in local revenue.

This is how it worked in Alameda County. Nearly 30 landowners applied for preservation status for their land. Had they not done so, the market value of the land would have been at least $116m. Under the Act, however, the land was appraised on the basis of the income which was being received, not what the land was worth on the open market. As a result, vast ranchland acreage in remote areas that had a value ranging from $200 to $1,000 an acre, but was earning only $3 an acre, was devalued in the assessments. The value was written down to about $16m., with a property tax liability reduced from $3.5m. to $480,000. The Jarvis-Gann effect was to further reduce the liability down to $160,000, yielding a net saving for the landowners of $3.3m. Yet only 9,500 acres were considered to be prime agricultural land worthy of conservation. This did not stop practically everyone getting in on the act, however, from owners of cattle and timber holdings, oil fields, mountains, gun clubs, riding academies, golf courses and half-acre homesites. 'It was a haven for speculators who bought up property not ready for development, but whose prices steadily rose while property taxes were negligible. Landbanking it's called,' wrote Don DeMain, an *Oakland Tribune* reporter.[33]

One of the selling points used by Jarvis in his progaganda campaign was that reduced property taxes would mean lower rents for tenants. This forecast was based on unsound economic premises. If, as is generally agreed, a tax on economic surplus (rent) cannot be passed on by the landowner, it also follows with equal certainty that a reduction of taxes on land values results in that saving being incorporated into rents (or capitalised into selling prices). If a tenant was willing to pay $x p.a. before Proposition 13, he would have little option but to continue paying that sum even if the landlord's tax bill was reduced.

As could have been predicted on the basis of economic theory, the reductions — amounting to an estimated saving of $1.2bn. for California's landlords — were not swiftly passed on to tenants. On the contrary, tenants who had been paying the tax on the properties they occupied found themselves confronted with rent increases! The increases were equivalent to the tax saving. The demand for rent control was rejected by the state's governor, Jerry Brown,[34] but he urged that 'The landlords better respond to the call' — which, if they did, would have been the result of philanthropic rather than economic imperatives.

Not even the home-owning voters were destined to be the primary beneficiaries of Proposition 13. The constitutional change resulted in two-thirds of the benefits going to big corporations, a proportion which increased over time. This is because one of the clauses of the new law ensured that when a property was sold, its taxes would be assessed on the new (higher) sale price and not on the 1975 base value. Since commercial properties changed hands less frequently than houses, the relative tax burden shifted further on to homeowners.[35] A further inequity arose between neighbours with identical homes of similar value: they found that they had tax liabilities which differed because some of them bought their houses after 1975.

Proposition 13 had the direct effect of turning home-owners into specu-
tors, but the thrill of turning their homes into investment assets was short-
ved. The market weakened in 1980. The elation, however, disguised the
ality. Owners were reluctant to cut their prices, which had moved up
arkedly since 1978. To encourage a turnover of properties, therefore,
llers started to offer low interest loans to potential buyers. This trapped
ousands of families in a vicious network of debt that was passed off under
e guise of 'creative financing'. Mortgage defaults climbed to $2bn. in
982, and according to mortgage banker William Heath:

> Creative financing is a razor at our throat. California today is at the same
> point Wall Street was in 1929 when the big crash came. Homes have been
> purchased on margin, as stocks were 53 years ago. Eventually the whole
> thing has to come tumbling down around our ears. And when that
> happens, it will be like the 1930s again — only this time it will be
> Californians heading for Oklahoma.[36]

The anomalous outcome of Proposition 13, only a few elements of which
ave been itemised here, raises the perplexing question: how could it happen?
ne explanation is that obfuscation pays. Ernest Engelbert used restrained
rminology to describe this: 'More often than not property owners are wary
f highly efficient and scientific tax procedures at the local level since this
sters impersonality and reduces bargaining power with assessors and
oards of appeal'.[37] Prof. Gaffney, however, was more blunt:

> We hear a lot these days about cutting fat out of the public sector, but there
> is lots of fat in the private sector too. 'Fat' I interpret to mean paying
> someone for doing nothing, or nothing useful. Most economists agree that
> paying people for holding title to land is a non-functional income, since the
> land was created by nature, secured by the nation's armed forces, and
> improved by public spending and the progress of society. 'Economic rent'
> is the economist's term, but in Jarvis-talk we may call it the fat of the land
> or 'land-fat' ... Howard Jarvis has said that the policeman or fireman who
> risks his life protecting the property of others has his 'nose in the public
> trough', but it has seemed to generations of economists that the owner
> whose land rises in value because public spending builds an eight-lane
> freeway from let us say, Anaheim to Riverside, and carries water from the
> Feather River to San Diego, is the first in the trough...[38]

We have now established a continuity of practices from the beginning of
e 19th century until the 1970s: of official encouragement to private
eculation in rent, which in turn induced recessions which undermined
rowth and created personal hardship. The Americans who worked for their
ving have had to struggle against malevolent economic forces which are
enerated by the private pillage of the public domain by a privileged class of
eople who continue to live off the 'fat' of the land.

The rational reform would have been to lift taxation from wages and t income from capital, and place it on land. Had the politicians adopted t strategy in the late 19th century, at the outset of industrialisation, the N World would have been a happier and more prosperous haven for t immigrants who fled the corrupt European economies.

This is a sweeping claim to make. Would land-value taxation ha neutralized the macro-economic impact of speculation and improved t prospects for the new industrial economy? In the final half of this study, test this hypothesis by investigating the history of Japan, and subjecting t land tax — and the socialist alternatives — to close scrutiny.

Notes

1   Letter to Henry S. Reuss, the Democrat Representative for Milwaukee, cited latter's Press Release dated 11.1.79.
2   T. Le Duc, 'History and Appraisal of US Land Policy to 1862', in *Land U Policy and Problems in the US*, editor: H. W. Ottoson, Lincoln: University Nebraska Press, 1963.
3   *Ibid.*, p. 9.
4   *Ibid.*, p. 15.
5   *Ibid.*, p. 17.
6   *Ibid.*, p. 18. Many soldiers, however, succeeded in beating the speculators at th own game. For example, after the war of 1812, the grants of Illinois land soldiers made by Congress were sold to speculators for an average of about 62 cents to 72 cents an acre. The true market value of the land at the time w appraised by Walter Kuehnle for the purposes of an Indian land claim. He valu the land as worth, at most, 35 cents an acre. Thousands of speculators sold out what little they could get, disappointed at not making the anticipated pro W. R. Kuehnle, 'Appraisal of Royce Areas 147 and 148 in Illinois and Wiscons — 1829', Chicago, 1958, pp. 114-15.
7   P. W. Gates, 'The Homestead Act: Free Land Policy in Operation, 1862-193 in Ottoson, *op. cit.* Prof. Gates has laconically noted how 'land attorneys, w were sometimes ex-congressmen or former officials in the General Land Offi seemed to be more successful in breaching the laws than they had formerly be in drafting them'. 'Homesteading in the High Plains', *Agricultural Histo* Vol. 51, 1977, pp. 109-110.
8   Le Duc, *op. cit.*, p. 27.
9   T. Le Duc, 'Public Policy, Private Investment, and Land Use in Americ Agriculture, 1825-1875', *Agricultural History*, Vol. 37, 1963.
10 *Ibid.*, p. 5.
11 *Ibid.*, p. 6.
12 *Ibid.*, p. 9.
13 T. C. Cochran, *200 Years of American Business*, New York: Basic Books, 197 p. 30.
14 *Ibid.*, p. 92.

15   *Chicago Daily News*, 21.10.70.
16   H. Tideman, 'A System of Land and Building Taxation for Urban Housing', in *Urban Housing*, editor: V.Kouskoulas, Detroit: Wayne State University, 1973, p. 106.
17   Condit, *op. cit.*, pp. 97-8.
18   *Chicago Daily News*, 10.12.70.
19   Cullerton's chief consultant, Thomas McCracken, stated at a Press conference that he could not cite any case in which an Objection I suit supported by Cullerton had not been granted by the Circuit Court.
20   *Ibid.*, 21.10.70.
21   *Ibid.*, 7.10.70.
22   Rubloff was one of the key men in the 'Real Estate Men for Cullerton' campaign organisation, which donated substantial sums of money to secure the assessor's re-election in 1970. As Mike Royko, a *Daily News* columnist, observed: 'There is something about Cullerton that brings out great warmth and affection in big real estate men'. The chairman of the boards of two major Illinois banks issued a statement declaring that 'one of the most important factors contributing toward the dynamic growth of our city has been the manner in which Cook County real estate and personal property taxes have been administered by P.J. Cullerton'. *Chicago Daily News*, 26.10.70. Other cities enjoyed a dynamic growth in construction without the benefit of sympathetic treatment from the local assessors' offices!
23   Walter R. Kuehnle, of Walter R. Kuehnle & Co., in communication to the present author, 21.2.79.
24   M. Clawson and H.S. Perloff, 'Alternatives for Future Urban Land Policy', in *Modernising Urban Land Policy*, editor: M. Clawson, Baltimore: John Hopkins University Press, 1973, p. 237. See also Dick Netzer, *Impact of the Property Tax - Effect on Housing, Urban Land Use, Local Government Finance*, National Commission on Urban Problems, Research Report No. 1, Washington, DC: US Government Printing Office, 1968, p. 46.
25   *Final Report of the Task Force on Housing Costs*, Washington, DC: US Dept. of Housing and Urban Development, May 1978, p. 17.
26   *Ibid.*, p. 19. This is yet another example of double taxation, because under-assessment in a period of escalating prices results in a reduction in taxes on land. During the 10 years up to 1975, the share of property taxes in GDP fell in most OECD countries. This increased the attractions of land as a medium for investment, and so pushed up its price. Thus, as well as paying higher land prices, people had to make up the short-fall in government revenue out of extra taxes on their income from labour and capital.
27   'Market Value Versus Speculative Value', *op. cit.*, p. 795.
28   J. McMullen, 'Real estate still good tax shelter', *Chicago Sun-Times*, 9.2.79.
29   M. Rawson, *Property Taxation and Urban Development*, Washington, DC: ULI Research Monograph 4, 1961, p. 7.
30   M.N. Danielson, *The Politics of Exclusion*, New York: Columbia University Press, 1976.
31   The history of this litigation is summarised in *Fair Housing & Exclusionary Land Use*, Washington, DC: ULI Research Report 23, 1974.
32   M. Gaffney, 'Tax Limitation: Proposition 13 and its Alternatives', paper read at The Center for the Study of Democratic Institutions, 25.8.79 (unpublished) p. 4.
33   *The Analyst*, Vol. XI, No. 9, 1978.

34 D. F. Salisbury, 'California landlords a target', *Christian Science Monitor*, 20.7.78.

35 A further ironical consequence was that the public expenditure on administering assessments had to rise, because existing computerised mass appraisal methods lost their utility. Re-assessments had to be conducted on the basis of facts peculiar to each property. Labour intense appraisal methods therefore had to be adopted.

36 R. Yates, 'California Bust: Boom to Time Bomb in the Golden State', *The Washington Post*, 21.8.82.

37 E. E. Engelbert, 'The Political Aspects of Real Estate Taxation in Relation to Metropolitan Growth and Planning', in *Land and Building Taxes*, editor: A. P. Becker, Milwaukee: University of Wisconsin Press, 1969, p. 100.

38 *Op. cit.*, pp. 6-7.

THE JAPANESE 'MIRACLE'

11

Spirit of the Samurai

Shady land deals brought down Premier Kakuei Tanaka in the biggest political scandal in Japan's postwar history. But Tanaka is important not because he can be added to the long list of corrupt people who exploited the wealth of others to his own ends through the monopoly of land; he has more general significance in the quest to understand the malfunctionings of the industrial economy.

Kakuei Tanaka embodied the spirit that betrayed the aspirations of the Japanese who, in 1867, liquidated the parasitic class of feudal land lords. The mechanism which was selected to achieve this result was simple, and it was executed reasonably smoothly. Rent which had formerly been levied upon the rural peasants to support the warrior class and its conspicuous consumption was switched into the coffers of the nation's exchequer and used to finance an industrial revolution.

Two hundred and fifty *daimyo* (feudal lords) were rendered redundant, and Japan embarked on the path of industrial growth until, finally, she attained supremacy in the field of modern economic enterprise. This was achieved, at the outset, on a foundation of land value taxation. Something, however, ultimately went wrong. Our study of Japan will analyse the processes that created the opportunities for the Japanese to industrialise, and will reveal how and monopoly undermined that grand determination and left the people living in a miserable physical environment even while they stacked up the material goods that poured out of their factories.[1]

But at the outset we must note that, to the leading Japanese land speculators, there was nothing mysterious in the forces that served to unhinge attempts at harmonising the process of modernisation with a civilised social system and stable ecological environment. Their appreciation of their power to hinder the creation of new wealth and higher living standards, in the pursuit of unearned rental income, is neatly summarised in the book which sold a million copies and helped its author, Kakuei Tanaka, to become Prime Minister of Japan.

The contents of the book, *Building a New Japan*[2], are summarised in its sub-title: A Plan for Remodeling the Japanese Archipelago. In it, Tanaka describes objectively how the process of land monopoly dislocated the growth of urban centres like Tokyo, priced decent homes out of the reach of wage-earners, deterred the creation of new factories, distorted the locational pattern of industries, and inhibited the development of agriculture. In this one book, then, Tanaka affirmed the essential features of the thesis that land monopoly is the major agent blocking the creative efforts of people and their capital. And yet, ironically, modern Japan was built on a fiscal foundation that provided her leaders with the unique opportunity for avoiding the destructive path of the land values cycle that manifested itself in other industrial nations. What were the distinctive contributions and promises of the Japanese land tax, and how were they eclipsed by the grasping claims of the land monopolists?

The political power of the Tokugawa *shogun* and his supporting structure of *daimyo* and their dependent *samurai* was wiped out by the restoration to power of the Emperor in 1867. This transformation of the Japanese political system was the prelude to a rationalisation of the economy, a programme specifically designed to industrialise an agrarian economy to meet the challenge from the Europeans and Americans who demanded that there should be free trading access to the Japanese market.

Japan, at this point, was in a backward state. The agrarian society operated on a configuration of traditional values and loyalties which were no match for the thrusting merchants who threatened to follow Commodore Perry's gunboat. To resist this threat, Japan had to modernise her political and economic institutions. But to build a new superstructure, she had to change the method of extracting agricultural surplus. Rents and taxes had up until then been paid in kind by peasant cultivators. This was unsuitable for a modern economy. Taxes, to facilitate the creation of a new economic infrastructure, had to be paid in cash. Marx feared the worst:

> If the foreign trade, forced upon Japan by Europeans, should lead to the substitution of money rents for rents in kind, it will be all up with the exemplary agriculture of that country. The narrow economic conditions under which that agriculture is carried on, will be swept away.[3]

Marx's prediction proved to be wrong. Agriculture did not fare any worse than under the feudal system; indeed, within two decades Japan had completed the transition to modern economic growth[4] and was ready to take on all-comers!

The Meiji reformers reconstructed the land tenure system through the Land Tax Revision Act (1873). They had no axe to grind. They were technicians determined to produce solutions to the problem of strengthening the economic base of their society, rather than rigging the results in favour of the landlords. Nonetheless, the law which they enacted suffered from a number of shortcomings. These — and their effects — we need to examine in detail.

The Meiji land tax, as we shall see, has been criticised on a number of counts. These criticisms, however, have been misdirected; they imply, or explicitly state, that the land tax *per se* is a deficient instrument for accomplishing the desired goals. But on the contrary, problems arose in Japan because the tax was technically inadequate and incomplete. These concessions, however, far from counting against land taxation, provide those who formulate policies today with a clearer understanding of what they need to accomplish if they wish to maximise the prospects for constructive development.

The Meiji reformers devised a formula which led them to believe that their tax fell on net produce (in contrast to the Tokugawa land tax, which was a proportional levy on gross farm produce). Net produce, correctly defined, is economic rent. The tax is still commonly regarded as falling on land values by modern scholars.[5]

The law required that a *standard value* of cultivated land should be established. To arrive at this figure, certain costs were deducted. These were the cost of seeds and fertilizers (15% of the value of gross output), and the national land tax (3%) and local land tax (1%). Income was calculated by taking local market prices averaged over the previous five years.

It is evident from this that the Meiji formulation of taxable income made no allowance for the wages of farmers to compensate them for their labour inputs. The tax, then, fell on both rent *and* wages, and was evidently not a tax on net produce. Few students of this crucial fiscal feature of early modern Japan have noted, let alone elaborated upon, the consequences. Ranis, for example, settled for parenthetically noting that 'implicit wages not deducted' in a footnote to his otherwise excellent quantitative study.[6]

Yet the authorities realized that their formula failed to untax wages, for they had a second method for determining the value of land.[7] This was to capitalise the rent actually paid to landlords, that is the surplus *after* allowing for the wages (and other overheads) retained by a tenant farmer. The problem for the authorities was that, using this method of arriving at net income, there would be a disparity in taxable income. For — using the same rate of interest to capitalize income, to arrive at the value of land — they would get two different figures, depending on whether a piece of land was owner-occupied or farmed by a tenant. Instead of imputing the cost of wages under the first formula, they dealt with this problem by using two different rates of interest. They assumed that the income of the tenant was one-third and the rent was two-thirds of taxable income. So they decided that rental income should be capitalised by using a rate of interest which was two-thirds (4%) of the figure used to capitalize owner-cultivated land (6%). This ensured that the 'land' value would turn out to be identical on the same property whether that land was owner-occupied or cultivated by a tenant.

Now, while a tax on wages has an obvious effect on family incomes — reducing purchasing power, and so restricting the domestic market for consumer goods — the overall effects on owner-occupiers need not have been serious, given that the land tax did not take away the whole of economic rent. This state of affairs, however, held true only for so long as the price of rice remained buoyant. As soon as it started to come down it had a serious effect on incomes. This was what happened in the mid-1880s. The price of rice rose steadily until 1881, then started sliding, reaching its lowest point in 1887.[8] From 1883 to 1890, over 367,000 producers suffered forced sales for arrears in the payment of the land tax. The total amount in arrears was 114,178 yen , and the area of land auctioned or confiscated was nearly 116,000 acres.[9]

The distress in the countryside was the product of an imperfectly formu-lated land tax. The payments were inflexible obligations even compared with the Tokugawa system. In the feudal period, if harvests were poor (leaving a smaller economic surplus), the official who was charged with the duty of collecting the taxes told the farmers how much the payments would be reduced: this provided immediate relief. There was no administrative reason why the centralised Meiji bureaucracy could not have emulated this procedure.

The sale of all or part of a farm in the 1880s, then, provided more than just the cash with which to discharge immediate tax obligations. For the farmer, as a tenant, could deduct his wages from the gross product before paying the remainder, as rent, to the landowner. This shifted the tax burden onto the landlord: he, however, was destined for long-run prosperity as the price of rice recovered. The Meiji land tax, however, was levied at a uniform rate 'without regard to bumper or lean years',[10] which meant that tenants and landowners retained part of the economic surplus in the bumper years, but the landowning farmers had to dig into their wages to meet tax obligations during lean years.

The limitations placed on the land tax guaranteed that, at the macro economic level, the 'miracle' of the Japanese model was to be betrayed by th 18-year cycle of destruction. The first cycle will be examined here because i lays bare the defects in the Meiji land tax. The last cycle, which brought to close the major phase of unimpeded growth in the decades after the Second World War, will then be fully investigated in Chapter 12. This will demon strate that, without a 100% tax on annual land values, the hard work an high-level entrepreneurial skill of the Japanese workers and management their flexible working practices and adaptive institutions, are ultimately defeated by those who monopolise the earth's natural resources.

How do we date the beginning of any 18-year cycle in land values that might have been present in the early Meiji period? The obvious starting point would be 1873 (rather than the first year of Restoration, 1868), for this was the year of the great land settlement which established new rural relationships and provided secure legal title to land for those who formerly held it by custom. Money rents and legal titles ensured the creation of a market in land.

If there *was* a cycle of land values, it ought to have brought its palsied hand down in 1890: and that is precisely what happened. Rents rose to an extraordinarily high proportion of total factor income,[11] and in 1890 the people were confronted with what Norman characterised as 'this first economic crisis of modern Japan'.[12]

How did the Meiji reformers unwittingly hand over their economy as a hostage to fortune?

TABLE 11:I

Relative Shares in Japan's Agricultural Sector

	Percentage of Total Product		
	Landowners	*State*	*Tenants*
1868	18	50	32
1873	34	34	32
1874-76	55	13	32
1877	50	18	32
1878	56.5	11.5	32

	Percentage of Net Agricultural Product		
	Rent	*Taxes*	*Tenants*
1878-82	60.4	16.9	22.7
1888-92	56.0	15.5	28.5
1898-1902	50.7	12.1	37.2
1908-1912	55.1	12.5	32.4
1918-22	59.1	9.2	31.7
1928-32	57.9	9.7	32.4

Source: G. Ranis, 'The Financing of Japanese Economic Development', *Econ. Hist. Rev.*, XI, 1958, Table 5, p. 448. Norman [*op. cit.*, p. 150, n. 29] gives 56% to landowners and 12% to the state for 1877.

When the 3% land tax was instituted, payable in cash, the state took about one-quarter of the produce from farmland.[13] Thereafter, however, the distribution shifted in favour of landowners. From Table 11:I, we can see that landowners received an increasing proportion of agricultural income at the expense not of the tenant, but of the state.

This re-distribution of income, in an opposite direction to the one which we would have advocated, ensured that all the speculative motives and structural dislocations associated with the European land market would be at work in Japan.

The state unwittingly conspired with the landowners in the interests of the latter. R.P. Dore has emphasised that those who controlled policy after the Meiji Restoration were not landed gentlemen — unlike the situation in England at the comparable state of industrialisation — but were bureaucrats who depended for their income on salaries.[14] 'They had, therefore, no personal interest in protecting agricultural incomes at the cost of slowing the growth of industry.'[15] But with the growth in the demand for democracy, the landlords were able to drive a wedge into the disinterested administration of the affairs of State:

> As soon as they were allowed representation in the national Diet their main interest was directed towards reducing their tax burden. This pressure on the national budget slowed the growth of agricultural research and extension services and of the developmental subsidy system. If the voice of the villages in the Diet had been the voice of practising farmers these things would not have been neglected.[16]

In 1878, the land tax was reduced to 2.5%, but rents were not lowered for tenant farmers.[17] In 1884, the government abandoned the original plan to reassess land values every five years: this meant that, with the rising price of rice, an increasing proportion of economic surplus remained with landowners. By 1889, the economic privileges of the new landowning class were institutionalised in the political system. In that year, the franchise in national elections was granted to men over the age of 25 years. Of a total electorate of 453,474, only 13,491 qualified to vote on the basis of income tax payments. The majority, 97% of the total, were landowners who qualified on the basis of land tax payments.[18] Appropriately enough, the economic crash the following year, in 1890, bore witness to the underlying influence exercised by the landlords over the economy.

The transfer of political power to the landlords was accompanied by reduction in the contribution of land taxes to total government revenue. In 1872, land taxes were 72% of revenue. This share declined to about 46% in 1890, and sank to 15% just before the outbreak of the First World War. When we dig behind the statistics, we find a pattern of behaviour which has now become depressingly familiar. There was corruption; local governors who learnt, in their official capacities, of intentions to build railways, bought land and re-sold at inflated prices to the construction companies.[19] Land was the most secure investment, yielding a rising income: it therefore attracted money and entrepreneurial skills from both the rural and urban sectors that would otherwise have been devoted to fixed capital formation in industry.[20]

The 'extremely high rent' demanded by landlords reduced the domestic market for factory-produced consumer goods.[21] Even more serious, however, was the impact on investment. For during this period construction (excluding military investment) accounted for over 50% of gross domestic capital formation,[22] and there came a point where buying or renting land for erecting buildings, roads, bridges and railways reached deterrent levels.

Thus, the level of the land tax, although significant from the point of view of landowners, was a declining proportion of gross rents and was ultimately insufficiently high to deter the land monopolists from influencing the process of economic growth. The incorrect interpretation of these facts, then, would be to arrive at the conclusion that a land tax cannot ultimately thwart landlords from having a causal influence on the directional growth of the economy. The correct interpretation is that a 100% recovery of annual rental income is a necessary pre-condition for stable, sustained development.

The Meiji leaders had a perfect opportunity to realign their policies in the 1890s. The onset of the first severe structural recession induced by the termination of the 18-year cycle in land values was the beginning of five years of severe hardship.[23] There were demands for reforms. One of the options was the establishment of a consistent and thorough-going programme of land value taxation. Henry George's *Progress and Poverty* appeared in translation in 1891, and it created a considerable impression.[24] The virtues of the tax were vigorously promoted, and one of its advocates was an American missionary, C. E. Garst — affectionately known as Tanzei Taro ('Single-tax Joe'), 'who stumped the country with a proselytizing zeal primarily directed towards the propagation of the gospel according to Henry George'.[25] The landowners, however, were by now exercising power in the political system, and the idea of capturing the full value of land for the benefit of the community — offset by a reduction in taxes on wages and consumption — was not adopted.

Recovery began in 1895. Was this the start of the second of the 18-year cycles? The peak in the new cycle should have been in 1913. This was, indeed, the case.[26] But although land values began to slump, the structural recession did not occur: the preparations for World War I intervened to provide the economy with an extraordinary buoyancy. Had this influence not come into operation, report Ohkawa and Rosovsky, 'it is entirely possible that 1909-12 would have developed into a full-fledged downswing'

in the economy, for in that period the growth rate of private capital formation 'falters'.[27]

And so the price of ignoring Henry George's solution was not paid. A
world war saved the economy from the effects of the land values cycle — as it
did in Britain in the 1930s — but few would deny that mass slaughter and a
profitable munitions industry are high prices to pay for neutralising the
influence of land monopoly. Land values quickly recovered, and were on
course for a termination in the early 1930s, neatly dovetailing the deficiencies
of the domestic economy with the identical problems that were converging in
the leading industrial systems. It was the same story in the postwar years, as
we shall now see.

Notes

1   J. Woronoff, *Japan: the Coming Economic Crisis*, Tokyo: Lotus Press, 1979.
2   K. Tanaka, *Building a New Japan*, Tokyo: Simul Press, 1972, first English
    edition, 1973.
3   *Capital, op. cit.*, Vol. I, p. 140.
4   H. Rosovsky, 'Japan's Transition to Modern Economic Growth, 1868-1885'
    in *Industrialisation in Two Systems*, editor: H. Rosovsky, J. Wiley & Sons, 1966
5   E. H. Norman, *Japan's Emergence as a Modern State*, New York: Institute o.
    Pacific Relations, 1940, p. 141; R. P. Dore, *Land Reform in Japan*, London
    Oxford University Press, 1959, p. 15, and T. Fukutake, *Japanese Rural Society*
    Ithaca: Cornell University Press, 1967, p. 10.
6   G. Ranis, 'The Financing of Japanese Economic Development', *Economic His
    tory Review*, Vol. XI, 1958, p. 445, n. 1.
7   J. I. Nakamura, *Agricultural Production and the Economic Development of Japa
    1873-1922*, Princeton: Princeton University Press, 1966, p. 190.
8   Norman, *op. cit.*, p. 144, n. 15.
9   Norman, *ibid.*
10 Norman, *ibid.*, p. 142.
11 C. Clark, *The Value of Agricultural Land*, Oxford: Pergamon Press, 1973, p. 8{
12 *Op. cit.*, p. 166.
13 Norman, *op. cit.*, p. 141, n. 10, and p. 143, n. 14.
14 R. P. Dore, 'Land Reform and Japan's Economic Development', *Developin
    Economies*, Special Issue, Vol. 3, 1965; page references are to the reprint ?
    Peasants and Peasant Societies, editor: T. Shanin, Harmondsworth: Pengui:
    1971.
15 *Ibid.*, p. 381.
16 *Ibid.*, p. 385.
17 A. Waswo, *Japanese Landlords*, Berkeley: University of California Press, 197
    p. 22, and Dore, *op. cit.*, p. 17.
18 Waswo, *op. cit.*, p. 33, n. 65.
19 W. W. McLaren, *A Political History of Japan during the Meiji Era 1867-191*
    London: George Allen & Unwin, 1916, p. 129.

20 Waswo, *op. cit.*, p. 76, Norman, *op. cit.*, p. 111, and Dore, *op. cit.*
21 Norman, *op. cit.*, pp. 165-166.
22 K. Ohkawa and H. Rosovsky, *Japanese Economic Growth*, Stanford, California: Stanford University Press, 1973, pp. 16-17.
23 Dore, *op. cit.*, p. 63.
24 Y. Jamasaki, 'The Influence of Henry George's Ideas Upon Modern Japan', *The American Journal of Economics and Sociology*, Vol. 21, 1962.
25 Dore, *op. cit.*, p. 67.
26 *Ibid.*, p. 20, for the price of rice land, and Clark, *op. cit.*, p. 99, Table 39.
27 *Op. cit.*, p. 33.

12

The Conquest and Collapse

Japan lost the war but won the peace. What she failed to do with battleships she did with her factories: capturing the world with competitively-priced high-quality goods. Western entrepreneurs marvelled at the diligence of the Japanese workforce. They worked hard, made reasonable demands for wages and they cooperated with innovative managements in a constructive way. The capitalists did not demand inflated rates of return on their investments; they could not do so, because they wanted to compete in the market place against all comers.

And so it was that the mighty Japanese industrial machine conquered. No-one could smite down the giant — except the home-grown land speculators. Yet if we were to believe conventional economic analysis, we would have to exonerate land speculators from any responsibility for the great crash that originated in Japan in 1973.

Edward Denison and William Chung, while recognising that land values rose dramatically, conclude:

> Availability and ownership of land obviously condition the composition and distribution of output. But in the absence of changes in the quantity of land available for use in production, the contribution of land to the growth rate of total output is necessarily zero. This is the case in all countries.[1]

As they estimated that the quantity of land available for use in Japan had not changed,[2] they arrived at the view that the slight negative influence of land on the growth of the economy was due to the increase in the population (which meant less land *per capita*).[3] No allowance is made for the effects of land monopolists who can manipulate the supply of land to their advantage: this influence is assumed not to exist — or at any rate, not to have a causally significant impact on growth trends.

Two other leading experts on the Japanese economy, Ohkawa and Rosovsky, have noted the 'great inflation in land prices', which they characterised as 'another stumbling block' obstructing the achievement of goals such as the provision of better homes and roads. But they, too, do not consider the performance of the land market to be of fundamental importance.[4]

Does this mean, then, that the hypothesis which explains the slumps in the US and British economies does not apply to the Japanese system? If the answer is in the affirmative, then the theory does not enjoy general significance. And if this *is* the case, do the postwar land reforms instituted in Japan provide a model to be safely emulated by developing countries?

In confronting these two questions, the first problem is to establish the starting date for any long-run economic cycle that might have operated. Economists generally agree that it took about a decade for Japan to restructure her war-devastated economy and recommence normal economic growth.[5] Ohkawa and Rosovsky, in their exhaustive study of Japanese business cycles over a period of 100 years, conclude that the period of rehabilitation came to an end in 1952-54.[6] This accords with the official view that 1955 was the year 'when the Japanese economy was about to begin its high postwar growth'.[7]

The year 1955 also fits neatly with events in the agricultural sector; the conditions were recreated for growth in the real value of land. Although rent controls still existed, these were circumvented by the black market. Tenants who acquired ownership of land under the reforms forced through by General MacArthur, the Allied Supreme Commander, were pleased with the £54m. in subsidies and grants-in-aid earmarked for agriculture. Rural incomes recovered their pre-war levels. In addition, the system under which farmers were compelled to supply a quota of their rice output to the government at controlled prices was terminated, giving farmers a freer hand to sell their produce on the black market. The government provided credit to farmers to buy land,[8] which established a buoyancy in the market for sales.

The former tenants were not slow to cash-in on the need for development land. It was in 1955, at a congress of dispossessed landowners, that the complaint was heard that

> land which was taken from them 'for the price of a sparrow's tears' was now being sold as building land at 500 times the purchase price by tenant beneficiaries in growing urban areas.[9]

And in 1955-1956 the few remaining landlords, who had suffered psychological as well as economic distress during the previous decade, disclosed signs of a renewed offensive ... to get back their land',[10] the turning point in attitudes which was to prove significant in the land market.

The test of the fundamental importance of a theory or set of empirical observations is whether useful predictions can be derived. What do Ohkawa and Rosovsky tell us? They completed their study in 1972. After taking into account considerations such as the rate at which Japan was assimilating imported technology, changing attitudes of workers and the threat of protectionism against Japanese exports, Ohkawa and Rosovsky predicted a slowdown in the rate of growth of Japan's national product toward the end of the 1970s.[11] In fact, the economy was going into a nose-dive in 1973, the very year in which their book was published. And 1973, of course, is 18 years after the beginning of the postwar cycle in land values. Before seeking to establish the causal connection between land values and the performance of the economy in the downturn of the business cycle, it is necessary to trace the movements in values over the cycle.

First, agricultural land. Between 1960 and 1971, the national average price of middle-grade paddy land increased sixfold, at a compound annual rate of increase of 18.1%. The increase was on an accelerating trend, reaching an annual rate of over 20% after 1967. A study by the Food and Agricultural Organisation recorded the effect:

> Such a rise in the price of land, which has surpassed by far the rate of increase in prices of agricultural products or in the cost of living, has hindered transactions in farm land. Farmers tend increasingly to retain their land as valuable property rather than as a factor of production.[12]

As a result, there was under-use of both farm labour and capital equipment.[13] High land values also altered the pattern of output on the farm, deterring, for example, the production of beef-type cattle, and so inhibiting the full liberalisation of international trade in products such as beef.[14] The explosive rise in rents and land values, however, was not paralleled by a similar rise in the wages of farm labour. In the absence of an adequate fiscal penalty on under-used land, it paid farmers to turn into part-time urban wage-workers, sitting on their land in the expectation of future capital gains. Genuine full-time farmers received the lowest average income *per capita*.[1]

Now, urban land. Under the influence of roaring inflation, the price of land rocketed by a factor of 26 between 1945 and 1950. This, however, represented a loss in real value. During the same period, wholesale commodity prices rose by as much as 82 times. The adjustment in relative values occurred between 1951 and 1955. Land prices maintained their upward trends, while wholesale commodity prices stabilized. In September 1955 the price increase ratios of wholesale commodities and land were 326 and 325 respectively when compared with those of 1936. The market had returned to a state of pre-war normality, and so 1955 has been used as the basic year for comparing urban land price movements.[16]

Between 1955 and 1975, income levels increased by six times.[17] Land prices, however multiplied 30 times: an enormous gap appeared between the wealth and purchasing power of landowners and the rest of the community

The cycle of urban land prices peaked in 1973, when prices leapt 34.7% in 12 months. They then levelled off and slumped (for the first time) by 9% in 1974. The 18-year cycle terminated in a frantic bout of speculation during 1972-73: in those two years, property companies and individuals poured ¥5 to ¥10 trillion (US $25-50bn.) into speculative land purchases.

A survey by the Real Estate Companies Association of Japan showed that the supply of residential building land peaked in 1971 (2,210 hectares), then started a downward course.[18] People preferred to hold land idle in the expectation of even greater capital gains in the future.

The burden of the land market on individual households can be seen with reference to the problem of providing decent homes. Despite its phenomenal material achievements, Japan has one of the worst housed populations in the industrialised world. People live in wooden structures, cramped for want of space, and most lack basic amenities such as sewage. The Government slogan of 'one house, one family' was not achieved by the late 1960s because of the soaring price of land.[19] According to the Japan Real Estate Research Institute, the average price of urban land increased by 2,200 per cent between 1955 and the first half of 1973.[20]

Another cost to the welfare of Japanese society has been the ecological damage of the postwar years. This has generally been blamed on economic growth *per se*.[21] The distinctive contribution of land speculators has been overlooked by scholarly investigators; the link, however, has been made by journalists, and the problem can be viewed by examining a particular aspect of the land boom associated with Kakuei Tanaka.

Tanaka had enjoyed a successful career as a land developer by the time that he assumed the reins of power as head of the Liberal Democratic Government in July 1972. His big dream was to remodel the archipelago, shifting people and jobs away from the areas of high concentration and intense pollution to the more remote, less densely populated regions of the countryside. In June 1972, Tanaka published a book, *Building a New Japan*, which unfolded his plan. It was instrumental in boosting him into the Prime Minister's office. The cost of the plan was estimated at US$1 trillion, and the target date for completion was 1985. This was the signal for renewed efforts by the speculators:

> Many companies, seeking quick profits from the national remodeling, have invested so heavily in real estate as to pose a threat to the plan itself. The land-buying spree began right after publication of Tanaka's book, and it has pushed prices up by as much as fifty percent in some places. The government anticipated a twelve percent increase in land values in the fiscal year ending March 31, but prices shot up an average of twenty percent in the first half. Hideo Edo, president of Mitsui Real Estate Development Co., says with great dismay: 'In the past, increases were

mostly in a few big cities. Now they extend from one part of the country
to another.' Much of the speculation involves land earmarked for new
towns and factory sites, but astronomical land prices could sabotage many
remodeling projects. The land grabbing has stirred public controversy
over the Tanaka Plan. During recent parliamentary elections, opponents
accused the premier of personally profiting from land deals.[22]

It was all for nothing. The speculators were buying land at the top end of the
18-year cycle. They were to be denied the big profits that they sought at
double-quick time, but in the process they caused ecological havoc. They
chopped down forests, which dislocated water-tables and thereby reduced
the level of water in the wells; and they slapped down asphalt, but weeds
rather than houses sprouted.[23]

The speculative binge had spawned *tochi narikin* (the *nouveaux riches*
peasants who made fortunes by selling pieces of their land). But the people
who according to the Tanaka Plan were to quadruple industrial output — the
families seeking larger homes in healthier environments, the retailers and
entrepreneurs seeking modern, spacious shops and factories — could not fit
the rents and the price of buying land into their budgets. The land stood idle.

The economy turned down in 1973, before the oil crisis struck in the dying
months of that year. The speculators were caught in the classic squeeze, of
having to finance the large loans which they had taken out to buy land. The
bubble of inflated land prices burst. The biggest corporation to crash in
Japan's history, the Kohjin Co. Ltd., had built its empire on textiles. Then it
moved into land speculation in the early 1970s, and by 1975, with land
valued at ¥54bn., it crashed under the weight of interest payments on its
borrowings.

As for Tanaka, the popularity of his Cabinet had slumped to 20%
according to opinion polls taken in April 1973. People gave the price of land
as one of the reasons for their dissatisfaction with their political leaders.[24] The
Prime Minister, seizing on the oil crisis which struck in November-Dec-
ember 1973, announced a national state of emergency. Two laws were passed
to freeze commodity prices and the distribution of petroleum; the land
market, however, was not blamed for the country's ills.

Tanaka, however, was to be called to account for his part in the big land
boom. Earlier allegations about his involvement in shady land deals crystallised in October 1974 when a respected literary magazine, *Bungei Shunju*,
published the results of its investigations. One of its disclosures was that
Tanaka, on reaching the top office of the Liberal Democratic Party, had
released public land as a reward to his friends, who were able to buy huge
tracts at bargain prices. Another allegation was that Tanaka, a multi-
millionaire, had speculated in land, which he had then re-sold to the

Government at high prices.[25] He resigned on November 26, 1974, in public disgrace.[26]

The so-called 'miracle' economy was unable to avoid the distress of the late 1970s, which was officially attributed to the OPEC oil price explosion. Economic trends are today measured in terms of the 'pre-oil crisis' and the 'post-oil crisis'.[27] The autumn of 1973 is regarded as the dividing line. Although the government's Economic Planning Agency characterises the oil price rise as 'a turning point', it fails to grant sufficient causal significance to other factors. For example, it does not come to terms with the temporal problem. If the oil price rises *were* to be of primary importance, then we must ascribe (and explain) a remarkable facility for foresight to Japanese households and entrepreneurs. They started unwinding vital parts of the economy a full nine months before the oil price rises — and well over a year before those prices started filtering through the economy in higher factor and consumer goods prices.

Yet the Economic Planning Agency's reports faithfully document all the facts to support the theory that land speculation is the primary cause of industrial slumps.

To start with, the rate of return on capital investments in Japan's leading enterprises, high in 1955, started a long-term downward trend and reached its nadir in 1972 and 1973, at which point the interest rate had become unsupportably high 'due to excessive borrowings (for such purposes as speculation in land)'.[28] In noting that 'land prices are already extraordinarily high in big cities', the agency correctly predicts that 'a rise in land prices makes it difficult for people to own detached houses' — which was linked to the fact that Tokyo, where people could not afford to buy building land at the asking prices, suffered a slump in construction of private dwellings.[29]

The cost of buying a home rose beyond the reach of family budgets in 1972-73,[30] with the result that there was a downturn in the building industry in the first quarter of 1973.[31] The government's economists were aware of the macro-economic consequences: 'Expansion of housing investment is necessary to provide demand for stable economic growth'.[32] So with the slump in construction a full 12 months before the oil price rises, the Japanese economy was destined for a recession of severe proportions whatever the decisions taken by the oil sheikhs.

Output fell more heavily in Japan than other economies. Domestic consumption showed a marked downturn in 1972, and the rate of increase in bankruptcies of firms accelerated throughout 1973 (and actually *declined* as oil prices fed through the system in 1974). Investment in plant and equipment peaked in mid-1973, while inventories accumulated throughout the year for want of effective purchasing power, when people were forced to spend more on land and housing.[33]

Thus Japan, the envy of the rest of the world, fell victim to the land tenure and fiscal system. We have seen that there was a measurable contraction in the supply of land to the families who needed homes, and to the entrepreneurs who wanted to invest their capital, and that the curtailment in activity satisfactorily explains the onset of the recession. Yet modern critics of Henry George nonetheless maintain (despite the available quantitative evidence) that such a contraction does not occur. They therefore erroneously conclude that George's theoretical system is fatally defective, and that his policy prescription 'has been justly relegated to the museum of colourful but untried ideas'.[34]

The policy of land value taxation had, in fact, been well tried in Japan in the early decades of the Meiji Restoration, and it is to this that we can ascribe the 'miracle' of the Japanese economy. For the institutions that originated in this period determined the shape and pace of the Japanese economy in the 20th century. But it is also true that land taxation did not figure in the land reform programme after the Second World War, and we now know the results of that omission.

The postwar reform sought to eliminate the despised landlords, by increasing the number of owner-occupiers (a policy orientation that can be traced back to the Hirota Cabinet of 1936). But in merely transforming tenants into owners, the 'reform' succeeded in consolidating the system of land monopoly, with the privileges enjoyed by an enlarged class. There is no such thing as a society free of landlordism, when the benefits of publicly-created land values are privately appropriated. When the fiscal system permits monopolists to exploit the land market to their advantage, society becomes the tenant of the owner-occupiers.

So it was with Japan in the postwar years. The hard work of employees and the entrepreneurial skills of managements suffered an unwarranted setback with the collapse induced by the speculative boom of 1972/73. The government, alarmed by the effects of the land market, passed a Progressive Sales Tax on land transactions in 1974 — after the proverbial horse had bolted, for land prices started coming down in that year.

The Meiji land tax had been allowed to degenerate into a system which reinforced speculation and the misallocation of land. Scarce agricultural land for example, on which urban-based families and industries relied for expansion in that exceedingly mountainous archipelago (80% of the supply of raw land for housing development is agricultural land), was taxed at only 0.5% to 1% of the rate on residential land. The incentive, then, was for rural landowners to keep their acres ostensibly in agricultural use, while their properties appreciated inexorably in value. Then, those who mistimed their sales — having failed to off-load properties before the peak of the cycle — were encouraged to hold onto their land by the Progressive Sales Tax.[35] Wh sell (if there is no fiscal inducement to do so, whatever the demands of the market) when you can postpone the transaction into the future, when the tax may be removed?[36]

The mix of tax policies and large-scale public investment in housing (designed to re-stimulate the depressed economy) ensured the premature recovery of the level of land prices, which started accelerating upwards again in 1977. The Keynesian pump priming, which began with the announcement of an extra £3bn. public sector spending in 1975, set the Japanese economy on course for a rapid return to the recession levels of 1974.

The Japanese landowners, then, like their counterparts in Britain and the USA who were rescued by governmental and central bank 'lifeboat' operations, were effectively insured against the costs of their own misdeeds. Land values were held buoyant, instead of being the most seriously depressed of all factor prices. The people of the Land of the Economic Miracle were destined to enter the 1980s in poor shape.

And so it came to pass, and the social despair could be measured in the daily Press reports of the alarming increase in the deaths of whole families. The heads of households murdered their children and then committed suicide to escape the forces which, unseen, were creating unbearable depths of anguish. The economic grief was entirely home-spun and could not be attributed to the foreign land speculators. For although some industries were opened up to foreign competition in the 1967-71 liberalization programme, real estate was designated as one of the seven 'restricted' industries. Automatic approval was granted for foreign investment only if the amount of investment per foreign investor was under 10% of the total equity of the firm, with aggregate foreign ownership of not more than 15%. The land speculation of the early '70s, then, originated as a domestic phenomenon. It was not under 1981 that Japan lifted its restrictions on the purchase of real estate by foreign investors with the introduction of Foreign Exchange & Foreign Trade Control Law.

What encouragement is this to the leaders of the poor Third World countries? If the powerful Japanese economy could not survive its 'internal contradictions', might it not be better to eschew capitalism in favour of its anti-thesis, communism? Such a conclusion is superficially attractive, but is based on a misdiagnosis of the fundamental causes of the Japanese crisis. But if the Japanese themselves, and the leading economists of the Western world, are incapable of correctly identifying the San Andreas fault in the structure of the fastest growing capitalist economy, how can we expect the political leaders of developing countries to do any better?

Notes

1   E. F. Denison and W. K. Chung, *How Japan's Economy Grew So Fast*, Washington, DC: The Brookings Institution, 1976, p. 77.
2   *Ibid.*, p. 33, Table 4-4.
3   *Ibid.*, p. 52, Table 5-1.
4   *Op. cit.*, p. 243.
5   See, e.g. Johnston, *op. cit.*, p. 306, and W. W. Lockwood, 'Japan's "New Capitalism"', in Lockwood, *op. cit.*, p. 448.
6   *Op. cit.*, pp. 20-24.
7   Economic Planning Agency, Japanese Government, *Economic Survey of Japan 1976/1977*, Tokyo: The Japan Times, 1977, p. 84.
8   Dore, *op. cit.*, pp. 304-305.
9   *Ibid.*, p. 436. Dore, who undertook an extensive field trip into the Japanese countryside in 1955-56, confirms the complaints of the ex-landords. *Ibid.*, p. 439. In 1957 the ex-landlords decided that it would be a good idea if their former tenants were heavily taxed on the profits arising from the sale of land acquired under the land reform! *Ibid.*, p. 440.
10 *Ibid.*, p. 194. See also pp. 431-443 for an account of the development of aggressive tactics by the landlord and ex-landlord class.
11 *Op. cit.*, pp. 233 and 246.
12 FAO, 'Case Study of Japan', in *Growth and Adjustment in National Agricultures*, editor: J. P. O'Hagan, London: Macmillan, 1978, p. 38.
13 *Ibid.*, pp. 41-43.
14 *Ibid.*, pp. 27, 36.
15 *Ibid.*, p. 47, Table 1.15.
16 A. Takanashi, of the Mitsui Real Estate Development Co., Tokyo: personal communication.
17 Data in this paragraph taken from 'Japan's Land Development Policy and the Real Estate Industry: Problems and Prospects', paper presented by H. Tsuboi, to the 20th Annual Congress of FIABCI, the International Real Estate Federation, 1.6.79, Tokyo, Japan.
18 The rate of conversion of farmland for all uses, including industrial facilities roads and railways, peaked in 1970. *Economic Survey of Japan 1976/1977, op. cit.* p. 151, Chart II-4-8.
19 P. B. Stone, *Japan Surges Ahead*, London: Weidenfeld & Nicolson, 1969, p. 14
20 P. Hazelhurst, 'Japan's human sacrifices at the altar of GNP', *The Times*, 8.8.73
21 See, e.g. the FAO's 'Case Study of Japan', *op. cit.*, p. 22.
22 L. Kraar, 'Japan Sets Out to Remodel Itself', *Fortune*, March 1973.
23 R. Whymant, 'Japan's rural rides back to the land', *The Guardian*, 20.11.79.
24 'Boom time for major industrial states', *The Times*, 14.5.73.
25 Another allegation, investigated by the Government's Administrative Management Agency in 1975, was that the Construction Ministry had changed the course of a river bank in Northern Japan to increase the value of riverbed land bought earlier by a company founded by Tanaka. The investigation was terminated when officials found that they could not come to final conclusion: certain vital documents were missing from the official files. 'Documents missing *The Guardian*, 11.9.75.
26 Tanaka was subsequently charged with receiving £1.25m. in bribes from the Lockheed Corporation. In April 1980 the government took possession of lar

and a country house pending payment of Y480m. (£750,000) tax claim against the former Premier.

27   See, e.g. Economic Planning Agency, Japanese Government, *Economic Survey of Japan 1977/1978*, Tokyo: The Japan Times, 1978, Ch. IV, Sec. 1.

28   *Economic Survey of Japan 1976/77, op. cit.*, pp. 94-96.

29   *Economic Survey of Japan 1977/78, op. cit.*, p. 100.

30   As a result, with the onset of the speculative boom, people reduced savings intended for the purchase of land and/or house (*Economic Survey of Japan 1976/77, op. cit.*, p. 108), despite the strong demand for owner-occupation.

31   *1977/1978 Survey, op. cit.*, p. 99, and *1976/1977 Survey, op. cit.*, p. 23, Chart I-1-15.

32   *1977/1978 Survey, op. cit.*, p. 96.

33   *Ibid.*, p. 90.

34   See, e.g. C. Collier, 'Henry George's system of political economy', *History of Political Economy*, Vol. 11, 1979, p. 93.

35   Tsuboi, *op. cit.*, p. 6.

36   The 1974 Progressive Sales Tax was similar to the UK's betterment levy, introduced by Harold Wilson's Labour Government in 1967; it had a similar effect, of discouraging sales by landowners who correctly anticipated that a subsequent Conservative Government would remove the tax. In the Japanese case, the tax was proportional to plot size; it therefore encouraged the sale of small plots, a fragmentation of units of land not designed to create optimum efficiency.

THE SOCIALIST MODELS

13

Marxist Theory and Soviet Experiment

Nationalisation of the means of production was the socialists' catch-all solution to the shortcomings of 19th century industrial society. The instability of the capitalist system could be rectified by the public sector. An enlightened bureaucracy equipped with planning powers was popularly believed to be the most effective instrument for dealing with the afflictions of cyclical crises that were internal 'contradictions', harbingers of the imminent collapse of private enterprise.

Yet when Henry George emerged to shape political philosophy in the 1880s, there was a prospect that Western capitalism would be reformed internally, made consistent with the original Smithian tenets of a free market, private enterprise and consumer sovereignty. Although Karl Marx scorned *Progress and Poverty*, calling it 'the capitalist's last ditch',[1] the book raised the level of popular awareness of economic issues. The consciousness of radicals of the left was certainly heightened. From Eugene V. Debs, the Socialist Party presidential candidate in the USA, to Sidney Webb in Britain, they acknowledged a debt of gratitude for the new visions opened up by Henry George. George Bernard Shaw observed: 'When I was thus swept into the great Socialist revival of 1883, I found that five-sixths of those who were swept in with me had been converted by Henry George'.[2] In 1884, Frederick Engels predicted 'a meteoric role' for George.[3]

Marx himself poured scorn on the use of the concept of economic rent, which he regarded as a category of bourgeois economics.[4] Nonetheless, he saw that land materially contributed to the process of production. In the agricultural sector, soil fertility could produce unequal yields from two plots of land of equivalent size onto which identical labour and capital inputs had been deployed. Rent as a surplus income, however, was determined by the market, in which competition equalised prices down to the costs of production. And this model did not find acceptance within Marx's ideological system.

The virtue of the competitive market model is that it enables the decision-makers to calculate the relative contributions of various factors, and so maximise efficiency. Orthodox Soviet economists, however, preferred to hold the view that only workers created wealth, an illusion inspired ironic- ally, by Marx's treatment of the labour theory of value in Vol. 1 of *Capital*.[5]

The Soviet wisdom, however, is a vulgarised form of Marxism. Marx himself did not exclude land from the process of value-creation. His descrip- tion of rent in Vol. III of *Capital* is a valuable contribution to economic literature. And in his *Critique of the Gotha Programme* he firmly declared: 'Labour is not the source of all wealth. Nature is just as much the souce of use- values (and surely these are what make up material wealth?) as labour'[6]. To achieve optimum efficiency in the allocation of resources, it is necessary to have an accurate measure of the relative contributions of the different factors of production. The market solution to this problem was unacceptable to Marx, but this was because he had failed comprehensively to appreciate that land monopoly was the fundamental source of the problem: his solutions consequently addressed themselves to secondary issues.

Accordingly, the natural riches which fell under the geo-political influence of Moscow have been systematically squandered. The dogmatic view of Marxist economics had prevailed. Because land was not a product of labour, it was not accorded value. And so for 60 years the costs of its use were not taken adequately into account by the planners.

But the result has been more than a profligate use of natural resources. The failure to attribute accurate rental value to each and every piece of land, rural and urban, distorted the allocation of capital and labour. Bad investment decisions have been responsible for an unquantifiable degree of waste. For example, Soviet economists have calculated that the annual losses caused by the maldistribution of buildings alone in the USSR amounted to 1,000m. roubles in the early 1960s (over 0.5% of national income).[7] Extensive rather than intensive use of land was the order of the era. Volume of output rather than value of production, efficiency and quality, has been the guiding principle and yardstick for success. By spreading available resources far and wide in their dash for growth, the Soviet planners condemned the citizens to lower living standards than were otherwise attainable, and to deep-seated problems — such as soil erosion on marginal agricultural land that ought never to have been tilled — which could have been avoided.

The miscalculations were due entirely to the absence of those economic signals which, in the free market, are known as prices. Marxist planners have had to rely on their intuitions. The role of intuition in the extensive investment of capital in the Polish iron and steel industry over the period 1961-65 has been studied. One-third of the investment projects was based on intuition and 'guesswork', one-third was partly documented and no more than one-third was properly worked out and supported by documentation.[8]

The Polish experience is illuminating. The attempts to fulfil the aspirations of the Polish workers in the 1970s were valiant, but they were bound to fail. Billions of borrowed dollars were poured into new investment projects. But according to Wilczynski:

> The omission of land made the initial effectiveness of the investment outlay appear unduly high, because the increase in production seemed to be due only to this outlay, as if there were no contributions from land. Then, additional investment outlays on labour and capital appeared to lead to disproportionately low increments to production in the project in question. This only exaggerated the extensive approach to investment, because new projects on other land promised higher returns on paper.[9]

The misdirected investment resulted in the crisis in industrial relations in 1980, culminating in the victory for Lech Walesa and Gdansk workers who led the demand for free trade unions.

Edward Gierek, the Communist Party leader, had come to power in 1970 as a result of widespread social discontent. His programme of massive investment landed the country with a $20bn. foreign debt without raising living standards because the resources that flooded into the country were not put to their best use. Gierek was bound to fail, because of the adherence to Marxist methodology rather than through a lack of good intentions. In public statements the Communist leaders finally admitted that there had been serious economic mistakes, especially in relation to the investment programme. Shortly after Gierek was replaced as party leader, Henryk Kiesel, the Planning Commission chief and former Finance Minister, confessed that 'ineffective investments' contributed to the crisis.[10]

On August 30, 1980, the Polish Communist Party endorsed the demand for free trade unions and the workers' right to strike. This was the first major fissure in the hegemonic power of Moscow's communist ideology. Poland's auto-critique was subjected to an orchestrated attack from other European communist leaders. But the economic lessons were not lost on the Chinese communists, who followed a Marxist line that was independent of Moscow. In the following month, the Chinese abandoned their 10-year Plan because — according to Chairman Hua Guofeng — its target aimed 'too high, the scale of capital construction was too large and comprehensive balance was lacking'. Marxist national accounting had enabled the Eastern bureaucratic planners to set goals that were not realistically underpinned by the costs of the available resources. The extensive spread of these resources led to a miscalculation that did not augur well for the experimental return to economic co-operation with the West. The events in Poland quickly compelled Peking to review her strategy. During the four months leading to the announcement of an interim budget in March 1981, the Chinese Government cut the allocation for capital construction by 40% from around $36bn. to about $20bn.[11] Among the projects identified as wasteful and mislocated, and which was subject to a severe cutback, was the $2.4bn. Baoshan iron and steel complex.

The economic inefficiency of the Marxist methodology has been emphasised, but could this be an acceptable price to pay, if communism nonetheless secures social justice in the distribution of natural resources? We have, after all, censured the Western model because of its inequities in the distribution of unearned rental income. Has this problem been solved in the East? Yugoslavia presents us with a fair opportunity to weigh the question, because she is not dogmatically plugged into the conventional wisdom of Moscow, she recognises market incentives for workers, and yet constitutionally she indubitably harbours socialist egalitarian ideals.[12]

Here we find two distinct land markets. Rural land is operated almost entirely on Western principles. About 85% of the land is privately owned. There are legal limits to the size of individual holdings, ranging from 15 hectares for arable land up to 70 hectares on poor-quality land in hilly terrain. As in the West, owners of land on the periphery of urban centres have been replacing their farming activities with the inert role of the speculator, dividing up their holdings and selling off parcels to town-dwellers. The compensation paid to owners for land that is expropriated for public-sector purposes is calculated on the basis of free market values. In theory, that part of land value which can be attributed to natural or social factors — such as the existence of infrastructural facilities, the demands for land from urban areas, irrigation installations, etc. — are deducted from the compensation. If applied consistently, this would mean that the whole of economic rent would be removed, leaving the farmer with the value arising from his capital and labour investments. In fact, however, the farmer does retain part of Ricardian rent.

The urban economy fuses socialist planning with the unique Yugoslavian system of self-management and individual incentives. Proprietary rights in urban land, however, were nationalized in 1958. The law applied to 860 towns and various industrial, mining and tourist centres. By 1980, nearly 50% of the population lived in the country's 510 major municipalities. The policy aimed to provide land at the right time, in the right place and at the right price (taking into account both social and economic criteria).

In theory, there was no room for private appropriation of economic rent. One official exception was allowed to this rule. A municipality could waive its right to appropriate economic rent if the land user agreed to invest the money in socially useful projects such as new factories or urban infrastructure. Otherwise, the municipality levies a tax on rent to redistribute the surplus value between all its citizens through the public sector. This ethic is egalitarian, but does it work in practice? The answer is in the negative, and the failure arises from the inadequacies in the structure of the socialist economy.

Officially, there is no market in urban land. Rents are determined according to bureaucratic criteria. These criteria are arrived at on the basis of 'intuition'. They include location, availability of infrastructural facilities and recreational amenities, environmental attractions, and the general quality of urban life. The urban area is then divided into residential and commercial zones. Monthly rental payments are computed on the basis of so many dinars per square meter of floor space. The dinar rate is uniform throughout the zone, irrespective of variations in the characteristics of individual plots within a zone which influence the real economic value of land.

The result of the application of the subjective intuitions of bureaucratic planners, however, is that the rents actually paid by those who possess land are less than the true economic value of the sites. Consequently, the belief that there is no market in land values is a constitutional fiction: a black market emerged to enable the possessors of land to exploit economic rent.

This is what happens. Urban land users own the buildings (homes, shops and so on). In the residential market, each individual can own two large or three small apartments. When they decide to sell, they add a premium onto the price of the structure. This premium is the capitalised value of that part of economic rent that is not appropriated by the municipality. The premium represents the value of the land as perceived by the prospective occupiers of the site. *They* know how to put a cash value on the attributes of the land, and they do so on the basis of competing with other prospective users. The highest realistic premium which this black market is willing to realise is the capitalisation of economic rent, after discounting for the monthly rental payments which the possessor is obliged to pay to the community for the privilege of possession.

The value of land in Belgrade rose rapidly in the 1960s. The municipal authorities, because they had to rely on their intuitions, were not able to track the movements. The available statistical data was inadequate. As a result, the municipalities did not rapidly adjust their rental charges upwards. Had their land taxes risen in line with real values, the selling price of land would have been zero (the constitutional theory). In fact, individuals and institutions had to pay considerable sums of money to get the land they needed for commercial and manufacturing activities (the economic reality).

Four deficiencies in the Yugoslavian model can now be highlighted.

1. The intention of socialising urban land values has not been achieved. People in favoured locations are able to retain significant portions of economic rent. We find, therefore, in a socialist economy, the institutionalisation of economic inequality based on the failure to use free market principles. An increase in municipal land taxes would enable Yugoslavia's

economy to grow faster, through the reduction of income taxes. This would meet what Dr Janić, the Director of the Yugoslav Institute of Town Planning and Housing, called 'The absence of a market for many urban goods and services'.[13]

2. Inequities exist between land users. Because the monthly rent payments are based on a crude calculation, they fail to take account of all the factors which in a free market would influence the decisions made by individuals. This can be illustrated with location and the costs of transportation. Some people in favourably located residential areas save on the money they have to pay to travel to work. Others, in outer areas, have to bear extra costs of transportation. In a free market, these additional costs would be taken into account when determining the economic surplus available for payment of rent. But in Yugoslavia there is official discrimination in favour of the privileged. Again, this is an unintentional byproduct of the system for determining land values.

3. The land tax is actually a general property tax. Monthly rental payments fall not just on land but also on capital improvements upon it. The rent is calculated on the basis of so much per square meter of *floor space* in the building, and not by the square meter of occupied land. The physical expansion of premises is thereby discouraged, at the expense of improved productive capacity.

4. Scarce capital resources are not efficiently allocated because of the rigidities in the land market. People who occupy land but fail to put it to optimum use are under no fiscal pressure to take action. In fact, the longer they wait, the higher the premia they can eventually extract from others. There is, then, a positive inducement to inertia in the occupation of urban sites. Potential users are excluded from desirable locations, and the overall result is an economy producing fewer consumer goods and services than would otherwise be possible.

By the turn into the 1970s, the municipal authorities grew alarmed at the way in which citizens were able to manipulate the land market to their advantage. Had a realistic annual land tax been levied, there would have been no financial incentive to speculatively postpone the sale of houses.[14]. The 'remedial' action in 1972 was to increase to nearly 80% the tax on the gains from the sale of residential properties. House owners resisted the tax by declining to sell. The house market dried up. Owners were aware, of course, that by sitting tight they would eventually win. The value of the land which they occupied would continue to rise, along with the premia they would charge for moving out. By 1980, the municipal authorities were persuaded that they ought to reduce the tax rate to stimulate the sale of houses. The socialist land speculators — the ordinary home-owners — were winning.

According to the Yugoslavian constitution, land is a resource which had to be managed rationally in the social interest. The absence of effective market prices (which constitute signals based on the incomes and preferences of all citizens) thwarted this principle. In the early 1980s, the Yugoslav Institute of Town Planning and Housing in Belgrade set about promoting objective criteria for measuring surplus income (rent). This objectivity, however, was still based on bureaucratic criteria. Empirical research was conducted which suggested that the turnover of commercial enterprises was a good indicator of urban rents, and could therefore replace the subjective criteria developed by the intuitions of the bureaucrat. But while this might tell the municipal authorities something about the prosperity of commercial areas, it still leaves a big gap in the knowledge of the tax authorities about the industrial and residential areas.

Marxist economists may now be awakening to the need to put realistic prices on land which could then be taken into account in project-appraisals. But the analytical tools at their disposal are shaped by ideology. The bureaucratic planner's method of cost-accounting, rather than market-determined prices, are still officially endorsed as the desirable system for adoption. As a consequence, the Soviet approach to socialised land will continue to retard the optimum use of productive resources and so fail to raise the level of consumer satisfaction. Not until the Marxists revise their attitudes towards the concepts employed by 'bourgeois' economists will they have reached the stage where they can begin to exercise value judgements about a fair and effective system of social and economic organisation.

The dishonesty that underpins Marxist economics can be illuminated by examining the Soviet housing sector. It illustrates the size of the distortions arising from the failure to measure and charge the full market rent. A privately rented flat that costs £47 a month would be rented out by the public sector for £5.[15] Low rents are considered an achievement of 'real socialism', and were laid down in 1928 at the rate of one square metre of living space for the equivalent of 10p. In those days, this would represent 10% of a family budget, whereas today it takes on average 2%.

Subsidised rents cost the USSR £5.5bn. a year. The deception is that citizens are told that the State provides the subsidies that enable them to live cheaply. The reality, of course, is that wages are centrally fixed at low rates, so that the resources can be used to provide public housing. All that has happened here, is that the bureaucrats spend the income instead of the citizens; they exercise the choices that are (or ought to be) made by individual consumers in the West.

Thus, although the Western model built on the existing land tenure and fiscal system is deficient, reformist solutions will not be found by moving geographically or philosophically eastwards.

It is a tragedy that, 200 years after the industrial revolution, it should be necessary for us to even contemplate whether lessons could be learnt from the Marxists. This suggests that Western liberal democracy is inadequately equipped to handle the scale of the reforms that are necessary if capitalism is to survive in a recognisable form. This would be an incorrect assumption, for change along the Georgist lines became a prospect in Britain. Ironically, the socialists were instrumental in preventing the internal reform: the story is worth recounting briefly in the context of this appraisal of the prospects of permanent reforms within a socialist framework.

The British Liberal Party, which dominated Parliament for most of the years at the turn of the 19th century, wrote George's land tax into its constitution. In the early years of the 20th century, distinguished Liberals like Winston Churchill took the message to the hustings.[16] As the most mature of industrial economies in the world, Britain was ripe for the experiment. But while the political will was present, the grasp of economic fundamentals was lacking. Lloyd George, the Chancellor of the Exchequer, simply did not know what he was about.[17] The House of Lords chose to make their final stand in defence of their aristocratic control over landed property; the gauntlet was picked up by the commoners, who trounced the opposition through the ballot box. Lloyd George, however, in his 'People's Budget', introduced duties on land that bore no resemblance to the land value tax recommended by Henry George.

The bungling by the Parliamentary draftsmen who produced the Act in 1910 that sought to introduce the 'land value taxation' system has been analysed by Sir Edgar Harper, the Chief Valuer to the Board of Inland Revenue who had an intimate knowledge of those fateful years.[18] After a gruelling 10 years, the attempt to institute land taxation as a coherent fiscal policy was abandoned. This was not surprising. Instead of using the 'market value' definition for land values, the Act introduced five different values which had to be determined for each property: Gross Value, Full Site Value, Total Value, Assessable Site Value and the value of the land for agricultural purposes. There were four duties instead of one *ad valorem* tax on the value of land. Two of them, Reversion Duty and Mineral Rights Duty, were not even taxes upon land values. The third, Increment Value Duty, was a charge upon only a part (usually a minor part) of the land value, levied at irregular intervals determined by death or sale. The fourth, Undeveloped Land Duty, was a small tax and subject to so many deductions and allowances that proved difficult to collect and almost impossible for taxpayers to understand. The cost of instituting the programme of valuing land was increased unnecessarily by the cumbrous conditions laboriously spelt out in the Act, and the valuation records were never open to public inspection (in striking contrast to the valuations made for rating purposes). Harper concluded:

... not one of these miscalled 'land value duties' in any way resembles the tax on the unimproved value of land advocated by Henry George. Therefore to say — as our more unscrupulous opponents do — that the Taxation of Land Values has been tried in Britain and has failed, is not only untrue, it is the reverse of the truth!

Except for the Mineral Rights Duty, the duties imposed by Part 1 of the 1910 Act were repealed by the Finance Act 1920. The attempt to destroy land monopoly was not still-born: it had not even been conceived.

But all was not lost. The Labour Party supplanted the Liberals as the main opposition party, and they retained a strong interest in Henry George's land value tax. A socialist Chancellor, Philip Snowden, introduced proposals to tax land values in his budget in April 1931, but this was lost after the collapse of his minority government in the mid-summer crisis that led to the formation of a National Government.[19] A substantial number of Labour MPs continued actively to support the policy, but the party determined to change course. Led by Clement Atlee, Labour won a landslide victory at the general election in 1945. The opportunity for an internal reform of the free market was abandoned. Instead, the socialists now favoured an emphasis on socialist planning and the nationalisation of land, establishing the so-called mixed economy.

Was this a correct strategy for the British socialists who abandoned Henry George? Could straightforward nationalisation be successfully grafted onto the existing system? Would the 'mixed economy' secure both equity and economic efficiency? The Western socialist model has to be examined before final conclusions can be drawn on land value taxation as the only viable solution to 'the land problem' that has plagued industrial society for 200 years.

Notes

1 H. M. Hyndman, *Record of an Adventurous Life*, New York: Macmillan, 1911, p. 268.

2 Cited in A. G. de Mille, *Henry George: Citizen of the World*, Chapel Hill: University of North Carolina Press, 1950, p. 2.

3 Engels to A. Bebel, letter dated Jan. 18, 1884, in *Marx and Engels: Selected Correspondence*, Moscow: Progress Publishers, 1975, p. 346. Lawrence described George as 'the godfather of British socialism'. E. P. Lawrence, 'Uneasy Alliance: The Reception of Henry George by British Socialists in the Eighties', *The American Journal of Economics and Sociology*, Vol. 11, No. 1, 1951, p. 61.

4 K. Marx, *The Poverty of Philosophy*, Moscow: Progress Publishers, 1955, pp. 134-144.

5 For a fuller treatment of the deficiencies in Marx's approach, see F. Harrison, 'Gronlund and other Marxists', in Andelson, *op. cit.*, pp. 206-208.

6 K. Marx, *The First International and After*, Harmondsworth: Penguin, 1974, p. 341.

7 J. Wilczynski, *Socialist Economic Development and Reforms*, London: Macmillan, 1972, p. 37.

8 *Ibid.*, p. 185, n. 2.

9 *Ibid.*, p. 184.

10 L. Colitt, 'The rare frankness of an economic chief', *Financial Times*, 10.9.80.

11 C. MacDougall and D. Housego, 'China's perplexing economic U-turn', *Financial Times*, 2.3.81.

12 Data for this part of the study of socialist land economics draws heavily on papers by, and a personal interview with, Dr. Miodrag Janić, at the World Congress on Land Policy, Cambridge, Mass., June 23-27, 1980. Opinions expressed are those of the present author.

13 M. Janić, 'The Operation of Urban Land Market in Belgrade', *Ibid.*, p. 1.

14 In 1972, about 360,000 acres of prime agricultural land were reported to be standing idle in one region alone, the Vojvodia, Yugoslavia's granary. J. Steele, 'Tito's harvest moan', *The Guardian*, 1.9.73. This would not have been possible if the tax system had socialised the full annual value of agricultural land.

15 M. Frankland, 'How to raise rents without being noticed', *The Observer*, 26.9.82.

16 Cameron Hazlehurst notes the 'fluency and remorselessness of [Churchill's] attacks on land monopoly' in his introduction to W. S. Churchill, *The People's Rights*, London: Jonathan Cape, 1970, originally published 1909.

17 Lord Douglas of Barloch, 'Land Taxation: Victim of a Vague Socialism', *Land & Liberty*, Sept.-Oct. 1980.

18 Sir E. Harper, 'The Lloyd George Finance (1909-10) Act, 1910: Its errors, and How to Correct Them', Fourth International Conference on Land-Value Taxation, Edinburgh, July 29-Aug. 4, 1929, Paper No. 11.

19 Douglas, *op. cit.*, pp. 200-208.

14

Nationalisation & the Mixed Economy

John Maynard Keynes gave academic respectability to the idea that the state could intervene in the economy to promote the welfare of the under-privileged classes. As a development in political consciousness, this was an advance on the mercantilism that marshalled the law behind a few merchants. Keynesianism was a halfway house. Because it appeared to work, it helped significantly to promote the notion of the mixed economy. Even capitalists came to accept that the public sector was a necessary component of modern industrial society. And so the philosophical acceptance of the state's right to partial ownership of the means of production was diffused throughout the West with very little opposition. One of the pillars of that philosophy has been the concession that the state has the right to own a significant portion of the land. Could land nationalisation be a more effective solution than the one advocated here — of simply collecting the full annual rental value of land within a strictly free market framework?

Socialist land policy has been associated with two goals. One has been the recovery of 'betterment' values which arise from the increased selling price of land that follows the grant of planning permission. The other has been a regulatory function: ensuring a flow of land onto the market to meet the needs of developers. A third criterion for a successful land policy, that it should benignly support the macro-economy, has been totally ignored, for the simple reason that few people have considered this to be necessary. Our examination begins with Britain's experiences.

Repeated attempts were made by the Labour Party in the postwar years to alter the balance in the land market in favour of the public sector. These began in 1947 with the Town and Country Planning Act, which reserved all development rights for the state on payment of *ex gratia* compensation (which could be bought back by a development charge on the private developer). A fund of £300m. was set aside for the payment of compensation. The scheme failed, because it left landowners with no incentive to make land available. It was abandoned in 1952.

Next came the Land Commission, in 1967, which acquired the statutory right to buy the freehold of land which could then be leased back to a developer. Again, it foundered. One reason was that landowners declined to release their land for development; they preferred to squat (there being no cost for doing so) until sympathetic political attitudes intervened to restore their former rights. This happened in the guise of Edward Heath's Conservative Government, which assumed power in 1970.

Then, in 1975, under Harold Wilson's final premiership, the Labour Government introduced the Community Land Act. The primary objective of this was to assign public ownership of development land. This aspect of the Act was repealed by Margaret Thatcher's Government in 1979. Undaunted, however, the Labour Party immediately promised to 'tackle the land problem through public ownership'.[1]

Despite the consistent application of the socialist ideology, the 18-year land values cycle was free to operate: the socialist attempts had failed to neutralise the impact of land monopoly, and the recession of the post-1973 years was inevitable.

But objections may be levelled against this conclusion. Labour's policies were relatively short-lived. Could they have worked if they had not been sabotaged by the Conservative Party in its role of defender of the landowning interests (and in pursuit of the objective of a 'property-owning democracy')? Could the problem lie not with the intrinsic defects in the socialist programme *per se*, but with the failure to apply it in a sufficiently extensive manner? There were clear economic defects which discredited the British experiments; nonetheless, there is some force to these objections. We must therefore search further.

Israel offers us a fine opportunity for studying the influence of socialist policy on the land market, and for gauging whether extensive state intervention can thwart the speculator.

From the late nineteenth century, Jewish philanthropists poured money into funds out of which to buy land in Palestine. The strategy was to re-settle the Jews from the Diaspora in the Promised Land. By the 1970s, the land was classified in this way: 1m. hectares were unused (largely desert); 880,000 hectares were publicly owned, and a very small proportion, just 150,000 hectares, were privately owned.

The late Dr. Haim Darin-Drabkin, who at the time was Director of the Institute for Land Resources Planning in Tel Aviv, assessed the influence of this large-scale public land ownership on the Israeli economy:

> ... the extensive programme of public land development did not exert any essential influence on the private land market in the big cities. The rates of land-price increase in Jerusalem and Tel Aviv have been some of th

highest in the world. Because of its location, privately held land had the decisive impact on land prices.[2]

The degree of public ownership was unmatched in other European industrial economies. Yet the speculator had a field day. One reason was the tax system. 'The taxation system has encouraged the holding of vacant land in urban areas by not taxing land profits as other profits,' stated Darin-Drabkin. This led to a shortage of land on the market in urban areas, and consequently price increases of 20-30% p.a.

But it could not even be argued that extensive public ownership was neutral, for 'the restriction in the size of the private sector due to extensive undeveloped public land holdings has also encouraged speculation'.[3] And so the state's involvement in the land marked directly aggravated the rate of increase in prices. This was a bonus for landowners, because their advantage — the fixed aggregate supply of land — was supplemented by an additional limitation. It was, in a classic sense, a seller's market. Furthermore, the fiscal system reinforced speculation, for the longer they held their land, the lower the eventual taxes paid when selling at a speculative profit.

In Tel Aviv, between 1951 and 1971, the price of land increased by over 20% p.a., compared with the consumer price index of 6% and an increase in the GNP *per capita* of 5.9%.[4] The people who wished to settle in the Promised Land and create new forms of employment for the refugees from Europe had to pay a price to the private landowners out of all proportion to the real value of land. But, the defender of the socialist solution might persist, Israel is not a fair test of the potential effectiveness of nationalisation. For 47% of strategically-located land in or near urban settlements is privately-owned. Is it surprising that they could influence price trends? But what would happen if the community owned the key development sites? Would that not be a fairer test of the nationalisation model?

Through Sweden's social democratic party, the philosophy of socialism is the dominant political creed. The economy is a profit-oriented one, which means that land values respond to free market pressures. At the same time, Sweden has the longest tradition of extensive land banking. Stockholm is the municipality with the largest land bank in Western Europe, and most development in Greater Stockholm is on land owned by the public sector.[5] Stockholm's landholdings outside its boundaries in 1970 amounted to over three times the total surface area of the city itself; public officials administered 40% (30 sq. miles) of land publicly-owned within the city borders, plus 100 sq. miles in the suburbs. This city, then, appears to offer a fair test of the public ownership approach to land policy.

There were two objectives behind the advance purchase of extensive tracts that would one day be needed for urban development. First, the land would be bought at low agricultural prices, rather than inflated speculative prices.

Second, the municipality would release the land, either by selling it (to hold down prices), or by leasing it (so that families could secure decent homes when these were needed) to developers. Were these aims achieved? If so, at what cost?

Darin-Drabkin has suggested that Sweden's 'land policy played a dominant role in the relatively slow rate of land prices increase and the low level of land in housing costs in comparison with other European countries'.[6] This is certainly the common assumption in Stockholm, but an exhaustive study by Ann Strong led her to the conclusion that it was impossible to verify whether this was true or not.[7] The following, however, are the facts for the postwar years.

In the 1940s, laws were passed that were intended to stop speculation: they proved to be inadequate.[8] There was undoubtedly an element of speculation present in the regional economy. In the 1960s, the municipality went on a land-buying spree. Between 1964 and 1969, over 21,500 hectares were bought at rapidly-increasing prices. Indeed, from 1955 onwards, the price of land increased faster than the cost-of-living index.[9] So the start of the Stockholm land cycle was synchronised with the general cycles traced in the leading capitalist economies; it peaked 18 years later, in 1973. Thus, while it might be hypothesised that land banking did not aggravate the land market, the policy undoubtedly failed to neutralise the underlying macro-economic impact of the land values cycle.

First-time occupiers of new houses built on municipally-owned land did benefit from moderate prices. The official policy of not directly profiting from rising land values through rental revenue was determined as far back as 1908. Leasehold rents for residential properties, therefore, were not only fixed for 60-year periods, but they were initially set below the cost of the land purchased by the municipality. Land not required for development was leased for agricultural use at nominal rents. Revenues to the community were designed to cover interest costs, site planning, ground improvements, infrastructure and administrative costs, but not the original capital outlay, which was not to be amortized. The philosophy behind the policy was that, with land rising in value all the time, the municipality could not lose: it would eventually sell the land and could, if it so wished, do so at a huge profit.

There was a dual result. First, the income from the leases amounted to 'only pocket money'.[10] Revenue was lost to the community. More than that, however, the capital costs were borne by the general taxpayer, rather than the home-occupying beneficiaries. There were also inequities among lessees. Two families in homes of equal size and quality could find themselves paying considerably different rates, depending on when they signed their leases. The second point, however, was that the original leaseholders could sublet their interest to others at a premium, the latter being the untaxed rise in the value of land upon which the building was situated. Thus, the philosophy which inspired the land bank policy in the first place — decent homes at moderate prices — was undermined.

Stockholm's city fathers were, nonetheless, able to release sufficient land to meet the housing needs of the population. Even here, however, problems arose which manifested themselves in a paradoxical way. In other urban centres, land speculators stifled construction by pricing home-seekers out of the market. In Stockholm, although the outward signs were similar — a growing volume of unoccupied new homes — the reason was different. Quite simply, people did not like the high-density high-rise apartment buildings favoured by the planners. The vacancy rate in Norra Botkyrka reached 10%. Observed Ann Strong:

> Had the city not had such absolute control of the development process, starting with ownership of land, the planners and other officials might have solicited and responded to public opinion. Their early sensitivity to human needs seems to have been lost in recent years in an absorption with quantification of individual components and with technological possibilities.[11]

Thus, the citizens of Stockholm seem to have lost out on all counts. The aggressive land-buying policy failed to neutralise the effects of the land values cycle, and the economy plunged into recession in the 1970s. The 'ruinous and politically motivated'[12] lease policies forced them as taxpayers to carry financial burdens that were properly the obligation of people who directly benefitted from the use of land. For potential home occupiers, their consumer satisfaction fell short of preferences: choice was arbitrarily restricted by the unresponsive bureaucrats.

Although data on market rents for residential properties was available, Stockholm's political masters deliberately ignored it. As a result, the land bank model failed to resolve the triple goal: social equity among all citizens, including those who did not possess land; economic efficiency in the allocation of resources; and consumer satisfaction.

In 1973, the Real Estate Office decided to base lease rates on the market value of land. Once again, the remedial action came after the damage was done. The economy slumped, and Stockholm's plight during the mid-'70s was similar to that in the other Western capitals. Like London and Washington, cities built on privately-monopolized land, Stockholm — which relied on income taxes rather than property taxes for its principal revenue — was in parlous financial plight. The story would have been different if the city had tapped the full value of its rich land holdings. That could have been accomplished without the direct intervention in the land market. Full recovery of the annual value of the land would have been sufficient: as well as raising its revenue it could have removed major obstacles (high income taxes and bureaucratic red tape) to an even faster rate of economic growth.

Try hard as we may, then, it has proved impossible to accept socialist policy as the effective alternative to private monopoly.

There are examples of how public intervention can improve the functioning of the land market. The pooling system employed by some municipalities in the Perth region of Western Australia improved site assembly and development. Archer has described the way the pooling system works:

> The council assembles the private and public lands in the pooling area without paying compensation, services and subdivides it into building sites, then sells some of them to recover its outlays and costs, and passes the other sites back to the landowners.[13]

This overrides the inertia of speculators, and helps to finance infrastructural developments out of rising land values. The main beneficiaries, however, are the landowners, for most of the net land value increases generated by the public projects are passed to them.[14]

The unambiguous conclusion is that the mere transfer of *proprietary rights* is neither sufficient nor necessary to secure an efficiently functioning land market. What counts is the distribution of the economic benefits arising from the use of land over time. If a portion of economic rent can be privately appropriated, the fact that legal title to the land is vested in the community cannot upset the process of dislocation caused by the pursuit of speculative gains from the possession of land. If an efficient land market is an essential component of a smoothly operating industrial economy, the socialist system is as much condemned to fall short of its goals as its capitalist opposite.

Notes

1 *Labour Manifesto 1980: Draft*, London: Labour Party 1980, p.22.
2 H. Darin-Drabkin, *Land Policy and Urban Growth*, Oxford: Pergamon Press 1977, pp.287-288.
3 *Ibid*.
4 *Ibid*, p.77, Table 4.1.
5 A.L. Strong, *Land Banking: European Reality, American Prospect*, Baltimore John Hopkins University Press, 1979, p.43.
6 *Op. cit.*, p.341.
7 *Op. cit.*, p.46.
8 *Ibid*, p.63.
9 *Ibid*, p.54.
10 P. Heimbürger, 'Land Banking — The Case of Stockholm', World Congress c Land Policy, Cambridge, Mass., June 23-27, 1980, p.3.
11 *Op. cit.*, p.46.
12 *Ibid.*, p.93.
13 R.W. Archer, 'Land Pooling for Planned Urban Development in Perth, Weste Australia', *Regional Studies*, Vol. 12, 1978.
14 *Ibid.*, p.407.

LAND VALUE TAXATION

15

The Single Tax and Laissez Faire

Henry George's attempt to remove the destabilising elements in the economy was a direct challenge to the distribution of power and patronage. That was why it was very necessary for the diehard enemies of the left and the right to take time off to attack him as a common foe, for he threatened their cosy entrenched interests.

On the right, landowners (indiscriminately categorised as 'capitalists') attacked George as a 'socialist' and 'communist'. Associating themselves with the attempt to discredit the American economist, the socialists, including Marx, sought to denigrate and dismiss George as an apologist for the capitalist system. This unholy coalition is the best proof that George held no brief for either of the conventional orthodoxies; that he in fact offered a genuine alternative to those which, through fair trial and repeated error, had successfully discredited themselves.

Henry George did not fit neatly into any of the established categories of political philosophy. He insisted that the private creation of wealth meant that capital could be individually owned. This located him on the right, in Marxist terms. Marx placed the burden of blame for the excesses of 19th century industrial society on capital (hence the title of his book, *Capital*). But George's uncompromising stand against the individual appropriation of the socially-created value of natural resources alienated him from the right, and appeared to lend some force to the argument that he was a socialist.

He did suggest that a full tax on land values, aligned with the removal of taxes on other sources of income, would produce a society that could be called socialism. But he was not an anarcho-socialist (it was Marx who proclaimed the withering away of the state'). George saw a continuing but benign role for government, which would collect land values and spend them for the collective good of the community.

We should reach the ideal of the socialist, but not through government repression. Government would change its character, and would become the administration of a great co-operative society. It would become merely

193

the agency by which the common property was administered for the common benefit.[1]

Even so, George was closer to the capitalist, for he ardently advocated the virtues of the free market (which, if permitted to operate freely, was nothing except the neutral mechanism for expressing the totality of preferences of people as consumers and wealth creators). He located the fundamental obstacle to this model in the land tenure system. Winston Churchill was to echo his critique in these terms.

> It is quite true that land monopoly is not the only monopoly which exists, but it is by far the greatest of monopolies — it is a perpetual monopoly, and it is the mother of all other forms of monopoly.[2]

Churchill, as President of the Board of Trade, delivered this scathing commentary on the Tory land monopolists at the hustings. He employed his oratorical talents to inform the people that 'the unearned increment in land is reaped by the land monopolist in exact proportion, not to the service but to the disservice done'. Churchill had no doubt how profoundly evil land-lordism was and how it affected the economic system.

> It does not matter where you look or what examples you select, you will see that every form of enterprise, every step in material progress, is only undertaken after the land monopolist has skimmed the cream off for himself, and everywhere today the man or the public body who wishes to put land to its highest use is forced to pay a preliminary fine in land values to the man who is putting it to an inferior use, and in some cases to no use at all. All comes back to the land value...[3]

But was Henry George trying to get the best of both worlds? Was he utopian? Did he create a vision of a Great Society which could never be realised? No. His reforms were not so impractical and abstract as to safely enable people of all political persuasions to pay lip-service to the ideals while conveniently pursuing other courses of action.

George made great claims for the one major fiscal reform that he advocated. A single tax on land values was to accomplish more than income re distribution. It was also intended to lay the foundations of an enhanced mora and social life. Was he over-stating his case? In building up our examinatio of the charge that he was utopian, we must begin with single issue problem and then work up to the total picture. To this end, we can take as an issu a major contemporary problem, the quality and availability of housing.

Sociologists and psychologists have now documented sufficient evidenc for us to take it as proven that poor housing contributes to a deterioration i both family life and the behaviour of individuals who are relegated to slum Most societies aspire to the provision of good-quality homes for all the citizens in the belief that this is a human right. Yet this goal eludes even the technologically most advanced economies, which have the potential capacity for making such provisions. Can we seriously claim that by eliminating a tax on capital improvements, and offsetting the loss in revenue by raising the income from land values, we would achieve this aspiration? We do not have to rely on theory for an answer. The empirical evidence suggests that this one simple reform would, indeed, make a measurable contribution to the achievement of decent accommodation for every family.

The Australian state of Victoria between the years 1966 and 1978 can be taken as a case study. Twenty-seven metropolitan cities used site value rating (SVR: represented in Table 15:I by Moorabbin, Oakleigh, Malvern and Camberwell). Fifteen cities based their local property tax on the net annual

TABLE 15:I

Victoria Metropolitan Cities, 1966-1978

Numbers and values of building permits issued in selected cities
grouped according to rating basis

| | | Dwellings | | Alterations and additions |
		Nos.	Values $000	$000
A. *Moorabbin, Oakleigh, Malvern* *and Camberwell*				
Site Value Rating	1966-1969	6,774	49,960	15,364
	1969-1972	5,683	57,271	18,064
	1972-1975	4,667	69,462	22,990
	1975-1978	2,704	74,228	29,714
B. *Caulfield*				
SVR	1966-1969	4,685	26,694	2,183
Composite	1969-1972	1,565	15,053	2,700
	1972-1975	1,650	25,451	3,057
	1975-1978	656	22,990	5,566
C. *Brighton, Prahran,* *St. Kilda*				
NAV	1966-1969	6,716	49,577	4,107
	1969-1972	4,864	35,861	4,365
	1972-1975	2,254	31,424	5,816
	1975-1978	642	23,887	12,288

value (NAV) of both land and buildings. These cities are represented by
Brighton, Prahran and St. Kilda. Before analysing the story as summarised in
the statistics, we should note that 1973 saw the peak in the cycle of land
values.

Between the censuses of 1971 and 1976, the number of new dwellings built
by private enterprise increased on average by 12.9% in the 27 cities that
taxed only land values. In the 15 cities that also taxed buildings the average
growth in dwellings was a mere 2.8%; eight of these cities showed
decreases in their total dwellings.[4]

Because of the escalating price of land in the early 1970s, the absence of a
tax on buildings in the SVR cities was not sufficient to offset the effects on the
house building programme. The land price boom pushed the price of
completed homes beyond the reach of many aspiring owner-occupiers, and
the construction of new houses declined. The drop, however, was far less
marked in the SVR cities than in the NAV cities. In 1975-78, the number of
building permits issued was 39.9% of the 1966-69 figure for the SVR cities;
but the comparable figure for those areas that taxed buildings was 9.5%.

So, as people were priced out of the house-buying category, they turned to
renovating older properties, and 'making do' with their existing homes. Not
surprisingly, the value of improvements trebled in the NAV cities, while
they only doubled in the SVR cities. This was because more people in the
latter areas were able to buy their way into the quality of homes that they
desired: they were not deeply locked into their homes. This fact is verified by
the value of new dwellings: the figure increased dramatically for the SVR
areas, whereas they slumped badly in the NAV cities.

Caulfield is interesting because it illustrates what happens when a city shifts
its property tax onto buildings. The city is one of eight predominantly
residential cities. The other seven surround or adjoin it, and are the ones
identified in Table 15:1. It can, therefore, be fairly compared with its
neighbours.

In 1969-70, Caulfield switched from the site-value basis to the 'composite'
basis of taxation (popularly known as the 'shandy' system) under which half
of the rates are on site value and half on the value of land-plus-improvements.
The immediate consequence was a dramatic drop in the number of building
permits sought by developers. Although building permits issued for 1969-7.
dropped by 16% over their level in the previous period for the SVR cities
they dropped by 66% in Caulfield. This sensitivity to the property tax ha
been traced in other urban areas in Australia. Usually, however, the marke
change has been in the opposite direction; with the progressive untaxing o
buildings by local authorities switching to site value rating, there have bee
sudden increases in the number of applications for building permits.

The second point to note about Caulfield relates to the value of buildin permits. The composite tax system is in an intermediate position between SVR and NAV. This is reflected in the figures for the value of building permits, which were worse than for the SVR cities but better than for the NAV cities.

The dramatic lesson to be derived from this is that if a government wishes to encourage new construction, it needs to shift the burden of taxation onto land values. If a government is perverse, however, and wishes to stifle house-building and the quality of the physical environment of its citizens, it should retain — or shift to — a system of property taxes that penalises capital improvements upon the land, the normal practice in the West.

This conclusion would not go unchallenged, however. Homer Hoyt would claim that the loss of profit from land would destroy rather than rejuvenate the construction industry.[5] Coming from such an authority, this is a serious challenge that requires scrutiny.

Hoyt's contention is that developers rely almost exclusively on the increase in the value of land to turn a project into an economically viable one. 'If the full increase [in the value of the land] were taxed (single tax) the developer would have no incentive to build a shopping centre, or to build houses, offices, etc. He would make a profit on sale of houses but I doubt that incentive would be enough,' wrote Hoyt.

Hoyt's argument rests on the assumption that landowners sell their land for less than the full economic rental value capitalised into the highest selling price that the market will bear. It may be that, in some cases — because of imperfections in the market — landowners sell for less than the full residual value of a project after all the development costs (including the developer's normal profits) have been taken into account. In such cases, the developers — the capitalists — enjoy a bonus; they reap some of the economic rent that would normally go to the land monopolist. But would the developer be willing to pay the full economic rent for the opportunity to engage in a viable commercial project? 'In principle he will be prepared to have to pay it all: competition within the development industry will drive developers' profits down to the normal rates for entrepreneurial endeavour. This theory is supported empirically.'[6] This conclusion has been authoritatively endorsed recently by British ministerial advisors.[7] What the evidence amounts to is that developers are already paying the full land tax — the beneficiaries, however, being the land monopolists rather than the community. Landowners capitalise that portion of economic rent that is not already taxed by government, and impose the levy on final consumers through the construction industry.

It would be fair to say that Homer Hoyt understands these facts. When he wrote to the present author that 'My large vacant tract near Washington is being developed and houses are selling rapidly at peak prices', he did so not as developer but as landowner. It is inconceivable that, through ignorance, he willingly allowed the developer to capture part of the untaxed economic rent that Hoyt could lawfully claim as his share of the proceeds. Yet the developer was apparently willing to build the houses — and find a market for them at prices that must have yielded him a satisfactory return on the capital that he had invested in the project. Hoyt's objection cannot be explained in terms of ignorance. To what, then, do we attribute it? The answer must be ideological, which is why he labelled Henry George's system as communism.

If it is now conceded that land value taxation is a practical fiscal reform that generates desirable results, why do we have to insist that it flourishes best when associated with a free market economy? If it is such an efficient medium for both raising governmental revenue *and* creating social conditions close to the ideal, why should we deny the socialist the opportunity to improve his model by adopting this fiscal reform?

We have already documented part of the answer to this question. Socialist national accounting, central planning and the process of determining the relative distribution of income are inconsistent with an efficient land market. And even if this part of the problem could be overcome (by inconsistently allowing a free market in land), we could not expect Henry George's fiscal reform to be sufficient to compensate for the remaining defects in the socialist model. This conclusion is theoretically sound, but we can draw upon empirical evidence to substantiate it.

Jamaica, under the Premiership of Michael Manley, attempted to combine land value taxation with socialism. The preparatory technical work of valuing land and compiling registers was successfully completed, but the distortions in the economy can be ascribed entirely to the political decision to introduce socialism in the other sectors of the economy.

The transition to land value taxation was completed in 1974. The Land Valuation Act (1957) introduced the system, but it was initially applied to rural land alone. During the 1960s, the value of urban land spiralled at a rate of increase as high as 25% to 30% per annum, causing political embarrassment as the government abandoned important investment programmes because of the price of land.[8] The level of unemployment rose from 12% in the 1950s to 24% in 1972. The return to power of the People's National Party in 1972 added new impetus to the land valuation programme, and system of computer-based records for the island's 500,000 parcels of land was finally completed. By 1974, the authorities were ready to tax urban land which constituted over half of total values.

The Jamaican version of land value taxation differs from the model prescribed by Henry George, in that it is not a uniform tax for all land capable of yielding an economic surplus. Politicians, responding to pressures from the electorate, instituted a tax which took a little less than 1% of annual site value to about 4.5% at the upper end of the scale of values. Furthermore, pa of the tax liability can be legally avoided: agricultural land receives a 75% 'discount', i.e. landowners are required to pay only a quarter of the tax assessed. And hotel properties are allowed a 25% reduction. These concessions raise serious questions about the equity of the tax, for nearly 50% of the potential yield of the land tax has been eroded by reliefs of one kind or another. This shifts an unnecessary (and inequitable) burden onto wages and capital, which retards the development of the country's economic base. This criticism, however, is of the way in which the tax is administered; it does not raise objections to the intrinsic nature of the tax itself.

What happened to the level of land values, which were formerly deterring capital investments? In the first six years of the operation of land value taxation, up to 1980, the prices of vacant sites fell by as much as 50% in some cases.[9] The dramatic increase in the cost of holding land vacant had an impact. But it is not possible to explain the whole of this decline in prices in terms of the tax effect. The six years under review were a period of political and economic turbulence. Michael Manley's socialist policies worried many middle class people: talk of nationalising banks, for example, encouraged many owners of capital to migrate, with the result that the demand for urban land declined. This would have had an impact on prices. Agricultural land values remained fairly steady, however, reflecting the favourable tax treatment as well as the emphasis on the agrarian solution to the problem of rural poverty.

Jamaica's Commissioner of Valuations during this critical period, O. St. Clair Risden, foresaw that from the middle of 1980 the price of land would start to rise again. 'But it seems unlikely that the holding of vacant lots as a hedge against inflation will ever regain its earlier popularity,' he predicted.[10] Nonetheless, the full benefits of land value taxation were not reaped, because the tax rates were too low. As Risden observed:

> If the rate of tax or if the progressivity of rate of tax is not steep enough, no dramatic redistributive effects can be expected and other advantages of the site value system will be nullified.[11]

At the same time, the flight of capital and the 33% level of unemployment created a political crisis. Manley's row with the International Monetary Fund (he claimed that their loan conditions conflicted with his socialist objectives) resulted in the withdrawal of financial support. His plea for help from Fidel Castro of Cuba and Premier Alexei Kosygin of the USSR did not yield the kind of rescue operation that could save his left-wing government. Manley was defeated at the elections in November 1980.

The new Prime Minister, Edward Seaga, promised a return to the principles of the free market. Jamaica entered the 1980s with an opportunity to test her partial taxation of land values within a new framework.

Finally, we must now confront what is the most fundamental challenge to Henry George. The earliest critics argued that the Single Tax was not capable of raising anything like enough revenue for the national exchequer. If true, this would destroy one of the major principles on which George built his vision of the liberal society.

There are various ways in which this contention can be refuted. One is to question the statistical data and curious assumptions employed by George's original opponents. As this exercise has already been performed,[12] we can move on to a fresh approach.

We will advance our case by first dealing with the statistical misrepresentations in the national income accounts, and then proceed to the theoretical argument which demonstrates the truth of George's claim that a Single Tax would raise enough revenue for the public sector.

The objection that the budget could not be balanced is made without taking into account the legitimacy of some forms of public expenditure. If the state insists on stacking up piles of nuclear weapons at an annual cost of many billions of pounds, this can hardly count against the equity or sufficiency of land value taxation. Indeed, even the conventionally acceptable forms of taxes are inadequate: hence the deficit financing that caused inflation. Having made this point, however, it is still necessary to deal with the argument that rental revenue would not be able to meet even the basic cash needs of the public sector.

The inadequacy of land as the sole source of public revenue is a myth that only the paucity of data permits to survive. The astonishing fact is that, while we can reliably state how much income is earned by labour and capital, we do not know — within a tolerable margin of error — how much is enjoyed by the recipients of the economic rent of land.

Attempts have been made to quantify land values and rental income. In the United States, the Conference Board estimated that the asset value of all land in 1975 was $1,284.8bn.[13] That figure seriously misrepresents income derived from land, and an attempt to set the record straight has been made by Steven Cord, the Professor of History at the University of Indiana Pennsylvania.[14]

Cord first classified the reasons why the 1975 figure was a serious under estimate. Tax-exempt land and mineral land were excluded; market values were under-assessed by tax authorities; corporate landowners declare original buying prices rather than current market values; and there was no allowance for the rental income that can be imputed to organisations such as radio and TV stations.[15] Cord then made some assumptions which enabled him to calculate, on a very conservative basis, that rental income for 1975 was $228bn., approximately double the income that is implied by the Conference Board data. Then, extrapolating forward, he showed that the figure for 198 would have been at least $440bn., but could have been as high as $600bn., a sum exceeding the combined revenue from state and local taxes, or 48% of all taxes paid in 1978.

Cord's exercise was not without error. But the single over-estimate was the capitalisation of existing property taxes. He took property tax revenue as $51.5bn., but this would have included taxes on personal property that should have been excluded. This problem arose because of the deficient collection of data. Government Census reports disclose data for all property (real and personal) taxes combined. For 1975, a more reliable estimate for the value of real property revenue was $43bn.[16] Cord's error, however, is more than offset by the extremely conservative assumptions he employed in his calculations. Indeed, in subsequent calculations, he was able to conclude that in 1982 a 100% tax on US land values would have reaped about $1,020bn.[17] This sum was nearly double all government revenue. Even this estimate, however, understated the true value of natural resource revenue, because it reflected the ruling prices of energy. These were largely controlled, and below the free market levels. Had the world prices been used, Cord's estimate would have been even higher.

A similar exercise, drawing on more reliable base data, has been undertaken for the Australian economy. In 1976/77, the revenue actually collected as a percentage of total site rent potential as officially defined by the tax authorities, was 35%: see Table 15:II. The Australian data has been monitored by the Melbourne-based Land Values Research Group. The calculations reported here draw heavily on the work by the Group's Research Director, Allan Hutchinson.[18].

The fiscal year 1976/77 is taken for the purpose of examining the fiscal magnitudes. Federal, state and local government tax revenues from all sources were A$24.8bn. The revenue from land value taxes, local authority rates on land, and lease rents, totalled just over A$1.6bn. (col. 1 in Table 15:II). This figure does not include the A$206.2m. royalties from publicly-owned mines and forests. This is a small proportion of public revenue. But if the full assessed value of all sites were taxed for the community's benefit, the sum raised would be A$4.5bn. This figure is arrived at by calculating the portion of site values left in private hands (col. 2). This is done by taking the total unimproved capital value of rateable land in private ownership, which was A$59.5m., and calculating that at 5% (the figure used in municipal valuations), the potential site rent remaining in private hands net of rates and land taxes was A$2.9bn.

The figure of A$4.5bn., however, seriously understates the true potential annual income to be derived from land in Australia. The sum would have to be increased substantially for at least three reasons.

First, official valuations understate the value of land. Revaluations are not

TABLE 15:II

Australia: Land Rental Values and Taxes, 1976/77

State or Territory	Portion publicly collected (1)	Portion not publicly collected (2)	Total Site Rent Potential (3)	Revenue collected: % of total (4)
	Australian dollars: millions			
New South Wales	799.620	1,283.995	2,083.615	38.37
Victoria	368.893	1,110.557	1,479.450	24.99
Queensland	205.084	197.492	402.576	50.94
South Australia	93.296	180.866	274.262	34.01
Western Australia	105.964	110.460	216.424	46.20
Tasmania	17.747	38.183	55.930	31.73
Aust. Cap. Territory	15.598	42.448	58.046	26.87
Northern Territory	4.405	9.185	13.590	32.41
TOTALS	1,610.606	2,973.186	4,561.445	34.99

Source: A.R. Hutchinson, *Land Rent as Public Revenue in Australia, 1976*, London ESSRA, n.d. [1981].

on an annual basis, but vary from periods between two and ten years. When land values are rising rapidly, as in the 1970s, this leads to serious distortions Hutchinson has calculated that the under-estimates can vary from 59% (Queensland) to 108% (Tasmania).[19]

Second, the values given for rateable land do not include those for mines for which rights to royalties are usually reserved to the State government concerned. They also exclude a substantial proportion of holdings that ar exempt from municipal rates and land taxes. These comprise properties hel by the Commonwealth and State governments, religious bodies, hospital and charities. The total value involved for all states is unknown, but the figur for Queensland is published. In 1976/77, rates foregone on exempt propertie equalled 12.9% of the total general rate revenue collected. The proportio exempt would be greater in N.S.W. and Victoria, with their larger cor centration of government organisations. This, and other valuation short comings, would increase the real site rent of Australian land, in Hutchinson view, to over A$5.2bn., excluding mineral and forestry royalties received public revenue from publicly-owned lands.

Third, and this is the most important point — yet the one least capable of quantification at the present time — land values would rise significantly under a new tax regime. If taxes on wages and capital were reduced in line with increases in land value taxes, part of the privately-retained income would be spent in such ways as to increase the demand for land. People's tastes change as their incomes rise. They want more spacious houses, access to better recreational facilities, and so on. Land values would rise along with the demand for land. Higher incomes mean greater consumption. The level of economic activity would rise to accommodate the increased personal prosperity. This would increase the demand from the commercial and industrial sectors for land which they needed to expand their productive capacities. The increased competition would drive up land values. Under these collective influences, land values would rise markedly and so benefit the community through the increased revenue received by the exchequer.

Given the present state of knowledge, it would be difficult to predict with precision the amount that would be raised as public revenue in Australia in 1976 under a Single Tax regime. However, the *current* gap between the annual income from land, and total exchequer receipts, would not be narrowed just by increasing the revenue side of public accounts. Public expenditure would be reduced. Governments, at the new level of household prosperity, would need to spend much less on public health, education and welfare programmes, as families exercised their personal preferences based on their increased ability to buy what they wanted without the support of the public sector.[20]

But even on the basis of a static analysis, taking the Australian economy as it was constituted in 1976, it can be argued that rental income *would* have covered public expenditure. This is the conclusion to be drawn from Book VI, Ch. 1 of *Progress and Poverty*, where George argues that *current* tax revenue from all sources is at the expense of rental income. If this hypothesis is correct, a Single Tax society would reap public revenue comprising both current tax revenue from all existing sources *plus* the outstanding economic rent still retained in private hands : there would be an embarrassment of riches for the state! This startling perception follows logically from the Ricardian theory of economic rent. This states that the rate of wages throughout the competitive economy is determined on zero-rent marginal land, the least productive land on which labour and capital can work to yield an acceptable minimum income. On more productive land, which is more fertile and/or more advantageously located, income above this rate is captured as rent.

The theoretical implications, once taxation is introduced to threaten the minimum acceptable returns to labour, are extremely significant. We would expect people to take current levels of taxation into account when bargaining over wages and interest. So their present net incomes would be the proportion of national income acceptable to them in the alternative tax-free regime. In such a society, the difference would be attributed wholly to land.

Adam Smith anticipated this analysis when he noted that taxes on wages and the products of labour were ultimately at the expense of economic rent. They were passed on through higher prices until they eventually reduced the surplus that could be appropriated by landlords.[21]

Conversely, it follows that if we reduce taxes on wages and interest, we do not automatically or permanently increase the real returns to labour and capital. The land monopolist eventually mops up the extra income in higher rents and the selling price of land, as when taxes were dramatically reduced in the US in the 1920s and the 1960s.

Thus, the Single Tax, seen from this perspective, far from being an inadequate source of income, would in fact embarrass us by providing revenue for the public exchequer far in excess of existing expenditure. For example, government expenditure in the US in 1982 was \$540bn. Given Prof. Cord's conservative computations, government expenditure would on the face of it have to be *tripled* if we changed to a Single Tax society. Neglect of this insight led Samuelson to undertake a revision of Henry George's philosophy.[22] Starting with his guess that economic rent was 'probably' only about 5% of GNP, he concluded that 'if Henry George were alive today and facing the need of government for more than 25% of GNP, he would perhaps change his movement's name from "the single tax" to "the useful tax on unearned land surplus"'. On the contrary, George would probably argue that economic rent could be defined as being over 30% of GNP, and therefore quite adequate to meet existing public sector expenditure.

At the heart of the issue is the taxable capacity of an economy. This is a slippery concept, because it requires an identification of the 'subsistence' standard of living of a population; the sum above this level becomes the taxable capacity, or economic rent.

> How is subsistence income to be defined? In biological, economic or cultural terms? It would be absurd to assume that the minimum of subsistence is the same for an Englishman as for a native of New Guinea or the Mato Grosso.[23]

The subsistence level of an industrial country is above that of the agricultural economy, which in turn is above that of the rudimentary hunter / gatherer society. Why? Because the different modes of production dictate the expenditure of different amounts of income on health and education. For example, a complex urban society needs to spend much more, *per capita*, on pollution control and technological training than a rural community in Western Samoa, in order to function. It also requires a rate of return on investments that ensures the replacement of the capital that is at the heart of its system of production.

Thus, for industrialised societies, subsistence levels have to be largely defined in economic rather than biological terms. If we bear this in mind, the dynamic fiscal processes that have been described above still apply. To begin with, industrial workers defend their wages by shifting forward increases in taxes which threaten to reduce their living standards below what is perceived to be a 'subsistence' level. This is a fact that is ignored by most economists because, according to Vito Tanzi, the Director of the Fiscal Affairs Department of the International Monetary Fund, it 'gives results inconsistent with the fiscal policy recommendation that one would get from the application of orthodox Keynesian analysis'.[24] Pay bargaining, however, is not constrained by the prejudices of professional economists, and upward movements in taxes do get shifted forward.[25] These taxes show up as increased labour costs and therefore higher product prices, which reduce competitiveness in the international markets. This was understood by the English pamphleteers of the mid-18th century who opposed Horace Walpole's strenuous attempts on behalf of the landlords to eliminate the land tax by substituting a tax on the salt consumed by workers.

The original shift in the tax from rent to wages ultimately had to be at the expense of rental income, of course, because wages were at biological subsistence levels. In 1688, as the fiscal reformers of Britain began to discuss the idea of the income tax, government revenue, at £3m., was estimated by Gregory King to be 6% of the national product; rental income was over 25%. In 1982-83, the state spent over £114 bn., 45% of the annual product. An additional £9 bn. was raised by local governments through the property tax. Rental income was about 5%. The intervening 300 years of tax history is the story of the switch of the burden from land to labour and its products. But this was merely a process of diminishing the portion of rental income that could be appropriated by the *private* sector; a growing portion was needed to fund the state sector.

The logic of this long-run transformation has escaped the attention of statisticians and economists. Once we take it into account, however, the difficulties in explaining the discrete jumps in employment incomes, and the apparent diminution of rental income, evaporate. This is illustrated by the explosive growth of public spending in Britain in the 1920s, which was induced by social welfare legislation on health, housing and unemployment insurance. This programme was financed by taxes on labour and its products. The effects can be traced in Table 15:III. Factor incomes had been constant over the 50 years up to the First World War. Thereafter, there was an apparent leap in the share received by employees. The reason was that gross wages were pushed up to enable wage-earners to pay the new taxes and leave

TABLE 15:III

UK: Distribution of Income and Government Expenditure

	Factor shares, % of national income			Government expenditure: percent of GNP at current prices	
	Employ- ment incomes	Rents	Profits, interest and mixed incomes		
1860-69	49	14	38		
1870-79	49	13	38		
1880-89	48	14	38		
1890-99	50	12	38	1900	14
1900-09	48	11	40	1910	12
1920-29	60	7	34	1920	26
1930-39	62	9	29	1928	24
				1938	30
1948-57	72	4	24	1950	39
				1955	36

Sources: Factor shares — Deane and Cole, *op. cit.*, Table 80, p. 301, citing estimates by various authorities; government expenditure — A. T. Peacock and J. Wiseman, *The Growth of Public Expenditure in the UK* (1961), p. 86.

themselves with a net income which would maintain their 'subsistence' standard of living. This was at the expense of the privately-appropriated rental income.

Employees are not completely successful in shifting forward the tax burden, however. We have seen that, in Britain, after-tax incomes as a share of employers' revenue slumped dramatically over the years 1955 to 1981 (Table 6:V, p. 82). Thus the political attacks on trade unions, vilifying them as anti-social, are misdirected: the loss of profits and markets must be attributed to government fiscal policy, the result of a determination to combine high taxes on labour and its products with a low or zero tax on land values.

We now consider what happens when taxes are reduced. If the government simultaneously reduces its spending, one of two things can happen. If that expenditure was formerly on the provision of goods and services that were part of the 'subsistence' needs of society (e.g. an educational system up to university level), then wage earners will resist attempts to capitalise these tax savings into higher land values. For they will require higher net incomes to meet the provision of all their needs. Their overall living standards, however, would not be increased. On the other hand, if the reduction in public spending amounts to the elimination of what is recognised as wasteful xpenditure, there will not be a rise in net incomes. One clear-cut saving is the xpenditure on the bureaucracy. If fewer civil servants are required to dminister a smaller public sector, the elimination of their jobs would not ave wage-earners with the feeling that their vital living standards were eing undermined. The savings from this quarter, then, would ultimately be ppropriated into higher land values.

But the strongest modern impetus to higher land values through cuts in axes arises when the government does *not* concomitantly reduce the size of ie public sector. In this case, existing services are simply financed through ie inflationary expedient of increasing the money supply. Thus, the wage arner does not have to receive a higher real net income to maintain his living tandard, which is unaffected; so the tax cuts are drawn into land values.

The animosity which is directed against the size and efficiency of the public ector is justified in part. There is nothing sacred about public services, lthough socialists — in defence of entrenched interests — seek to instil such n uncritical view as a means of intimidating free market reformers. But we ave to accept that public services were provided because, since the beginning f the industrial revolution, the vast majority of citizens were denied the pportunity of buying adequate health and education services with their ubsistence incomes. Poverty and the humanitarian sensitivities of a handful f reformers (as well as the imperative needs of the industrial economy) lowly brought the state sector into existence. Although public expenditure s indirectly financed out of rental income, present forms of taxation create bstacles to both production and consumption. They amount to legislated onstraints on the wealth-creating process. Not until we finance the public ector by the direct route, explicitly taxing the market value of all land, will ve succeed in eradicating the structural defects in the economy that condemn nillions of families to poverty. Only then can we contemplate dismantling ssential services merely to reduce the burden of taxes on incomes.

The foregoing analysis of what happens when exchequer revenue is cut pens up a realistic debate and points towards the prospect of a diminution in he size of the public sector; but a precondition for this transition is the reation of a tax on land values, to ensure that the benefits are spread equally mong all citizens rather than the privileged monopolists.

Overall, then, when we take into account the dynamic macro-economic effects, we have to conclude that Henry George's Single Tax formula for a reformed free market is vindicated. Where the reductions in existing direct and indirect taxes are not transformed by income earners into higher net wages and salaries (to ensure continuity in the provision of necessary goods and services through the private sector), the surplus income generated by society (economic rent) is sufficient to finance a smaller public sector.

One would have thought that this tax reform would have attracted mass support, out of pure self-interest. For example, Raymond Crotty, an authority on the Irish economy, attempted to interest the Irish trade unions in land value taxation. He had the best possible evidence to present to them: he calculated that the Single Tax would raise more than sufficient to wipe out the IR£1bn. appropriated in income taxes.[26] Furthermore, Irish governments would appear to have had good reason to embrace this policy for political reasons. Dublin was the scene of massive public demonstrations in 1979 by employees who objected to the way in which the fiscal system discriminated against them and in favour of property owners, especially the farmers. Nonetheless, the proposal failed to generate any interest in land value taxation in Eire.

Why Henry George's reforms have been over-looked is one of those perplexing historical puzzles. Students of economic history have to fall back on irony. As one bemused City of London stockbroker put it:

> Thanks to his combination of radical thought, impeccable logic and practical understanding, George's ideas have been largely ignored by professional economists.[27]

As we shall record, there is little evidence that the political decision-makers have entered the 1980s with a greater determination to pursue enlightened policies through a greater clarity of thought than existed over 100 years ago when George put down his pen and set the metal type himself to print the first edition of *Progress and Poverty*.

Notes

1   *Op. cit.*, p. 456.
2   *The People's Rights, op. cit.*, p. 117.
3   *Ibid.*, p. 121.
4   'Victorian Local Government Rating Study', Melbourne: Land Values Research Group, 1979.
5   Correspondence with the present author, letters dated Dec. 23, 1976, and Jan. 14 and 27, 1977.
6   N. Lichfield and H. Darin-Drabkin, *Land Policy in Planning*, London: George Allen & Unwin, 1980, p. 71.
7   *Commercial Property Development, op. cit.*, p. 51, para. 7.8.
8   O. St. C. Risden, 'A History of Jamaica's Experience with Site Value Taxation', in R. W. Bahl, *op. cit.*, p. 252.
9   O. St. C. Risden, 'An Assessment of Land Taxation measures against a background of political and economic change: A Case Study of the Jamican experience in the decade of the Seventies', World Congress on Land Policy, June 23-27, 1980, Cambridge, Mass., mimeo, p. 8.
10 *Ibid.*, p. 9. Risden adds (p. 11) that premature subdivision for speculation had virtually disappeared, and the larger agricultural properties were tending to be broken up among a larger number of cultivators.

11 'A History...', *op. cit.*, p.261.

12 One of the most influential of those critics was William Hurrell Mallock. For a critique of his statistical computations and arguments, see Andelson, *op. cit.*

13 J. Kendrick, K. Lee and J. Lomask, *The National Wealth of the United States by Major Sectors and Industry*, New York: Conference Board, 1976, p.68.

14 S. Cord, *Catalyst*, Indiana: Henry George Foundation of America, 1979, pp. 59-61.

15 Wavelenths are a scarce natural resource that would be included in the economist's definition of 'land', the returns to which are economic rent.

16 W. Wünderlich, *Facts About US Landownership*, Washington, DC: Economics, Statistics and Cooperatives Service, USDA, Agricultural Information Bulletin No. 422, 1978, p.18.

17 'Land Rent Fund Underestimated', *Incentive Taxation*, May-June 1982, p.2.

18 A. R. Hutchinson, *Land Rent as Public Revenue in Australia*, London: Economic and Social Science Research Assn., n.d. [1981].

19 Personal communication, 2.2.80.

20 For a general consideration of the way in which public accounting would be affected by a 100% capture of annual land values, see F. Harrison, 'Longe and Wrightson: Conservative Critics of George's Wage Theory', in Andelson, *op. cit.*, pp. 84-90.

21 *The Wealth of Nations, op cit.*, pp. 393-394, 400-401. For a recent elaboration of the principles involved, see M. Gaffney, 'Adequacy of Land as a Tax Base', in D. M. Holland (editor), *The Assessment of Land Value*, Madison; University of Wisconsin Press, 1970, esp. pp. 187-192. It is unfortunate that Ricardo, the one classical economist who might have done most to alert us to this process of income redistribution, actually side-tracked fiscal theorists. This was because he denied that taxes on wages were passed on in higher prices, and ultimately depressed the size of rental income. Part of the explanation for Ricardo's error must be attributed to the confusions induced by his acceptance of the Wage Fund theory, which maintained that wages were paid out of some source established by capital. His second reason for rejecting Adam Smith's original argument is that some farmers worked on marginal land; they did not pay rent, and so they could not recoup the costs of taxes on their wages out of reduced rents. See C. S. Shoup, *Ricardo on Taxation*, New York: Columbia University Press, 1960, esp. Chapter X. What happens, of course, is that taxes which reduce wages and/or interest below minimum acceptable levels simply lead to marginal land being withdrawn from use. Ricardo clearly understood this: "A tithe on land which cannot afford a rent will prevent that land from being cultivated until the price of corn rises" (*ibid.*, p.45).

22 *Op. cit.*, pp. 538, 566.

23 V. Tanzi, 'International Tax Burdens', in *Taxation: A Radical Approach*, London: Institute of Economic Affairs, 1970, p. 10.

24 V. Tanzi, *Inflation and the Personal Income Tax*, Cambridge: Cambridge University Press, 1980, p. 132.

25 *Ibid.*, pp. 132-142.

26 R. Crotty, 'Submission to the Commission on Taxation', Dublin, Feb. 1981, p. 15, mimeo., reported in F. Harrison, 'How to Abolish the Income Tax', *Land & Liberty*, July-Aug. 1981.

27 J. Roberts, 'Oil & Gas Report', London: Rowe & Pitman, December 1980, p. 11.

16

Academic Strictures: a Critique*

Few economic theories are as simple, as symmetrical and as sound as the one advocated as a fiscal policy by Henry George in *Progress and Poverty*. A university philosopher has described it as 'a thing of such elegant simplicity as to be intellectually beautiful'.[1] Yet contemporary academics, with a century of scholarship upon which to draw, still succeed in distorting the remedies promoted by George. Until the learned people are able to get their facts straight, we can hardly expect the policy-makers to adopt a radical approach to the problems arising from the ownership of property and the distribution of income.

There is widespread misrepresentation of the theory, and it is a matter for regret that we have to review these rather than immediately elaborating how a 100% *ad valorem* tax on land values would dramatically alter the dynamic mechanisms of the industrial economy in the capitalist West and, by inference, solve (or drastically ameliorate) many psycho-social problems that have economic origins.

On the whole, Henry George is dealt with in dismissive terms by authorities of disciplines such as economic theory and urban studies. Four criteria were employed in the otherwise random selection of examples that are examined here. First, George's critics were selected for the means that they afford us to explore vital aspects of his theory. Second, the writers are teachers in higher education. Third, a geographical spread was considered useful, given that the problems dealt with are universal, and require global action. And fourth, authors were selected in order to obtain a spread of views right across the political spectrum.

Murray Rothbard's *For a New Liberty: The Libertarian Manifesto*, has become the 'bible' for the new Libertarian Party in the United States

---

* This chapter is a review of academic misrepresentation of Henry George's thesis which may be safely passed over by readers who prefer a less abstract exposition of the subject.

Rothbard justifies the exclusive proprietorial rights in land on the basis of the homesteading model. Provided no traceable person is wrongfully deprived of a piece of land to which he had prior legal claim, then one could assert the right to ownership of the land without impediment from the state.

Our interest is not so much in Rothbard's own theory of property (the internal contradiction, of course, is that the liberty to own beneficial interests in land is not generalised for the benefit of all, without exception), as of the impression that he creates of Henry George's alternative. Rothbard suggests that George wished to carve up the land surface of the globe in equal portions:

> ... it is obviously impossible for every person in the world to exercise effective ownership of his four-billionth portion (if the world population is, say, four billion) of every piece of the world's land surface. In practice, of course, a small oligarchy would do the controlling and owning, and not the world as a whole.[2]

The issue about who would control the land under the Georgist system is dealt with below. The main point here is to note that George did *not* advocate the physical reapportionment of land, on an equal basis or otherwise, among the world's population. His concern, through the fiscal system, was to reallocate the *value* of natural resources through the national exchequer.

But according to Graham Hallett, a senior lecturer in economics at University College, Cardiff, the introduction of Henry George's tax would destroy the value of land: *ergo*, there would be nothing to reallocate through the exchequer. Dr. Hallett states that the tax, 'by eliminating all net rent, was designed to reduce the value of land to zero'.[3] This is an astonishing conclusion for an economist to draw. If the whole of the annual value (i.e. economic rent) were transferred from the private to the public sector, through the tax system, then the *selling price* of land would certainly be reduced to zero; but the rental value would be unaffected, except insofar as the tax would destroy that portion that constituted the speculative element of asking prices.

Dr. Hallett, however, is not finished with his interpretation of George's words:

> If all profits from land use are eliminated, there is no incentive for any change in land use to take place. In other words, the price system would be eliminated as a means of allocating land between competing uses, and it would be necessary for all development and allocation to be undertaken on a purely administrative basis by the State. This, ironically, was quite contrary to Henry George's ideals; he somehow thought that his land tax would permit a system of unrestrained private enterprise, and this confusion has continued down to the present.[4]

The confusion, however, rests with Hallett. The price system — in this case, the market-determined rental levels — *would* continue to determine allocation. Land users would continue to possess the land so long as their economic returns were such as to enable them to compete with others for the retention of the right to possession. In other words, so long as they could afford to pay the annual land tax (= economic rent, which is what tenants in town and country pay to landlords prior to the introduction of land value taxation), they can continue to keep the land in its present use. When, however, through the growth of productivity and know-how, better uses for the land emerge which push up its value, *then* existing users are obliged to compete by adapting the use to which they put the land — or relinquish their possessory titles in favour of others. By better use, we mean those uses which would yield a higher income for everyone, including the community through the fiscal system.

A cornerstone of Henry George's system was the requirement that man, in order to remain free, needed to distance himself from a socio-economic model which necessitated bureaucratic controls. The socialist model was anathema to George, and he proposed a modification of the existing capitalist system because this would enable men to retain the service of the free market system. But this does not mean that his alternative socio-economic framework could not accommodate a certain amount of land use planning.

In recent decades, the planners in the city halls of the world's great urban connurbations have come to recognise the importance of efficient land use. Their solution has been a proliferation of plans, in which geographical zones are designated for different uses. These plans are negative, telling people what they may not do rather than encouraging them to do something better with the land. But our immediate concern is not with the value of such negative plans: they can be taken as a datum, in the same way that land speculators take them as given. The point, however, is that land value taxation, if it is to make a major contribution to the living environment, must be capable of making positive contribution to urban society. It is with interest, then, that we can turn to the views of Leonie Sandercock. In addition to being a teacher of urban studies, in Melbourne, she comes from the Australian continent which has a long tradition of municipal taxation of unimproved site values. We would therefore expect her to have a sound appreciation of Henry George prescriptions.

In *The Land Racket*, Sandercock claims that Henry George proposed the taxation of land 'at different rates according to the different uses to which was being put'.[5] This is an elementary error, but urban economists do not seem too anxious to pay due regard to the facts so far as Henry George solutions are concerned.[6] In fact, George proposed a uniform *rate*: namely 100% tax on the current market rental value of all land, whatever its present use. George knew that a variable rate would distort the pattern of land use

Owners would be encouraged — against the market trends, which are simply collective signals of the people's preferences — to re-schedule the use of their land to achieve the lowest tax liability, rather than the optimum current use.

Sandercock dismissed George's solution as 'much-too-neat' and utopian.

> It bears little relevance to the nature of today's land issue, which has less to do with whether it is being productively used and more to do with its unequal distribution and with the inequalities that that distribution then produces, particularly in large cities.[7]

The existence of vast tracts of vacant land in the hearts of our cities surely warrants appropriate recognition from a land economist? That such a vital issue can be glibly dismissed tells us a great deal about the shortcomings in present knowledge about the social and economic costs of vacant urban land, which no-one has satisfactorily quantified.

But let us turn to the issue that Sandercock considers to be most important. She takes the view that the distribution of land is the major cause of our problems — hence her proposal for partial nationalisation.[8] If the whole of the economic value of land (rather than the land itself) is appropriated from the current possessors, does this not solve the unequal distribution? A full land tax reallocates the economic surplus but it safeguards against the fragmentation of holdings. Is this not eminently practical rather than utopian?

We now move to a class of criticisms of the proposal to tax land values which are practical. The most important of these is that a pure land value tax could not be implemented because of the difficulty of isolating economic rent.

Prof. Richard Lipsey, in his best-selling textbook on economics, correctly notes that a tax on economic rent cannot be passed on to consumers: it falls exclusively on landowners.[9] But he then claims that identifying economic rent is 'At best...difficult, at worst, it is impossible'. Most of the rental income of a modern economy derives from the urban sector, where, as Lipsey notes, 'The high payments...are largely economic rents'.[10] The value of city land arises exclusively from locational advantages. If, then, we can accurately value this land, the tax authorities could capture the full unearned rental income.

We can rebut the suggestion that such an exercise in valuation is difficult by pointing out that the highly-qualified profession of valuers and surveyors have built their skills on a tradition which can be traced back to classical antiquity.[11] Alternatively, we can point to Denmark, which since it passed the Land-Value Tax Act (1922) has employed modern methods to value land apart from buildings and has levied a higher rate on the former than the latter. The value of urban and rural land is published on maps, which are available for taxpayers to scrutinise and challenge if they think that the valuers have erred in their judgments. A minute proportion of the valuations become the subject of litigation.

Denmark uses capital values rather than annual income for the purpose of valuation. This basis has been defended by K. J. Kristensen, a former chief of the Valuation Department of the Directorate of Assessments, Denmark, in the following terms.

> Since tenancy is exceptional it was not thought advisable to assess the annual value. Annual value will, perhaps, be found the better basis in countries where the landlord-and-tenant system is prevalent and possibly also when we approach the point at which the greater part of economic rent is taken in taxation for public purposes.[12]

Professional valuers, acting on behalf of both private landowners and taxation authorities, perform valuation exercises as a matter of daily routine, but this is not a very interesting objection to the Lipsey criticism. More illuminating, for discerning the directional influences of land value taxation, is our contention that *without* the ability to value land, property owners would not be able to decide when to pull down a building that had lost its value in relation to the value of the land on which it stood. If economic rent was, in practical terms, elusive, this would be a serious constraint on the ability of the free market to renew the structures in our cities. This critical problem can be evaluated by reviewing evidence from both the private and public sectors, in the process of which we will see that accurate assessments of economic rent are constantly being made by those who perceive a gain in doing so.

During the boom of the early 1970s, 'asset-stripping' became a vogue activity among land speculators. They were able to calculate that many industrial and commercial companies were failing to reap a rate of return consistent with their capital investments *if the true value of their proprietorial rights in land were taken into account.* These companies were ripe for take-over bids. As soon as the companies were bought, the strippers redeveloped the properties in order to realise the full value of the land. Clearly, these operators were able to value the land apart from the buildings that stood upon them. But in case it should be thought that speculators have access to methods that are denied to taxation authorities, we can review the case of Johannesburg.

In 1919 the city fathers of this, the largest South African city, introduced site value rating (the local property tax). Since that date, not a penny has been raised on the value of capital improvements on the land. In the postwar years a succession of official and commercial inquiries (including two by the Chamber of Commerce in 1948 and 1953) evaluated site value rating and endorsed its continuation. This is not surprising. It meant that entrepreneurs were not deterred by the tax system from constantly up-grading the capital investments on which they depended for productive success — by re-investment in new buildings or renovating aging structures. This is the theory: what are the facts?

In 1973 John McCulloch, the City Valuer of Johannesburg, was assigned the task of raising the valuation roll of 140,000 properties — a larger number of parcels than in Boston, Massachusetts — to something close to market values. He reports that the up-dated valuations were within 5% of market values.[13] Objections resulted in only 42 slight reductions 'as a result of factors such as unregistered servitudes and nuisance problems'.[14] Land in Johannesburg is valued 'as though vacant', and that value should represent the market value in terms of actual rights *or potential* irrespective of what is on the site at the time of valuation.

As a result of site value rating, states McCulloch, 'The development of Johannesburg has been continual, despite minor economic slumps, whereas in other cities where improvements are taxed, development has been sporadic in terms of minor economic booms and slumps'.[15] What were the problems associated with the process of valuation?

> Land value estimation is no great problem using the residual technique and vacant land sales. Fortunately, many central-city properties are bought for the land only, and the buildings, though in many cases very substantial are demolished. This category of sale is treated as a vacant land sale or as a demolition sale, and the courts have accepted this demolition sale category as depicting vacant land value.[16]

Because of the incentive to continually improve the capital investments, a global survey of office rents in 1980 revealed that, while London topped the league table at £20 a square foot, the cheapest city was Johannesburg at a mere £3.85.[17] Despite the low rents, entrepreneurs found it profitable to invest in buildings at a faster rate than comparable modern cities. The consequences for economic prosperity — the ease with which people could start new enterprises — are self-evident.

Finally, moving to North America, we can consider the graded property tax employed by Pittsburgh, Pennsylvania, where land and buildings are assessed separately. As 1979 drew to a close, the city needed an additional $23.2m. in taxes to balance its budget. The city council wanted to raise the whole amount by further raising the tax on land, which was already higher than the tax on buildings. They voted 8-1 to increase the tax on land by 48 mills,[18] and to increase the wage tax by only 0.25%. This meant that 80% of the tax increase was placed upon land, almost doubling the tax on land to 97.5 mills (while leaving the tax on buildings at 24.75 mills). The average cost to homeowners was an additional $84 a year, compared with $225 for average wage earners if the income tax had raised the same revenue. One reason for these savings was that the land tax fell heavily on absentee owners who owned much of the city's prime property.

Pittsburgh had taxed land at twice the rate of improvements since 1925. When, in 1979, the city taxed land at nearly four times the rate on buildings, some critics predicted a negative effect on construction. A preliminary study of trends in the first 12 months after the marked increase in the land tax revealed a rise in the rate at which people were willing to improve their homes, and an increase in the sale of vacant sites.[19] These trends were in the direction predicted by the theory. The local citizens were evidently satisfied, for a year later (1980) they raised the land tax to 125 mills.

How much more satisfied those citizens would be if the full burden of the property tax fell exclusively on land values. Prof. Mason Gaffney, a leading expert on the US property tax, reported that 20% or more of Milwaukee would be rebuilt immediately in the absence of a tax on buildings.[20] He arrived at this conclusion by taking into account the rise in land values compared with the combined values of land and old buildings. The implications for the regeneration of derelict inner cities are enormous. At present, governments are spending billions of dollars which are levied out of earned incomes to subsidise the rehabilitation of the physical environment of the great urban centres. Yet all they need do is switch the tax emphasis to impose a cost on those who choose to under-use the land that they monopolise: private capital would then respond by voluntarily replacing worn-out structures with new buildings at no cost to the payer of income taxes.

This fiscal strategy was promoted by a sub-committee of the US House of Representatives' Committee on Banking, Finance and Urban Affiars, which noted:

> Real estate taxes in most US jurisdictions favour speculative land holders over builders or land users. In Alabama the drastically low property tax (effective rates below 1%) contributes to (1) large land holdings, so that only five corporations own over half the undeveloped land in Jefferson County surrounding Birmingham; (2) absentee ownership; and (3) underdevelopment — the nation's largest iron ore reserves are lying fallow and iron workers are laid off.[21]

The perverse and discriminatory effects of US tax policy can be illustrated by reference to commercial and industrial properties. These are assessed at rate 32% higher than the vacant land held by speculators.[22] It comes as no surprise to learn that 22% of all privately-owned land was vacant in central cities with a population of over 100,000 in 1968.[23] This was matched in the 1970s by figure of 24% of land held vacant on the fringe of American cities.[24]

We have now seen that the empirical evidence proves that land value taxation is administratively feasible. Critics who oppose the policy would d better to argue that speculation has not been abolished from cities like Johannesburg or Pittsburgh, where there is a measure of fiscal discrimination against income from land. Given the force of this point, we need to address ourselves to the defects in the property tax, which explain the shortfall in results and point the policy-maker in the direction of the appropriate reforms.

The first issue concerns the way in which the present law relating to the assessment of values is observed. One leading US tax authority, Prof. Dick Netzer, has noted that great advances would be made in the operations of the land market if the professionals did 'what the laws say should be done; assessors have long antedated the White House staff in presuming that laws need not be obeyed'.[25]

US federal and state governments lose billions of dollars through under-assessment of land values. The facts are known to the politicians, yet inertia — and corruption — has operated in favour of the speculator.

> To their discredit, some state legislatures deal with illegal assessments and related irregularities, not by correcting them but by legalizing them. Powerful landed interests in Alabama frustrated court-ordered assessment improvements throughout the 1970s, ex-Mayor Vann asserts, by creating 'a jumble of computation that no one can yet untangle'.[26]

But even when the authorities record accurate assessments, the level of tax rates are too low to neutralise the malign effects of the 18-year cycle in land values. The impact may be somewhat reduced, but not banished. For example, in 1973 Johannesburg's city valuer, John McCulloch, paid a tax bill of 0.56% of the market value of the land underneath the house in which he lived. This was less than the amount that he paid for water and electricity, the removal of rubbish and sewerage services. This rate is not designed to exploit the revenue-raising potential of the land tax, let alone expect it to yield additional dynamic benefits like thwarting speculators.

We can conclude that the evidence suggests that only a full recovery of all the economic rent will eliminate the incentive to speculate. This conclusion on a free market solution is offered, here, as provisional: we have yet to explore all the evidence. But what now appears to be beyond dispute is that existing treatments of Henry George's thesis have to be treated with considerable caution. If the socialist models for coping with the land market are inadequate, then the capitalist system will have to begin a fresh reappraisal of the free market options; and that means that the policy-makers will not find much of the existing literature on land value taxation helpful in their reassessment of how the land market ought to operate.

Notes

1   H. Steiner, 'Liberty and Equality', mimeo., University of Manchester, April
    1980, p. 14.
2   M. N. Rothbard, *For a New Liberty: The Libertarian Manifesto*, New York:
    Collier, revised edn., 1978, p. 34. For a full critique of Rothbard's previous
    writings on Henry George, see C. Lowell Harris, 'Rothbard's Anarcho
    Capitalist Critique', in R. V. Andelson, *op. cit.*
3   G. Hallett, *Housing & Land Policies in West Germany & Britain*, London:
    Macmillan, 1977, p. 112.
4   *Ibid.*, p. 113.
5   L. Sandercock, *The Land Racket*, Australian Assn. of Socialist Studies, 1979,
    p. 79.
6   For example, P. N. Balchin and J. L. Kieve, in *Urban Land Economics* [London:
    Macmillan, 1977, p. 124], claim that George 'proposed a 100% tax on *increased
    rents*'. John Stuart Mill had certainly proposed that unearned *increments* over and
    above existing rental levels should be appropriated, but Henry George
    advocated that the whole of current rental income should be redistributed for
    the benefit of everyone.
7   *Op. cit.*, p. 79.
8   *Ibid.*, p. 95.
9   R. Lipsey, *Positive Economics*, London: Weidenfeld & Nicolson, 5th edn., 1980,
    p. 370.
10 *Ibid.*, p. 369.
11 O. A. W. Dilke, *The Roman Land Surveyors*, Newton Abbott: David & Charles,
    1971.
12 K. J. Kristensen, 'Land Valuation and Land-Value Taxation in Denmark', paper
    presented to the Eleventh International Conference on Land Value Taxation and
    Free Trade, New York, Aug. 30 - Sept. 5, 1964.
13 J. McCulloch, 'Site Value Rating in Johannesburg, South Africa', in R. W. Bahl,
    editor: *The Taxation of Urban Property in Less Developed Countries*, Wisconsin:
    University of Wisconsin Press, 1979.
14 *Ibid.*, p. 264.
15 *Ibid.*, p. 267.
16 *Ibid.*, p. 265. Seventy-nine South African towns raised their property taxes from
    site values alone in 1982. In New Zealand in 1981, assessments of unimproved
    land values were the basis for the property tax levied by 189 county, district and
    town authorities (81% of the total).
17 'World Rental Levels', London: Richard Ellis, January 1980.
18 One mill is $1 tax per $1,000 of assessed value, equal to 0.1%.
19 Report by the Center for Local Tax Research, New York, 'Pittsburgh tax shift
    yields promising trends', *Land & Liberty*, Sept.-Oct. 1980.
20 *Compact Cities: A Neglected Way of Conserving Energy*, Joint Hearings before
    the Sub-Committee of the City and the Sub-Committee on Oversight and
    Investigations, Ninety-Sixth Congress, First Session, Dec. 11 and 12, 1979,
    Washington, DC: US Govt. Printing Office, 1980, p. 241. See also M. M
    Gaffney, 'Property Taxes and the Frequency of Urban Renewal', Harrisburg
    Penn.: National Tax Association, n.d., paper presented to the 57th National
    Tax Conference, Pittsburgh, Penn., Sept. 14-17, 1964.

21   *Compact Cities: Energy Saving Strategies for the Eighties*, Washington, DC: US
     Govt. Printing Office, 1980, p.61.
22   *Ibid.*, p.64.
23   A.D. Manvel, 'Land Use in 106 Large Cities', in *Three Land Research Studies, op.
     cit.*, p.20, Table 1. This result was confirmed by a study of 86 cities in 1971.
     R.M. Northam, 'Vacant Urban Land in the American City', *Land Economics*,
     Vol. 47, 1971.
24   Brown *et al.*, 'Land Ownership...' *op. cit.*, Table 18.
25   D. Netzer, 'The incidence of the property tax revisited', *National Tax Journal*,
     Vol. 26, 1973, p.535.
26   *Compact Cities, op. cit.*, p.65.

17

Equity and Creative Financing

When Benito Mussolini ordered the construction of Rome's first underground railway track, he did more than make the trains run on time. His plan pinpointed the locations where property would rise in value; and sure enough, the speculators moved on to the prime sites adjoining the stations to reap the benefits of the massive investment which connected Rome with the buildings where Mussolini had hoped to stage a world fair in 1942.

That government spending increases the value of land is a well-established fact.[1] But the justification for the private appropriation of this value is a generally neglected issue. This brings us to a consideration of equity, a concept which neatly embodies the two issues of central concern to us here. It is a moral concept that alludes to fairness. At the same time, its economic content refers to the value over and above charges outstanding against a property.

It seems fair to argue that if public projects cause the value of adjoining land to rise, then the community is entitled to capture that value. The landowner has no moral or financial claim on the enhanced equity of his property. Would it not make sense to finance those projects directly out of the increased value of affected land? Would this not be a shrewd way of overcoming the shortage of capital that is given as the principal reason why projects vital to social well-being have to be deferred into the future? These questions can be examined in relation to the global need for energy conservation, the relief of congested highways and the reduction of pollution through the provision of new systems for mass transit.

From Mexico City to Singapore, the town planners entered the 1980s determined to devise efficient means for transporting people from their suburban homes to the cities where they work and play. But no sooner do such plans get laid and the taxpayers' money allocated, than the speculators move in to capture the financial benefits by capitalising them into higher land prices. For example, from the day that the location was identified in 1966 land prices around Tokyo's controversial Narita Airport started rising. The had escalated by a factor of 30 by 1980, most markedly along the line of the Hokuso railway, which was to connect Chiba New Town with the airport.

Government plans are aimed at reducing psychological stress and physical discomfort, improving economic productivity and conserving scarce natural resources (from the consumption of finite energy to the curbing of urban sprawl on to green pastures). The benefits will go almost wholly to the land monopolists.

> If we now focus on urban movements, benefits due to incremental improvements in transportation (either in cost, time, or stress) beween residence and work in a centralized city such as New York seem to be reflected fairly unambiguously in increases in residential rent and land values. Thus, the user benefits only marginally unless he is also the landowner at his residence; as a renter, he may even be put at a disadvantage.[2]

A dramatic illustration is the Metro system built in Washington, DC. In 1980, senators approved a $24.8bn. federal subsidy programme for US mass transit systems, the money to be spent during the following five years. The senators themselves were well-acquainted with the attractions of efficient systems, because the underground railway being built in and around the American capital was the most advanced in the world — what *Fortune* dubbed the solid-gold Cadillac of mass transit'.[3]

The original cost of the Metro was put at $2.5bn. From the day of the first ground-breaking, in 1969, the cost escalated to $7.2bn., and 80% of that money was to be paid out of federal funds. By 1980, taxpayers across the continent had generously contributed to the commuting comfort of the residents living within short distances of Capitol Hill.

For the benefit of the *residents*? A congressional staff survey discovered that land values around Metro stations had increased by $2bn. in the five years since the first train slipped out of Farragut North in 1975.[4] This was a calculation based on the most conservative assumptions; the true figure was somewhere up to $3.5bn. Thus, the wage-earners of America had paid their taxes to the federal government, who in turn created an air sprung subway system the financial benefits of which went into the pockets of landowners! Is this a sound way to finance public projects? Is it the *morally*-correct way to distribute the benefits?

The equitable way to finance mass transit systems (as with any public project) is to do so out of enhanced land values. That such values do result from public investment is recognised in an official report which concluded that there were substantial social benefits (such as the conservation of oil) to be enjoyed by main line electrification of Britain's railway system.

There is evidence that this has occurred with previous electrification schemes, but it has not been possible to assess the magnitude of the effect which might arise from a large electrification programme.[5]

That the increase in land values from such investment is considerable was testified to by property developer Nigel Broackes in a letter he sent in June 1982 to the Secretary of State for the Environment (Michael Heseltine). Mr Broackes, the chairman of the London Docklands Development Corporation, justified the expenditure of £65m. of taxpayers' money on a light rail system connecting the East End with the centre of London on the grounds that the impact on land values, 'though impossible to quantify, will in my judgment be considerable, providing benefit to the Treasury on our own land and enhance land values generally to private owners'.

The alleged difficulty of monitoring the increase in land values[6] did not deter the Hong Kong government, which in 1980 selected this method to finance the HK$7bn. Island Line extension to its railway system. Of the total cost, $5bn. was to be raised through the profits on property development around the 13 underground stations. To a criticism that this was a 'somewhat bizarre' way of financing the railway, the chairman of the Mass Transit Railway Corporation replied:

> I would have preferred the description to be progressive or realistic...
> World experience as well as that in Hong Kong indicates that property
> values in the vicinity of newly opened underground railway stations tend
> to increase dramatically. By allowing the corporation to develop the air
> space above stations and depots, the government has diverted a portion of
> the profits arising from such an increase in property values towards the
> financing of the railway. What is bizarre about that?[7]

Thus, the community creates equity in land which it then captures to finance the original project. No-one loses, but everyone gains through access to the improved transportation system.

Examples can be found of this form of creative financing. In the past 30 years Bogotá, in Colombia, has used special assessments on land value (called 'valorization' taxes) to finance much of the capital's urban infra structure.[8] Each plot of land is assigned a prescribed benefit calculated on the basis of proximity to the project, the size of the plot, frontage, and anticipated changes in use due to improved economic activity. The tax is a lump-sum payment, which from the equity point of view is a shortcoming. For the benefits in the form of increased land values continue after the project has been completed. The continuing benefits, however, remain with the land owners.[9] This is not the case with an *ad valorem* tax on the annual value of land, in which the benefits accrue to the community in perpetuity.

Another problem concerns the price of land. With the valorization tax, the lump-sum payment does not reduce the rate of return to land after completion of the development. The price of land will therefore not be directly affected. It will remain as expensive as ever to first-time users. Under land value taxation, however, the initial cost of land is reduced for potential users. The buying price is reduced by the amount that has to be paid in the form of the annual tax.

The irrigation districts of California afford an outstanding example of how the annual tax on land values overcomes the problems associated with once-for-all lump-sum taxes.

In the early 1880s one of California's legislators, C. C. Wright, realised that the huge ranches owned by the cattle barons would be more productive if water was channelled into the semi-arid zones. In 1887 the 'Wright Act' (known officially since a 1917 amendment as the Irrigation District Act) was passed to deprive large-scale landlords of what Henley called 'a traditional veto of progress'[10]. The purpose was to transform a 'semi-arid land from its normal permanent slumber as an area of absentee baronies to one of prosperous independent farms and rural cities offering social as well as economic rewards'.[11]

The districts created their network of irrigation canals out of money raised through a tax on the value of land that benefited either directly or, according to court decisions, indirectly (land in neighbouring towns was held to rise in value because of the rural prosperity). In 1909 an amendment provided for the exemption of improvements, such as orchards and buildings; a tax on these were held to be a disincentive to new investment.

The big landlords tried to resist the measure. One of then, Henry Miller — the Cattle King who could drive his herds from Oregon to Mexico and camp each night on his own land — branded the Act 'a communist device'. He appealed all the way to the Supreme Court, but lost. The transformation from extensively-used ranches to intensively cultivated small farms was rapid. In three counties (Modesto, Turlock and Stanislaus), a vast semi-arid treeless tract of 81 played-out wheat farms became over 7,000 family-sized farms with an average size of about 30 acres. The change did not come through political controls, land appropriation and arbitrary bureaucratic allocation. The free market provided the framework, and the tax on the value of land simulated the action. Henley neatly summarized the dynamic forces propelling the landowner.

> He is nudged from behind by the assessment on his land to do something that will permit him to pay it. At the same time he is beckoned by the promise that his effort and investment to make the land produce will not be penalized, since such improvements are not taxed.[12]

The cattle barons were not able to use all of their land to its full potential, so they relinquished some of it to others, and in the process the correct distribution of land (consistent with the local conditions) was attained.

Lest it be thought that the whole of California benefited from such enlightened fiscal action, the story of Kern County Land Co. is worth recounting. In 1877 two speculators, Lloyd Tevis and James Ben Ali Haggin gained title to 150 square miles in the San Joaquin valley through a masterful fraud.[13] Unknown to most people, Congress had hurriedly passed the Desert Land Act, which authorised the disposal of arid public lands in 640-acre holdings to persons who promised to provide irrigation. Haggin and Tevis arranged through their political friends to have the San Francisco land office opened on Saturday for their exclusive use. Scores of henchmen were then organised to enter claims to 640 acres each. These holdings were then transferred to Tevis and Haggin. Settlers already on the land (some of it, located near the Kern River, was fertile) were dispossessed. There was a public outcry, but the evil deed was done.

In 1880, the two men incorporated their holdings under the name of Kern County Land Co., on whose land oil was discovered in 1936. The company was acquired in 1967 by Tenneco, the Houston-based conglomerate. Their fiscal obligations to the community can be measured by looking at the year 1970. California's Williamson Act produced an estimated property tax reduction of $136,911. The federal crop subsidy bestowed $1.3m. on Tenneco, along with an unknown sum conferred by way of a water subsidy under the California Water Project. The value of Tenneco's land holdings in the valley was soaring. The corporation reported profits of $73.8m. But according to documents on file with the Securities and Exchange Commission, far from paying federal income tax that year, it enjoyed a federal income tax *credit* of $20m!

Thus, while we can demonstrate the administrative feasibility and economic efficiency of land value taxation, we are still left with the political problem. How long will the public continue to tolerate the maldistribution of socially-created income? According to Harold Dunkerley of the World Bank:

> Recent international discussions have served to underline the widespread conviction that surplus [land] values which are unearned in the sense of not being due to the savings of the private holder should accrue to the public since this surplus is primarily due to public investments or community development or monopolistic practices.[14]

Despite this optimistic assessment, the monopolists continue to retain their grip over the land; and they do so by turning the argument for equity against the reformers. Their most effective weapon is to deny that landowners have the ability to pay, one of the key Smithian tenets of a sound tax. And the most emotive obstacle placed in the way of fiscal reform is this: 'What about the little old lady living in a cottage on a high-value site? She does not have the income to pay the high tax based on the market value of her land. Is it fair to drive her out of her home during her years of retirement?'

There are indeed many cases of old age pensioners living on valuable tracts in urban growth centres. From the viewpoint of efficient resource allocation, it would be desirable that they moved to less commercialised locations in residential districts with lower land values. But a delicate principle of individual freedom is held to be involved here.

Should the old lady be free to remain where she is without let or fiscal hindrance? Or does the freedom and welfare of the majority take precedence? If a means can be found to overcome this problem, then the public accept-ability of the principle and equity of land value taxation is enhanced. Such a solution exists in the form of deferred assessments.

Prof. Donald Shoup has described how political support can be raised for specific public projects that are to be financed out of enhanced land values, *if the tax payments can be deferred until the property is sold and the benefits of the investment have been capitalised into the selling price*. His model relates to special assessments for one-off projects,[15] but its principles can be extended to meet the general issue.

Shoup cites, as an example, the decision to bury underground the utility wires which were blighting an old, largely owner-occupied neighbourhood. The project costs \$10,000 per house, and everyone agrees that this amenity would increase house values by more than this sum. Nevertheless, some owners would oppose the proposal if their incomes did not enable them to meet the tax payments. Their objections, however, would be overcome if they could defer the tax payment until the day that they sold the house. Thus, the beneficial investment could be undertaken by the government, using borrowed cash, which then amortizes the debt by annual assessments. Those who deferred their tax payments would have to pay interest at a market rate on the outstanding money when they eventually realized the equity in the property. If a market interest rate is charged on deferred assessment debt, the present discounted value of repayments equals the initial special assessment, so the government loses nothing by the delay. The home owner could reduce his debt at any time (as when his salary rose through professional advance-ment). If, however, the homeowner died, the government would not lose out: there would be a legal charge on the estate.

Thus, the little old lady on her high-value plot in the middle of a busy commercial district could opt to remain in her home. Payment of the full tax on her land could be deferred until the equity in the property was realised either when she decided to move, or at her death. Something similar to such a scheme exists in California, where the Senior Citizens Property Tax Post-ponement Law permits owners to delay payment of their local property taxes, and the State recovers the debt plus 7% annual simple interest at the point of the sale of the property. Not only is the income stream of the pensioner raised at a time of life when income-earning prospects are at their lowest, but the exchequer does not lose revenue in the long-run. The land may, in some cases, not be put to its best economic use immediately, but the legitimate claims of the community on the value of the land have been — or will be — met.

And so we can now conclude that there are no inherent administrative, theoretical, social or moral problems associated with the implementation of land value taxation. The empirical evidence demonstrates that imposing a cost on the possession of land moves economic activity in a desirable direction. This review, however, has been restricted to a partial analysis. We now need to address ourselves to the issues from a macro-economic perspective. Fortunately, the impact on a whole economy can be gauged by an examination of Taiwan, which applied land value taxation a full century after the first experiment in Japan.

Land value taxation was absorbed into Chinese thinking through two channels — the one philosophical, the other through what economists today call 'the demonstration effect'. They both feature Henry George in their origination, and they both finally converged on Sun Yat-Sen (1866-1925), the nationalist philosopher and leading member of the Kuomintang.

Sun Yat-Sen incorporated his ideals of land equalisation and land taxation into Kuomintang policies after reading the works of Henry George and John Stuart Mill.[16] In addition, however, he was able to examine at first hand the influence of land value taxation in action *on Chinese soil*. In 1898 the Chinese Government leased the 200-square mile district of the Kiao-chau to Germany. The principal urban centre was Tsingtao, a fishing village on the mouth of the Chiao-chou-wan. The man appointed as civil commissioner was Dr Ludwig Wilhelm Schrameier, an admirer of Henry George.[17]

During the 16 years of German occupation, the colony more than tripled its population. The central policy of the colony was that all land rent should be available for public use. Land was taxed according to its assessed value. The initial rate was 6%. Land bought from the government and not immediately put to proper use was taxed on a scale which rose from 9% to 24% according to the length of time which the land was held idle. Not surprisingly, therefore, there was rapid development and no speculation. Ironically land taxation was abolished during the Japanese military occupation of Tsingtao (1915-1922).

Schrameier was invited by Sun Yat-Sen to be his adviser. He went to Canton to assist in drafting the land law and land registration regulations, the draft of which was nearly completed and required only 10 days more to be put into its final form when Schrameier was killed in a car accident on January

5, 1926.[18] In any event, Henry George's ideals lived on through Dr. Sun's *San Min Chu-I* (Three Principles of the People). When the nationalists fled from the communists and took refuge on Taiwan (then called Formosa) in 1950 under the leadership of General Chiang Kai-shek, the *San Min Chu-I* formed the centrepiece of the strategy for economic development.

By the mid-'50s, Taiwan had undertaken the most successful of postwar land reforms. Through the land-to-the-tiller programme, rural incomes were progressively equalised.[19] A quarter of the land was redistributed, and was used more efficiently. Government revenue increased from land taxation, and resources were switched into the industrialisation programme.[20] By 1969-72, industry was growing at an annual rate of over 21%.[21] GDP rose at an annual rate of over 10% in the decade up to 1974.

In 1967, C. F. Koo, the President of the Chinese National Association of Industry and Commerce, reviewed the evidence, and concluded that industrialisation was critically influenced by land reform. Previously, he said, few landlords were willing to invest money in industry. As a result of the government's measures, however, 'capital which used to be active in land transactions or frozen in land has been given over to growing industry since the land reform and thus increased the rate of industrial employment'.[22] And he did not subscribe to a cultural explanation for the pre-industrial state of the Chinese mode of production.

> The reason why China could not catch up with the pace of industrial-isation in occidental countries in spite of contacts made with Western countries during their period of overseas expansion in commercial and industrial markets, was not because of her backwardness in agricultural production, but because of the restrictions imposed on industry by the traditional rural-productive relationship. The land reform abolished this irrational rural-productive relationship and the unreasonable tenancy system, thus removing the obstacle that stood in the way of industrial development and creating a remarkable change in the structure of the social economy.[23]

In spite of her undeniable achievements, however, Taiwan's experiment fell short of its full potential. Land value taxation was not applied either fully or consistently. The average tax rate has been under 2% on assessed value and the actual average rate on estimated market value has been under 1%.[24] Nor was the land value increment tax, which falls at differential rates at the point of land transactions, eliminated speculation in land on urban fringes. The government sought to deal with this problem with the Statute for Equaliz-ation of Land Rights (1977). This introduced a new device: a 10% penalty on the value of land sold on which no improvements had been made, and a 20% reduction in the tax on the value of land sold on which improvements had been made. There are administrative problems associated with implementing this formula. In addition, the statute appeared to fly in the face of its title — the equalisation of land rights — by removing the penalty on absentee ownership, and reducing the preferential rate for owner-occupied residential land from 0.7% to 0.5% on urban land up to 3 acres and on rural land up to 7 acres. The ideal solution, which would have removed the anomalies and generated an even more successful realisation of the goals set by Sun Yat-Sen, would have been a 100% recovery of annual rental income.

By 1980, the leaders of Taiwan's land reform programme had grown to appreciate that social tensions were emerging as a direct result of unequal rights to land.[25] Although an authoritarian system, Taiwan's politicians expressed a wish to modify their tax system to re-establish harmony, but it seems that the partial solutions ultimately advocated by J.S. Mill (such as taxation of *future* increases in land values), were to succeed over the pure model advocated by Henry George.

The failure to develop the taxation of land values to its logical conclusion can have serious consequences. In Japan it led to a mitigation of the miracle, through the creation of a new landlord class; the economic impact of the speculative motive is in no way ameliorated just because the opportunities for cashing in on unearned rental income are diffused among a larger group of people. The truth of this proposition can be tested against the important evidence that is provided by the history of Australia.

Notes

1   C. L. Harriss, editor: *Government Spending & Land Values: Public Money & Private Gain*, Wisconsin: University of Wisconsin Press, 1973.
2   M. O. Stern and R. U. Ayers, 'Transportation Outlays: Who Pays and Who Benefits?', in Harriss, *ibid.*, p. 118.
3   H. Nickel, 'Washington's Metro is the solid-gold Cadillac of mass transit', *Fortune*, 3.12.79.
4   L. M. Simons, 'Value of Land Around Metro Leaps Dramatically in 5 years' *The Washington Post*, 24.1.81.
5   Department of Transport/British Railways Board, *Review of Main Line Electrification, Final Report*, London: HMSO, 1981, p. 76, para. 42.
6   *Ibid.*, p. 77, para. 43.
7   N. S. Thompson, 'Tunnel vision on the MTR', *Far Eastern Economic Rev* 30.1.81.
8   W. A. Doebele, O. F. Grimes Jr and J. F. Linn, 'Participation of Beneficiaries i Financing Urban Services: Valorization Charges in Bogotá, Colombia', *Lan Economics*, Feb. 1979.
9   Doebele, *et al.*, state: 'the landowner nearly always emerges with a net gain *Ibid.*, p. 90.

10   A. T. Henley, 'Land Value Taxation by California Irrigation Districts', in Becker, *op. cit.*, p. 144.
11   *Ibid.*, p. 145.
12   *Ibid.*, p. 144.
13   P. Barnes and L. Casalino, *Who Owns the Land?*, Berkley: Centre for Rural Studies, n.d. p. 15.
14   H. B. Dunkerley, 'Urban Land Policy Issues and Opportunities — An Overview', in *Urban Land Policy Issues and Opportunities*, Vol. 1, World Bank Staff Working Paper No. 283, 1978, p. 40.
15   D. C. Shoup, 'Financing Neighbourhood Public Investment by Deferred Special Assessment', Los Angeles: School of Architecture and Urban Planning, University of California, 1980.
16   A. M. Woodruff, 'Progress and Poverty: a Hundred Years' Perspective', in *Henry George and Sun Yat-Sen: Application and Evolution of their Land Use Doctrines*, Cambridge, Mass., Lincoln Institute, 1977, and C. Cheng, *Land Reform in Taiwan*, Taipei: China Publishing Co., 1961, p. 10.
17   T. Hsiao, 'Land Tenure in Tsingtao and Henry George's Ideals', in *Henry George and Sun Yet-Sen, op. cit.*
18   *Ibid.*, p. 127, n. 6.
19   Professor Woodruff has emphasised that this came about not by cutting the top incomes, but by forcing up at a faster rate the incomes of the least affluent people. 'The land reform built the prosperity of the country from the bottom up.' A. M. Woodruff, 'The application of Georgist ideas in Taiwan, Republic of China', paper presented to the Conference marking the centennial of the publication of Henry George's *Progress and Poverty*, San Francisco, Aug. 1979, pp. 9-10. See also K. Griffin, *Land Concentration and Rural Poverty*, London: Macmillan, 1976, Ch. 7, and J. C. H. Fei, G. Ranis and S. W. Y. Yuo, *Growth with Equity: The Taiwan Case*, Washington: The World Bank/Oxford University Press, 1979.
20   G. Ranis, 'Industrial Development', in W. Galenson, editor: *Economic Growth and Structural Change in Taiwan*, Ithaca: Cornell University Press, 1979, p. 214. See also E. Thorbecke, 'Agricultural Development', *ibid.*
21   T. H. Shen, 'Land Reform and its Contribution to Rural Development in Taiwan', in *Henry George and Sun Yat-Sen, op. cit.*, p. 80, Table 4.
22   C. F. Koo, 'Land reform and its impact on industrial development in Taiwan', in J. R. Brown and S. Lin, editors: *Land Reform in Developing Countries*, Hartford, Conn.: University of Hartford, 1968, p. 374.
23   *Ibid.*, p. 375.
24   W. King, 'Republic of China's System of Land Taxation', in *Henry George and Sun Yat-Sen, op. cit.*, p. 60.
25   Interview with Dr. R. C. T. Lee, chairman, Council for Agricultural Planning and Development, Taipei, Republic of China, at World Congress on Land Policy, Cambridge, Mass., June 23-27, 1980.

18

Australia: a Case Study

Monopolists successfully create the illusion of scarcity. No matter how mu
land is available, when it is locked away behind an anti-social system of tenu
and taxation, people starve. So it was in Australia, where the tax o
unimproved land values was first introduced in 1884 in an attempt to unlo
the land for the benefit of settlers. Today, the property tax is based e
clusively on the value of land in two-thirds of all local government uni
covering 93% of land under municipal jurisdiction. Speculation, alas, has n
been banished, and the reason is to be found in the low incidence of the ta

In 1976, Sydney's rate was 2.199 cents in the $ of assessed capital valu
plus another 1.10 cents in the $ on residential properties for water, sewera
and drainage levied by separate corporations. This brought the combin
rate to 3.30 cents. For properties with a substantial minimum unimprov
value, there was also a state land tax. This is a progressive tax, and properti
at the top end of the scale paid over $20,000 plus 3 cents for each $1 of t
taxable value over $880,000 of unimproved capital value.

The local, corporation and state taxes certainly combined to produce a
incentive to develop which was absent elsewhere; the intensive developme
of the central business district has been attributed to the land taxes.[1] Noneth
less, the evidence amply demonstrates that so long as a good proportion of t
value of land remained to be exploited by the private sector, the speculato
would move in to work their influence.

We can trace the macro-economic effects of land speculation from t
earliest period of European civilisation on the continent. Australia's develo
ment is significant because despite the land value tax, her evolution into
industrial state parallels the experience of the metropolitan countries th
gave birth to it. The big question is whether, given a high rate of land ta
Australia's evolution might have taken a different course.

The first major land booms, in the 1830s and 1850s, preceded the init
phase of industrial growth and capital formation which took place betwe
1860 and 1900.[2] The first decade of this period does not fit our model of t

18-year cycle for a variety of reasons. This was a time for consolidating holdings at the expense of the public domain, rather than speculating in land that was already privately monopolised. Under the auspices of official policy, land was auctioned off in a process that was designed to 'unlock the land'. Because wool yielded the highest profits, the squatting pastoralists were favoured by the banks for loans. According to the law, settlers who acquired land were obliged to live on it for three years before they could finally own — and therefore alienate — the land. This minimised speculative buying and selling.

But the tempo changed in the 1870s. In New South Wales, 4m. acres of Crown land had been sold for £2.35m. between 1862 and 1871; but from 1872 to 1876, 11.5m. acres were sold for £6.66m. Amending Acts in 1875 and 1880 eased the rules for squatters to buy land. Agricultural income from wool and wheat started to rise dramatically. In 1869, 2m. lbs of canned meat were exported: the figure leapt to 16m. lbs in 1880.[3]

During the two decades ending in the late 1880s, land values increased steadily. Speculation became the pre-occupation of many frontiersmen who saw the personal advantage to be gained by getting in first and extorting a premium from subsequent generations of settlers. Infant industries, however, would have been better served by entrepreneurs developing opportunities for fresh capital formation. The gigantic splurge in land speculation in the 1880s was followed by the most severe depression experienced on the continent in the 19th century. The role of the speculator during this period has been most carefully studied in Melbourne, Victoria,[4] where 'land speculation extending well ahead of building'[5] was a general phenomenon. The distortion in the allocation of resources skewed the economy: there was inadequate industrial and commercial activity to support the sprawling urban centres.[6]

We can see from Table 18:I how the returns to cash invested in land far outpaced yields from alternative sources. The average net rate of return on subdivided tracts reached a staggering 94.8% in 1887.[7] The land market started its decline in 1888. Speculators found themselves short of liquid cash with which to finance mortgages, and many defaulted on their repayments as they realised that they would not secure the high prices which they had paid no matter how long they hung on to their properties. Prices slid fast in 1890 and the depression struck 12 to 24 months later.

Building societies were the main lenders of cash, and their fortunes paralleled the rise in land values. In Victoria, there were 47 societies in 1880, reaching a peak of 74 in 1888. Then, as land values started to slither from their speculative peak, they dragged down 14 societies in the space of just three years.[8]

In 1888 the *Journal of Commerce* reported: 'A very simple calculation of the number of allotments reported to have been sold during the past twelve

TABLE 18:I

Average Rate of Return on Urban Land Investment in Melbourne as Compared with Victorian Interest Rates and Market Yields, 1881-1891

	Average rate of return on urban land investment %	Trading bank deposit rate: 12 month deposit %	Commercial paper rate 90 days %	Trading bank overdraft rate %	Mining stock yields %
1881	4.1	3.5	5.5	7.0	27.9
1882	49.7	4.8	6.3	8.0	29.8
1883	41.4	6.0	7.0	9.0	31.8
1884	10.0	5.3	6.5	9.0	31.2
1885	46.5	5.0	6.5	9.0	33.7
1886	50.3	5.5	7.3	9.0	25.9
1887	78.3	4.5	7.0	8.5	31.2
1888	38.4	5.0	7.0	8.5	27.2
1889	30.2	5.0	7.0	9.0	26.7
1890	18.2	4.0	7.0	9.0	6.2
1891	8.4	5.0	7.3	8.5	11.8

Source: R. Silberberg, 'Rates of Return on Melbourne Land Investment, 1880-92' *The Economic Record*, 1975, p. 216.

months, will show that with a population of a million, provision has been made for five millions'.[9] Australia had reached a period of mature land speculation. Coincident with the depression of the early 1890s, Henry George's *Progress and Poverty* stimulated the call for reforms. George had accepted an invitation to undertake a lecture tour of the continent,[10] and by 1900 many communities had adopted the practice of levying rates on site values.[11] This brought some order to the use of land. The threat to the vested interests invited the inevitable retaliation, and one of the victims was an influential exponent of George's fiscal reform, R. F. Irvine, who was forced to resign his post as economics professor at Sydney University. He was agreed both friend and foe, too radical in his public pronouncements for the liking of those who controlled the political system.

There is clear evidence that the tax on land values did have an impact on absentee landlords. Even while the imposition of a new tax was being discussed at the hustings in 1910, many of them took fright and sold up

Thereafter, the number of absentee owners, and the size of their estates, declined measurably.[12] But the range of state and municipal taxes and rates on land failed to halt speculation. For the level of taxation was, and is, too low; the scope for making huge unearned fortunes out of land still existed.

Postwar Australia was clearly subjected to the vicissitudes of the speculator. The economy was synchronised into the major events of the other industrial economies,[13] but not just because of her trading role as a food exporter. Her timing of the domestic land values cycle coincided with those in the UK, USA and Japan. The 18-year cycle began in 1955. Between the end of the Second World War and the mid-'50s, the number of years of average male earnings required to buy a house of average price was declining: the turning point was in 1955.[14] A major reason why land prices were initially restrained after the war was that speculative sub-divisions were discouraged. Politicians were aware that earlier sub-divisions extending back over many decades had not been put to use: in 1947, vacant land with water and electricity in the county around Sydney could have supported 250,000 more people. Thousands of residential plots with roads and services were available but still vacant, a clear cost of wasted resources. Planning controls were therefore used to limit fresh sub-divisions, along with a financial deterrent: developers were required to invest in roadworks as a condition of planning permission being granted.[15] Ultimately, however, these half-hearted attempts could not thwart the cycle in land values. For, as Max Neutze put it:

> As long as the demand for building sites remained strong, these cost increases could be recovered from the buyers of developed sites without depressing developer profits or the price they could pay for raw land. When the demand weakened in 1974 the rate of land development slackened and the price of raw land stabilised or fell.[16]

The rise in land values peaked in 1973,[17] dead on target — 18 years after it began to corrode its way through the economy. The pattern conformed to the cycles described for Britain, the USA and Japan — the inexorable upward rise in land values after the Korean war, a squeeze on the profit margins of manufacturers,[18] political scandal and the collapse of the economy after 1973 into the worst depression this century. In place of the REITs in North America and the fringe banks in the UK, the financial institution that emerged in Australia was the property trust, which originated around 1968/9.[19]

Average rents for modern air-conditioned buildings in the central area of Sydney increased by 128.5% between 1957 and 1971; for the same period, the city's consumer price index rose by 19%.[20] The rate of increase of land values accelerated in the second half of this cycle. Average industrial land prices per acre for sites in the central area, for example, were A$56,000 in 1962, rising to A$115,000 in 1967 and leaping to A$185,000 in 1972[21] — and the speculative boom continued into 1973, pushing prices further before the collapse of the economy. The Institute of Real Estate Development of NSW has estimated that the cost of residential land per acre rose by 350% in the 10 years to 1969.[22] Average real estate transactions consistently out-performed Stock Exchange shares — compounding at an average rate of 7¾%, compared to 7%.

Town planners conveniently assisted speculators by outlining the geo-graphical areas to be favoured by development. These 'corridors', radiating outward from the metropolitan centres, sharply focused the activities of the speculators.[23] Murphy has listed the benefits to landowners.[24] First, the published plans reduce the uncertainty involved in sub-dividing land for development. Second, they specify the locations where land should be bought, and by preventing sub-division outside the zoned area, buyers have an assured market — because *bona fide* developers may be forced to buy land from them. Third, existing landowners, mainly farmers, are encouraged to hold out for above-market prices, for developers have little option but to buy in their localities.

The price of land squeezed house building. The average cost of land per house rose by 161%, whereas the cost of erecting the house upon it rose by only 24%, between 1967/8 and 1971/2.[25] The percentage of land cost to the total (land and house) cost, rose, from 26% to 42.5% over this period. This contrasts with the rise of 28% in the average income of a family with one bread-winner: there can be no doubt that there was an alarming squeeze on family budgets in the pre-slump phase of the post-war Australian economy.[26]

Developers' profit margins were squeezed by the escalation in land prices and associated land development costs imposed by state authorities.[27] So there can be no doubt as to who enjoyed a rising rate of profit: established landowners whose properties had been zoned for development, and the speculator who was able to move in quickly, buy in advance of demand and sit tight until the unearned fortunes were poured into his bank account. The same trends were suffered in each of the other five state capitals, where housing costs rose faster than the sum of the other expenditure items[28] (the widening gap between the two was all the more alarming because govern-ment statistics actually understate the rate at which housing costs had risen[29]).

According to the State Planning Authority's *Sydney Region Outline Plan*, proposed increase in population of 2.75m. required an increase of 250,00 acres, yielding an increase in value to landowners of A$1,000m. by the end of the century. This prediction, coupled with the boom in land values at the time, led the government to propose a 'betterment tax' on land in the non urban area of Sydney. A 30% levy not dissimilar to those twice abandoned unworkable in the UK during the postwar years was supposed to fall on new increments in land values after January 1, 1970. The Hon. P.H. Morton, Minister for Local Government, declared when announcing the Land Development Contribution Bill:

> ...the capital gain in the value of land into which Sydney is expanding arises not from the initiative or investment of the owners of such land, but rather from the decisions taken and investments made by the community as a whole. The appreciation in the value of these lands is, therefore, in the nature of a 'windfall' gain and, in the view of the Government, a strong case has been made for a proportion of this gain to come back to the community which creates it.[30]

The 'betterment' levy was supposed to yield A$300m. by the year 2000. Although Morton confidently declared that 'We are satisfied that no better alternative exists', historical evidence in Britain suggested that *such a levy could somehow be passed on by landowners to homebuyers*, as was quickly made plain by Australian commentators.[31]

A number of official enquiries investigated the alarming increase in land values since the Second World War, but they failed to propose sufficiently drastic action to finally cure the problem. The McCarry Report, for example, described how the activities of speculators were instrumental in forcing up raw land prices and ultimately plot prices, by restricting supply and artificially inflating demand.[32] The proposals for land taxation contained in the report, however, have been assessed as 'too timid in relation to the problem'.[33]

A rate on annual unimproved land values, as suggested by the Housing Industry Association,[34] would have accomplished the government's policy objectives, provided it was a uniform rate on the value of all land. Otherwise, owners could avoid it by adopting tactics like refusing to put their land on to the market, claiming that they wanted to use it for purposes which would not realise optimal cash returns if developed for housing, and so on... until the levy was removed as unworkable.[35]

That Australia has not exploited its fiscal system to its maximum potential is a great pity. Certainly its tax authorities cannot fall back on a traditional bureaucratic excuse for inactivity — the lack of verifiable information about the consequences of change. For the decision to transform the small town of Canberra into the continent's capital afforded a rare opportunity to monitor the growth in land values and quantify the effects of land speculation. There was to be an accelerated growth of mainly public-sector activities after 1958, and a determination to retain public ownership of land within the growth area. Private development could take place only as a result of the purchase of 99-year leases.

By controlling the rate of development, the National Capital Development

Commission was able to obliterate the usual responses of urban growth: the speculative withholding of land until prices had reached an acceptably high level, the associated sprawl of construction, and the private appropriation of values created by the community.[36] By auctioning leases, the Commission was able to use the value of land to finance the infrastructural development of the city. But even without the distortions caused by speculators, the demand for the land as the scarcest factor inevitably resulted in a natural rise in values. Between 1958-9 and 1970-1, the average price of each site rose from A\$775 to A\$3,215, an average increase of 22.5% p.a. This compares with the 2.3% p.a. increase in Canberra's consumer price index for the same period.[37] The increase in land values arose through the demands of an expanding city. The authorities claimed that they did not restrict the supply of building land (the supply of sites for private housing rose from one site per 12 persons of population increase in 1958-9 to one per 5 persons of population increase in 1970-1). Thus, because the municipal authority levied its rates on the unimproved capital value of land, the community's essential services were financed annually out of a source of income which grew as a direct result of the collective efforts of all the people living in Canberra.

In the early phase of Canberra's growth, however, speculative influences did help to push up land values sharply. In 1962, therefore, the Department of the Interior introduced a new class of auction which was restricted to people building their first homes in the city. Bidding was limited to those who had not owned a house site lease for a specified period. In this way the speculator-builder was eliminated from a sizeable number of the auctions. The average price of A\$2,071 per site paid for the 618 sites sold at the restricted auctions in 1970-1 compared with the average level of about A\$3,200 per site paid for the cheaper house sites in the five largest state capital cities on the continent.[38] This difference of over A\$1,000 was largely attributable to the power of speculation.

This measure of speculative effect is a rough-and-ready one. There are two reasons why it understates the true proportions. First, the Canberra figure reflects a relatively high demand arising from determined public sector expansion. The rise in the rate of growth of land use was higher in the capital than the rate existing in the other cities arising from the natural growth of population.

Secondly, there was some evidence that the authorities *did* artificially restrict the supply of land to push up premium payments[39] (the sum over and above the figure used to determine annual rental payments). Critics argued that the public authorities operated as 'land sharks' in the old-fashioned sense of the private land monopolist to boost their revenue. Thus, prices paid at restricted auctions might have been lower but for the bureaucratic attempts to regulate supply.

TABLE 18:II

Relative Movements in Land Prices
and Average Earnings: 1969-73

		Annual percentage changes in		Number of years' earnings required to buy site
		Land Prices	Average earnings	
Sydney	1969	12	9	1.7
	1970	14	9	1.8
	1971	20	12	1.9
	1972	28	8	2.3
	1973	34	12	2.7
Melbourne	1969	8	9	1.2
	1970	2	8	1.1
	1971	20	12	1.2
	1972	22	8	1.4
	1973	46	12	1.8
Perth	1969	9	9	2.5
	1970	-3	9	2.2
	1971	7	14	2.0
	1972	21	5	2.4
	1973	22	12	2.6
Canberra	1969	4	9	0.8
	1970	-9	9	0.7
	1971	50	12	0.9
	1972	73	8	1.4
	1973	34	12	1.7
Adelaide	1969	6	8	0.7
	1970	6	9	0.6
	1971	-3	12	0.6
	1972	22	8	0.6
	1973	46	14	0.8

Source: Urban Land Prices 1968-1974; An Urban Paper, Department of Urban and Regional Development, Canberra: Australian Government Publishing Service, 1974.

A comparison of Canberra's performance with that of Sydney, Melbourne, Adelaide and Perth (Table 18:II) lays bare the contagious malaise of the speculator. There was a uniform rise in average earnings. However, marked differences are revealed in the number of years' earnings required to

buy sites. Although this factor doubled in Canberra, from 0.8 in 1969 to 1.
in 1973, the latter figure still lagged behind Melbourne (1.8), Perth (2.0
and Sydney (2.7). The brakes on consumption and investment, th
cumulative effects of tens of thousands of household decisions all influence
by the downturn in spending power, were evidently slammed on hard
outside Canberra, in the cities where public policy failed to minimise th
acquisitive functions of the land speculator.[40]

The striking exception was Adelaide, and the explanation for this has to b
sought in the origins of the state of South Australia.[41] In the early decades o
this century, the South Australia Housing Trust rapidly emerged as th
largest land developer in the state. It built up land banks well in advance o
demand, in a conscious effort to eliminate the shrewd dealings of speculato
who tried to anticipate the trust's development plans. For these plans caused
rise in the value of land — and adjoining tracts — favoured with developmen
According to Alex Ramsey, the trust's general manager, it was not wholl
successful: 'No matter how far ahead we bought, we always bought bac
some of the unearned increment because there would be some speculato
who had bought right beyond that need'.[42]

Because the trust was able to supply a large part of the needs of the lan
market, however, the cost of land in Adelaide remained low. The speculato
had been all but beaten, and he did not like it. This was why, when Goug
Whitlam's Labour Party assumed governmental power in 1972, the spe
ulators succeeded in persuading the 'socialist' politicians that the trust ough
to be compelled to reduce its share of the housing market (which had, in fac
markedly declined in favour of private developers). Successful lobbyin
permitted 'most land and building prices to drift upwards, as the lobbyis
intended. Of the workers who have set up house since, many must have lo
more money to that decision than they gained from all the other policies o
that government', bitterly records Hugh Stretton, professor of history at th
University of Adelaide.[43] Partly due to the successful political pressure
Adelaide's land prices leapt by 46% in 1973, matched only by an equivaler
increase in Melbourne. That political influence culminated in a row tha
illustrates yet another mechanism for 'privatising' socially-created lan
values, and so it is worth noting in passing.

In 1973, 61 blocks of residential land were bought on the Morningto
Peninsular, about 70km south of Melbourne, by Grosvenor Nominees Pt
Ltd. This company managed a property trust for the family of Philip Lync
Australia's Treasurer.[44] The deal subsequently reaped a profit of A$74,00
there was nothing illegal in the operation, but the political row which ensue
resulted in Lynch's resignation from the Government in 1977. His mi
fortune was to be associated with two men who had succeeded in makin
handsome profits out of selling land to the Victorian Housing Commission.

public body whose task it was to erect cheap houses for low-income families.[45] A public inquiry was instituted into the VHC deals,[46] but the affair did not prevent Lynch's re-election in October 1977, or his return to Malcolm Fraser's Liberal-National Country Party coalition government.[47]

And so throughout the first century of industrial society in this vast outpost of European civilisation, the refugees from the metropolitan countries who sought a better life were betrayed by land speculation. The original philosophical foundations of Australia had promised something better. An early campaigner for social and economic justice was Sir Samuel Griffith (1845-1920), a former Prime Minister of Queensland. Born in Wales, he migrated in 1853 and retired as the first Chief Justice of the High Court of Australia in 1919. He introduced into the Queensland Parliament a Bill entitled To Declare the Natural Law relating to the Acquisition and Owner-ship of Private Property (1890). The philosophy which shaped the definitions of the economic terms embodied in that Bill were straight out of *Progress and Poverty*. It did not succeed, however — one of the earliest of a long line of honourable attempts by enlightened politicians who sought to capture the socially-created portion of wealth for the benefit of the community.

Today, politicians have to remain alert to the forces of reaction which want to shift the property tax back on to capital improvements. The failure to administer the existing tax system properly is arousing public irritation and creating electoral support for regressive change. For example, the lobby organised against the land tax in Victoria in 1977-78 (led by the Urban Development Institute of Australia) was encouraged by the introduction of 1974 valuations. Had valuations been revised annually, landowners would not have been hit so forcibly by sharp upward increments in their payments, and there would have been no public expression of dissatisfaction.

A progressive increase in the land tax would have transformed modern Australian history, and strengthened her against the storms that engulfed the industrial economies of the free world in the 1970s. The existence of speculation in the continental economy has been interpreted as proof of the ineffectiveness of the land tax *per se*.[48] But all that this demonstrates is that the authorities had failed to pitch the tax at a deterrent level and to administer it intelligently.

Higher land tax revenue would have permitted a reduction in taxes on wages and capital.[49] These, in turn, would have stimulated consumption and investment, raising domestic living standards well above their present levels. Even so, Australia would have felt a degree of economic discomfort due to her heavy dependence on exports of primary goods, but this would have been a relatively mild set-back to the vigorous process of sustained growth. She would have been well-placed to shift the pattern of investment in favour of extending the domestic manufacturing sector, thereby displacing some of th imports and ensuring a healthy balance of payments from international trad And the higher level of disposable incomes would have provided a larg domestic market for manufacturers, thereby reducing Australia's dependen on foreign trade.

As it was, Australia went through the protracted recession of the 197 and '80s, and only when she applies her tax consistently on the market valu of land, and at a uniform and deterrent rate, will she achieve the level prosperity that is on offer on the bountiful continent.

Notes

1   R. W. Archer, *Site Value Taxation in Central Business District Redevelopmen* Washington, DC: Urban Land Institute, Research Report 19, 1972. The mun cipal rate and the state land tax amounted to about 5% of annual site value Owners were compelled to put their land to its best use. The fiscal pressure w illustrated by an examination of some properties which had yet to be improve The land taxes alone absorbed between 28% and 83% of estimated gro incomes. After redevelopment, the ratio of site value taxes to gross annual incon dropped to between 8% and 13%. *Ibid.*, p. 30.

2   N. G. Butlin and H. de Meel, *Public Capital Formation in Australia*, Canberr Australian National University, 1954.

3   A. G. L. Shaw, *The Economic Development of Australia*, London: Longma Green & Co., 1944, 3rd edn., 1955, Ch. IX.

4   M. Cannon, *The Land Boomers*, Melbourne: Melbourne University Press, 196

5   L. Sandercock, *Cities for Sale*, London: Heinemann, 1976, p. 9.

6   N. G. Butlin, *Investment in Australian Economic Development 1861-190* London: Cambridge University Press, 1964, p. 213.

7   R. Silberberg, 'Rates of Return on Melbourne Land Investment, 1880-92', *T Economic Record*, 1975, p. 208, Table II. The upward trend in the rate of retu on investment in land flowed against the general tide of prices: the Melbour wholesale price index indicates that the general price level fell during t 1880s. *Ibid.*, p. 204, n. 4.

8   R. Silberberg, 'Institutional Investors in the Real Estate Mortgage Market Victoria in the 1880s', *Australian Econ. His. Rev.*, Vol. 18, 197 p. 165, Table 1.

9   Quoted by Silberberg, *ibid.*, p. 209.

10 For a critical account of George's influence on Australia, see J. M. Garlan *Economic Aspects of Australian Land Taxation*, Melbourne: Melbourne Universi Press, 1934, pp. 24-29.

11 For resumé of early legislation, see M. Hirsch, *Land Value Taxation in Practi* Melbourne: Renwick, Price, Nuttall, 1910.

12 Garland, *op. cit.*, pp. 182-4.

13 P. F. Parry and C. W. Guille, 'The Australian Business Cycle and Internatior Cyclical Linkages, 1959-1974', *The Economic Record*, 1976.

14 M. Neutze, *Urban Development in Australia*, London: George Allen & Unwin, 1977, p. 162.
15 *Ibid.*, p. 210.
16 *Ibid.*, p. 211.
17 *Ibid.*, p. 158, Figure 6.5.
18 C. Clark, 'Inflation and Declining Profits', *Lloyds Bank Review*, No. 114, 1974.
19 D. G. Murphy, *Economic Aspects of Residential Subdivisions*, Canberra: Australian Institute of Urban Studies, 1973, p. 15. The distinctive financial-cum-property developing institution which developed in France was the *Sicomis*, which was granted tax advantages which enabled them to attract funds for developments — and sub-let to industrial tenants who had a right to eventual purchase of the property.
20 *A Memorandum of Property Investment in Australia*, Melbourne: Richard Ellis, Sallman & Seward, 1972.
21 *Ibid.*, p. 37.
22 Quoted in *Housing and the Future Shape of Sydney*, Melbourne: Housing Industry Association, 1969, p. 11.
23 *Land Taxation and Land Prices in Western Australia*, Report of the Committee Appointed by the Premier of Western Australia on the Taxation of Unimproved Land and on Land Prices, Perth, 1968, p. 26, called the Perth Metropolitan Region Planning Scheme 'a speculator's guide'. For some examples of how re-zoning boosts the sale price of land, see *Report on Land Tenures* (chairman: Justice Else-Mitchell). In one case, a site was bought in Penrith, NSW, for A$20,000 a hectare in December 1970, rezoned in October 1971, and sold in March 1972 at A$155,000 a hectare (profit: A$135,000). Planners do not 'create' values when they re-zone land. Legal restraints are a means of altering (for better or worse) the pattern of land use. This results in prices being artificially distorted (in some cases boosting the value of land which would otherwise have been avoided as unsuitable for use). When land is re-zoned prices adjust to their latent levels.
24 *Op. cit.*, p. 2.
25 A. S. Tyler, *The Price of Land*, The Institute of Real Estate Development, 1973, p. 12. The price of house sites 10-15 miles from Sydney's centre rose from between A$2,900-5,000 in November 1964 to A$12,000-30,000 in September 1972. R. W. Archer, *The Rising Price of Land for New Housing*, Canberra: Metropolitan Research Trust, 1972, Table 1, quoting *Housing in Australia*, Commonwealth Savings/Trading Bank, London.
26 *A Study of Land Costs in Australia*, Melbourne: Housing Industry Association, 1971, p. 8.
27 Tyler, *op. cit.*, p. 19, and *A Study of Land Costs in Australia, op. cit.*, p. 2.
28 Commonwealth Bureau of Census and Statistics, *Consumer Price Index*, March 1973.
29 G. M. Neutze, 'The Cost of Housing', *The Economic Record*, 1972.
30 Quoted in *Housing and the Future Shape of Sydney, op. cit.*, p. 14.
31 See, e.g. J. Pullen, 'The NSW Land Development Contribution Act 1970', *Royal Australian Planning Institute Journal*, January 1971, and Tyler *op. cit.*, p. 9. In fact, the levy is not 'passed on'. What happens is that owners side-step the levy by not selling. This shrinks the supply of developable land, which consequently increases prices. These increases are assumed to be equivalent to the 'betterment' levy. The net result is that the land monopolist is not worse off.
32 *Land Taxation and Land Prices in Western Australia, op. cit.*

33   A. R. Hutchinson, *Land Rent as Public Revenue in Australia*, London : Land
     Liberty Press, n.d. [1968], p. 26.

34   *Housing and the Future Shape of Sydney, op. cit.*, p. 15.

35   The Land Development Contribution Act, with its 30% betterment levy, h
     predictably been allowed to lapse on the grounds of its ineffectiveness.

36   R. W. Archer, 'The Public Land and Leasehold System in Canberra, Australi
     The American Journal of Economics and Sociology, Vol. 36, 1977.

37   *Ibid.*, pp. 356, Table 1, and 362, Table 3B.

38   *Seventh Annual Report of the Secretary, Dept., of Housing, 1970-71*, Canber
     1971, p. 7.

39   F. Brennan, *Canberra in Crisis*, Canberra: Dalton Publishing Co., 1971, pp. 1€
     66, who provides the best historical account of the origins of the Canberra la
     tenure system.

40   We do not claim that the Canberra solution to the private acquisition of public
     created values is an equitable one. For example, the abolition of the annu
     land rent charge was explained in a Department of the Interior pamphlet *Yc
     Crown Lease in the Seventies* (quoted by Archer, *The Rising Price of Land for N*
     Housing, op. cit., p. 366) in the following terms : 'Rapid rises in land values ov
     the past few years have created anomalies in land charges paid by Canber
     leaseholders. People with similar blocks in similar locations have been payi
     widely different annual land rents. When land rent was reviewed in ea
     twentieth year of the lease, payments often increased many times over'.

41   R. J. Roddewig 'Australia: Land Banking as an Emerging Policy', in N.
     Roberts, editor : *The Government Land Developers*, Toronto : Lexington Boo
     1977, pp. 130-35.

42   Quoted by Roddewig, *ibid*, p. 132.

43   H. Stretton, *Ideas for Australian Cities*, Melbourne : Georgian House, 2nd edi
     1975, p. 177.

44   'The Lynch Affair', *The National Times*, Sydney, Nov. 21-26, 1977.

45   For an account of one transaction involving the VHC, which was obliged to p
     urban prices for a tract of rural land in the Latrobe Valley, see Sandercock, *o*
     cit., 236-7.

46   *Report of the Board of Inquiry into Certain Land Purchases by the Housing Con*
     mission and Questions Arising Therefrom, Victoria, 1978.

47   Under questioning during the election campaign Prime Minister Malcolm Fras
     admitted that his family, too, had a trust, but that it existed to keep proper
     in the family, and not as a tax-avoidance device. *Daily Telegraph*, Londo
     24.11.77.

48   R. O. Harvey and W. A. V. Clark, 'Controlling Urban Growth : The New Ze
     land and Australian Experiment', in R. B. Andrews, editor : *Urban Land U*
     Policy : The Central City, New York : The Free Press, 1972, p. 245.

49   For a discussion on the amount of revenue to be raised under a full land tax
     Australia, see Chapter 15.

THE POVERTY OF POLITICS

19

1974-1978: Operation Lifeboat

The Bank of England lent credence to the fashionable idea that Arab oil price increases were responsible for the recession that struck the world economy in 1980. Along with the Organisation for Economic Cooperation and Development,[1] it noted how low industrial profits had 'recovered only modestly from the very low level to which it sank after the 1973-4 "oil crisis"', and that cost pressures on industry — and particularly the rapid rise in oil prices — had squeezed the finances of industry.[2]

The reasoning that led to the wrong conclusion on such a vital issue may be excusable in journalistic writings, which require drama to flavour the harsh facts, but it is indefensible in what purports to be serious economic analysis. The Bank did not intend to mislead; but without knowing it, the Old Lady of Threadneedle Street *did* have something to conceal. For, along with others, she had directly contributed to a configuration of forces that prevented the British economy from recovering, and thereby helped to transform what would otherwise have been a short and sharp recession into an unnecessarily prolonged economic disaster spanning the decade and reaching into the 1980s.

A similar misdiagnosis of the problem in Washington led ultimately to policies that distorted the US economy. The orthodox perceptions of the problem by the politicians and their advisors misled them on the nature of the difficulties confronting consumers and entrepreneurs.

On January 30, 1980, President Jimmy Carter submitted his Economic Report to Congress, in which he declared that Britain and the US would be the only important Western economies to plunge into recession during the following 12 months. Blame for Britain's sharp decline was attributed to the tight financial policy pursued by Prime Minister Margaret Thatcher. The report declared:

> The UK's fall in output does not derive principally from the rise in oil prices but from the very sharp shift towards restrictive monetary and fiscal policies instituted by the new government.

There are problems with this analysis. For the UK economy started its downward slide before Mrs Thatcher came to power; her disciplined monetary policy did not *cause* the recession. The Thatcher strategy was to reduce the rate of inflation, not deal with low productivity and unemployment. In any event, by the end of 1980 the financial authorities on both sides of the Atlantic were forced to concede that their attempts to restrict the growth in the money supply to target levels had failed.[3] The recession, therefore, could not be blamed on tight monetary policy.

The turning point in Western economic fortunes was 1978, the year in which, in Britain, all the outward signs pointed to a hopeful recovery. Average earnings remained stable through to late 1979, and the Treasury's index of unit labour costs (the measure used to gauge the relative international competitiveness of British labour) remained constant around 94.0 throughout 1978, not rising significantly until the spring of 1979 (second quarter: 110.9).[4] Interest rates were also tolerable; they had not taken off to the record heights achieved in 1980. Yet the foundations of the economy began to buckle under some apparently irresistible strain. Why?

Before looking at the facts, we need to recall the theory of the 18-year cycle in land values. In previous structural recessions, land values collapsed heavily. This facilitated the subsequent recovery, by readjusting the distribution of income among the factors of production. Rental payments were reduced to a level consistent with the true economic surplus of the economy, and there was little point in speculating in the selling price of land unless one were willing to tie up funds for 10 to 15 years. As a result, investors were attracted by the increased yields accruing to capital: this led to fresh investment, new jobs, and the engine of economic growth restarted itself, with the cycle in land values beginning at the low point and making its way back to a peak 18 years later.

This time, however, something unique happened. Following the 1973/74 collapse at the end of the previous cycle, land values recovered rapidly reaching their 1973 speculative peaks within five years *and during a period of on-going recession*. So the shake-out which is the usual prelude to fresh economic growth was stopped dead in its tracks. The evidence on the distribution of wealth and national income endorses this explanation, viewed in terms of yields from assets, capital values and the distribution of the national product.

Initially, rents and land values declined in all sectors — agriculture, retail, industrial and residential. This facilitated the process of setting up new industries and expanding commerce. Employees were left with larger net disposable incomes, which meant that the consumer market could expand.

Then, industrial profitability started to recover on a world-wide basis. In Britain, profit shares (see Table 9:IV, page 126) rose from 10% in 19 to 19% in 1977; net rates of return rose from 3.5% to 8% in the same period. *The industrial economies were set on a new course of sustained growth which, on the basis of historical experience, ought to have continued for 18 years.* Something went wrong, however, and this new lease of economic life was suddenly stillborn: the economy returned to the recession from which it was never effectively released.

OPEC was quickly singled out as the 'fall guy', but this interpretation is implausible on *timing*. Oil producers grew increasingly angry when they saw Western oil companies boosting their profits by selling crude oil on the Amsterdam spot market at rates much higher than they had bought it for. By November 1979, the official price for Arabian light oil (the grade used as a reference for price fixing by OPEC) was still $18 a barrel, when large volumes were sold on the spot market for $40-50 a barrel to buyers who evidently considered that consumers were willing and able to pay much more than the rates determined by OPEC. So official OPEC prices were pushed up. But the rise did not begin until the second quarter of 1979. In fact, since the major price rises early in 1974, the cost of oil in relation to manufactured goods had declined. From 1976 onwards, UK consumers were paying *less* for crude oil, in real terms. Allowing for a three-month time-lag before the rises fed through into higher prices in the shops, the impact of the new oil price rises would not have been felt until the third quarter of 1979. Yet the profitability of UK companies peaked one year earlier, in the third quarter of 1978, and then started sliding rapidly. Over the 12 months from mid-'78, the real pre-tax rate of return on net trading assets fell from 5.9% to 4.1%[5] — sliding on down to the 3% level achieved in the trough of the 1975 slump. Gross domestic fixed capital formation fell in the last quarter of 1978. Companies sank into the red to the tune of £2.5bn. in the first half of 1979, which the Bank of England considered to be a possible under-estimate.[6]

As in 1973/4, therefore, OPEC can be absolved from playing anything but a secondary role in recession. Its influence through the price level began *after* the grand slide into the trough.

The economic downturn that began in late 1978 was blamed by the Treasury on 'bad weather and industrial disputes',[7] an explanation that neatly accommodated the twin British pastimes of blaming the natural elements and trade unions for all the country's problems. This assessment, however, was as reliable as the daily weather forecast in a temperate climate. We have to seek our answer in more fundamental economic analysis, not least because the consumer confidence that affects profits in the High Streets began spiralling downwards earlier in 1978.[8]

A starting point for our investigation is to consider the level of rents and and values at the end of the last cycle. These, as can be seen from Table 19:I, made an unprecedented recovery. After sliding through what transpired to be

TABLE 19:I

Recovery of the UK Land Market, 1972–1979

Housing

	Land: price per plot[1] 1975 = 100	House-price/earnings ratio[2] 1975 = 100
1972	94	—
1973	146	4.11
1974	145	3.47
1975	100	3.17
1976	100	3.08
1977	106	3.04
1978 1st half	118	3.39
2nd half	142	
1979 1st half	168	3.74*
2nd half	202	

Commercial rents[3] (1965 = 100)

	Shop	Office	Industrial
1972	150	155	116
1973	178	123	135
1974	180	217	152
1975	152	171	138
1976	142	143	131
May '77	131	124	123
Nov. '77	136	123	124
May '78	145	126	123
Nov. '78	156	128	126
May '79	165	130	132
Nov. '79	163	125	130

Agriculture[4] England (1973 = 100)

	1978	1979
Jan.	131	199
Feb.	132	205
Mar.	137	212
Apr.	142	205
May	144	208
June	149	213
July	157	213
Aug.	160	214
Sept.	165	216
Oct.	167	220
Nov.	177	221
Dec.	192	222

* Estimated

1 Dept. of the Environment
2 Housing Trends: Fourth Quarter 1979, London: Nationwide Building Society.
3 Investors Chronicle / Hillier Parker Rent Index, No. 5, Nov. 1979. Adjusted for inflation.

a shallow trough (1975-6), they recovered with breath-taking speed: and *they reached the historically high 1973-4 levels within two years, i.e., in the second half of 1978.*

The recovery in the price of a plot of land for house building in the second half of 1978 to the speculatively high 1973 level was disastrous. It arrested the decline in the houseprice/earnings ratio. What happened in the following 12 months was quantified by Tom Baron, a former advisor on housing to the Conservative Party and Chairman of Christian Salvesen Properties. House buyers paid out over £1 bn. more than they would have done had the flow of land onto the market been responsive to the needs of consumers.[9] Compared with 1970, every new house cost £2,000 more than it ought to because land values had been forced up by the scarcity of building plots. About 350,000 first-time purchasers were affected, paying an average of £1,600 more than they need have done. About 575,000 owners moving to their second homes gained from the increased price of their first houses, but even so they paid an average of £800 more than they would have done if there had been no artificial land shortage. Thus, a staggering slice of consumer power was shifted away from shops. Retailers in turn, cut back their purchases from the factories. Entrepreneurs, finding themselves with growing stockpiles in the warehouses, cut back on their investment programmes — all at the expense of the level of employment.

The artificially-inflated house prices, however, did not benefit the construction firms and their craftsmen. Wage-earners found it increasingly difficult to buy homes at the ruling prices. So from 1978, fewer private-sector houses were built. The importance of the construction sector in the national economy has already been stressed. In Britain in the late 1970s it was the largest industry whether measured in manpower or output. Apart from the 1.25m. directly employed in the industry, hundreds of thousands more were indirectly involved through the production of materials, equipment or services. In output, construction represented about 11% of GNP. So a deterioration in the well-being of this one sector — over 300,000 construction workers were unemployed in 1981 — had a deep-seated influence on the rest of the economy.

Commercial rents also recovered remarkably well. Office rents, especially in London and the south-east, exceeded the previous peak levels in current prices, while shop and industrial rents matched the 1973 levels. The figures, however, do not give the full picture for industry and commerce. For on top of the rents paid to landlords we have to take account of the effect of rates, the local property tax, on the outgoings from businesses. In the 19th century, these were both low and constant. They did not, therefore, contribute usually to the business cycle. This changed in the period following the Second World War.

Over the medium term, increases in rates (insofar as they fall on land values) are offset against rent demands in negotiations between landlords and tenants. In the short term, however — and especially within the framework of an uncompetitive land market — an accelerated increase in rates falls on the entrepreneurs who occupy the business premises. Under modern leases, rents are fixed for five years. Therefore, although rents are the major cost (there is a 60/40 ratio of rents to rates), a sudden increase in the growth of rates can in the short term impose a non-transferable burden of dangerous proportions in a time of economic instability.

In 1962, non-domestic rates as a percentage of gross trading profits (after deducting stock appreciation) were 12.8%.[10] The burden rose to 19.5% in 1973. In the face of an artificially restricted supply of land, the users of land could not fully compensate for this by negotiating down their rental payments to landlords. The collective rise in rents and rates hammered profits, resulting in the recession in 1974. Again in 1978, the recovery of profits was undermined by the rates burden combined with the rapid recovery of rental levels. Non-domestic rates as a percentage of gross trading profits in 1978 were 18.2%, rising to an estimated 27.3% in 1980. Rates on office blocks rose by an average of 26.%, well above the rate of inflation. Rates in London's office centres were about 43% of open market rents in 1980, whereas in 1973 they represented just over 20% of rent.[11]

Rates were predicted to rise by over 25% to £4.2bn. in 1980/81,[12] and while these were partly reflected in the slowdown in the rise of rental levels at the turn of the decade, the damage was already done. Profits (excluding North Sea oil activities) sank to around two to three per cent, and the rates burden (taken in conjunction with the level of rents) were isolated as a deterrent to the formation of new businesses, especially small firms.[13]

The recovery in land prices cannot be explained in terms of economic prosperity, for GNP growth rates were historically low. So what caused the artificial resuscitation? Initially, OPEC may have helped to cushion the drop in land values through its participation in the market during the early post '74 period when it enjoyed large financial surpluses. But their investments in equities, property, etc., in Britain declined to $400m. in 1977 and $100m in 1978[14] the critical year from the viewpoint of general recovery. So the major explanation for the land phenomenon must be sought in domestic policies.

What we discover is a massive effort by the authorities to buoy up the value of assets held by landowners. This action created an unwarranted optimism in the land market which thwarted the adjustments in the income distribution which were vital for long-term recovery. The land market was set to collapse by early 1974 in the way that it had traditionally done after speculative orgy. But the Bank of England, towing along the main High

Street banks, floated a £1.3bn. 'lifeboat' operation to support the fringe banks that had helped to fuel the speculation. Twenty-six fringe (or 'secondary') banks were thrown financial life-lines, and subsequently only eight of them went into liquidation. Had they all gone bust, many more property companies would have sunk with them. The market would have been flooded, and land values would have been depressed to economically realistic levels. The financial authorities were not willing to let this happen, however. They acted swiftly to provide the cash resources that were needed by the speculating institutions to satisfy creditors.

The politicians played their part, too. Harold Wilson's government spent millions of pounds of taxpayers' money on the inner cities, which inflated the expectations of landowners — both private individuals and public corporations — and encouraged the hope that land prices would rapidly recover. They did — with a vengeance!

A similar configuration of banking and political policies aimed at camouflaging the property market were at work in the USA. The Federal Reserve encouraged the banks to support the REITs, whose shaky foundations would otherwise have swallowed many more of them.

'Instead of selling at today's distressed values,' said Campbell in an address to the Economic Society of South Florida on December 8th, 1975, 'REITs tend to hold on to the problem assets until "true value" asserts itself. So both banks lending agreements and REIT psychology is preventing the diffusion of these problem loans through the economy.'[15] Campbell estimated that in 1976 there were over 80,000 'distressed' condominium units in the hands of REITs alone, and that they were overpriced by about 25% in the market as it existed in its post-boom condition. But because of the support from the banks, they were able to hold out for the prices which they had set during the heady days of the boom.

The banks that were forced to repossess properties sold some of these off in the market. 'If they were suddenly dumped onto the market en masse, they would push a reeling real estate industry into complete disaster,' noted Thomas. So, cannily, 'the business of unloading and buying distressed properties is being conducted in the most discreet way possible.'[16]

Washington felt obliged to make its contribution. In 1976, the politicians stepped in with their Tax Reform Act, which made REITs attractive as tax shelters.[17] This drew money into what should have been a depressed property market — money which would otherwise have been spent on capital goods or consumer products.

Policies with a similar logic but with local variations contributed to the recovery of landowners' income all over the Western world. In France, for example, the government decided to de-control housing rents in 1978; rents doubled and tripled. In Australia, the slump in land values in 1974 was mitigated when government funds available for land acquisition and development were raised in 1975/6 to A$130m.[18]

This global rescue operation amounted to the public being forced to underwrite the risks of the losses that might have been incurred by land speculators. The rapid revival in values brought unexpected fortunes. And it was not just the bare surface of sites that were sold. In New York, property owners sold the air space above relatively low-rise buildings to their neighbours for large sums. Tiffany's, famous as a store selling luxury goods, sold its 'air rights' over its 10-storey building in Fifth Avenue to a property developer who wanted to build a skyscraper on an adjoining site. Tiffany's transferred its rights to build into air space for $5m., a get-rich-quick technique that became popular in the late 1970s.[19] In July 1980, Pan Am agreed to sell its 59-storey building in New York for about $400m., the largest real estate deal for a single building in recorded history. At the same time, in London, British Petroleum clinched another record deal by agreeing to pay £93m. for a property in the City, which on a per-square-foot basis was even greater than the Pan Am deal.

But if the politicians and bankers wrote out the insurance policies that protected the speculators, the premiums were paid by consumers and industrialists in the form of reduced spending power and fewer jobs. The detailed elements of the crisis were visible for anyone to perceive, as a closer look at the UK economy will demonstrate.

Consumers found that, by 1978, instead of being able to expand consumption, their household budgets were hit by having to spend a growing proportion on mortgage repayments and rent. House prices rose twice as fast as consumer prices, and out-paced the increase in personal disposable incomes. The consumer market contracted.

As early as January 1978, housebuilders identified the shortage of reasonably priced land as the major constraint on output. By April, 87% of the firms surveyed by The House-Builders Federation placed this problem at the top of their list, far out-stripping difficulties posed by labour shortages and planning obstacles.[20] The Department of the Environment continued to insist that, based on a study of land with planning permission, land was in ample supply. But an official study of land availability in Greater Manchester revealed that, of the 27,500 plots originally thought to be available over three-year period, only 17,200 (62%) could in fact be developed. And one of the obstacles to achieving the rate of output to which the builders aspired was identified by their Federation in these terms:

Ownership problems reduce production, particularly in areas of shortage which experience rapidly rising land prices. Land owners have n incentive to sell quickly, and developers tend to eke out land stocks when replacements are uncertain.[21]

The estimates of plots of land with planning permission for housing owned by builders stood at about 336,000 in 1977. The stocks slumped to 290,000 (1978), 286,000 (1979) and about 220,000 in the first half of 1980.[22]

Business was good for the speculators, however, and industrial land was one of their targets. For example, attempts to revive Britain's inner cities with expanded output and improved living conditions was proving a failure: firms still wanted to move out. This afforded opportunities to speculators, who were willing to pay well over £300,000 an acre, and in some cases close to £400,000 an acre, for prime locations. 'This reflects an institutional and developer orientated interpretation of the demand from companies within the Inner Cities, wishing to relocate', reported a firm of surveyors and valuers. 'It is widely assumed that these companies are now prepared to stomach higher rentals than those which were traditionally charged.'[23]

For companies which found their profits diminishing, and employees who faced the threat of unemployment, the prospects were not so rosy. Official indicators failed to give early warning of what was happening, which is not surprising since they failed to take account of the dominant variable: land values. Thus in Washington, the policy-makers failed to take remedial action in time precisely because they did not know what was happening under their feet.

In September 1979 an economist at the Commerce Department admitted that Washington's index of leading economic indicators had to be used with caution. He said: 'The leading indicators index underwent its baptism of fire this year. It didn't give us a real good indication we were sliding into a recession... We got fooled.'[24] Throughout 1978 the index predicted continuing economic activity, effectively disguising the underlying adjustments which were portents of troubled times to come. During the year, the number of bankruptcies — which had steadily declined over the previous two years — started an upward climb on the graph. Faced with enormous increases in land prices, the house-building industry slowed down its rate of production before collapsing early in 1979. The speculators, however, were not deterred, and there was no shortage of advice for prospective dealers of a do-it-yourself sort.[25]

Consumption continued at a high level, but this was in part attributed to the willingness of income-earners to raise billions of dollars by borrowing against the increased value of their properties: home mortgage increases rose from an annual rate of $20-25bn. in the early 1970s to over $100bn. by the end of the decade.[26]

But while purchases of durable goods for the home continued to rise in

1979, consumption of non-durables, and cars, started their downward spiral. It was not until the second half of 1979 that the smoke signals went up. The *Wall Street Journal*, noting the decline in corporate income, asked: 'How are the gaps in saving and investment going to be filled so that economic growth can continue?'[27] *Business Week* headlined its analysis (September 19, 1979): 'An eerie resemblance to 1974'.

The anxieties that emerged in mid-'79 were not shared in California, where the State's business and political leaders believed that they were sheltered from the storm clouds which were passing by. The buoyant real estate market fostered the feeling that the sun would continue to shine through. But land values bore no relation to real economic growth. Productivity grew at a pitiful 1.1% p.a. between 1973-78. 'Most Californians reinvest their housing profits in more real estate, adding to the price spiral,' reported the *Wall Street Journal*. 'But coming up with a down payment is just half the problem. Meeting monthly payments has also become a struggle, with home prices so high and interest rates often at more than 11%.'[28]

The 1976 Tax Reform Act had increased the attractions of real estate as a tax shelter, and money poured into this sector of the Californian economy from people anxious to reduce tax liabilities and concurrently stake a claim to a future fortune.

Where criticisms were levelled at land speculation these were directed at a convenient target: the foreigners.[29] The continuing slide in the value of the dollar did give foreign buyers a bidding edge over American land speculators. It is also true that they were dislocating the economy. In Los Angeles, for example, some locally owned businesses in the downtown area were being shut down by 'skyrocketing lease rentals and land costs'.[30] But land speculation and artificially inflated land prices, if they have the ability to disrupt an economy, will do so irrespective of the nationality of the person whose name goes down on the contracts. California did not escape the recession as was augured by the drop in construction from July 1979. Observers drew the connection between rising land costs, escalating prices of houses, and the cut back in the rate at which poorly-housed people could secure decent homes. But as ever, the blame was shifted away from the true causes, and onto convenient whipping boys like 'Government red tape'.[31]

In Britain, the danger signals were not flared until the meeting of the National Economic Development Council in August 1979. Sir Keith Joseph, the Secretary of State for Industry, submitted a departmental paper warning of the low rate of profitability. This document claimed that 'it is impossible to demonstrate beyond any doubt the causes of the UK's declining profitability',[32] although Sir Keith himself had little personal doubt as to the causes of the problem. Three days earlier, in a radio interview, he listed six 'poisons' and principal among these were a politicised trade union movement and the state institutions that had emerged to ameliorate the condition of the working class.[33]

While people began to brace themselves for an increase in unemployment, asset-holders were busily switching into land. Firms that needed to increase investment — and therefore productivity — were rapidly starved of funds. This was quickly recognised: the warning came from the Bank of England,[34] the NEDC[35] and data released by the Central Statistical Office.[36]

The Confederation of British Industry accurately predicted a downturn in the real rate of return to 3%, with the concomitant depressing effect on investment and the creation of new jobs.[37] But the purchasers of industrial and warehouse sites were not so pessimistic about their prospects. It paid to invest in the soil under the factory rather than in the machines upon it. For gross trading profits of industrial and commercial companies (after deducting stock appreciation) was down £261m. in the first quarter of 1979 compared with the same period in the previous year, whereas rent and non-trading income was calculated by the Treasury to have risen by £230m.[38] Thus, investors who accepted the recommendations given by advisors in the property world and switched to land,[39] helped to buoy up prices at levels which were unrealistic within the framework of a depressed economy.

One of the heaviest class of borrowers was the farming sector, whose indebtedness rose to £2.5bn. by August 1979. The money went mainly into the purchase of land, the rapidly rising value of which proved an attractive security to the banks. This indebtedness was then used by the agricultural lobby to press for further tax concessions. Their case was exposed by Alister Sutherland, the director of economic studies at Trinity College, Cambridge.

> In agriculture the increase in the already high capital intensity reflects the *increased* earning capacity of each acre; and the fact that the *same* net profit in total can now be achieved on fewer acres. Contrary to what happens in other industries, a low yield happens in agriculture because the net income (rent) prospects are high, and *not* because the replacement cost of man-made machinery is high relative to the profit that can then be earned by using that machinery. That is, far from any increase in the capital intensity of agriculture reflecting a struggle to maintain competitiveness against new production employing capital intensive techniques in other countries, the increase in the capital intensity in agriculture reflects the increase in protection given by the EEC agricultural arrangements, and by the tax advantages that flow from owning land. Consequently the 'low yield on assets' does *not* mean that the agricultural industry is hard pressed for cash. On the contrary, *it is just because the expected profit stream has risen (in relation to itself, but not of course as a percentage of 'capital')* that the yield is low.[40]

Sutherland challenged the conventional wisdom that agriculture was heavily in debt, and he pointed out that the returns to tenant capital — i.e. non-land assets — were not low. With remorseless logic, he pressed his case home to its conclusion:

> Thus in effect the UK consumer is being asked both to pay higher prices for food, and so, even allowing for farming cost increases, to generate higher farm profits: and then he is asked to release the farmer from the standard capital transfer tax consequences of the increases in farmer wealth that follow from those higher food prices.[41]

Sutherland's comments were in a report to the Northfield Committee of which he was an official adviser. The report was attacked by the National Farmers' Union and the Country Landowners Association, and it was not published as an appendix to the final document which was submitted to Parliament by the Committee.

In October 1979 the Wall Street stock market panicked, reviving memories of the great 1929 crash just 50 years earlier. The beginning of 1980 saw the world's industrial production at a zero rate of growth. The price of gold rocketed to unbelievable heights, and people queued up outside goldsmiths shops in London's Hatton Garden to sell off their rings and heirlooms.

How the economies fare will depend on a variety of factors. Will governments and the banking system allow land values and rents to decline to realistic levels? What will happen to the revived cash surpluses (estimated to be around $100bn. in 1980) held by OPEC countries? Will they flow rapidly into Western real estate, sympathetically reinforcing official policies in favour of land speculators? Whatever the answers, the politicians and institutions that influence the course of Western economic activity can be indicted for collaborating with the speculators to turn the 1970s into a repeat performance of the 1930s, that erea of economic horror that was supposed to have been eternally banished by Keynesian demand management.

But were the policy-makers the tools of the land monopolists? Culpability is supposed to depend on a conscious affirmation of the consequences of the decisions that are taken. A case study will help us to evaluate the process of policy formation, and it is to this that we now turn.

Notes

1 *Economic Outlook*, Paris: OECD, July 1979, pp. 8-9.
2 Bank of England Quarterly Bulletin, Vol. 19, No. 3, Sept. 1979, pp. 256-7.
3 The Conservative Government's monetarism is critically evaluated in *Monetary Policy*, Third Report from the House of Commons Treasury and Civil Service Committee, London: HMSO, 1981.

Hansard, 3.7.80, col 676.

Bank of England Quarterly Bulletin, Vol. 20, No. 2, June 1980, p. 191.

Ibid., Vol. 19, No. 4, Dec. 1979, p. 366.

Economic Progress Report Supplement, Dec. 1979, London: HM Treasury.

D. Churchill, 'Growing mood of optimism', *Financial Times*, 19.8.80.

T. Stevens, 'Planning cost for house buyers', *Estates Gazette*, 20.9.80, quoting
T. Baron, 'Planning's biggest and least satisfied customer: Housing', mimeo.,
Town and Country Planning Summer School, Exeter, 1980.

C. D. Foster, 'The Decline of Local Government', paper delivered to Association
of Municipal Authorities' Conference, Manchester, 11.9.80, p. 32, Table 12.

Debenham Tewson and Chinnocks, 'Office Rent and Rates 1973-1980',
London, April 1980, p. 9. At the same time Sir Horace Cutler, the leader of the
Conservative-controlled Greater London Council, warned property owners
that an insistence on 'excessive' rents would kill off the 'golden goose' — the
millions of office jobs located in the capital. See M. Cassell, 'Rates burden gets
heavier', *Financial Times*, 25.4.80.

Confederation of British Industry, 'Local Government Finance and Expenditure', London, C 30 80.

Coopers & Lybrand Associates Ltd., *Report on Non-Domestic Rates with
Particular Reference to Small Firms*, London, 1980. The impact on the use of
capital of a tax on buildings was tragically illustrated in 1982, a year in which the
depression flooded the market with 168m. sq. ft. of vacant industrial floorspace
in England and Wales. Industrialists were estimated by King & Co., a leading
London estate agency, to be paying £60m. in rates on these empty premises (see
P. Finch, 'King & Co optimistic on vacancy rates', *Estate Times*, 1.10.82). Some
industrialists avoided this tax by destroying their buildings — 10m. sq. ft. of
space in the distressed Midlands alone (B. Phillips, 'Void rating lifts the roof',
The Times, 13.9.82), and the national figure was probably double this amount.
While making short-term financial sense for the individual entrepreneurs, this
fiscally-induced destruction had serious consequences for both the waste of the
existing capital stock, and the speed with which new businesses could be housed
in premises once the economy had begun to recover.

Bank of England Quarterly Bulletin, Vol. 19, No. 3, Sept. 1979, p. 276. Investments in the USA dropped from $5.3bn. (1977) to $3.1bn. (1978).

K. D. Campbell 'Issues and Interpretations', *Real Estate Review*, Vol. 6, Spring
1976, p. 10.

D. L. Thomas, *Lords of the Land, op. cit..*, p. 289. REITS adopted accounting
practices to conceal the disastrous drop in the real value of their properties. See
J. B. Levy, 'No Bargain Basement: REIT accounting Compounds the Risk for
Investors', *Barron's* 13.6.77.

T. D. Englebrecht and J. L. Kramer, 'Tax Breaks for REITs Under the Tax
Reform Act', *Real Estate Review*, Vol. 7, Spring 1977.

M. Neutze, 'Urban Land', in P. Scott, editor, *Australian Cities and Public Policy*,
Melbourne: Georgian House, 1978, p. 80, Table 5.1.

D. Lascelles, 'How Tiffany's made $5m. out of thin air', *Financial Times*, 9.7.80.

The House-Builders Federation Press Notice, 31.8.79, Table VI.

*Study of the Availability of Private House-Building Land in Greater Manchester –
1978-1981*, Vol. 1, London: DoE, n.d., p. 17.

'Private enterprise Housebuilding', London: DoE. Press Notice No. 353,
28.8.80.

23 *Report on the Industrial Property Market*, London: Grant & Partners, Ju 1979, p. 7.
24 G. Conderacci, 'Index of Leading Indicators Can Mislead, Commerce Depa ment Economists Warn', *Wall Street Journal*, 4.9.79. Some real estate investme analysts, however, *were* alarmed early in 1978, and they said so. One of these w Charles Kirkpatrick (see 'A long wait for collapse', *The Tribune*, 19.8.79) a J.W. English and G.E. Cardiff, who published their predictions in *The Comi Real Estate Crash*, New Rochelle: Arlington House, 1979.
25 See, for example, G. Nicely, *How to Reap Riches from Raw Land*, Prent Hall, 1978.
26 In 1978, aggregate US wealth came to $4.18 trillion, 51.7% of which was r estate. See 'The "Ultimate Index Fund"', *Fortune*, 3.12.79.
27 'Truth in Taxation', *Wall Street Journal*, 23.8.79.
28 V.F. Zonana, 'Basic price of $100,000 for 3-bedroom houses prevails in so areas', *Wall Street Journal*, 17.8.79. Rents and mortgage repayments were taki an increasing share of household incomes by 1978. Between 1973 and 1977 value of an owner-occupied, single family house rose 53%, whereas the inco of houseowners rose 39%. 'Value of homes rose faster than incomes of own in mid-'70s', *Wall Street Journal*, 16.8.79.
29 See, e.g. 'Buying America from overseas', *San Francisco Examiner*, 18.8.79.
30 R. Herbert, 'Downtown pulls foreign capital to L.A.', *Los Angeles Tin* 3.9.79.
31 See, e.g. J.W. Anguiano, 'Government Red Tape blamed by builders for adc costs', *Los Angeles Times*, 2.9.79.
32 Company Profitability: Memorandum by the Secretary of State for Indust NEDC (79)41, 26.7.79.
33 J. Langdon, 'Joseph lists unions among "six poisons"', *The Guardian*, 31.7.'
34 J. Elliot, 'Bank gives warning on industrial investment', *Financial Times*, 2.8.'
35 Profitability and Investment: Memorandum by the Director General, NEI (79)42, 25.7.79, p. 10.
36 Institutional Investment: First Quarter 1979, CSO(79)57, 26.7.79.
37 Profitability and Investment — The Short-term Outlook: Memorandum by President of the CBI, London: NEDC(79)43, p. 5.
38 Industrial and Commercial Companies' Appropriation Account, Londo CSO(79)56, 23.7.79, Table A, p. 5.
39 See, for example, *Property Investment Report*, London: Richard Ellis, 1979
40 'Capital Taxation and Farm Structure,' mimeo., 1979, London: MAFF libra p. 107.
41 *Ibid.*, p. 108.

20

1979: the Reagan-Thatcher Myth

Political decisions made in 1979 proved to be critical to modern economic history. The recession produced an electoral swing to the right, giving the so-called free market a last chance to prove itself. If people could be rescued from the chasm of unemployment and the social humiliation of redundancy, Western society would shift away from its flirtation with mild socialism in the form of the mixed economy and demand management. Free enterprise would be vindicated. The formulation of policies, however, did not augur well for the experiment.

In California, ex-Governor Reagan put the finishing touches to his plan to capture the primaries and win the nomination as Republican candidate in the 1980 presidential election. In the event, he overpowered the incumbent President Jimmy Carter, and moved into the White House in January 1981.

President Reagan's approach to the US slump was to cut back severely on public spending. He proposed a 30% reduction in personal income taxes, spread over three years (in 1981 this was revised down to 25% in the face of resistance from Capitol Hill), associated with budget savings of nearly $56bn. in 1982. Here was the chance to test the proposition that the capitalist free market could deliver the goods if only the politicians would stop interfering. More would be saved out of post-tax wages; this in turn would stimulate investment which would provide the formula for economic recovery. Allied with this expectation was the view that it would only work if the Federal government accepted its budget-balancing responsibilities and avoided the deficit financing that caused inflation.

Would it work? Most observers were unwilling to commit themselves. They played a wait-and-see game. The signs of failure were there to be detected, but the commentators did not know which clues to look for. They should have known that when the US finally climbed out of the trough of the recession, this would be *despite* President Reagan's efforts, and at the expense of considerable suffering among wage-earners of unemployment and reduced living standards. For Reagan's policies were not designed to free the economy from the grip of the land monopolist. This was evident at an early stage.

President Reagan did not regard land speculation as immoral. He himself had made a million out of land deals in California, and had used the law to reduce property taxes on his million-dollar 680-acre ranch down to a trifling $908 in 1979 (a fact of considerable irritation to actress Jane Fonda, who paid about seven times more on her 180-acre California property).

Politically, President Reagan wanted the support of a segment of the American population that was imbued with the 'Go West Young Man' mentality of carving up public lands for private profit. The so-called Sage-brush Rebellion that swept the country — a militant demand from the States that they should be given greater access to Federally-owned land — was sympathetically received by the President. To reinforce his attitude that the public domain was to be alienated in favour of the private sector, he appointed James Watt as his Secretary of the Interior, who favoured local control over Federal resources.

And the first major administrative decision on the use of natural resources reinforced the view that the Reagan policy was not designed to free the economy from the monopolists. When member countries convened at the UN in New York in March, 1981, they discovered that Washington had put a block on the Treaty of the Seas which would have confirmed that the value of mineral resources was 'the common heritage of mankind'. Proposals such as a global revenue-sharing scheme were alien to the Reagan Administration philosophy, and the US mining companies successfully lobbied the President's men into adopting the view that the treaty should be reviewed. This effectively scuppered seven years of negotiations that could have culminated in a tax on the value of minerals that would have been shared out in favour of the poor countries.

But a diagnosis would not just rely on these elements to predict that the new Administration's philosophy was a futile one. It was possible to draw upon evidence from across the Atlantic, where the same policy intentions had been carried out for nearly two years in Britain.

For when Mrs Margaret Thatcher led the Conservative Party to victory at the general election in May 1979, she was presented with the chance to use Britain as a laboratory. With a majority in the House of Commons of 43, she pushed through policies that would test the theories of free market economists. The results, as unemployment headed for 3m., exposed the fallacy that the old-style capitalism fostered by Adam Smith and his heirs was sufficient to resuscitate the depressed economy. And in July 1981 even supporters of the Reagan Administration began to feel uneasy about the Conservative strateg as they watched the TV newsreels of Britain's cities aflame as unemploye people rioted in the streets. Here was the anatomy of the looming America experience writ large, and yet the Reagan Administration failed to benefit from the lessons in time to correct its mistakes.

Mrs Thatcher was not out on an ideological limb. Her professed aim was to implement the monetary policies shaped by Prof. Milton Friedman, the doyen of a branch of economics that was known as the Chicago school. Her approach, in varying degrees, was simulated by leaders in many other industrial countries. For at their meeting under the aegis of the Organisation for Economic Cooperation and Development in June 1979, it was agreed 'that the right response to the inflationary impact of higher oil prices was non-accommodating monetary policies and tight fiscal policies'. This was to be coupled with a programme designed to persuade people to accept lower living standards, a necessary concomitant — it was argued — of the rise in oil prices.

The emphasis on lower wages dovetailed neatly with Mrs Thatcher's philosophy. Thus, when the news broke a year later, in August 1980, that over 2m. people were unemployed in Britain, the Prime Minister remained steadfast in her commitment. But she was placing more than the electoral prospects of her party at risk. For if she ultimately failed, the full force of people's bitteness would be channelled against the 'free enterprise' system that she loudly eulogised.

Unfortunately, her model of *laissez faire* did not entail a challenge to the monopoly power of landowners, the daddy of all monopolies. By failing to equalise the balance of bargaining power, a reduction in the cost of employing people merely translated into higher land values. This was no help to the entrepreneurs who wanted to create new businesses.

Mrs Thatcher promoted the myth that the market could be stimulated by reducing taxes and the size of the public sector. Her policies were doomed to failure because she did not take account of the macro-economic effects of the law of rent. Ironically, indeed, instead of promulgating fiscal policies that would increase the availability of land and reduce its price, the Government adopted a strategy that directly subverted the regeneration of the British economy. How did this happen?

Mrs Thatcher's chief in-house theoretician in this critical formative period was Sir Keith Joseph, who held the key post of Minister of Industry. He recognised that the establishment of small businesses was crucial for the revival of the flagging economy.[1] What were the problems that confronted the entrepreneurs who wished for nothing more than to be free to put their talents to good use?

Despite the recession in the late 1970s, the supply of building units to accommodate small firms fell short of the demand. Entrepreneurs were constrained from setting up their work-benches, were prevented from taking people out of the dole queues, because they could not find suitable structures in which to set up shop.[2] And yet, according to a study for the Department of Industry, the provision of such units 'offers opportunities for profitable investment by both public and private agencies'.[3]

Why, then, was this investment opportunity not exploited by developers? A study of industry in Warrington illuminates the problem. Despite 'a considerable amount of privately owned land potentially available for industrial development', the major constraint on firms that wanted to expand was the *shortage of land*.[4] Some of the vacant land was owned by statutory bodies. One of these, British Rail, wanted to sell surplus land, but it found that the Development Land Tax was an obstacle to fresh development on its holdings. This tax, a once-for-all impost on capital investment, was introduced by the Labour Government in 1975, but Mrs Thatcher's government merely reduced it from 80% to 60%. This failed to remove the obstacle to new development — at any rate, so far as British Rail was concerned.[5] And in any event, some of the land that it did sell was merely hoarded by speculators![6]

Thus, while businessmen were desperately seeking premises, many of them were thwarted by the failure of owners to provide land. Or, if the land was ostensibly available, its price was set at speculatively high levels which effectively meant that it was out of the reach of entrepreneurs.[7]

What was the Conservative Government's response? The blame was placed squarely on public sector landowners. Mrs Thatcher and her ministers did not take the view that private landowners would want to withhold land from use if it could yield an income. Holding land vacant, failing to derive an income from it, is irrational, and is not accommodated by the conventional economic theory of the perfectly competitive market in which people are viewed as profit maximisers rather than spoil-sports.

Superficial analysis suggests that the Conservative Government's attitude was plausible. An examination of the London Borough of Tower Hamlets, however, uncovers the reality. Alice Coleman, geography lecturer at King's College, London, and director of the Second Land Utilisation Survey, has characterised the creation of derelict urban land as 'Britain's biggest growth industry'.[8] In Tower Hamlets, one of the most depressed Inner London boroughs, between 500 and 600 acres of land were derelict.[9] Only 62 acres were privately owned — a small proportion indeed. But the current figure disguise the historical facts. The council, in keeping with the postwar philosophy of extending public control, purchased privately-owned vacant land which *it* then allowed to remain vacant. This land-buying programme, general throughout the country, was a key determinant in holding (or pushing) values up above the realistic levels, thereby pricing potential users out of the market.[10] Furthermore, the data on vacant sites disguised the scandal of waste. For example, inner London alone contained about 25m square feet of empty commercial premises.[11]

The Department of the Environment, under the command of Michael Heseltine, did perceive the importance of the role of land in regenerating the economy. But before this perception could be used to achieve results, three things had to be accomplished. First, the facts had to be established. Second, the supply of land had to be increased. Third, the price of land had to be reduced to levels consistent with the current earning capacity of labour and capital. The thrust of the government's policies, however, far from facilitating these objectives, actually worsened the problem to the advantage of speculators, the men whose bank balances were destroyed when the land boom collapsed in 1974, but who decided to come out of retirement in 1980. There was, in fact, a fatal ambivalence in government policy.

To obtain facts, Michael Heseltine ordered a survey of derelict land and the compilation of the data in registers. The fact gathering, however, was restricted to the public sector. From this, we could be excused for thinking that the government did not regard private land monopolists as dogs in mangers. If (as orthodox conservative philosophy postulated) they were responsive to the price mechanism, land was not arbitrarily withheld from use. If that were true, there would be no need to catalogue the quantity and location of vacant land in the private sector. Yet Whitehall circulars which sought to cajole local authorities into taking action when landowners failed to respond to the price mechanism, was a confession that the private land market was *not* effective.

The forms of action that were recommended included 'being prepared to acquire compulsorily land needed for development which an owner is unwilling to sell'.[12] These circulars, according to the Land Authority for Wales (which in 1980 found that land was being developed at an alarmingly faster rate than the increase in the supply), 'have consistently failed to engineer the release of land in areas that mattered'.[13] One enterprising builder, Barratt Developments, overcame the supply problem by paying a minimum of $12m. for the Californian-based American National Housing Corporation, which had a land bank sufficient for three years.[14] But despite the strength of sterling against the US dollar at the time, such a solution was not open to most British construction firms.

On the price of land, the government's philosophy precluded it from taking decisive action. Market pressures were supposed to adjust supply to demand. But because of the monopolistic nature of the land market, the paradoxical situation prevailed in which vacant sites — *apparently* available for use — were associated with rising prices. Rising prices, while signalling a shortfall in the supply relative to demand, do not say anything about *potential* availability. In the land market, they indicate an unwillingness of vendors to sell below speculatively high levels, which during a recession effectively means that there is no realistic attempt at reaching agreement on a transaction.

In Tower Hamlets the land potentially available for development is painfully obvious to the eye: nonetheless, 'property developers recognise that, due to the high cost of land in Tower Hamlets, private housing schemes are normally unprofitable'.[15] There was no shortage of readily-usable land in Britain in the 1970s. Over 130,000 acres were officially classified as derelict but reclaimable. In addition, 250,000 acres in towns and villages stood dormant,[16] an area equivalent to Birmingham, Derby, Glasgow, Hull, Liverpool, Manchester, Nottingham, Portsmouth and Southampton combined! This astonishing waste meant that agricultural land was being eaten up at an unwarranted rate. According to Reading University's Centre for Agricultural Strategy, up to 80% of urban land requirements to the year 2000 could be met from this idle land.[17] Government policy, however, instead of forcing this land into use (by fusing the market mechanism with fiscal policy), ultimately increased prices instead. Because of the absence of any tax liability on idle land, no rational land use strategy was pursued. As a result, about 50,000 acres of farmland were lost every year to sprawling urban centres. This represents a net loss of agricultural jobs: and by reducing the output of domestically grown food, the country's foreign currency has to be spent on importing food.

The incoherence of official policies was not due to ignorance of the Ricardian law of rent. The *mechanism* for converting income into higher rents and land values was well-understood by senior Cabinet ministers. The problem was that they did not recognise the macro-economic impact of artificially-inflated rental levels and land values. The influence of the Conservative government can be illustrated by examining the 'enterprise zones' which it created as models of how to release the energies of private enterprise.

In his 1980 budget, the Chancellor of the Exchequer, Sir Geoffrey Howe, announced the first six of twenty-two zones, each of approximately 500 acres. They would enjoy freedom from planning controls, and in particular there would be tax concessions for 10 years. Construction firms would be free from the Development Land Tax, and there would be total exemption from rates, the local property tax. Here we had a controlled experiment which removed the impediments of bureaucracy and socialist-style planning. The zones, then, would throw into sharp relief the role of the land market in the productive process.

The Prime Minister jubilantly announced that there would be a flood of applications from entrepreneurs. Estate agents warned, however, that 'if everyone flocks to these zones then rents could rise quite dramatically and the benefits of paying no rates could be lost'.[18] The anticipated rise in rents and land values, however, was not a responsive one — a rational adjustment of the supply price of land in the face of heavy demand. The rise *preceded* the stage at which the actual demand from firms for sites could be calculated. The rise the price of land, in fact, occurred on budget day — immediately the Chancellor announced the tax concessions. The sites for enterprise zones had not even been designated, at this stage. But landowners who anticipated that their sites would be selected knew that the tax concessions would be capitalised into higher values. So, in fact, the entrepreneurs who were supposed to receive a head start by benefitting from lower rents and property taxes, were to enjoy no such concessions.

Professional organisations warned the government of this effect. The Rating and Valuation Association declared: 'There is little doubt that the enterprise zones will attract speculators who will take advantage of the various allowances and grants by realising the enhanced gains before moving on to alternative fields of investment. It is suggested that the operation of the zones should be closely watched in order to prevent excessive speculative gains being made in the short term'.[19] When the threat of speculation was raised in the House of Commons, the Financial Secretary to the Treasury, Nigel Lawson, said that firms would benefit to the tune of between £25m. and £30m. in rate relief and capital allowances. Who would be the ultimate beneficiaries? Mr Lawson conceded:

> Once an area has been designated an enterprise zone, it is likely that land values will then rise. But that is not the end of the world. That is no terrible thing. It is an extraordinary suggestion that we should not rescue these areas from dereliction because land values might rise. It is almost inconceivable that they will not rise if these areas are to be rescued from dereliction.[20]

Yet unrealistically high land values were the major obstacle to new development in the run-down areas of the cities which the government said that it wished to revive. There was no shortage of voices to remind the government of that fact.[21]

New and small firms rarely own or build their premises. They rely on rented accommodation, and it was clear from the outset that they were to be denied the tax concessions which were apparently intended to bring them into existence. The subsidies that were supposed to stimulate an increase in employment were capitalised into higher land values, much to the dismay of prospective tenants.[22] Thus the barriers to the creation of new jobs were consolidated.

The government, however, far from publicly deprecating the actions of landowners, actually condoned them. Just a few days before the jobless youths of Brixton (London) and Toxteth (Liverpool) challenged authority and attacked property, a Junior Minister at the Department of Environment wrote: 'So long as the result is to bring the zones into development, increased rents seem perfectly acceptable'.[23]

But who benefitted? Economic theory informs us that, under the existing fiscal regime, the benefits accrue to the land monopolists, the very people who are strangling the productive efforts of the economy.

Well-meaning local politicians, however, taking their cue from the government's strategy, helped to compound the problems of the businessman. The West Midlands County Council, with 124,000 people out of work (9% of the workforce), decided to allocate £150,000 as cash aid for new firms. The money was to be paid in the form of a 'Rent and Rates Grants Scheme'. People who agreed to rent or buy premises in certain priority areas would receive grants of up to £2,500 over three years.[24] Landowners in the Birmingham area had to be philanthropists if they decided not to increase their rents or the selling price of their land to absorb these grants.

The politically-inspired buoyancy of land values were not only at the expense of prospective firms, however. In the enterprise zones, the local authorities were assured that the lost revenue from rates of between £5m. and £10m. would be made up out of Treasury funds. Thus, the taxpayers' burden was increased for the benefit of landowners. As this occurred at a time when the depressed economy was desperate for a revival of consumption in the High Streets, government policy was economic suicide — for consumers and producers, that is, but not for landowners.

When unemployment reached two million in August 1980, the Prime Minister had no doubt who was to blame. According to her analysis (which was sustained by her Treasury ministers' as unemployment reached for 3m. towards the end of 1981[25]), wages were too high in relation to output. This was as spurious as the argument that high wages and trade union power engineered the 1974 slump: real wages between 1970 and 1972 were on a downward trend[26] at the same time as those key adjustments — a declining house-building sector, collapse of profits and speculatively high land values — were undermining the economy. In 1978, the year that saw an end to the recovery from the recession of 1974/75, wages remained constant.[27] Yet entrepreneurial profits slumped, while rental income rose dramatically. Between 1972 and 1980, property outperformed equities and fixed-interest investments, and over the course of 1976-1980 property beat both the inflation and earnings indices.[28] Given the low yields on capital, the concept of property — when reflecting on these results — should be understood to mean land.

In the face of these trends, Mrs Thatcher's prescription was that unemployed workers ought to move to areas where job prospects were brighter. She failed to explain how workers could abandon their homes (many of them council houses with subsidised rents), and compete for high priced houses at a time when record interest rates prevailed in the mortgage market. In the US, the problem of labour mobility was solved for top executives in the big corporations: employers made the cash available to overcome the cost of switching homes.[29] This option was not available to the redundant docker of Merseyside.

Had the Chancellor of the Exchequer announced in his budget a high *ad valorem* tax on the value of all land, the situation could have been transformed: more urban land would have come onto the market, rental levels would have slumped, and entrepreneurs would have been confronted by a benign environment. Instead, however, the fiscal pressures were moved in the opposite direction, as can be seen by a decision announced in the House of Commons on May 15, 1980.

Under the General Rate Act (1967), local authorities had been given the power to levy 50% of the rate on the owner of unoccupied property after three months of vacancy. Formerly empty properties escaped the property tax entirely, even though the local services — fire and police protection, for example — were still available to the owners of the properties. In 1974, after a protracted public row over empty buildings (especially the vacant Centre Point skyscraper that dominated the corner of Oxford Street and Tottenham Court Road), the Local Government Act had removed the 50% figure and left the proportion to the discretion of individual authorities. Many local governments exercised their discretion, and increased the levy to 100%.

The deficiencies in the British rating system guaranteed that the intentions behind void rating would be thwarted. By itself, the rate burden was not heavy enough to act as a deterrent against the speculative motive. And because the tax also fell on the value of capital improvements, it could be avoided by destroying the functional value of the buildings — it certainly could not encourage the refurbishment of old structures. The Minister for Local Government, Tom King, finally announced that the 198 authorities that were using their discretionary power were to lose the right to levy rates on vacant property.[30] Rates on unoccupied properties had raised about £55m. in 1979/80, but had singularly failed — according to the Minister — to persuade owners to bring their properties back into use. Furthermore, he announced, some owners had preferred to demolish properties rather than continue to pay the rates.

There are other examples of how the government undermined its publicly-proclaimed goals. For instance, in his budget in March 1981 the Chancellor of the Exchequer, Sir Geoffrey Howe, extended the tax privileges enjoyed by agricultural landowners. Relief from the capital transfer tax which was already accorded to owner-occupied land was extended to tenanted land, a decision which enhanced the attractions of land as a haven against tax and inflation, and consequently increased its selling price. Money and entrepreneurial skills that ought to have gone into new productive machines were diverted into land, and the dole queues lengthened to a chorus about the need to erect trade barriers against Japanese imports. Passions were channelled in irrational directions because the dominant ideology distracted people from an informed appreciation of the causes of their problems. This was the intention of the vested interests that laid the foundations of the modern political state. So long as their values and analytical terms are preserved, effective remedial action is bound to be frustrated.

And so the British economy slithered into the 1980s. Housebuilders offered to lead the nation out of the recession, but the pre-condition for this strategy was the release of more land. The Director of the House-Builders Federation correctly identified the *motive* which was more important than whether the land monopolists were from the public or private sectors:

> Local authorities must sell land at realistic prices to house-builders, rather than acting like 'property speculators', if the potential private sector contribution is to be realised.[31]

London's small entrepreneurs also became aware that the supply of land was intimately linked to their fortunes. They wanted to bring into use the 30 square miles of vacant land in the capital. This, they suggested, should be done by enabling businessmen to bid at auctions for land which had been held idle by the public sector for over 10 years.[32]

But there was little prospect of the Conservative Government taking comprehensive action. For as one of the Prime Minister's closest advisers said with resignation, on the second anniversary of Mrs Thatcher's rise to power: 'She has fallen into the very trap she promised she never would. She has come under the influence of the layabouts and the landowners of the party'.[33]

In Washington, President Reagan continued to court Mrs Thatcher as his closest international ally; their political philosophy and economic ideology dovetailed perfectly, and the mounting social tensions within their two nations failed to dissuade them from their course. The US economy slumped into a recession six months after Reagan entered the White House.

But Reagonomics was not entirely to blame for the new downturn in the protracted depression: the seeds were re-sown in the mid-'70s, when official policy came to the rescue of the land speculators. A boom in house price began in 1975, as people switched money into the best of all assets: land.[3] But the profit for a few was the loss of the many. The boom in house price meant that mortgage payments increased faster than other components of th cost of living. Between 1970 and 1980, the after-tax cost of home ownershi rose by 52%, in real terms, compared with the increase in median famil incomes of 6.5%. With land values held unrealistically high, the housin market began its slide in 1979. Three years later it slumped to the lowest lev since World War II. The rise in the cost of housing struck family budge severely. There was a cut-back in consumption, and especially in th purchase of new cars. The drag on the economy promised a new recession in the early 1980s, yet the policy-makers failed to take corrective action.

And so President Reagan fought a losing battle with his election promises. As agricultural landowners signalled their gratitude for the passage of $11bn. in subsidies, poor families lost $700m. in food stamps as the President tried in vain to make sense of the Federal finances. The nation's statesmen who had grudgingly accorded the President initial support were outraged when the Budget Director, David Stockman, confessed to a journalist in the *Atlantic* magazine (December 1981), that Reagan's supply-side economics was 'essentially guesswork'. The guessing game took interest rates to record levels, successfully bankrupting many firms.

The rich financial institutions, however, were able to borrow money at interest rates below the prime level and divert the funds into land. And as the speculators braced themselves for a fresh spate of deals, the President reaffirmed his faith in the litany of the New Right. Enterprise zones would be established to demonstrate the superiority of the free market; the government would quit interfering with the private sector; welfare programmes would be pruned back. At the end of President Reagan's first year in office, unemployment touched 9.5m, the highest since the 1930s, and then crashed through the sensitive 10% barrier in September 1982.

The New Right failed before they had time to institute the reforms to which they aspired, and this was no more evident than in the fiscal goals. President Reagan was elected on a promise to balance the budget in 1984. Instead, his defence expenditures and tax cuts directed the 1982 budget to a forecasted deficit of $99bn., soaring to over $160bn. by 1984. As for Mrs Thatcher, her desire for lower taxation was interred in the new Tax and Price Index which she introduced; this revealed a progressive annual rise from the day that she assumed power in 1979, thanks to a rise in the tax burden under her stewardship.

These two political allies failed because they were unable to analyse the source of the economic problems confronting their nations. It was inevitable that their policies would be buried along with the jobs of millions of innocent employees who asked for nothing more than the opportunity to work for their daily bread. And so it is towards an appropriate programme of action that we must now turn, to consider how the global economy can be rescued from the economic debris of the 1970s.

Notes

1   D. Penfold, 'Joseph plea for small businesses', *Estates Gazette*, 5.4.80
2   Coopers & Lybrand Associates with Drivers Jonas, *Provision of Small Industrial Premises*, London: Department of Industry, 1980, p.ii, para. 8.

3   *Ibid.*, p.ii, para. 10. The report asserts the obvious: 'The provision of premises on suitable terms has undoubtedly itself had the effect of stimulating the formation of new firms and the growth of existing small firms'.

4   'Inner Warrington Industrial Survey', Warrington Borough Council: Development Services Committee, 20.5.80.

5   T. Glover, 'Break-up nearer for PO and BR assets', *Estates Gazette*, 19.7.80.

6   'Hoarders mop up rail land sales', *Land & Liberty*, July-August 1981.

7   The Town and Country Planning Association noted that 'experience has shown that suitable locations and premises are often not available in densely developed areas, or are available at prices or rents which small firms cannot afford'. 'Draft Circular on Development Control — Policy and Practice', London: Town and Country Planning Association, 17.10.80, p.5.

8   *Op. cit.*, p.14.

9   R. Nabarro and D. Richards, *Wasteland*, London Thames TV Report, n.d. (1980), p.14.

10 'Land Values and Planning in the Inner Areas', Report of a Working Party of the Royal Town Planning Institute (chairman: Prof. G. Smart), London, March 1978, p.22.

11 *Ibid.*, p.39.

12 'Land for Private Housebuilding', London: Department of the Environment, Circular 9/80. The responsibility for dealing with the failures of the private landowners were also conveniently shifted to local authorities by government advisors, e.g. Coopers & Lybrand, *op. cit.*, p.40, and *Structure and Activity of the Development Industry*, Report of the Property Advisory Group, London: HMSO, 1980, p.13, para. 4.13.

13 *South Wales housing land availability study 1980*, Cardiff: Land Authority for Wales, para. 7.32(3).

14 'Barratt'ṣ Californian venture undeterred by poor US outlook', *Estates Times*, 11.4.80.

15 Nabarro and Richards, *op. cit.*, p.25.

16 *Urban Wasteland*, Civic Trust, London, 1977.

17 *Land for Agriculture*, CAS Report 1, 1976, p.11.

18 'Property News', London: Bernard Thorpe & Partners, No. 544, 27.3.80.

19 'RVA criticises the principle of rate exemption in enterprise zones', R & VA Press Release, London, 3.6.80.

20 Debate on the Finance (No. 2) Bill, *Hansard*, 4.6.80, col. 1516. Nigel Broackes, chairman of the London Dockland Development Corporation, insisted that the increase in land values had been exaggerated; he estimated, in a letter to the *Financial Times* (14.9.81), that the increase was in the order of 50% over former prices.

21 The Town and Country Planning Association issued a memorandum noting that 'the greatest block to development comes from the way in which land is valued at an artificially high level which bears no relationship to either its current unproductive state or the amount of money which is needed merely to bring the sites up to a condition which allows construction on them'. Quoted in *Estates Gazette*, 21.6.80, p.1075.

22 C. Tighe and J. Tucker, 'Rent rises undermine spirit of enterprise, *Sunday Times* 5.7.81

23 Letter dated 25.6.81 from Lord Bellwin to Walter Goldsmith, director-general of the Institute of Directors. The government's attitude was not wholly benign

however. On Nov. 18, 1981, the Local Government Minister (Tom King) described developers who were cashing-in on the absence of the property tax as 'greedy'. Quoted in *Estates Gazette*, 28.11.81, Vol. 260, p. 864.

24 'Cash aid for new firms', Birmingham: West Midlands County Council Press Notice, 14.7.80.

25 J. Lewis, 'No crock of gold for wages, says Lawson', *The Guardian*, 13.6.81.

26 W. E. Martin, *The Economics of the Profits Crisis*, London: HMSO, 1981, p. 218, Chart 3.

27 Employers did not assign blame to 'greedy' workers for the alarming rise in unemployment. See M. Crawford and J. Fryer, 'Two million: who's really to blame?' *Sunday Times*, 31.8.80.

28 *Property Funds for Pension Schemes*, London: Metropolitan Pensions Association, 1981, p. 5.

29 A. M. Morrison, 'The Going Gets Lusher for Employees Who Move', *Fortune*, 16.6.80.

30 *Hansard*, 15.5.80, cols. 1132-3.

31 R. Humber, 'Housing Crisis Caused by Local Authority Policies, Not Public Expenditure Cuts', The House-Builders Federation, London: Press Notice A. 81.40.

32 *30 Square Miles of Waste-land*, London: National Federation of Self Employed and Small Business Ltd., 1981.

33 S. Winchester, 'You see before you a rebel', *Sunday Times*, 3.5.81.

34 The rate of return on a typical house bought in 1973 and sold in 1978 was from 12% to 21%, depending on how the calculation was made. This far out-stripped returns from bank deposits, government bonds and stocks and shares. See S. A. Seelig and J. L. Freund, 'The Homeowner's Best Investment', *Real Estate Rev.*, Vol. 11, No. 2, 1981, pp. 75-76.

21

1980s : Policies for Recovery

The third century of industrial society dawned in a world afflicted with total uncertainty. All reference points had been destroyed by the worst global recession since the 1930s. Paradoxically, the dominant economic strategy was destined to re-create, to the last detail, the devastating pre-war conditions. The Reagan-Thatcher determination to balance the budgets and burn inflation out of the system to restore the value of currencies, if successful, would re-establish the final feature of that unhappy era, in which high unemployment and poverty co-existed with a stable and even declining level of prices.

Today, as in the 1930s, there is no coherent rescue plan. Some global nightmare, such as the threat of another world war, might induce the feverish activity that would pull the great industries back into full employment, but would it be rational to wait for such an eventuality ?[1] The price would be too high, in any event, as it was when Adolf Hitler and Emperor Hirohito came to the economic rescue of the world in the 1930s and unleashed a holocaust the like of which was never before experienced by mankind.

In this chapter, we describe a humane and practical programme for economic recovery which would also ensure sustained growth beyond yet another 18-year cycle and cataclysmic collapse at the turn into the 21st century. The problem can be crystallised by considering the ways in which the level of business profits can be raised.

Profits can be raised by improving productivity, or by reducing the share paid out as wages, salaries or rental income, or some combination of these alternatives. The idea that rental income should be reduced has not been a policy option. In Britain, the government's Property Advisory Group claimed to have perceived a drop in the share of income going to land-owners,[2] but the Cabinet's policies were designed to undermine any such tendency (see Chapter 20). Policies were intended to increase productivity and reduce wages.

The 'shake-out' of 30m. people into unemployment in the OECD countries by the early 1980s did result in a small increase in productivity.[3]

But this was not expected to make any significant difference for any of the economies except the few (especially Japan and Germany) that have traditionally invested heavily in new capital and in research and development. The gains in output per manhour did not realise sufficient *additional* income for entrepreneurs to enable them to reinvest out of internal funds. Against the gains in *per capita* productivity through de-manning, however, have to be set the cost of the lost output through unemployment and the extra burden on taxpayers who were obliged to finance additional state welfare programmes.

Slight gains in productivity were also achieved through changes in work-practices which were successfully forced upon trades unions. The balance of power on the shopfloor shifted in favour of employers as the dole queues lengthened. Some employers felt confident enough to take unilateral action. Where agreements were secured, these were underpinned by the coercive threat of redundancies. Perhaps the most dramatic challenge to union power was President Reagan's dismissal of 11,500 air traffic controllers who went on strike in 1981. This effectively destroyed their union. But again, while there may have been marginal improvements in output, these were minimal short-term gains against which we would have to offset the losses that were threatened by increasingly resentful workforces, many of which can be expected to take revenge when circumstances eventually shift back in their favour.

In sum, then, profit levels and investment could not expect to benefit to any significant degree by the productivity advances that were realised in the trough of the recession. While this caused some dismay, it was not considered the only recipe for improved profits. For conventional wisdom linked profits with the movement in wages, an association which in anything but the very short term is a fallacious one. In view of the confusion even among senior economic advisors, it would be as well to re-examine some of the elementary principles of the capitalist system before proceeding to an account of our solution.

The profit motive is at the heart of the Western economy. Its function is a dual one. First, the prospect of accumulating profits generates entrepreneurial activity: it compels the businessman to consider how best to satisfy consumer preferences. Second, profits provide the funds for the re-investment that enables entrepreneurs to expand their operations. This investment financed out of internal funds expands output, holds down prices and increases employment. The pursuit of profits, then, is an honourable one, individually gratifying and socially beneficial insofar as the price mechanism correctly directs the attention of the wealth-creators towards the needs of the consuming public.

The global crisis of the 1980s is monitored by the insufficiency of profits.

Unless a formula can be devised to re-establish a growth trend in profits, unemployment will continue to rise. *A reappraisal of why profits have slumped must be at the centre of any attempt at fresh policy formation*, yet the debate is not illuminated by an appreciation of the full historical facts.

Why are profits so low? On September 24, 1981, Mrs Thatcher's chief economic advisor, Professor Terry Burns, addressed America's National Association of Business Economists in Washington DC. In his speech he made the following statement:

> The rate of return to industrial and commercial companies fell from around 8%, to 2-3%, during the 1970s. This fall in profitability has been concentrated on manufacturing. There is *no easy explanation* of why profit margins have deteriorated so badly. The *most identifiable factor appears* to be the bargaining strength of UK labour relative to employers in part deriving from the high unionised portion of the labour force, the legal privileges of UK trade unions and the vulnerability of monopoly nationised industries to high wage demands.

The power of unions, then — through their ability to increase that portion of GNP paid out in wages and salaries — was assigned the chief role in the process leading to 'a sharp fall in real rates of return upon companies'.

The statement by Prof. Burns has two phrases which have been italicized. The concession that there was 'no easy explanation' was an honest admission of ignorance. The British Government's chief economic advisor felt obliged to fall back on *appearances* in his search for an answer to the historical problem of the collapse of profits; and the 'most identifiable factor' *appeared* to be the bargaining strength of trade unions. After two centuries of refinements to the economic theories of Adam Smith, and despite at least three decades of complicated model building with the aid of computer technology, the Western world's leading politicians rely on impressionistic evidence to formulate the policies which determine the welfare of hundreds of millions of people.

The Burns impression is one that has not been substantiated. Nor can it be correct. The slump in profits struck simultaneously: market economies that are highly planned, with detailed annual agreements on the apportionment of the national product between labour and capital (e.g. Sweden); a country in which 'company' unions are noted for their collaboration with managements (Japan); countries with a union structure, the strengths of which — across the economy — are doubtful, to say the least (USA); and a country which, in the popular view at any rate, has a destructive trade union system (UK).

But the *belief* that unionised employees were responsible for the decline in profits was sufficient to enable policy-makers to propose that the value of non-property incomes should be reduced in the 1980s. This was accomplished by reducing income transfers (such as pensions and other state welfare benefits, such as food stamps in the US); by the use of intimidation in wage bargaining, backed up by the threat of redundancy; and through the covert use of inflation, which reduced the real value of wages and salaries.[4]

In the United States, the cold figures reveal the success of this configuration of policies. In 1980, over 29m. people were classified as living below the poverty line, a staggering 13% of the population and an increase of 3.2m. over 1979.[5] But it was not just the families at the lowest income levels that suffered. The median family income in 1980 was $21,020, which was 5.5% lower in real terms than the previous year. This was the largest decline since World War II, and a drop of $1,330 over the 1973 median income ($22,350).[6]

The sustained attack on the living standards of families since the collapse of 1974 was foolhardy in the extreme, for it deflated the economy. The result was a decrease in the demand for the goods and services at a time when the economy desperately needed an increase in consumption. Profits did not benefit at all. After-tax profits of non-financial corporations in the US, for example, were down to 4%, the lowest level since 1948 (except for 1974, the beginning of the recession when the rate was 2.6%). What, then, needs to be done?

The problem is to expand the opportunities for labour and capital to produce the goods and services that are demanded by consumers. To try to do so by reducing wages is absurd, for two reasons. First, this does not work. We have seen that the share of the value of national output paid in wages and salaries is constant over a long time. This remains true (averaging roughly 50% in the manufacturing sector) under varying conditions.

> That this should be so in all principal industrial countries is an impressive indication of the strength of the operative underlying economic forces in spite of the wide variety of technology, size of operation and industrial structure. In this respect, the experience of economies as different in structure and management as those of the USA and USSR, Britain and Hungary shows a remarkable similarity.[7]

Secondly, one of the major initial problems is to increase *effective* demand — the public has to have the money with which to buy new goods and services and this can be obtained by them only by prior production. The short-term effect of any kind of wage-suppressing incomes policy is to cut immediate consumption, and therefore discourage production.

The rational strategy is to reduce rents and the buying price of land in locations where firms might start up or expand; and reduce taxes on wages and interest, to stimulate new capital formation and higher productivity. This is the policy that meets the diagnosis of the world's problems by the

Organisation for Economic Co-operation and Development, the influential mouthpiece for the industrialised world:

> The reasons for the protracted deterioration in the employment situation in many countries are complex, and not fully understood. But it would seem that a range of structural factors have been important in various countries, including significant and perhaps growing inflexibility in labour and product markets, the emergence of major imbalances in the share of aggregate income, and a shift in the tax burden to employment and investment. (*Economic Outlook*, Paris: OECD, July 1982, p. 6)

Land value taxation, this one pivotal policy, has the direct effect of loosening the rigidities in the markets (by increasing opportunities and compelling competition); it changes the share of aggregate income in favour of wages (to boost consumption) and interest (to stimulate investment); and it permits a reduction in the tax burden on employees and investors. There is no one other policy for challenging the problems that confront the West in such a comprehensive way.

We present our model in the belief that the general despondency that afflicts the West — the acceptance of high unemployment and low growth rates for many years to come — is unwarranted. The impact of land value taxation is schematically illustrated in Diagram 21:I. The key assumption here is that, ultimately, taxes are at the expense of that surplus called economic rent (the value over and above the costs of labour and capital: see pp. 203-7). In the diagram, then, the returns to labour and capital are shown net of taxes, and everything above the line YD is economic rent. Government revenue derived by the current tax system is that part of the rent above the line WZ, leaving landowners the portion WYZ for their income.

The first point to notice is that the present taxation contributes directly to the artificial restriction on the amount of land made available by the owners (OB rather than OC). This happens because the aggregate rental income is reduced throughout the economy, making some land 'marginal' — that is it does not yield any rent to the owners. The reason is that the taxable capacity (AZD) of those firms which could occupy the land BC as commercially viable concerns, would be exhausted by existing taxes, leaving them unable to pay the landowners rent.

Why, then, under the prevailing tax structure, should the landowner put his holdings to use, even if unemployed labour needs it? Sites in our major cities as well as the poor agricultural land in the far-flung foothills testify to the fiscal foolishness of taxes imposed directly on labour and capital, which are then passed on in the form of higher consumer prices. Thus, the potential output denied to the economy is represented in the diagram by the

DIAGRAM 21:I
The impact of taxation on the economy

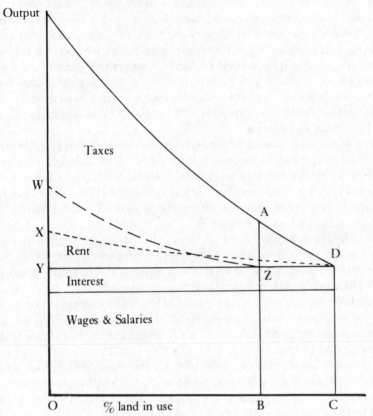

area ABCD. Lost government revenue (assuming a 100% tax on annual land values) is represented by the amount AZD.

A change to land value taxation at a rate of, say, 80% (represented on the diagram by the line XD), turns 'marginal' land (BC) into rent-yielding sites. This would result from a carrot-and-stick impact on owners. First, because they would retain 20% of the rental value of this land, they would have a reason for putting it to use. Secondly, however, because they would be obliged to pay 80% of rental income as a tax, they would be *pressured* into releasing land surplus to requirements onto the market. The overall consequence would be a restructuring of land use and values. Ultimately, towns would become more compact, and so on. In the short-term, rents in populated areas would come down and people would have an easier task when they set out to establish new enterprises. Output and consumption would rise, and unemployment would diminish. Firms which, *under the present tax system*, are not viable, would now find themselves making sufficient income to pay the ruling rates of wages, interest and rent (this is vital for firms competing in the export markets, as we shall see below), without requiring public subsidies.[8] Under competitive conditions, wage and interest rates would still be determined by their marginal products; but since the opportunities for productive employment would increase, the competition for labour and capital would rise, with a consequent beneficial effect for wages and interest.

The overall losers would be those hoarding land. Although additional land would now yield an income, a land value tax set at a deterrent level would reduce the income received by this class. In the diagram, the retained income (XYD) would be less than the former income (WYZ). But since the land owner *per se* contributes nothing to the process of wealth creation, his loss is not something to be lamented.

But the economic woes of the world cannot be conveniently cured by a few swift diagrammatic strokes on the theoretical economist's blackboard. Are we proposing a programme which is practical in *political* as well as economic terms? Democratic governments have four or five years in which to show results before they have to seek a new lease of life from the voters. How do we begin the enormous task of valuing land (minus unexhausted capital improvements upon it), and shifting taxes off labour and its products, within a tolerable period of time?

A complete transformation cannot be implemented within five years, although it might well be possible to do so through self-assessment (with suitable corrective adjustments at a later date). The change, however, could be comfortably achieved within the normal span of a two-term administration —eight to ten years. The first stage has to accomplish two tasks simultaneously: reduce unemployment, and equip the tax authorities with the capacity to value land and re-structure the fiscal system. This can be done by transforming the pay-as-you-earn tax into a corporate liability.[9] In Britain the consolidation of this employee-based income tax into a corporate impost would reduce the total number of annual assessments from 24m. to 1m. with the following advantages:

(1) Simplification of the tax records would result in smaller company wage departments; and a large army of accountants and lawyers would be released for more productive employment.

(2) Productivity would rise. Because employees would negotiate earnings on a take-home basis, the crucial connection between effort and reward

would encourage more productive work-practices, which would in turn translate into higher real earnings.

(3)   There would no longer be a need to pay earnings in the form of perks (expenses, company cars and the like) to avoid income tax. And the need for the tax-evading 'black economy' would also be eliminated, having a marked effect on public morality.

The initial influence of this strategy would be a measurable movement in output and domestic consumption, felt even before the tax burden was shifted away from the corporate sector and onto land values. The next most powerful effect, however, would be to expand exports, which are crucial for the regeneration of a sluggish economy. And countries which were quickest off the mark in transforming the tax structure would have a competitive edge over their rivals. The United States and Australia, for example, would be well placed to set the pace because — for existing property tax purposes — the value of land is already assessed separately from the value of buildings. It would therefore be a relatively simple exercise to up-date the values to current market levels, and shift the whole of the tax incidence onto land; whereas in Britain, for example, real property is assessed as a whole for tax purposes (and vacant sites are not valued at all, since they are not taxed).

That the initial edge would be enjoyed by the US, in particular, is not a bad thing. Even now, most of the weaker economies rely on a boom in the biggest of the capitalist economies for their own recovery. Those countries that then followed closely in restructuring their tax system would gain an advantage in the export markets. The truth of this can be illuminated by a look at Japanese fiscal policy.

The ratio of tax and national insurance contributions to national income in Japan in about 2% lower than in the US and over 15% less than most European countries. Personal taxes are lighter than any other major country except France. Furthermore, the share of output paid as wages to employees has been lower than in her competitor countries. (Loftus records an average ratio of wages to value added of 0.37 for 20 manufacturing industries in Japan compared with 0.49 for all countries[10].) We can derive two important lessons from this.

First, pricing. Lower gross wages translate into a competitive advantage in international trade. The legendary success of Japanese penetration into the European and North American markets bears witness to this. The Japanese success in the car markets in the 1970s was built on a ratio of wages and salaries to value added of 0.35 in the 1960s, compared with a ratio of 0.51 in the US and 0.61 in the UK.

And what of taxes? In the twenty years since the postwar cycle in land values began in 1955, individual income tax exemptions were increased in

TABLE 21:I

Economic performance and public sector finances in seven OECD countries, 1980

	Gross domestic product[1]	As percent of gross domestic product					Unemployment[2] 1982
		Gross fixed capital formation	Gross saving	Government final consumption expenditure	Current disbursements of government	Current receipts of government	
United States	-0.1	18.2	18.3	18.1	31.7	32.7	10.1
Japan	4.4	32.0	31.5	10.0	25.4	28.2	2.3
Germany	1.9	23.6	23.1	20.4	41.2	42.8	8.2
France	1.2	21.6	21.7	15.3	43.1	45.4	8.6
United Kingdom	-1.4	17.8	19.2	21.5	41.7	40.4	12.7
Italy	4.0	20.0	22.3	16.1	41.1	37.5	10.4
Canada	-0.1	23.1	21.5	19.5	37.7	37.1	12.2

1 Growth of real GDP at market prices, percentage change.
2 Percent of total labour force; data for August or September 1982.
Source: Economic Outlook, Paris: OECD, July 1982, pp. 142-153.

every year but three, individual income tax rates were reduced eleven times, and corporate tax rates were reduced six times. Supported by such a benign policy towards incomes, it is not surprising that Japanese workers were encouraged to work harder and better. Thus, a change to a policy of lower taxes would increase productivity (and therefore reduce the unit costs of labour) and decrease prices, leading to an additional competitive advantage in the world markets. An ailing car manufacturer like British Leyland, therefore, which survived into the 1980s only because hundreds of millions of pounds of taxpayers' money was poured into it (to offset the high UK taxes), would in these circumstances no longer be classified as a 'marginal' company. It would once again become an economically viable enterprise, able to meet all its costs of production without public subsidies.

The tax-effect on prices, competitiveness and employment can be appreciated by noting the findings of Hermione Parker, who revealed that in 1982 about 7.5m. people in Britain were suffering from 'tax-induced poverty'. And working from Department of Health and Social Security figures, she concluded that in almost every case the means-tested benefits payable to 1m. employees were necessary only because gross earnings were whittled away by income taxes and national insurance contributions.[11] This was a gift to Britain's competitors in the world markets, because prices had to be high enough to recover the total labour costs to employers (net wages plus employment-related taxes). And the bureaucracy was unnecessarily preoccupied with taxing away income and paying it back to the same people in the form of 'benefits'. The progressive elimination of these taxes would permit a reduction in prices (thereby raising real living standards) and a cut in the size of the bureaucracy to no-one's disappointment.

The next insight concerns land values. Since the shares received by labour and the public sector in Japan are lower than in competitor countries, we would expect a larger surplus to be captured by land monopolists. We believe this to be the case. The comparative data required to prove this is hard to come by, unfortunately.[12] Nonetheless, the thesis can be supported by facts such as the following. In the first half of the postwar cycle in land values (1956 to 1966), land prices increased by 6% in the USA, and by a staggering 19.9% in Japan.[13] As for wage earners, land as a proportion of the cost of a single family home was generally 20% to 40% in the large cities of the US; in Tokyo, in the 1970s, it reached 60% to 70% (and this was for an average plot of only 150-200 sq. metres, compared to 900 sq. metres in the US).

Japan's lower taxes and government spending (see Table 21:I), and lower wage rates, have as their reciprocal higher land values. The failure to neutralise the rent effect through land value taxation meant that Japan was vulnerable to the logic of the 18-year cycles, as we saw in Chapters 11 and 12. But although growth of the domestic economy was distorted (imagine what she would have achieved if the land monopolists had not been allowed to constrain economic activity), Japan was able to mitigate these effects through the competitive advantage that followed from her lower wages and income taxes.[14] Thus, after a decade of global recession, Japan's economy is racked by rents and land prices which would be insupportable but for her ability to out-perform her competitors. Although she has lost the overwhelming lead that she enjoyed in the 1960s and 1970s, she is still able to keep the growing rate of unemployment below the levels of her competitors. The price of doing so, however, is the worst housed workforce in the industrialised world.

So we see that a shift to lower taxes, unless it is accompanied by a simultaneous increase in a tax on land values, merely translates into riches for the land monopolists and misery for the workers. But a switch to land value taxation, in addition to neutralising the effects of land monopoly, would expand the tax base itself. This is a major consideration for a country like Japan, where a great deal of public money needs to be spent on infrastructural investments if the living environment is to be made tolerable for her citizens.

We are, then, proposing a strategy for building our way out of the recession of the 1980s in a literal sense: the house-building industry would play a central role in this programme. The relevance of this leading sector approach can be understood when we note that in the US in June 1982 the highest levels of unemployment were in construction, where it rose to 19.2%, followed by agriculture (16.3%). We presume that few people would challenge the direct dependence on land of these sectors.

But while we have seen that the house-building cycle in the past has been crucial to the trends in the economy as a whole, in 1980 there was a crude surplus of houses in the USA of about 9.6m. How can this sector hope to be the trend-setter in a 'boot-straps' approach to pulling the economy out of the slump? The answer can be documented by examining the case of the UK economy, where the construction industry developed both an acute awareness that the supply and price of land was at the heart of its problem *and* also a willingness to act as the leading sector capable of pulling the economy out of the recession. In this latter aspiration, the industry had the weight to be successful as the anchorman of the whole operation. It employs about 2m people, and accounts for 11% of Gross Domestic Product. In 1980, output was £22bn., and the value of exports was £3bn.

However, in 1980 there was also a crude surplus of nearly 1m. houses over the number of households. With a housing stock of 21.5m., then, it would be easy to make two initial assumptions. First, British families are content with the buildings in which they are housed. Second, there is little scope for expanding the activity in the building industry. Both these assumptions are false. According to an all-party committee of MPs, the measure of a 'crude housing surplus' was an unreliable guide to housing policy. It disguised the true position, as measured by the 2.2m. dwellings that, in 1976, either lacked basic amenities or were totally unfit for habitation. It also failed to take account of 'concealed households' (estimated in 1977 to be 250,000).[15]

According to Sir Peter Trench, one of the leading experts in Britain's housing industry,[16] a total of 250,000 dwellings per annum on average was the *minimum* requirement for the 1980s if people's aspirations were to be met. This was the irreducible minimum calculation of 'need'. If the economy could supply this number of new houses — as it would, if it were functioning freely — it would represent an increase in the housing stock over the decade of something like 10%. Such a massive investment would provide an increase in the quality of the household living environment, as people moved out of slums; it would stimulate the demand for skilled workers and labourers, as entrepreneurs expanded their operations; and it would have a generally beneficial effect on the economy, as labour mobility was increased in response to the supply of houses in locations where jobs could have been created but for the want of employees for hire.

In the face of the measurable need, worth a minimum of £21bn. for housing alone (at constant 1975 prices), we could have expected the building industry to respond to the challenge of the market place. Instead, however, the industry began to contract from 1978 (Table 21 : II). Why? The explanation can be summed up in one word: land.

By 1978, the price of a plot of land on which to build houses had regained the speculatively-high levels achieved in 1973.[17] A flood of reports alerted the authorities to the critical shortage of reasonably-priced land, both from official sources, charities and organisations concerned with the environment.[18] The warnings were reinforced by the housebuilders. In April 1981, 445 firms provided detailed answers to a survey which revealed that 85% of them were suffering from an acute shortage of land. Half of the builders said that their land supplies, at existing levels of production rates — the lowest since the 1920s — would last for less than one year. If, however, there was an upturn in the demand for houses, over 60% of the builders said that their land supply would last for less than one year.[19] The Federation of Master Builders issued its grim warning:

No one wants a repeat of the serious and sharp increase in prices which occurred in 1972/73. Yet that may happen if action is not taken to ensure that sufficient land is available at a reasonable price. If builders are as hard pressed for land, as shown in the survey results, they will obviously step up competition for whatever land is available in order to keep their firms in existence. This competition will intensify with any growth in demand for housing. The implication for housing costs is quite clear. On a rough average about 25% to 30% of the selling price relates directly to the cost of

TABLE 21:II
Great Britain, 1977-1981[1]

	Value of new orders obtained by contractors[2] £m.	Index: 1975 = 100	Housing completions (private: 000s)	Housing land prices per plot or per hectare 1975 = 100		Farm prices: average per acre: £		Unemployment (level in July) Millions	%
1977	6,096	94.6	140.3		106	1,022		1.5	6.6
1978	6,347	98.5	149.0		129	1,368		1.5	6.4
1979	5,681	88.1	138.1	1st half	168	1,828		1.3	5.9
1980	4,848	75.2	125.7	2nd half	202	1,904		1.8	7.7
1981 Q1	1,284	79.7	27.7	1st half	243				
Q2	1,295	80.3	25.4	2nd half	238				
Q3	1,230	76.3	29.3	1st half	247[3]	1,858	1st half	2.7	11.6

1 Data from the Department of the Environment, except for farm prices, which are derived from *Farmland Market* (and cover England and Wales only).

2 1975 constant prices, seasonally adjusted. Includes housing (excluding orders for home improvement work), and new work in public and private sectors.

3 Provisional.

the building plot on which the house stands. Any serious increase in land prices would therefore reflect heavily on the final selling price.[20]

Despite this weight of evidence, however, the government continued to believe that there was a 5-year supply of land available to builders. The main thrust of official policy — persuading public authorities to sell off surplus land to the private sector — was considered to be sufficient to meet all needs.[21] There were two defects in this policy, however. The flow of publicly-owned land into the hands of builders was at a derisorily low level,[22] wholly insufficient to meet production needs. Secondly, this was a once-for-all policy: once the authorities had released as much land as they were prepared to sell, the public sector as a source of supply would come to a dead end.

The British Government, while acknowledging the key role of the construction industry,[23] treated this sector in a cavalier fashion. It was accused by the all-party Select Committee of MPs of depriving itself of information necessary for sound decisions, and of treating public sector housing expenditure as a 'residual' item.[24]

Appeals for action from the housing industry were stone-walled. John Stanley, the Housing Minister, declared in January 1982: 'The message for the construction industry ... is that competitiveness is both the key to success and the only certain guarantee of survival'.[25] In fact, competition between builders — which is what the Minister meant — could not *begin* until the industry had wrested land from its owners: and that struggle had to take place under unequal terms, in an uncompetitive market.[26] The deprivation of reasonably-priced land prevented builders from erecting the houses that families could afford; builders were the major casualty in the 20% increase in bankruptcies heard in London's High Court in 1981.

Mrs Thatcher's government, having embarked on a monetary policy aimed at reducing inflation, was consistent in refusing to pump public funds into house-building. And in any event, such an approach would have been counter-productive. In France, for example, the socialist government of President Francois Mitterrand committed $5.85bn. to the construction sector in an attempt to reduce unemployment. The beneficiaries were the landowners, for subsidies of this size increase the attractions of land compared with other forms of assets.[27]

But the availability of *money* was not the crucial problem for the house-building industry. And nor did an increase in the supply of land depend upon the expenditure of a single penny of taxpayers' money: all that it required was the imposition of a tax on the annual value of land. The opportunity to consider such an approach was presented to Mrs Thatcher's Conservative Party when, while in opposition before the general election in 79, it committed itself to a radical review of the property tax. One of the options was to lift taxes off buildings and transfer them onto site values. Such a transformation would have been welcomed by both builders and house-purchasers, for it would have made buildings and land cheaper to buy and sell. But when the Conservative government published its Green Paper on the property tax, it did not contain one word on this policy option.[28] This silence reinforced the belief that the government, for all its rhetoric about the crucial importance of the construction industry, was unwilling to inform its policies with the facts.

Thus, the builders were helpless and the government was useless; the construction industry was *prevented* from discharging its historic role of coaxing life back into the rest of the economy on the basis of a plan that co-ordinated the industry's resources with the government's political leverage.

Sir Peter Trench, in reviewing the prospects for the industry and its customers, stated: 'If I have dwelt so long on this thorny question of land it is because I sincerely believe it to surpass in complexity any other constraint on housing supply that might exist'. And he concluded that by the end of the 1980s, the *need* for new housing would continue to be well in advance of supply. 'Supply,' he concluded, 'because of land, will be in a thorough mess.'[29]

Some public authorities made isolated attempts to increase the supply of land and override the uneconomic prices being demanded by private land-owners. In Britain, Liverpool Council encouraged inner city housing con-struction by providing land at subsidised prices. This enabled builders to provide homes at prices which were comparable to developments on 'green-field' sites. In the United States, the city of New York provided land on the Bathgate Industrial Park in the Bronx for industrial developments. This was designed to provide 1,500 new jobs, by making it possible to establish companies that were to pay rents which (at $2.50 a sq. foot) were nearly half the rents charged by the private sector.[30]

Although well-meaning, such efforts are inadequate and ultimately self defeating: they misallocate resources when the problem is viewed in the context of the whole economy and through time. The intervention of public authorities to over-ride the influence of land monopolists serves only to transfer economic rent to a new, favoured group — the ones who are given access to the land according to bureaucratic criteria.

Construction is a vital part of a programme of economic regeneration, but it has to be part of a rational strategy capable of reaping optimum advantage from all the factors of production — land, labour and capital — mixed in the correct quantities, in the right place and at the appropriate time.

We can now see how a switch in fiscal policy to land value taxation would not only increase consumption, through an increase in net household in-comes, and stimulate investment in fresh capital formation, through a increase in post-tax profits, but also thrust the construction industry into the role of the leading sector in the climb out of recession. This broad-front recovery operation turns on one simple fiscal device, the economic benefits of which are out of all proportion to the administrative changes necessary to realise them. Land value taxation was a policy that found favour with large builders, especially in the United States.[31] At the political level, however, the will was lacking. In Britain although 62 members of the Westminster and European Parliaments saw the wisdom of advocating a penal tax on vacant land, to generate economic development,[32] Mrs Thatcher's government was paralysed by philosophical inertia.[33]

Land speculators were the only beneficiaries of the global recession. The vast array of subsidies and tax advantages associated with land ownership helped in the short run to protect them against sluggish industrial economies, while the eventual recovery promised rich capital gains by the end of the decade.

It is never too late to reformulate policies, but this ought not to induce complacency among the statesmen who are instrumental in shaping popular opinion. For at stake in the 1980s is not just the issue of short-term tactics for economic recovery, but the political future of the West. The economic lessons of the past 200 years have not been learnt, and economics, as Marx noted, effectively determines much of socio-political life. The march of events appears to favour the eventual triumph of the Marxist vision, the continued potency of which was demonstrated once again when it successfully snuffed out the first beacon lights of freedom which were lit in Poland by the workers who were brazen enough to form themselves into a free trade union. It is to this philosophical issue, the nature of Western society and the way in which fiscal policy will be of vital importance, that we now turn to conclude this investigation.

Notes

1 Prime Minister Margaret Thatcher identified the munitions industry as a promising source of new jobs for Britain in the 1980s. J. Langdon, 'Arms drive aids exports, says Thatcher', *The Guardian*, 5.9.80. The defence budget was doubled from £7½bn. in 1978/79 to over £14bn. in 1982. In the US, President Reagan's 1983 budget set a record peacetime target increase in defence expenditure of $43.7bn. over the 1982 figure.

2 *Op. cit.*, p.13, para. 4.13.

3 *Economic Outlook*, Paris: OECD, July 1982, pp.20-21.

4 It was one of the ironies of this period that the representatives of organised labour implicitly endorsed the view that wages were at the source of the problem of low profits and investment. For example, Britain's Trade Union Congress agreed in

September 1980 to accept an incomes policy which would hold back the level of wage settlements and so reduce the real living standards of their members. This agreement was conditional on the return of the Labour Party to power at the following general election.

5   *Money Income & Poverty Status of Families and Persons in the US: 1980*, Washington DC: US Dept. of Commerce, Bureau of the Census, Aug. 1981. p. 3.

6   *Ibid.*, p. 1. In Britain, the decline in real personal disposable income in the year up to the third quarter 1981 was 3%.

7   P. J. Loftus, 'Labour's Share in Manufacturing', *Lloyds Bank Review*, April 1969, p. 17.

8   The present earnings-based taxes produce the absurd situation in which a company may need government subsidies to remain in business. The subsidies (or market restrictions which — by raising prices above their competitive levels — amount to the same thing), are necessary to offset the income tax yield. In other words, no-one wins except the bureaucracies which are kept busy trying to cancel out the negative influences of the tax structure!

9   E. Woolf and J. D. Allen, *Tax Restructuring: A Policy for Economic Regeneration*, London, July 1981, pp. 23-24.

10 *Op. cit.*, Table 6, p. 23.

11 H. Parker, *The Moral Hazard of Social Benefits: A Study of the Impact of Social Benefits and Income Tax on Incentives to Work*, London: I.E.A. Research Monograph No. 37, 1982.

12 A comparison of Tokyo's office rents with those ruling in London or Paris is made extremely difficult by the fact that Japan's rents understate the true cost of occupation to tenants. Tenants are required to pay very substantial deposits as well as rents. *International Property*, London: Richard Ellis, June 1982, p. 83

13 Darin-Drabkin, *op. cit.*, Table 3.4, p. 65.

14 The same explanation accounts for the buoyancy of the Hong Kong economy The maximum tax rate on profits is 17% and the maximum tax on individua incomes is 15%. Rents and the buying price of land, however, are the highest i the world. The British colony has been able to out-perform even Japan in th postwar years, but her success was built on extremely low wage rates, which ar made possible by an inexhaustible supply of cheap labour from Red China.

15 *Third Report from the Environment Committee*, HC 383, London: HMSO, 198 para. 18.

16 Sir Peter Trench was chairman of the National House-Building Council, director of the Nationwide Building Society and Chairman of Y. J. Lovell, th housebuilders and construction group.

17 *The Housebuilding Industry and Changes in the Market for Housebuilding Work: Review of the British Experience*, University of Birmingham, Centre for Urba and Regional Studies, Research Memorandum 87, June 1981, p. 23.

18 See especially D. C. Nicholls, D. M. Turner, R. Kirby-Smith and J. D. Culle *Private Housing Development Process: A Case Study*, London: Department of t Environment, 1981; *Countryside Management in the Urban Fringe*, Cheltenhar Countryside Commission, 1981, and *Waking Up Dormant Land*, Londo Council for Environmental Conservation Youth Unit, 1981.

19 *Future for Housebuilding*, London: Federation of Master Builders, June 198 Tables 2 and 3.

20 *Ibid.*, p. 2. This warning was verified by a detailed analysis of the accounts housebuilding firms, which concluded: 'Costs show little sign of easing and la

is coming into short supply. The resultant high price of land adds to the cost pressures'. See *Housebuilders: An Industry sector analysis*, London: ICC Business Ratio Report, 1981.

21 *The Government's Reply to the Third Report from the Environment Committee*, HC 383, London: HMSO, 1981 Cmnd. 8435, paras. 11-16.

22 *Future for Housebuilding, op. cit.*, Table 6.

23 John Stanley, 'The Government and the Construction Industry', Memo. by the Minister for Housing and Construction, London: NEDC (82)5, mimeo.

24 *Third Report from the Environment Committee, op. cit.*, para. 21. Public sector housing expenditure was reduced from 5.4% of planned total expenditure in 1980/81 to 2.9% in 1983/4.

25 'The Government and the Construction Industry', *op. cit.*, p. 16.

26 This point was forcefully made by housebuilder Tom Baron, a former adviser to Conservative Minister of the Environment Michael Heseltine, who stated: 'If land was more readily available and consequently cost less, we would be competing for customers instead of competing with each other to buy land'. *Chartered Surveyor*, January 1982, p. 333.

27 This fact was finally recognised by the French government. See D. Marsh, 'Keynesianism in a new guise', *Financial Times*, 28.9.82.

28 *Alternatives to Domestic Rates*, London: HMSO, Cmnd 8449, 1981.

29 'Sir Peter Trench foresees a decade of housing shortage', *The Building Societies' Gazette*, n.d. (June 1981), pp. 816-817.

30 R. Smothers, 'South Bronx Industrial Park Begins to Take Shape', *New York Times*, 18.12.81.

31 R.B. Andrews, editor, *Urban Land Use Policy: The Central City*, New York: The Free Press, 1972, p. 207.

32 A.D. Steen, *New Life for Old Cities*, London: Aims of Industry, n.d. [1981], p. 25.

33 The government did claim that it was studying the proposals contained in Steen's book. See *Hansard*, 7.12.81, col. 564. There is no evidence, however, that the land tax was one of the proposals under consideration.

CAPITALISM

22

Requiem or Revival?

The free market system was rescued in the 1930s by a world war. This military intervention distracted people who were tending towards the politics of extremism. After the war, a compromise was engineered on the basis of Keynesian principles. Capitalism was encrusted with a package of New Deal welfare programmes which entailed a massive redistribution of income and led to deep-rooted state control over people's homes, education, health and — as with the food stamps on which millions of American families rely — even their biological existence. The price of social security was increasing dependence upon bureaucratic administration.

The emergence of the New Right late in the 1970s sought to change all that. Unemployment and the instability of prices were to be cured through the reduction of tax levels and a decrease in the size of the public sector. More jobs, higher living standards and greater personal freedom were promised all round. The failure to live up to these promises has, once again, undermined the philosophical justification for the free market system, and has thrown open the question of social evolution. The free market, because of its cyclical failures, is on the defensive. And the fundamental principles of the non-communist world are now at stake.

People prefer a liberal democratic society free of bureaucratic controls. They want to generate independent forms of employment to challenge the corporations that have built their strength on the monopoly control of natural resources. They find repugnant the adversarial approach to industrial relations, which results from the creation of countervailing power-centres. They yearn for the eradication of poverty and the development of a social system that enhances self-esteem. Yet all of these ideals are thwarted by land monopoly.

This enquiry has demonstrated that neither of the extremes of political philosophy, nor a mixture of the two, can deal effectively with the problem at its source. Yet the realignment of property rights entailed by the introduction of land value taxation is not even on today's political agenda. Why?

293

The debate about the legitimate divide between private and social property is distorted by the misrepresentation of the alternative systems that are available. One is either a socialist, seeking to nationalise indiscriminately all the means of production; or a conservative, for whom all of the means of production must be privately owned. Thus, fiscal reform is resisted because it is interpreted as an attack on the sanctity of private property. Land value taxation does not fit neatly into this dualistic model of alternatives because it establishes property rights at a new level of sophistication. It guarantees individual *possession* of land on which people can put their labour and capital to best use; while people in society share on an egalitarian basis that portion of economic wealth that can be attributed to the distinctive contribution of nature and of the community to the process of wealth creation. This complex set of rights is accomplished by the simple device of a 100% tax on the rental value of the land, raising an income for the exchequer that is offset by a reduction in other forms of taxes.

This third model is neither communism nor conservatism. Nor is it a model of reform that most people would find either offensive to their libertarian aspirations or difficult to grasp in its administrative implications. Indeed, it merely requires a change measured in degrees. For people today lose a large portion of their *earned incomes* which are taxed away by the exchequer. A quarter, a half, or even three-quarters of earned income is removed from wage packets. To tax away the whole of the annual income from land instead, then, is only to adapt this sytem while leaving the present occupants in possession of the land and free to use it as they see fit.

We do not seek to disguise the redistributive character of land value taxation, which is a necessary price to pay for both economic efficiency and social justice. This does result in a change in the structure of property rights, a change that would require thorough public examination. Yet when it comes to discussing property rights to land, the intellectual community is struck by a strange infirmity of purpose. As individuals, some of them are aware of the truth that land ought to belong equally to all. As a group, however, they have clouded previous efforts at clarifying the issues by the simple device o obfuscation. Can this charge be substantiated?

The disposition to nurture the interests of landowners was built into th fabric of the Western political system, even when these interests wer perceived to be anti-social. The disposition was, indeed, a condition of th emergence of the modern state, which was born of violence and legitimate by the distortion of philosophy. The origins of this perverse tradition mu be uncovered if we are now to achieve any philosophical advance. We ca begin by looking back to the edicts of Sir William Blackstone, the author i the mid-18th century of the influential *Commentaries on the Laws of Englan* Blackstone chronicled the historical facts:

Necessity begat property; and, in order to insure that property, recourse was had to civil society, which brought along with it a long train of inseparable concomitants; states, governments, laws, punishments and the public exercise of religious duties.[1]

But he also saw that property rights in land rested on an unsound basis, for:

There is no foundation in nature or in natural law, why a set of words upon parchment should convey the dominion of land: why the son should have a right to exclude his fellow-creatures from a determinate spot of ground, because his father had done so before him.

Was it beyond the wit of man, even in the 18th century, to devise a system that neatly secured the property rights of individuals — based on the claims to value actually created by labour and capital — while protecting the collective interests of society? Hardly. But Blackstone would not countenance such thoughts — at least, not from ordinary citizens. For although the questions which he raised challenged 'the sole and despotic dominion' of the property holder, he concluded that they were 'useless and even troublesome in common life'. He invited people to leave the thinking to the philosophers:

. . . it is well if the mass of mankind will obey the laws when made, without scrutinizing too nicely into the reason for making them.

The 19th century saw the dawn of the age of the common man. Nonetheless, he was betrayed by the philosophers who inherited the Blackstone tradition. For example, in America, John Dewey and James Tufts, noting the rise in land values, saw clearly that 'from the standpoint of natural rights the reply would seem to be unanswerable: the community gives the increased value; it belongs to the community'. But they then invoked 'social welfare' to arrive at the conclusion that:

It might, for example, be socially desirable to encourage the owners of farming land by leaving to them the increase in value due to the growth of the country . . .[2]

This is not to say that land value taxation is lacking in advocates. Henry Reuss, who until 1982 was Representative for Milwaukee and a former Chairman of the House Committee on Banking, Finance and Urban Affairs, promoted the virtues of the reform in Washington.[3] In Britain a Cambridge professor advocated it in a letter to *The Times*,[4] and the Liberal Party endorsed its faith in the policy at its annual conference at Bournemouth in September 1982. Anthony Harris, a distinguished columnist on London's *Financial Times*, commended it as a technically feasible device for the budgetary needs of the European Economic Community.

Harris noted that the main burden of the Common Agricultural Policy could be borne 'by those getting the biggest uncovenanted benefit'.[5] A land tax, he wrote, had always seemed appealing in principle; it would fall exclusively on landowners, for in a competitive world it could not be passed on to consumers.[6] 'Now what the EEC has created, the EEC surely has some poetic right to take away; and I can imagine no more appropriate way of tapping the ridiculous values created by ridiculous policies than by taxing them.' But why, Harris asked, limit the tax to agricultural land? 'The arguments for taxing land values in general are just as strong, as is well understood in such countries as Australia and South Africa. It is a tax which falls on those best able to pay — indeed, they declare their own taxable capacity in every land deal; it is the perfect tax to balance regional problems. As a British Chancellor might well add, quietly, it has another greater merit as a tax base: you can't take it with you. A land tax produces no tax exiles.'

That rental income cannot be disguised and avoided is a matter of no mean importance. In the USA, for example, the Internal Revenue Service estimated that Americans were not declaring income from the 'underground economy' of between $100bn. and $135bn., thereby costing the government at least $19bn. in taxes. Thus, people who earned their income — creating wealth and rendering services to others — were branded as 'cheats'. Are not the landowners the cheats in society? But tapping their income was just one of the numerous merits of land value taxation, in Harris's view. And that, apparently was its defect: 'It is obviously far too sensible to stand a chance in the real world'. So, because of that paradoxical conclusion, Mr Harris — one of Fleet Street's leading commentators, a man of influence among the politicians who apply policies in 'the real world' — decided that there was therefore no point in writing further on the subject.

Thus, while the idea of the community sharing the value of land has not died, the stuffing has been largely knocked out of the men who generate and disseminate ideas.

The ability of landowners to intimidate did not rely exclusively on the use of coercive power: their most effective weapon, one allied with the unwillingness of philosophers to think and talk uncompromisingly, was the ability to suppress information. Without the raw data, the 'common' people are unable to detect why the economic system persists in dislocating society. For example, land reforms cannot be implemented without cadastral surveys and publicly accessible registers of ownership and values. Thus, because of the insistence on the right to privacy (that is, secrecy), the landowning class has succeeded in limiting the political action which would otherwise lead inexorably to the destruction of their economic — and therefore their political — power. In Britain, for example, the Royal Commission which was set up by the Government under the chairmanship of Lord Diamond to investigate the distribution of income, discovered that it was hindered in its analysis of land ownership because of what it called the 'remarkable' paucity of information.[7]

The paucity of data is nothing short of a scandal. We have to rely on amateur sleuths and impressionistic evidence to isolate the critical failures in the industrial junction boxes. We are told, for example, that 1.3m. acres in Britain are under-used, idle or derelict.[8] This is twice the area of Northumberland, on which could be built 34 new towns. Ought this data not to be available in the official records? Some authoritative material is available. For example, nearly 9,950 acres of land — over 5% of the urban area — stood idle in South Wales in the 1970s. The figure for Swansea was over 9%. The careful sifting of this evidence was undertaken at the behest of a private charity.[9] In the postwar years, furious rows in Parliament followed when the unemployment rate for labour rose above 2%; but the unemployment rate of land was deemed to be of no consequence at all, if the almost total silence is our guide. But who could cause a fuss when the statistics on land use were practically non-existent?

The absence of adequate data has muzzled all efforts at formulating coherent policies. With pin-point accuracy we can set the dials and head for the moon and Mars, but we cannot ensure full employment for every willing and able-bodied person on earth. And so, following the eclipse of Keynesianism, we continue to grope around in a philosophical hiatus.

But the common people will not be satisfied. They are the ones who are made redundant, walking the streets in search of jobs. From whom can they seek helpful directions? Marxism cannot provide a viable model of economic action because, in terms of the problem now defined, the Marxist critique is irrelevant. 'It consciously omits fluctuations, especially speculation, which now appear to play a dominant role in many cities.'[10] So the field ought to be open to develop a re-conditioned *laissez faire* system.

But Adam Smith's disciples are not equipped to meet the challenge, for they are as unaware as he was of the fatal vulnerability of the original model. In Britain, for example, the Institute of Economic Affairs has been immensely influential in promoting the efficacy of the free market, but it insists on treating land as precisely the same as other marketable goods.[11] Similarly, in the United States, the chief exponent of the free market mechanism, Prof. Milton Friedman, revealed that 'I do not agree that land represents a major objection to *laissez faire* or that economics has gone down a wrong track by failing to make a greater distinction between land and other capital goods.'[12]

So the macro-economic lessons of land speculation have escaped the politicians who formulate the policies. This is hardly surprising, since they were authoritatively told that there *was* no problem. In Britain, the Royal Institution of Chartered Surveyors, which considered itself 'perhaps uniquely qualified to offer a professional viewpoint on what ought to be the land policies of the future', declared:

> We do not believe that land speculation, windfall profits, land-hoarding or monopoly ownership are significant problems.[13]

Yet intuitively, the policy-makers *ought* to have known that the land question was the piece missing from their puzzle boxes. For example, Britain's Chancellor of the Exchequer, Sir Geoffrey Howe, was willing — in private — to concede that his experiment with Enterprise Zones was being spoilt by landowners who were more concerned with cashing in on their assets than creating jobs.[14] But because of the absence of a detailed critique of the role of land, the government remained blank-faced even as the nation's house-builders tried to expose as a 'myth' the official claim that the sale of *publicly*-owned vacant land would meet a large part of the needs of the construction industry.[15] Admittedly, in Canberra the Australian government did take some tough measures against land speculators; but not against speculation as such. Rather, the target was that favourite scapegoat, the foreigner. The economic objections to foreign-inspired real estate deals did not apparently apply to the domestic variety.

Yet it is one of the tragic ironies of our age that the intellectual leaders of the New Right *are* aware (parenthetically) that land speculation exercises a deleterious role on the productive economy. In the United States, for example, the book that voiced the philosophy that became known as Reaganomics identified land purchases as a 'sink', the effect of which was to divert cash and entrepreneurial skills away from the process of wealth creation.[16] And in Britain, Margaret Thatcher told a radio interviewer what she thought about the speculative fever that gripped the country in the early 1970s:

> We got an artificial boom, and do you know where the money went? It did not go into investment or expansion, it went into the biggest property boom we've ever seen and I don't wish to see the like of it ever again. I did the Conservative Party immense harm, it not only went into these enormous prices of property, the boom eventually collapsed, and in the meantime inflation rose and rose and the moment inflation goes up you are much less competitive and eventually unemployment rose again... Spending more money than you've got when you are already over spending is not the answer. What that does is to have another artificial boom, have prices going into property going up and up, and that would finish up with increased unemployment.[17]

Despite these insights, however, there was an unwillingness to confront land speculation as a problem requiring the urgent attention of reforming policy-makers. Mrs Thatcher, for example, would not admit that the disposition to speculate was an intrinsic feature of the existing land market. S blamed government deficit-financing for the speculation of the early 1970s. All that the policy-makers need do, then, is to restrain the temptation to finance public spending by printing money. This solution is spurious. During 1970-73, when US industries and household budgets were savagely battered by speculation, the country's deficit as a percentage of GNP declined consistently. It started an upward rise in 1974, by which time the economy had roller-coasted down into the trough of the depression.

If close regulation of the money supply and the banking system was consciously used as a weapon against land speculation, people would nonetheless find the means with which to continue to speculate. The existence of close substitutes for money, and the certainty of creating new institutions for channelling private funds from willing lenders, renders control of the established monetary system irrelevant. The Royal Commission which produced the Radcliffe Report (1959) documented the array of alternative sources of funds which were then available. In the 1970s, the 'fringe' banks in the UK, and the Real Estate Investment Trusts in the USA, emerged as testaments to the ingenuity of people who wished to marshall large sums of cash with which to speculate in land. As quickly as new devices are brought under legal or bureaucratic control, so others are created to serve the same purpose.

The only lasting solution is to remove all possibility of profiting from hoarding and trading in land. Then why is it that, apart from a few exceptions, there is no authoritative demand for land value taxation? The tax has not been short of endorsements from eminent economic scholars such as Nobel Prize winner Milton Friedman, who was moved to note: 'In my opinion the least bad tax is the property tax on the unimproved value of land, the Henry George argument of many, many years ago'[18]. Professor Martin Feldstein of Harvard, who was appointed chief economic adviser to President Reagan in 1982, took the following wisdom with him to Washington:

> One of the reasons that economists have long been interested in the tax on pure rental income is that it is a tax without excess burden. Because the owners of land cannot alter the supply of land, the tax induces no distortions and therefore no welfare loss.[19]

And Professor Bela Balassa, a World Bank consultant, urged Red China to adopt a tax on land values as a necessary part of its new economic strategy.[20] Few voices, however, were raised in favour of its incorporation into the Western economic model. The over-riding explanation is that land is not seen to be a major influence over the market system. This dangerous belief can be traced back to the writings of John Maynard Keynes, whose influence needs to be isolated, if it is to be expunged in the process of establishing a new philosophical framework for the 1980s and beyond.

Keynes, the apostle of the mixed economy, travelled from Cambridge to

Berlin in 1926 to pronounce *The End of Laissez Faire*. His lecture[21] to university audience was one of a series of death blows to the concept of completely free market economy, culminating in *The General Theory Employment, Interest and Money*.

Keynes was not qualified to adjudicate on the superior virtues of gover ment management of the economy. His impartiality as a judge must questioned. Despite his familiarity with the writings of Henry Georg which ought to have alerted him to the subversive influence of land monopol Keynes held the view that 'the land problem' no longer existed; there ha been, he told the Liberal Summer School at Cambridge in 1925, 'a sile change in the facts'. And in *The General Theory* he relegated the deleterio impact of the land market to earlier, agricultural-based social organisations

This myopia was also prevalent in the US, where 'popular faith in *laiss faire* had been greatly weakened'[23] in the period between the land speculatic fever of 1925 and the stock market collapse of 1929. The causal links betwee these two events were completely misunderstood, and the free market w held culpable.

Keynes ought to have known better. His conclusion was glib; it was n formulated on the basis of an examination of history, but was rather t] shallow view of conventional wisdom. He had failed to weigh all the eviden before delivering his guilty verdict against *laissez faire*. It was therefore like that his sentence — the need for bureaucratic and political 'fine tuning' of t] economy, to make up for the alleged deficiencies in entrepreneurial decisio making — would be an inappropriate remedy, a miscarriage of justice.

And so it was. But in promoting the need for a hybrid economy, Keyn was also a major architect of those political and economic institutions whi were designed to limit personal freedom in the name of altruism.

Western democracy can survive only if it is underpinned by an econom system consistent with its political tenets. The liberty of the soverei individual is the supreme principle. Institutions have been design accordingly. Thus, equal weight is given to political preferences by allocati one vote to each person. The reality conflicts with the philosophy.

The monopolistic foundations of the market economy are reflected in t power blocks that dominate the political processes. The manufacture associations and trades unions that try to compensate for the vulnerability capital and labour in the production process combat each other instead collaborating against the common enemy, the land monopolists whc interests go unchallenged. The distortions in the free market caused by la monopoly spawned the secondary, or derivative, power blocks; yet so w concealed are the motive forces that we are told by a distinguished econon historian that powerful interest groups are created by the democratic proce itself.[24]

Future generations will judge us on the basis of the choices which are now made — by design or default — to cope with the strains imposed by a capitalism on crutches. We have to undermine the disposition of industrial economies to surrender to those violent cyclical recessions which deepen the trough of human misery and encourage the rearguard actions which culminate in the creation of new defensive institutions that further negate the aspirations of the citizens of the free world.

The outlook is not bright. The failure of the General Agreement on Tariffs and Trade, meeting in 1982 to produce a forceful defence of free international trade, reinforced the growing demands for mean-minded protectionism. Autarky — the erection of border barriers, locking out the products of other people's labours ostensibly in the name of self-sufficiency — was the cry of the leaders of both workers and the owners of capital. Little did they appreciate that the Trojan horses were already deployed within their camps.

Alas, there is no coherent strategy for dealing with the exercise of the unique power that derives from the land. That power was poignantly reaffirmed when Kakuei Tanaka (labelled the 'shogun of the darkness' by opposition parties[25]) enjoyed the role of kingmaker in Japan's political process. Although he was driven from the Prime Minister's office because of his shady land deals (see pp. 165-7), Tanaka continued to wield power as leader of a 130-strong parliamentary faction. Yasuhiro Nakasone owed his move into the premier's office in November 1982 to the decisive backing that he received from Tanaka.

But would the free market respond constructively to the opportunities even if enlightened legislators promulgated a thoroughgoing land value tax? Sceptics continue to tell us that fiscal reform is 'ultimately flawed' by the historical facts: that when competing for the use of land, today's owners have an advantage over prospective users. From this, it follows that change can only be engineered through revolution, and the ultimate result would not be a system based on *laissez faire*.

In fact, the market would rise to the occasion and ensure that landowners would not retain their determinative influence over the distribution and price of land, *provided that the tax was pitched at a deterrent level*. Land value taxation would place the holders and potential users of land on an equal footing. The obligation to pay rent as a tax to the community would ensure that land holders put their possessions to optimum use, for otherwise they would have to pay their tax liabilities out of previous accumulations of capital, a sacrifice that could not be endured indefinitely.

In the new tax regime, a prospective employer of labour and capital can calculate what the economic surplus, or rent, would be after paying wages and interest. He can then bid this tax payment (the equivalent of the rent that he would agree to pay to a landlord under the present fiscal and tenurial system) at an auction against all-comers. If the existing possessor of the land is economically more efficient, and is willing to bid a higher rent for the right to retain possession, then everyone is satisfied. For the community benefits from maximum output at lowest prices from the use of the given resource endowments, and the people who lose at the auction are equal beneficiaries of higher exchequer revenue.

This defence of a reformed free market is tenable provided the entrepreneurial class is not a closed one. For if the system relied on the prior accumulation of private capital for the development of new economic enterprises, those who did not already enjoy access to property are indeed at a severe disadvantage. But the entrepreneurial class is not a closed one. For reassurance we need go no further than that well-known authority on capitalism, Karl Marx. He observed that

> the commercial value of each individual is pretty accurately estimated under the capitalist mode of production — it is greatly admired by apologists of the capitalist system . . . this circumstance continually brings an unwelcome number of new soldiers of fortune into the field and into competition with the already existing individual capitalists . . . [26]

A free market equalises the opportunities for people to demonstrate their individual worth, whereas monopolies are designed to prevent it from operating effectively for *everyone* and *at all times*.

The prospects for a radical reform are not high, but we should have a clear perception of the risks of trying to retain the present structure of the Western economy. The crudities of East European socialism may not enthral most reformers, but these will reign supreme if we do not define a practical alternative to the crippled capitalism that originated in Britain 200 years ago. Either that, or the Western economy will recover and enjoy 18 years of growth before tail-spinning into yet another deep-seated depression of even greater magnitude than the structural recession which began in 1974.

Eventually, however, if we are to achieve the civil liberties to which Western society aspires, we must reform the land market. Such a reform is both a necessary and sufficient step in the direction of economic stability and social sanity. Even Marx perceived that the destruction of the power of land monopoly would transform society. He understood that the power of capital was *derivative*; that it depended on an original monopoly — the private appropriation of land by a minority who were able to exclude others from equal access to the value of nature's products. In his *Critique of the Gotha Programme*, Marx wrote: 'In present-day society the instruments of labour are the monopoly of the landowners *and* the capitalists".[27] But he added in parenthesis: '. . . the monopoly of property in land is even the basis of the monopoly of capital . . .' There is no more hostile critic of capitalism than

Marx, yet he acknowledged that 'The nationalisation of land will work a complete change in the relations between labour and capital',[28] an observation that destroyed the logic of his call for the complete over-throw of the capitalist system by alienated workers.

Marx, because of his ideological commitment to socialism, prescribed nationalisation as a solution to the fundamental problem of the distribution of power and property. The evidence, however, favours the free market associated with an effectively-high tax on the value of land. Such a system would harmonise equity with economic efficiency; these are the twin achievements of most pre-industrial societies which are surely not beyond the wit of Space Age man?

Notes

1 *Commentaries*, Bk. II, Ch. I, p. 8.
2 J. Dewey and J. H. Tufts, *Ethics*, London: G. Bell & Sons, 1908, p. 565. Even Joseph Schumpeter, the socialist critic of capitalism, in his diagnosis of 'observable tendencies' towards socialism, in Western economies, noted in an address to the American Economic Association (Dec. 1949): 'Thus, a socialist regime in this country would have to be bold indeed if it ever thought of touching the subsidised independence of the farmer'. Reprinted in *Capitalism, Socialism, & Democracy, op. cit. p. 422.*
3 See *Compact Cities, op cit.* In 1979 Reuss urged the Secretary of Labour to compile an index of land values, which he described as a serious gap in the consumer and wholesale price indices. Until such an index is routinely compiled economic policy formation will continue to be critically impeded.
4 M. Chisholm, professor of geography, 'Derelict land', *The Times*, 5.3.80.
5 A. Harris, 'EEC's untapped resource bank', *Financial Times*, 22.3.79.
6 For an authoritative analysis of the principles supporting this statement (the truth of which is denied by lobbyists who seek to preserve the tax privileges of farmland owners), see Lipsey, *op. cit.*, p. 370.
7 Report No. 7, *op. cit.*, p. 152, para. 6.28, and p. 155, para. 6.37.
8 G. Moss, *Britain's Wasting Acres*, London: Architectural Press, 1981, p. 2. Vacant urban land was sufficient to house 5m. people. *Ibid.*
9 *Vacant Urban Land in South Wales*, Cardiff: University of Wales Institute of Science and Technology, 1981, report commissioned by an environmentally-concerned charity, the Prince of Wales' Committee.
10 T. A. Broadbent, *An attempt to apply Marx's theory of ground rent to the modern urban economy*, London: Centre for Environmental Studies, Research Paper 17, 1975, p. 25.
11 See, e.g., *Government and the Land*, London: IEA, 1974, esp. p. x, n. 4.
12 Letter from Friedman dated 26.5.80, to Dr R. J. Sandilands, Dept. of Economics, University of Strathclyde.
13 'A Land Policy for the Future', London: RICS, 1982, pp. 2-3.
14 'Chancellor wakes up to land profiteering', *Land and Liberty*, Nov.-Dec., 1982. That the lessons were not learned, however, is evidenced by such cases as

Belgium's decision to establish seven enterprise zones along the lines of the British model — property tax exemption and all.

15   'HBF Exposes Vacant Land Bonanza Myth', House-Builders Federation, London: Press Release, 19.11.82.

16   Gilder, *op. cit.*, who states of the US in the early 1980s (p. 20): 'The upper classes, normally the cutting edge of the economy — the source of most investment — fled to unproductive tax shelters and hoards of gold, real estate, and speculation. The demoralization of the elite, moreover, worsened the pains of the classes below.'

17   Independent Radio News, London, 30.11.80, transcript, p. 6.

18   Comment during public debate of the American Education League, quoted in *Human Events*, 18.11.78, p. 14.

19   M. Feldstein, 'The Surprising Incidence of a Tax on Pure Rent: A New Answer to an Old Question', *Journal of Political Economy*, Vol. 85, 1977, p. 357. For a critique of this article, see 'Reagan's adviser and the land tax, *Land and Liberty*, Jan.-Feb. 1983.

20   B. Balassa, 'Economic Reform in China', *Banca Nazionale Del Lavoro Quarterly Review*, Sept. 1982.

21   J. M. Keynes, *The End of Laissez Faire*, London: L. & V. Woolf, 1926.

22   J. M. Keynes, *The General Theory of Employment Interest and Money*, London: Macmillan, 1967, p. 241.

23   Galbraith, *op. cit.*, p. 160.

24   Sir E. Roll, 'The Wealth of Nations 1776-1976', *Lloyds Bank Review*, No. 119, 1976, p. 22.

25   'Shogun's mate', *The Economist*, 27.11.82.

26   *Capital*, Vol. III, *op. cit.*, p. 587.

27   *Op. cit.*, p. 343. Elsewhere, Marx notes that free access to land was dangerous for capital; in such conditions, 'the capitalist finds that his capital ceases to be capital without wage labour, and that one of the presuppositions of the latter is not only landed property in general, but modern landed property; landed property which, as capitalized rent, is expensive, and which, as such, excludes the direct use of the soil by individuals'. K. Marx, *Grundrisse*, Harmondsworth: Penguin, 1973, p. 278.

28   K. Marx, 'The Nationalization of the Land', in K. Marx and F. Engels, *Selected Works*, Vol. 2, Moscow: Progress Publishers, 1969, p. 290.

BIBLIOGRAPHY AND INDEX

Select Bibliography

Andelson, R.V., editor, *Critics of Henry George*, Rutherford: Fairleigh Dickinson University Press, 1979.

Archer, R.W., 'The Public Land and Leasehold System in Canberra, Australia', *The American Journal of Economics and Sociology*, Vol. 36, 1977.

— *The Rising Price of Land for New Housing*, Canberra: Metropolitan Research Trust, 1972.

— *Site Value Taxation in Central Business District Development*, Washington, DC: Urban Land Institute, Research Report 19, 1972.

Bahl, R.W., editor, *The Taxation of Urban Property in Less Developed Countries*, Wisconsin: University of Wisconsin Press, 1979.

Barnes, P. and Casalino, L., *Who Owns the Land?*, Berkeley: Centre for Rural Studies, n.d.

Bartlett, B., *Reaganomics: Supply Side Economics in Action*, Westport: Arlington House, 1981.

Becker, A.P. *Land and Building Taxes*, Milwaukee: University of Wisconsin Press, 1969.

Botha, D.J.J., *Urban Taxation and Land Use*, Report of a one-man Commission appointed by the City Council of Port Elizabeth, South Africa, 1970.

Brennan, F., *Canberra in Crisis*, Canberra: Dalton Publishing Co., 1971.

Broadbent, T.A., *An attempt to apply Marx's theory of ground rent to the modern urban economy*, London: Centre for Environmental Studies, Research Paper 17, 1975.

Brown, H.J., Phillips, R.S., and Roberts, N.A., 'Land Into Cities', Cambridge, Mass.: Lincoln Institute of Land Policy, 1980, mimeo.

Bruton, M.M. and Gore, A., 'Vacant Urban Land in South Wales', Cardiff: Dept. of Town Planning, University of Wales Institute of Science and Technology, Vol. 1.

Caincross, A.K. and Weber, B., 'Fluctuations in Building in Great Britain, 1785-1849', *Econ. Hist. Rev.*, 2nd series, Vol. IX, 1956-7.

Cannon, M., *The Land Boomers*, Melbourne: Melbourne University Press, 1966.

Cheng, C., *Land Reform in Taiwan*, Taipei: China Publishing Co., 1961.

Churchill, W.S., *The People's Rights*, London: Jonathan Cape, 1970.

Centre for Urban and Regional Studies, *The Role of the Local Authority in Land Programming and the Process of Private Residential Development*, Birmingham: Research Memorandum 80, April 1980.

Civic Trust, *Urban Wasteland*, London, 1977.

Clark, C., 'Prospects for Future Collaboration — the Universities' Contribution', in *New Horizons on Land and Property Values*, RICS Technical Information Service, March 1966.

— *The Value of Agricultural Land*, Oxford: Pergamon Press, 1973.

Collier, C., 'Henry George's system of political economy', *History of Politi Economy*, Vol. 11, 1979.

Cord, S., *Catalyst*, Indiana: Henry George Foundation of America, 1979.

Council for Environmental Conservation Youth Unit, *Waking Up Dormant Lar* London, 1981.

Cullen, M., and S. Woolery, *World Congress on Land Policy 1980*, Lexington: Lexin ton Books, 1982.

Darin-Drabkin, H., *Land Policy and Urban Growth*, Oxford: Pergamon Press, 197

de Mille, A. G., *Henry George: Citizen of the World*, Chapel Hill: University of Nor Carolina Press, 1950.

Denison, E. F. and W. K. Chung, *How Japan's Economy Grey So Fast*, Washingtc DC: The Brookings Institution, 1976.

Department of the Environment, 'Land for Private Housebuilding', London: Circ lar 9/80.

Derksen, J. B. D., 'Long Cycles in Residential Building: An Explanation', *Ecor metrica*, Vol. 8, 1940.

Dore, R. P., 'Land Reform and Japan's Economic Development', *Developing Ec omies*, Special Issue, Vol. 3, 1965.

Douglas, R., *Land, People & Politics*, London: Allison & Busby, 1976.

Dunkerley, H. B., 'Urban Land Policy Issues and Opportunities — An Overviev in *Urban Land Policy Issues and Opportunities*, Vol. 1, World Bank Staff Worki Paper No. 283, 1978.

Economist Intelligence Unit and Halpern and Partners, *Housing Land Availabil in the South East*, London: HMSO, 1975.

Economist Intelligence Unit, *An Analysis of Commercial Property Values 1962-19* London, 1977.

Engels, F., 'The Housing Question', in Marx and Engels, *Selected Works*, Vol. Moscow: Progress Publishers, 1969.

English, J. W. and G. E. Cardiff, *The Coming Real Estate Crash*, New Rochel Arlington House, 1979.

Federation of Master Builders, *Future for Housebuilding*, London: June 1981.

Feinstein, C. H., 'Income and Investment in the UK, 1854-1914', *Econ. Journ* 1961.

Garland, J. M., *Economic Aspects of Australian Land Taxation*, Melbourne: Melbou University Press, 1934.

Gates, P. W., 'The Homestead Act: Free Land Policy in Operation, 1862-193 in Ottoson

— 'Homesteading in the High Plains', *Agricultural History*, Vol. 51, 1977.

George, Henry, *Progress and Poverty* (1879), centenary edn. 1979, New yo. Robert Schalkenbach Foundation.

— *A Perplexed Philosopher* (1892), New York: Robert Schalkenbach Foundati 1946.

Gilder, G., *Wealth and Poverty*, New York: Basic Books, 1981.

Govt. Printing Office, *Compact Cities: Energy Saving Strategies for the Eight* Washington, DC: 1980

Grebler, L., 'House Building, the Business Cycle and State Intervention: I', *Int national Labour Rev.*, Vol. 33, 1936.

Hagman, D. and D. Misczynski, *Windfalls For Wipeouts: Land Value Capture and Cc pensation*, Chicago: American Society of Planning Officials, 1978.

Harper, Sir E., 'The Lloyd George Finance (1909-10) Act, 1910: Its errors a

How to Correct Them', Fourth International Conference on Land-Value Taxation, Edinburgh, July 29- Aug. 4, 1929, Paper No. 11.

Harriss, C. L., editor: *Government Spending & Land Values: Public Money & Private Gain*, Wisconsin: University of Wisconsin Press, 1973.

Harvey, D., 'Class-Monopoly Rent, Finance Capital and the Urban Revolution', *Regional Studies*, Vol. 8, 1974.

Holland, D. M., editor: *The Assessment of Land Value*, Madison: University of Wisconsin Press, 1970.

Hoyt, H., 'Bolshevism and the Laws of Property', originally published in *Open Court Magazine*, 1918, republished in *According to Hoyt*.

— *One Hundred Years of Land Values in Chicago*, University of Chicago Press, 1933.

— *The Urban Real Estate Cycle — Performances and Prospects*, Washington: ULI Technical Bulletin No. 38, 1950.

— *The Changing Principles of Land Economics*, Washington: ULI Technical Bulletin No. 60, 1968.

Hutchinson, A. R., *Land Rent as Public Revenue in Australia*, London: Economic and Social Science Research Assn., n.d. [1981].

Institute of Science and Technology, *Vacant Urban Land in South Wales*, Cardiff: University of Wales, 1981.

Jamasaki, Y., 'The Influence of Henry George's Ideas Upon Modern Japan', *The American Journal of Economics and Sociology*, Vol. 21, 1962.

Kamm, S., 'Inflation: Curbing Inflation in Residential Land Prices', *Urban Land*, Washington: ULI, Sept. 1971.

Khachaturov, T., *The Economy of the Soviet Union Today*, Moscow: Progress Publishers, 1977.

King, J. and Regan, P., *Relative Income Shares*, London: Macmillan, 1976.

Kondratieff, N. D., 'The Long Waves in Economic Life', *Lloyds Bank Review*, October, 1978.

Kraar, L., 'Japan Sets Out to Remodel Itself', *Fortune*, March, 1973.

Kristensen, K. J., 'Land Valuation and Land-Value Taxation in Denmark', paper presented to the Eleventh International Conference on Land Value Taxation and Free Trade, New York, Aug. 30-Sept. 5, 1964.

Land Authority for Wales, *South Wales housing land availability study 1980*, Cardiff.

Le Duc, T., 'History and Appraisal of US Land Policy to 1862', in *Land Use Policy and Problems in the US*, editor: H. W. Ottoson, Lincoln: University of Nebraska Press, 1963.

— 'Public Policy, Private Investment, and Land Use in American Agriculture, 1825-1875', *Agricultural History*, Vol. 37, 1963.

Leser, C. E. V., 'Building Activity and Housing Demand', *Yorkshire Bulletin of Economic and Social Research*, Vols. 3-4, 1951.

Levy, J. B., 'No Bargain Basement: REIT accounting Compounds the Risk for Investors', *Barron's* 13.6.77.

Lewis, J. P., *Building Cycles and British Growth*, London: Macmillan, 1965.

Lewis, W. A. and P. J. O'Leary, 'Secular Swings in Production and Trade 1870-1913', *Manchester School of Social and Economic Studies*, 1955.

Lichfield, N. and H. Darin-Drabkin, *Land Policy in Planning*, George Allen & Unwin, 1980.

Lindholm, R. W., and A. D. Lynn, *Land Value Taxation*, Madison: University of Wisconsin Press, 1982.

Loftus, P.J., 'Labour's Share in Manufacturing', *Lloyd's Bank Review*, April 1969.

Maiwald, K., 'An Index of Building Costs in the UK, 1845-1938', *Econ. Hist. Rev.*, 2nd Ser., Vol. VII (1954-5).

Manvel, A.D., 'Trends in the Value of Real Estate and Land, 1956 to 1966', in *Three Land Research Studies*, Washington, DC: National Commission on Urban Problems, Research Report No. 12, 1968, p.1.

Marriott, P., *The Property Boom*, London: Hamish Hamilton, 1967.

Martin, W.E., *The Economics of the Profits Crisis*, London: HMSO, 1981.

Marx, K., *The Poverty of Philosophy*, Moscow: Progress Publishers, 1955.

— *Capital*, London: Lawrence & Wishart, 1962.

— 'The Nationalization of the Land', in K. Marx and F. Engels, *Selected Works*, Vol. 2, Moscow: Progress Publishers, 1969.

— *Grundrisse*, Harmondsworth: Penguin, 1973.

— *The First International and After*, Harmondsworth: Penguin, 1974.

Melichar, E., 'The Relationship Between Farm Income and Asset Values, 1950-1977', Seminar on Food and Agricultural Policy Issues, Wayzata, Minnesota, 1978.

Menshikov, S., *The Economic Cycle: Postwar Developments*, Moscow: Progress Publishers, 1975.

Meyer, P., 'Land Rush', *Harper's* Jan. 1979.

Milgram, G., 'Estimates of the Value of Land in the US Held by Various Sectors of the Economy, Annually, 1952 to 1968', in R.W. Goldsmith, editor, *Institutional Investors and Corporate Stock — A Background Study*, National Bureau of Economic Research, 1973.

Moss, G., *Britain's Wasting Acres*, London: Architectural Press, 1981.

Murphy, D.G., *Economic Aspects of Residential Subdivisions*, Canberra: Australian Institute of Urban Studies, 1973.

Nabarro, R. and D. Richards, *Wasteland*, London Thames TV Report, n.d. (1980).

National Federation of Self Employed and Small Business, *30 Square Miles of Wasteland*, London, 1981.

Netzer, 'The incidence of the property tax revisited', *National Tax Journal*, Vol. 26, 1973.

— *Impact of the Property Tax Effect on Housing, Urban Land Use, Local Government Finance*, National Commission on Urban Problems, Research Report No. 1, Washington, DC: US Government Printing Office, 1968.

Neutze, G.M, 'The Cost of Housing', *The Economic Record*, 1972.

— *Urban Development in Australia*, London: George Allen & Unwin, 1977.

— 'Urban Land', in P. Scott, editor, *Australian Cities and Public Policy*, Melbourne: Georgian House, 1978.

Nicely, G., *How to Reap Riches from Raw Land*, Prentice Hall, 1978.

Norman, E.H., *Japan's Emergence as a Modern State*, New York: Institute of Pacific Relations, 1940.

Northam, R.M., 'Vacant Urban Land in the American City', *Land Economics* Vol. 47, 1971.

Norton-Taylor, R., *Whose Land Is It Anyway?*, Wellingborough: Turnstone Press 1982.

Ohkawa, K. and H. Rosovsky, *Japanese Economic Growth*, Stanford, California Stanford University press, 1973.

Phelps Brown, E.H. and B. Weber, 'Accumulation, Productivity and Distribution in the British Economy, 1870-1938', *Econ. J.*, 1953.

Prest, A.R., *The Taxation of Urban Land*, Manchester: Manchester University Press, 1981.

Radcliffe, W., *Letters on the Evils of the Exportation of Cotton Yarns*, Stockport, 1811.

— *Origins of the New System of manufacture commonly called power-loom weaving*, Stockport, 1828.

Ranis, G., 'The Financing of Japanese Economic Development', *Economic History Review*, Vol. XI, 1958.

Rawson, M., *Property Taxation and Urban Development*, Washington, DC: ULI Research Monograph 4, 1961.

Rosovsky, H., 'Japan's Transition to Modern Economic Growth, 1868-1885', in *Industrialisation in Two Systems*, editor: H. Rosovsky, J. Wiley & Sons, 1966.

Royal Town Planning Institute (chairman: Prof. G. Smart), 'Land Values and Planning in the Inner Areas', London, March 1978.

Sandercock, L., *The Land Racket*, Australian Assn. of Socialist Studies, 1979.

— *Cities for Sale*, London: Heinemann, 1976.

Schmid, A.A., *Converting Land From Rural to Urban Uses*, Washington: Resources For The Future, Inc., 1968.

Schulkin, P.A., 'Real Estate Investment Trusts in an Era of innovation', *Real Estate Review*, Fall 1972.

Shoup, D.C., 'Financing Neighbourhood Public Investment by Deferred Special Assessment', Los Angeles: School of Architecture and Urban Planning, University of California, 1980.

Smith, A., *The Theory of Moral Sentiments*, 1759; Indianapolis: Liberty Classics, 1969.

— *The Wealth of Nations*, 1776; Chicago: University of Chicago Press, 1976.

Stevenson, J. and C. Cook, *The Slump*, London: Jonathan Cape, 1977.

Strong, A.L., *Land Banking: European Reality, American Prospect*, Baltimore: Johns Hopkins University Press, 1979.

Tanaka, K., *Building a New Japan*, Tokyo: Simul Press, 1972, first English edition, 1973.

Tanzi, V., 'International Tax Burdens', in *Taxation: A Radical Approach*, London: Institute of Economic Affairs, 1970.

— *Inflation and the Personal Income Tax*, Cambridge: Cambridge University Press, 1980.

Thomas, D.L., *Lords of the Land*, New York: G.P. Putnam's Sons, 1977.

Turvey, R., 'The Rationale of Rising Property Values', *Lloyds Bank Review*, Jan. 1962.

Tyler, A.S., *The Price of Land*, The Institute of Real Estate Development, 1973.

Vallis, E.A., 'Urban Land and Building Prices 1892-1969', *Estates Gazette*, May 13, 1972.

Walker, L.A., 'Farm Finance and Real Estate Markets — Situation and Outlook', US Dept. of Agriculture, Washington DC (unpublished) 1978.

Walls, C., 'Property and the Operation of the Financial Markets', London: Simon & Coates, July, 1982.

Waswo, A., *Japanese Landlords*, Berkeley: University of California Press, 1977.

Wilczynski, J., *Socialist Economic Development and Reforms*, London: Macmillan, 1972.

Woodruff, A.M., 'Progress and Poverty: a Hundred Years' Perspective', in *Henry George and Sun Yat-Sen: Application and Evolution of their Land Use Doctrines*, Cambridge, Mass.: Lincoln Institute, 1977.

Wünderlich, W., *Facts About US Landownership*, Washington, DC: Economics, Statistics and Cooperatives Service, USDA, Agricultural Information Bulletin No. 422, 1978.

Index

313